# The Bipolar Child

The Definitive and
Reassuring Guide to
Childhood's Most
Misunderstood Disorder

DEMITRI PAPOLOS, M.D.,
AND JANICE PAPOLOS

THIRD EDITION

BROADWAY BOOKS  NEW YORK

PUBLISHED BY BROADWAY BOOKS

Previous editions of this book were published in 1999 and 2002 by Broadway Books.

A hardcover edition of this book was originally published in 2006 by Broadway Books.

Published in the United States by Broadway Books, an imprint of The Doubleday Broadway Publishing Group, a division of Random House, Inc., New York.
www.broadwaybooks.com

BROADWAY BOOKS and its logo, a letter B bisected on the diagonal, are trademarks of Random House, Inc.

Grateful acknowledgment is made for permission to reprint:
Excerpts from the *Diagnostic and Statistical Manual of Mental Disorders, Fourth Edition.* Reprinted with permission from the American Psychiatric Association. Copyright © 1994.
Excerpts from "I Couldn't Help My Daughter," by Swanee Hunt and Lillian Hunt-Meeks. Copyright © 1996 by Swanee Hunt and Lillian Hunt-Meeks. Originally published in *Good Housekeeping.* Reprinted with permission from the authors.
Excerpts from "Diagnosing Bipolar vs. ADHD: A Pharmacological Point of View," by Charles Popper, M.D. Reprinted from *The Link* 13 (1996). Reprinted with permission of the author.
Excerpt from "On Diagnostic Gore in a Child's Nightmares," by Charles Popper, M.D. From *The American Academy of Child and Adolescent Psychiatry Newsletter,* Fall 1990. Reprinted with permission of the author.
Venn diagram on page 44 from "Obsessive-Compulsive Disorder in Children and Adolescents: A Review," by Daniel Geller, Joseph Biederman, et al. From *The Harvard Review of Psychiatry,* page 265 of Volume 5, Issue 5. Reprinted with permission from Oxford University Press.
Lithium Dosing chart on page 82. Adapted from "Lithium Dosage Guide for Prepubertal Children: A Preliminary Report," by Elizabeth B. Weller, Ronald A. Weller, and Mary A. Fristad, from the *Journal of the American Academy of Child Psychiatry.* Reprinted with permission.

Book design by Jessica Shatan

Illustrated by Jackie Aher

Charts and graphs by Kris Tobiassen

Library of Congress Cataloging-in-Publication Data
Papolos, Demitri.
    The bipolar child : the definitive and reassuring guide to childhood's most misunderstood disorder /
Demitri Papolos and Janice Papolos.—3rd ed.
        p.   cm.
    Includes bibliographical references and index.
    1. Manic-depressive illness in children. 2. Depression in children. 3. Psychoses in children.
I. Papolos, Janice. II. Title.
RJ506.D4P36 2006
618.92'895—dc22

                                                                                            2005055312

ISBN 978-0-7679-2860-1

PRINTED IN THE UNITED STATES OF AMERICA

10 9 8 7 6 5 4 3 2 1

First Paperback Edition

For
Alex and Jordy,
and for
all the children

# Contents

## Part IV. Life Goes On

# Preface to the Third Edition

It is hard to believe that six years have passed since this volume first appeared on bookshelves. When it was launched in January of 2000 with a segment on *20/20,* it was the first time that the phrase "early-onset bipolar disorder" had ever been mentioned in prime time. The reaction was surprising even to our publishers.

Over six thousand people joined us online for a chat after the airing of the show, and thousands more e-mailed ABC and our website over the next few days. Many wrote that they sat stunned on the sofas of their living rooms as they learned that their children's wild and erratic behaviors had a name. Their children had an illness. They had not been acting volitionally; the parents themselves were not inadequate.

Since that night in 2000, much has changed to ease the burden of the children and families, and when our editor, Gerald Howard, asked us to consider another revision of the book, we felt extremely gratified to have a third opportunity to keep our readers abreast of all the advances. Let us outline some of the additions we've made to *The Bipolar Child, Third Edition.*

The first step to mood stabilization is finding the right treatment strategy for each child. In Chapter 4, "Prescriptions for Treatment," we've underscored the impact of seasonal change on the course of the illness. It has long been established that adult patients with bipolar disorder have pronounced seasonal episodes that require increased vigilance during these times of vulnerability and, commonly, medication adjustments. This is no less true for children. Mothers on Internet bulletin boards have dubbed these seasonal perturbations "March madness" and "September slumps."

These challenges to stability must be taken into account, or the child's previously stabilized mood may begin to disintegrate with the change of day/light and temperature cycles. If modifications are made to the medication regimen *prior* to these seasonal changes, destabilization might be staved off, ensuring a smoother, more grounded year for the child or adolescent.

In the previous editions of this book, we sounded an alarm about the dangers of antidepressant treatment for children with bipolar disorder. We observed (and parents reported) emerging manias, increased aggression, psychosis, and suicidal thoughts and behaviors after treatment with these drugs. Although formal studies were scarce, parents reported this phenomenon to us in overwhelming numbers. We went ahead and issued the warnings.

On October 15, 2004, the Food and Drug Administration issued a public health advisory to warn the public about the increased risk of suicidal thoughts and behaviors in children and adolescents being treated with antidepressant medications. The agency ordered manufacturers to add a black box warning to the professional labeling of all antidepressant medications to describe the risk and emphasize the need for close monitoring of young patients started on these medications.

Stimulants also can produce similar symptoms and behaviors in this population of children and adolescents, and again, we want to urge caution and careful monitoring. Although these medications are short-lasting, they are not always benign drugs for many youngsters with bipolar disorder.

On a brighter note, Chapter 4 includes a discussion of a new test that can locate an allele pattern in a child's genetic makeup that can gauge how quickly he or she will metabolize certain psychotropic medications. This test, and others in development, will no doubt prove very helpful to clinicians as they can make more informed treatment decisions that may reduce adverse side effects and improve treatment outcomes. (Major advances in molecular genetics are explained in some depth in Chapter 5, "The Genetic Aspects of Bipolar Disorder.")

Second only to the complexity of diagnosis and the medical treatment of juvenile bipolar disorder is the piece of the puzzle called school. With the reauthorization of the Individuals with Disabilities Improvement Act of 2004 (and its enactment in 2005), so many changes have been made to the laws governing special education that we have completely revised and expanded Chapter 9, "School: A Child's World Beyond Home." The information in this chapter will educate parents about the new laws that will impact their children in the academic setting and will help them work with their school systems to ensure that their sons and daughters receive a free and appropriate education. A new Individualized Education Plan (IEP) has been added, as well as lists of accommodations that might be added into the IEP. These accommodations are divided into four categories: those that might be needed as a result of the symptoms of the illness, the side effects of the medications, attentional problems, and specific learning disabilities.

We've also added sample letters to this chapter: one that will help parents request a complete evaluation of their child and another that will help parents personally introduce their child to non–special education teachers in order to spotlight the child's special gifts and needs in a warmer, less formal way. It is our hope that this kind of connecting will help strengthen the alliance between parents and teachers and make the student more comfortable in the school environment.

Chapter 10 is called "The Neuropsychological Testing of a Bipolar Child." The jumping-off point for neuropsychology is a test of general intellectual ability, and the Wechsler Intelligence Scales for Children—the WISC-III—has heretofore been the most commonly administered IQ test. The WISC-III has now been replaced by the WISC-IV, and we explain the battery of new subtests and what specific aspects of cognitive functioning they measure. This test and the other neuropsychological tests detailed in this chapter will bring to light the strengths and weaknesses of a student and guide accommodations and remediation strategies.

Also included in this chapter is a discussion of the difficulties many children and adolescents with bipolar disorder experience when asked to produce written work in the form of essays or expository writing. These common, co-occurring deficits of written expression render homework assignments a nightmare for the student and an agony for the parents who must supervise the work and attempt to motivate the balky child. We hope this new understanding of how difficult it is for these students to write in essay form will help take the onus off of the parents and help make it possible for them to work closely with the school system to modify the work and remediate the problem.

We have always felt that Chapter 8, "The Impact on the Family," was the heart and soul of this book. We have expanded its pages considerably to include many common but often unrecognized behaviors that come hand-in-hand with the illness and that have a profound impact on the interactions of the child with all of the family members.

Many of these children simply cannot get up in the morning (they suffer sleep inertia), and Monday through Friday mornings devolve into a battleground as parents urgently try to pull their children out of bed and get them off to school. In addition, these children and adolescents can be relentless in the pursuit of their own agendas—wearing down the parents in the process (one mother coined the phrase "mission mode" for this behavior). Moreover, these youngsters are often bored and subsequently become very provocative (often with siblings) in order to relieve these intolerable periods of boredom. These discussions should help parents better understand what is driving the youngsters and how to better deal with and to modify the behaviors.

Finally, we have added a new section: Chapter 11, "Navigating the Shoals of Adolescence." These soon-to-be young adults have very special concerns: Who do they tell? How? When? How will a boyfriend or girl-friend respond, and how will potential mates and future in-laws react to their having this disorder? Here a young man shares his feelings about his fiancée's telling him about her bipolar disorder, and offers some personal guidance.

When we look back to the time when we were writing the first edition of this book, it's hard to think that the only source of information and support in the country was Tomie Burke's listserv, BPParents. Today there are several national, Web-based organizations dedicated to providing support and information about the illness and educational issues. The Internet has vastly altered the playing field, and we are filled with admiration for the parents who never stopped searching for answers, found them, and then turned around to offer others reservoirs of support and information. The stories they offered to us have enriched every edition of this book, and there are no words to describe our gratitude.

Again, we would like to acknowledge the following professionals who graciously shared their time and expertise with us: Laurie Austin, M.S.W., Ross J. Baldessarini, M.D., Dana Z. Luck, Ph.D., Scott Franz,

Tiffany Ruby, Paul Schottland, Ph.D., Steven Mattis, Ph.D., and Kevin Walz.

A very special acknowledgment must go to Anne Marie Smith, M.A., for her huge contributions to the education chapter, and to Herb Lachman, M.D., for his patient and illuminating discussions about the newest findings in the field of molecular genetics. We are fortunate indeed to have had their input.

A number of people helped in ways that were extremely meaningful to us, and we would like to say thank-you to Rebecca Frazee, Cheryll Hart, Justin Sweeney, Jeanne Langer, Cheryl Matalene, and Karen Williams.

This entire project started with our extraordinary agent, Pam Bernstein, and was wisely shepherded through its last two editions by our esteemed editor, Gerald Howard. To both of you we offer our heartfelt gratitude. We hope you realize what a privilege it is for us to hand this third edition over to our readers.

Demitri Papolos, M.D., and Janice Papolos
Westport, Connecticut, 2006

# Preface

When we first moved to our town, we met a couple who had a seven-year-old child who was extraordinarily bright but was prone to strange and agitated awakenings in the night. During the day his need to not be separated from his mother was so great that he insisted she carry a walkie-talkie so that he could always be in touch with her. He preferred his mother in his sight lines at all times.

As a baby he could go for days without sleeping, and the "terrible-two" temper tantrums persisted through toddlerhood and seemed to grow proportionately with each birthday. He was extremely oppositional and his mother and father couldn't find a way to discipline him, although they tried every parenting technique and spent a great deal of time in parenting classes and family therapies. Friends began pulling away, and their home—and any semblance of a family life—was being destroyed by his explosive behavior and erratic moods.

One evening the couple told us their story over dinner. It seems that they had a family history of manic-depression (now called bipolar disorder) on both sides going back generations; their son was showing all the signs of early-onset bipolar disorder—bipolar disorder that seems to present with temperamental features even in infancy. After listening carefully to Demitri's discussion of the illness, they said that their son fit the clinical description "to a T."

A few weeks later the boy threw his television set through the window in a fit of rage, and they took him to see a colleague of Demitri's, who did in fact diagnose him with the condition.

After a time on a mood stabilizer the tantrums and erratic behaviors ceased and the parents began to pick up the shards of their family life. Their son was able to use his great perceptive abilities in therapy, and he began to monitor his own behavior at home and in school. While it hasn't been a perfect path, the before-and-after differences are significant and have made all the difference for the boy and his family.

It has long been thought in the psychiatric community that children could not be given a diagnosis of bipolar disorder until the mid- to late teens and that mania in children was extremely rare. But scientists in the research vanguard are beginning to prove that the disorder can begin very early in life and that it is far more common than was previously supposed. Because the illness looks so different in childhood, however, these children cannot be shoehorned into the adult criteria of the *Diagnostic and Statistical Manual (DSM-IV)*—the guidebook for psychiatrists. As a result, either they go undiagnosed or they are misdiagnosed.

When our book *Overcoming Depression* was first published in 1987, we included a small section on mood disorders in children. At that time little was known about bipolar disorder in the very young, and there was a handful of medication studies in this age group. But in 1996, as we began work on the tenth-anniversary edition of the book, the professional literature had mushroomed, and Demitri was involved in research focusing on bipolar disorder in children. There was so much to say, and although we did expand the discussion of childhood mood disorders in that edition, we felt that the subject of bipolar disorder in children deserved a volume of its own. Yet no book was published for either the layperson or the professional.

We decided to team up again and write a book that would be as comprehensive and reassuring about the childhood form of bipolar disorder as *Overcoming Depression* is about mood disorders in adults. We wanted to let parents know what is and is not known about the condition and how to get proper help for their children.

In the very early stages of this book, we were extremely fortunate to be invited to subscribe to BPParents, a listserv of several hundred mothers and fathers of bipolar children who e-mail one another. This group gave us permission to "listen" to their postings in order to let us see what living with the illness was really like. The extensive questionnaire that we had constructed (reprinted on pages 433–436) was displayed on the website Parents of Bipolar Children.

The response was overwhelming. The voices and written statements from parents all over the United States—from Maine to Alaska—and from Canada, England, the Netherlands, and New Zealand began pouring into our computer and mailbox. Each day over 175 messages were delivered to our e-mail address, and for over a year we sat in front of the computer screen and read and downloaded the postings, carefully noting the questions the parents asked.

Being members of this listserv offered us a unique vantage point from which to write about this disorder. In contrast to seeing a child once a month in a clinical situation, this was akin to watching two hundred children with bipolar disorder and their families in something like real time—hour by hour, day by day, season by season.

Because of the parents' frank and revealing postings, we got to "see" how these children woke up in the morning, whether the mothers could comb their hair that day, what outfit they insisted on wearing, and in what mood they boarded the school bus. We read about their activities and moods in the afternoon, what they would and would not eat for dinner, and their difficulties as the day came to a close. We learned how these children reacted on Christmas morning and at their birthday parties and how they handled unstructured time when school was not in session. Remarkably, several times mothers were online while their sons or daughters were raging in the background. Their graphic descriptions of the children's lengthy explosions seemed a way to preserve the parents' sanity—a sort of SOS to the only other people on earth who could possibly fathom what they were withstanding.

We got to see how lonely and isolated these parents had become before they discovered this cybercommunity, how they had blamed themselves for the difficult behaviors of their children, and how they worried about the effects of the illness on their well children. Yet they never stopped reaching out to one another to offer advice, share solutions they had found, and make other heartbroken parents only an e-mail address away feel less lonely and more supported and embraced.

These incredible women and men offered us the same support they offered to one another. Not only did they fill out our questionnaires carefully and thoughtfully, but from thirty-four states they sent hospital and school records, diaries and journals, charts of their children's mood disorders, and notes inviting us to call them and use "anything you think might help other parents and their children." We took them up on the offer and conducted over a hundred follow-up interviews on the telephone. When we had specific questions, we conducted minisurveys on the listserv and received intriguing answers that contributed to our data collection.

These parents as well as parents who were not on the listserv but who received the questionnaire from leaders of child and adolescent support groups or through our own professional networks and contacts gave us permission to quote them throughout this book. Their voices and the voices of their children have pride of place in these pages.

Toward the end of the year we spent writing, we transferred the information from the questionnaires to a database and crunched the numbers. The data revealed some very disturbing findings about the diagnosis and treatment of early-onset bipolar disorder. Because of the mixed-symptom picture of these children—many appear hyperactive and are oppositional or have obsessive-compulsive and anxiety disorders—most are being shunted off into these diagnostic groups without the possibility of a bipolar disorder even being considered (despite the fact that most of the children come from backgrounds with mood disorders). Many of these children were initially diagnosed as having attention-deficit disorder with hyperactivity (ADHD) and put on stimulant medications; or they were first seen in the throes of depression with little or no consideration of the opposite pole of a mood disorder. As a result, a shocking number of children were thrown into manic and psychotic states, became paranoid and violent, and ended up in a hospital—unstable, suicidal, and in worse shape than before the treatment began.

We want to state clearly that, given the accumulating knowledge in the field of research and the reactions of the children in our study, no doctor should prescribe a stimulant or antidepressant drug to a child whose family history reveals mood disorders without suspecting a "snake beneath the rock." Parents need to be warned of the possibility that these drugs may wreak havoc on a possible quiescent bipolar gene.

*In other words, bipolar disorder should be ruled out before any of the stimulant drugs or antidepressants are prescribed.* Instead, mood-stabilizing drugs such as lithium, Depakote, or Tegretol should be considered as a first line of treatment—early on—before episodes become more frequent, and the illness warps the psychological development of a child and destroys the life of a family.

We cannot imagine how families cope with this illness without an up-to-date resource at their fingertips. It is our fervent hope that this volume will shed new light on the enormous complexities of early-onset bipolar disorder, all the while offering support and intelligent solutions to family members. We also hope that these pages will create a new level of awareness about this illness and inspire further psychiatric research. This, in turn, will ensure more accurate diagnosis, better treatment, and a brighter future for all the children and adolescents suffering with this much-misunderstood disorder.

Demitri Papolos, M.D., and Janice Papolos
Westport, Connecticut, 1999

# Acknowledgments

Throughout the writing of this book, we were privileged to have the encouragement and support of so many people that it is with deep pride and gratitude that we acknowledge them here.

First, we owe the most profound debt to Tomie Burke, the founder of the online support group, BPParents. Several years ago, she created a safe haven on the Internet where parents of bipolar children could come together and share their grief, their struggles, and their triumphs. She was so supportive of this project that she introduced us to her listserv and urged the group to let us subscribe and receive its postings. In so doing, she—and they—opened the private world of the families of bipolar children and gave us the opportunity to write as truthful and compelling a book as possible. This precious community taught us more about heroic parenting, true love, and courage under fire than we could have learned in a lifetime, and we are grateful beyond measure. We would also like to thank all the men and women who filled out our questionnaire, gave us hours of their time on the telephone, and helped us collect invaluable data on the subject of early-onset bipolar disorder. In addition, we wish to thank the many children and young adults who generously discussed their personal experience with the illness and helped us to understand it from their point of view. In order to protect their privacy, we have changed all names and identifying characteristics.

Nine very special women must be mentioned next: Martha Hellander put all of her resources at our disposal, directed us to issues we needed to cover, and supplied us with important books, papers, and contacts. Karen Huckins, Jeanne Landry Harpin, Brenda Souto, Linda DiSantis, and Jennifer Burke made important contributions to these pages. Penny Smith, Linda N., Janice MacDonald, and Barbara Lurie Sand read the early drafts of the manuscript and provided much-needed insight and suggestions.

In our last book, we had the privilege of counting on the great medical expertise of Ross J. Baldessarini, M.D., of Harvard Medical School. His wisdom and keen eye are very much present in this volume also, and we are deeply indebted to him. We would also like to thank Charles Popper, M.D., also of Harvard Medical School, for his pioneering work in the field of early-onset bipolar disorder and for helping us track down some very elusive facts.

The other professionals we wish to acknowledge are: Nancy Austin, Psy. D., Julie Beckett, Deborah Bullwinckle, Trudy Carlson, M.S., Gianni Faedda, M.D., Max Fink, M.D., Shawn Fordham, Victor M. Fornari, M.D., Barbara Geller, M.D., Mark George, M.D., Julie Keys, Paul Kosowsky, L.S.C.W., Shalani Madon, Anna Papadorotheou, Norman Rosenthal, M.D., Andrew Stoll, M.D., Michael Strober, Ph.D., and Stephanie Welch.

We are particularly grateful to Suzanne Faustini, L.S.W., Elizabeth Jester, Esq., and Rosalie Greenberg, M.D., for their time, experience, and guidance.

A special thank-you to Andrew Skrilow, who spent months entering the data and crunching the numbers for us. His work was critical to this book.

Pam Bernstein, our literary agent of thirteen years and cherished friend, jump-started this project and brought it to the attention of editors in the most intelligent way. No two authors ever had a more indefatigable and able advocate. A special thank-you also to Donna Downing of Pam Bernstein and Associates, who was a trusted adviser throughout the project.

We met the team at Broadway Books on what was surely the coldest day of 1998, but we soon found the warmest, most supportive home there. Tracy Behar, our editor and the associate publisher at Broadway Books, should win awards for her insightful editing and responsiveness. We grew to admire her mind and expertise, and we were always grateful for the enormous care she invested in this book. Angela Casey was a pleasure to work with, kept us on track, and was a great source of moral support. Our being Broadway authors is particularly meaningful to us, because its esteemed publisher, William Shinker, originally acquired *Overcoming Depression* for HarperCollins in 1984. He has been the godfather of both these volumes, and we are very grateful for his belief in us then, and now.

We want to say a resounding thank-you to author Victoria Secunda, someone whose work we had long admired. Not only has she become the closest of friends, but she was always there for us, offering unfailing support and wise counsel from the proposal stage to the finished manuscript (even while racing toward her own book deadline). She also talked us through the many anxious moments that come with the writing of any book.

We were most fortunate to have a circle of people who anchored and sustained us and made very special and unique contributions. From the bottom of our hearts we thank Rose Belfiore Albicocco, Nick Granito, Carol Jessemy, Mervyn M. Peskin, M.D., Michael Porder, M.D., Wendy Queen, Nina Schorr, M.D., Irwin Sollinger, Ph.D., Laura and Mark Spector, Robert Shprintzen, Ph.D., Marlene Trotman, Marvin Wasserman, M.D., and Ruth and Alan Winnick.

And finally, we would like to acknowledge our two sons, Alex and Jordy, who tolerated their computer-bound, extremely preoccupied parents with patience and a good-natured humor. We would also like to mention that six-year-old Jordy took it upon himself to man the telephones, telling strangers and salespeople (and, unfortunately, sometimes even teachers): "They can *never* call you back. They have a lot of pages to write." We hope that someday this volume will make them proud.

# PART I

# Diagnosis and Treatment

# Voices from
# the Front

A few years ago Tomie Burke, a young mother in Pullman, Washington, developed a listserv (called BPParents) for parents of children with bipolar disorder. She was motivated to do so because when her six-year-old son first began experiencing the baffling and frightening symptoms of the illness, she searched community and university libraries, bookstores, databases, and Internet pages in her desperate desire to become educated about the illness and to help her child. She found little to check out, purchase, or download.

But eventually she did become extremely knowledgeable about the illness, and she wanted to reach out to other families—to provide information and assure them that they were not alone. She soon had an address on the World Wide Web called Parents of Bipolar Children. The site consisted of a home page, links to information about the disorder, and a guest book where parents could describe how they found the site, note whether they had a boy or girl with a diagnosis of bipolar disorder, and comment a bit about their situations.

The messages left by parents who visited convey a desperate need for information and sheer relief when they discover that they are not alone—that the illness is not uncommon and that it isn't caused by bad parenting. That first year thousands of parents came to the site seeking help for their children.

What is early-onset bipolar disorder, and why is it such a little-known illness? Most people have never heard of the expression, but it is actually psychiatry's phrase for manic-depression that occurs early—*very* early—in life. (Adults who used to be diagnosed manic-depressive are now also referred to as having bipolar disorder.)

Bipolar disorder in children is a neglected public health problem. It is estimated that one-third of all the children in this country who are being diagnosed with attention-deficit disorder with hyperactivity (ADHD) are actually suffering from early symptoms of bipolar disorder. Since close to 4 million children were prescribed stimulants such as Ritalin in 1998, that's over 1 million children who eventually will be diagnosed as bipolar. According to the American Academy of Child and Adolescent Psychiatry, a third of the 3.4 million children who first seem to be suffering with depression will go on to manifest the bipolar form of a mood disorder. Researchers in the field of early-onset bipolar disorder peg that figure closer to 50 percent. In the only large-scale epidemiological study done on the rates of bipolar disorder in adolescence, Dr. Peter M. Lewinsohn and his colleagues examined more than 1,700 high school students in western Oregon, and found that 5.7 percent of this group of adolescents—or ninety-seven students—suffered some form of bipolar spectrum disorder (they met criteria for the "Bipolar Not Otherwise Specified" category we will speak about in the next chapter). Amid all the dry statistics stand several million suffering children, as well as their mothers, fathers, brothers, sisters, and grandparents.

This illness is as old as humankind, and has probably been conserved in the human genome because it confers great energy and originality of thought. People who have had it have literally changed the course of human history: Manic-depression has afflicted (and probably fueled the brilliance of) people like Isaac Newton, Abraham Lincoln, Winston Churchill, Theodore Roosevelt, Johann Goethe, Honoré de Balzac, George Frederic Handel, Ludwig von Beethoven, Robert Schumann, Leo Tolstoy, Charles Dickens, Virginia Woolf, Ernest Hemingway, Robert Lowell, and Anne Sexton.

But until recently, manic-depression was thought to affect people in their early twenties or older. It was not viewed as an illness that could occur among children.

This has proven to be myth. The temperamental features and behaviors of bipolar disorder can begin to emerge very early on—even in infancy.

But because a vast majority of bipolar children also meet criteria for ADHD (and the focus of drug treatment strategies becomes the symptoms of ADHD), the bipolar illness is typically overlooked. As a result, drugs are prescribed to deal only with the symptoms of hyperactivity and distractibility. And, since many, many children initially develop depressive symptoms as the earliest manifestation of the illness, bipolar disorder may again be discounted as the primary diagnosis.

Childhood bipolar disorder can overlap or occur with many disorders of childhood other than ADHD or depression: panic disorder, generalized anxiety disorder, obsessive-compulsive disorder (OCD), and Tourette's syndrome, to name a few. And this mixed-symptom picture can be perplexing and confound diagnosis. Moreover, only in the past few years has bipolar disorder become the focus of research inquiry.

## The Illness in Adults

Bipolar disorder in children presents very differently from how it presents in adults. Adults typically experience a more classical pattern of mood swings. In the manic phase, the person experiences an increased rate of thinking, has surges of energy, and describes him- or herself as feeling more active, creative, intelligent, and sexual than he or she ever thought possible. The need for sleep diminishes as one idea after another bursts into consciousness and the person develops the expectation that he or she will be able to execute all the ideas that are flowing effortlessly into the mind. For many, a mild hypomania (less than manic state) is a period that brims with physical and mental well-being. It is often a time of great creativity.

Unfortunately, this enviable state does not last. A person experiencing the "highs" of manic-depression may make reckless decisions, go on buying sprees, commit sexual indiscretions, or bring financial ruin upon self and family. The mood of someone in a manic state is brittle and irritable; it may shift back and forth quickly, and the person may become very paranoid. If the hypomania escalates into a full-blown mania, the person can lose all touch with reality and become psychotic. In this stage (called stage 3 mania), a doctor may be unable to tell whether the patient is schizophrenic or manic-depressive without having the family history and other information about the patient's previous functioning.

Typically, after the manic energy is spent, the person plummets into the depths of depression. The mind slows down to such a degree that any decision seems almost impossible to make. Some depressed people will experience insomnia and early-morning awakening; others will begin to sleep excessively and yet never feel rested. In addition to mood, energy, and sleep disturbances, a person in a depression may feel bodily pains, such as headaches, backaches, and stomach problems.

Some adult patients will feel inordinate amounts of guilt; some will feel irritable, anxious, and hopeless. Depressed patients may feel they deserve only punishment and can become fixed on all the small mistakes they have made in their lives—losing any sense of past accomplishments. In the depths of depression, a person's thinking can become delusional and psychotic.

It is not unusual for adults to experience several weeks of hypomania or mania—very often in the spring or summer months—only to find their energy level ebbing as the days shorten in autumn. Individuals who experience depressions alternating with intense or psychotic manias are referred to as having the Bipolar I form of the disorder. Those who suffer depressions and experience only hypomanic episodes (they never get psychotic or lose total control) are referred to as being Bipolar II. Most adults will have well intervals in between the periods of heightened or lowered mood.

## BIPOLAR DISORDER IN CHILDREN

Children rarely fit this recognizable pattern. They have a more chronic course of illness where they cycle back and forth with few discernible well periods in between. Some tend to cycle rapidly (more than four times a year); some cycle within the week or month (and may be called ultrarapid cyclers). Many cycle so rapidly that they fit a pattern called ultraultrarapid (ultradian) cycling: They may have frequent spikes of highs and lows within a twenty-four-hour period.

Almost all bipolar children have certain temperamental and behavioral traits in common. They tend to be inflexible and oppositional, they tend to be extraordinarily irritable, and a large majority experience periods of explosive rage. They tantrum for hours at a time. Holes get kicked in walls, and parents and siblings and pets can be threatened or hurt.

Bipolar children don't often show this rageful side to the outside world. And because parents don't wish the outside world to see the child in this light, or to learn of their lack of control over the child—most people couldn't possibly imagine what actually goes on anyway—the illness stays behind closed doors as the parents try desperately to find some solutions to the fact that their lives are being turned upside down. As one woman described it: "We feel like we've been thrown into a tornado that is big, black, and powerful."

No one symptom identifies a child as having bipolar disorder, but if hyperactivity, irritable and shifting moods, and prolonged temper tantrums co-occur—and there is a history of mood disorders and/or alcoholism coming down either or both the mother's and father's line—the index of suspicion should be high.

Indeed, our study sample showed that over 80 percent of the children who developed early-onset bipolar disorder had what is known as "bilineal transmission"—substance abuse and mood disorders appeared on both sides of their families.

Perhaps the best way to get a "feel" for what the illness looks like in childhood is to listen to the voices of parents describing the temperaments and behaviors of their children.

## Difficulties in Infancy

Many parents recall that their children were different from early infancy. They seemed to sleep erratically and were irritable and difficult to settle:

> From the beginning he slept about four to six hours a night with virtually no naps other than that one span of sleep. This continued until he was four years old.

> He was very fussy, and some nights he did not actually go to sleep until 3:00 A.M. Then he would be up in the morning raring to go.

Many of these babies are referred to as "the wide-eyed babies of the nursery." One mother said that the nurse brought her baby to her after a twenty-four-hour isolation period and said, "Good luck! She's done nothing but cry for twenty-four hours and there was nothing we could do to soothe her."

Author Danielle Steel, whose son Nick Traina had early-onset bipolar disorder and who has written one of the few published accounts of how the disorder evolves from infancy, speaks about her child's surprising lack of a need to sleep in *His Bright Light*:

There was one thing about him that worried me then. He never slept, or not enough, anyway. Long before he was two I came to the realization that I couldn't give him a nap. If I did it meant that he'd be up all night, even long after me, and I work late at night. But he just didn't seem to need much sleep.

Many of the mothers we interviewed remembered their babies excessive activity even in utero. They seemed temperamentally different from their earliest days. Two mothers described it this way:

While my daughter was in the womb, she kicked so hard and so often that I had very little rest . . . much of the time it felt like she was in a fight—rolling and tumbling around inside me and then, when she was born, the nurse gave her a pacifier even though they were not permitted in the nursery. She kept all the other babies up all night with her screaming.

I too noticed signs that this was an extraspirited child. In fact, while I was pregnant, I remember saying, "Uh-oh, the baby is angry again." His kicks would last for an hour as I doubled over in pain toward the end of the pregnancy.

And a mother of twins told us that "at fourteen weeks the sonographer and obstetrician were unable to get a picture of Ian's face and could not sample the amniotic fluid due to 'constant, unpredictable activity.' "

## Precociousness

These children seem to burst into life and are on a different time schedule from the rest of the world right from the beginning. Many are extremely precocious and bright—doing everything early and with gusto. They seem like magical children, their creativity can be astounding, and the parents speak about them with real respect, and sometimes even awe:

She was always ahead of her time. She started talking at eight months with the words "kitty cat." She walked at nine months and was speaking in complete sentences by a year. She was writing small novels in the second grade. She acted and danced and sang way beyond her years.

At eighteen months he climbed out of the baby bed in the middle of the night, opened the fridge, got out three dozen eggs (it was Easter time), and proceeded to sit in his booster chair and crack three dozen eggs onto our hardwood floors. (He wanted to bake a real cake—he didn't like the toy mixing bowl I had given him to play with.) After the insurance company quit laughing they did pay to refinish our floors.

Another mother wrote that her son "has never been a child; he always thought like an adult. At the age of four he got very exercised and wanted to know, 'Why *can't* I have a phone in my room?' " Danielle Steel's son, Nick, "developed a passion for disco music at a year. His favorite was Gloria Gaynor singing 'I Will Survive,' and he would dance endlessly as we played records in my room. Our first serious argument came while planning his first birthday party, when he announced he wanted a clown and disco music, strange requests for a one-year-old."

## Separation Anxiety

Another behavioral trait often remarked upon is the infant's inability to be separated from the mother. Separation anxiety is often so extreme that mothers can't put the babies down. One mother remembers "cleaning chicken with her in a Snugli"; another hasn't forgotten "vacuuming with her in a sling"; and one mother described being "mauled, with his nails scraping down my chest as he struggled against being withdrawn by his father, who was trying to take him from me so that I could take a shower."

Indeed, this separation anxiety seems to arise long before and persist long after its appearance and disappearance in nonbipolar children. Lillian Hunt-Meeks, the daughter of Swanee Hunt, former U.S. ambassador to Austria, suffered early-onset bipolar disorder and had this to say about her separation anxiety in an article she and her mother wrote for *Good Housekeeping*:

For as long as I can remember, I was afraid of my mother leaving me. When I was little I would scream and cry every time she went away. Once, I remember, she went to Colorado Springs (just an hour away), and I spent the night at my best friend's house. I cried the whole time. The next day at school I was asked to write a story, and in my five-year-old handwriting scrawled on the title: "When My Mother Left and Went to Colorado Springs."

On the questionnaire that so many parents filled out and sent to us, we would find little notes scrawled in the margins of the pages saying things like "He is never more than a foot away from me"; "If he could crawl back into the womb, he would"; "She follows me into the bathroom; we seem joined at the hip."

Another mother e-mailed us about the separation anxiety her son was experiencing and had this to say:

> Right now Jamison can't be separated from me—it's like the umbil-
> ical cord grew back! I can't get him out of my room at night. If he
> falls asleep somewhere else, he ends up there eventually. I've stepped
> on him in the middle of the night many times. He hides under the
> bed with only his head sticking out. But he gets so anxious, and this
> relieves some of it.

Actress Patty Duke, who is quite candid about her manic-depression, wrote about separation anxiety in her autobiography *Call Me Anna*. She said: "When I was young, I had a dream, a child's nightmare: that I would be taken someplace away from my mother and never know if I was going to be with her again." She describes holding her mother's hand constantly whenever she was with her.

## Night Terrors and Vivid Nightmares

Many bipolar children suffer night terrors from which they awaken screaming with fright. Sometimes they cannot even be awakened but remain in a semiconscious state while they continue to experience some frightening event. When they reveal their nightmares, what stands out is the content.

They dream of being chased by sharks or monsters, but where typically a nonbipolar child wakes up just before the teeth pierce an arm or a leg, a bipolar child doesn't—the jaws surround the arm or leg, the massive teeth crunch into the skin, and bone and blood fill the water. Their dreams are often filled with blood and gore. As Dr. Charles Popper from Harvard Medical School wrote in an article titled "On Diagnostic Gore in Child's Nightmares":

> As bipolar children talk about these dreams, they report the explicit
> appearance of blood (not just imagined or inferred, but actually vi-

sualized blood) and descriptions of mutilations of bodies, dismemberment, and the insides of body parts. Their dreams are considerably more affectively intense than regular nightmares.

Dreams of fighting are quite common. In the fighting dreams of children or adults with mere anxiety, a knife may be pulled out and brought into attack, but the dreamer wakes up just before the knife enters the skin or rips the clothing. For bipolar children, the knife goes in, the blood is seen, and the dream may continue at considerable length and with explicit visualization of gore. . . . Where the "newsreel" of a dream story normally stops, the "newsreel" in the bipolar children keeps going.

Dr. Popper explains: "In these individuals, it is as though their unconscious sensors of painful affect are not working, even in their dreams."

Indeed, that may explain why some of these children say such shocking and almost sadistic things during the day. A nursery school director told us the story of a three-year-old boy who one day in the classroom said that "my father is going to come in and put seven knives in your throat." (And this was in response to her asking him to sit down.) Another youngster said to a teacher: "I'm going to put a rope around your neck and pull it till you bleed and your face goes white and your shirt is soaked with blood."

Perhaps the emotionally charged imagery of their nightmares is spilling over to the conscious mind during the day. Whatever the mechanism, these children are dealing with horrifying imagery of bodily threat, dismemberment, and death.

Danielle Steel noted with alarm that her son became "obsessed with Dracula . . . talking about him constantly. . . . At the same time he began drawing pictures of people killing each other, swords drawn, and dripping blood from severed limbs." These drawings, using only black crayons, pencils, and paint, were shown to doctor after doctor, and Ms. Steel was told by doctor after doctor that her son merely had a vivid imagination.

Other parents have told us that their children have never drawn a picture that does not include someone dying; and one mother described her son drawing human figures with huge, *Stegosaurus*-like blades on their backs.

It is small wonder that these children are afraid to go to sleep and that they need their parents to stay with them all through the night.

## Fear of Death and Annihilation

Accompanying these nightmares is a massive fear of death and annihilation. After her name was changed from Anna to Patty for professional reasons, Patty Duke recalls "a fear of death so powerful it precipitated anxiety attacks from the early 1950s to 1983. I was obsessed, truly obsessed with my mortality. All of a sudden the absolute realization of my mortality would hit and I just felt impelled to scream. Sometimes it was what I'd call a bloody-murder scream, sometimes words like 'No! No! No! No!' Inevitably, though, it happened at night, on the way to sleep. I'd scream every night of my life. I was overtaken by abject terror."

Ambassador Swanee Hunt noted something wrong in her daughter and said: "We were baffled by Lillian's preoccupation with death and separation. Even before she could write, the stories she told her teacher were laced with tragedy."

## Raging

Nighttime is terrifying for the bipolar child, but daytime becomes something of a nightmare for both the child and his or her family as rages begin to erupt. During these rages, which are typically triggered by a simple parental "no," the child goes into an almost seizurelike tantrum where he or she kicks, hits, bites, punches, breaks things, and screams foul language. This can go on for three hours at a time, several times a day, and can persist through adolescence if the child is not treated.

The child seems to have no control over the rage. One young woman who developed the illness early on told us:

It comes out so quickly; faster than a knee-jerk reaction. It's like electricity shoots through me. It's like being struck with lightning. I feel rage and hurt and need to strike back. It becomes primal— infantile.

I would throw things, smash a couple of frogs between rocks. I was raging all the time—every day, multiple times a day, verbally abusive, nasty, negative, but very careful not to show it to the outside world.

Another teenager described her rage this way:

I used to go to my room and punch the walls and I could not stop crying. The more I would cry, the more I couldn't stop. It was like a dream you can't recover in the morning: You know something bad and worrisome has been a concern somewhere in your brain, but you just can't remember it. Sometimes I felt so bad and would think: Why did I do that? And sometimes I'd actually feel better, like it cleared the air.

An eight-year-old boy explained that "when my moods shift, I am never prepared. It feels all tight around me. During a rage, I feel as though the real me is over on the stairway watching myself, but I'm powerless to stop it."

Indeed, the child seems to go into some kind of trancelike state. The parents describe it as "the look." The child seems to be in his own world, and the pupils of the eyes dilate and the eyes become wild-looking. One woman who was having difficulty describing "the look" said, "I finally came up with a word that fits. It's feral. He looks feral when he rages. Almost like a wild animal that is fighting for its life, territory, whatever. There is a certain shine in his eyes that is almost metallic. He just exudes this primal rage."

We have spoken to parents who haven't bought furniture in years because it all gets broken during one of these "affective storms." Their children are experiencing so much irritability and rage that the parents feel as if they live in a war zone. In Chapter 7 we will discuss some theories as to what is happening in the brain during these seizurelike rages, but on a daily basis parents and siblings are experiencing variations on the following:

Walking on eggshells would have been a treat compared to what life was like at our house. Even looking in her direction was seen as an attack. I was out of a job for a while last fall, and she spent part of every day belittling me—telling me how I was letting the family down by making a career change. The screaming, the foul language, and eventually the violence were devastating to our family.

Another mother described her seven-year-old thus:

He had major, major raging cycles. I'm talking going for several weeks, raging violently, throwing things, attacking me, throwing a chair out the window, going through a knife drawer saying he was going to kill me. I couldn't go to the bathroom, for fear he would hurt himself or me.

Friends, teachers, and the outside world cannot fathom what the parent is talking about (if the parent talks about it at all). But one mother who managed to catch an entire rage with a tape recorder wrote:

Many of our friends and even some of the professionals who work with us have not seen Robby in his full glory. They cannot believe that this sweet, charming, affectionate, and outgoing child could possibly be violent or bipolar. They just assume we are not firm enough with him, or pay too much attention to him.

So I got it on tape from start to finish—the screaming and yelling that he's going to kill me, kill the cats. . . .

Now anytime a friend says: "But he's so wonderful whenever we see him" I can pull out the tape and say, "Have a listen to this."

She went on to say:

How am I to have any kind of work life with this going on every day? It's impossible. After I dropped him off at school, I just had to cry as I have no one to talk to who could possibly understand the terror of living with a child like this.

Sir Isaac Newton's mother understood—even in the seventeenth century. As a youngster, Isaac visited his mother and stepfather and had such a rage attack that, in his own words, he threatened "to burne them and the house over them." He left home for boarding school at the age of ten, but not before terrorizing the household. In his diaries he describes: "Striking many"; "Peevishness with my mother and my sister"; "Falling out with the servants"; and "Punching my sister."

## Oppositional Behavior

In addition to the ADHD-like behavior, a significant number of these children exhibit behaviors of, and are diagnosed as having, oppositional defiant disorder (ODD). A child who meets the criteria for ODD typically argues with adults; is negativistic, disobedient, and hostile; and actively refuses to comply with requests made by adults.

But is this oppositionality really a separate diagnosis? Many psychiatrists in the research vanguard view this oppositional behavior as an aspect of the bipolar condition. These children seem incapable of making any transition or of complying with any request made by the parent. Their first reaction to anything is "no."

One father described how oppositional his nine-year-old son had become and told us that when he asked the boy if he wanted to go to the toy store to buy the toy he had been campaigning for, but informed him that they would first stop for pizza and ice cream on the way, his son's first response was "No! I'm not going!"

When presented as surprises, even much-desired experiences can seem threatening—a demand to reset the sequence of already integrated events. Transitions cause stress for these children, and stress causes meltdowns.

Children with bipolar disorder lack the flexibility that allows a smooth transition from one activity to another. In fact, parents soon learn to prepare their children for any transition well in advance so that they can integrate the idea of it.

Because any request or expectation may be viewed as a stressor, these children can become very adept at blocking out anyone else's agenda and become remarkably adept at clamoring for their own. Many parents feel beaten down by this persistence and oppositional behavior. Two women were commiserating with each other on the Internet and wrote:

My son is another future lawyer—argues and finds some slight difference in semantics to turn things around. I always thought of it as an OCD trait—had to get the last word in no matter what. I picture him as a future "My Cousin Vinny."

To which the other woman responded:

Ditto for my son. Maybe they could get together and form a company called "Battle Warriors, Inc." Their motto could be something like: "Whether you're right or wrong, we win every battle. Specialists in browbeating all opponents."

## Rapid Cycling

Beyond the oppositionality and extreme irritability, the majority of bi-polar children cycle rapidly from depression to mania and back again. Some cycle over a period of days; others seem to alternate mood states several times throughout the day. One seventeen-year-old girl, now treated, described it this way:

> My moods shifted constantly throughout the day. I can remember being so so happy, but after a while I wouldn't like it because I knew I would be coming down. It's so rapid. I'd be so happy and an hour later I'd say, "I'm so depressed."
>
> When I crash, I come down so hard, I can't do anything; I can't get up. I'm tired. I just have to sit down. My mom has to force me to go places. No words can describe it. It physically hurts your heart. You're so depressed that you actually feel that you're dying. You feel like you're wasting away—like you have cancer. When I'm de-pressed, I want to get high [manic], but then I worry about the com-ing depression. I always get depressed around the beginning to late afternoon. At six or seven I get hyper, happy. Sometimes I get a bad manic period. I feel angry and agitated and I feel I have to punch stuff. I just want to shake things. I have so much energy I feel like I want to jump out of my skin.

Because the mood shifts are so rapid, it is easy to see how children may become trapped in the switch process between depression and mania and develop what is called a *mixed state*. Their internal experience is one of marked agitation, anxiety, high energy, and constant restlessness. At the same time they feel worthless and self-destructive. While mixed states are not as common in adults unless induced by antidepressant treatment, they are a hallmark of the ultrarapid cycles found in childhood-onset bipolar disorder.

Dr. Barbara Geller of Washington University in St. Louis describes an example of depression and mania—a mixed state—occurring simultane-ously in a seven-year-old boy: "He was doing a Michael Jackson imitation at the diagnostic interview but was experiencing suicidal impulses at the same time."

## Sensitivity to Stimuli

Many parents describe their children as excruciatingly sensitive to stimuli of all sorts. The mother of one young girl describes her daughter as "very sensitive in the visual realm. She is drawn like a magnet to some designs, colors, beautiful paintings, landscapes, and repelled by others, as strongly as she reacts to odors and tastes. I always try to see the positive in these things—telling her that she would be a good interior or clothing designer, artist, chef, writer, or teacher."

Some bipolar children are so sensitive to stimuli that they cannot tolerate pockets in clothing or labels or collars on shirts. Backpacks must always feel a certain way, and we know children who will stuff them with books to approximate the "right feel" even if there is no homework given and no textbooks are required that day.

We've heard of mothers who've spent whole days shopping for socks that didn't have "nubbies" on the bottom; or for only blue clothing because "that is all my son would wear." Both mothers and fathers could be certified in the "Titration of Shoelaces" because their children have to have their sneakers tied at just the right tension or they can become explosive.

It's as if the arousal system of the child is set at such a threshold that any kind of physical sensation that is not "just right" is extremely irritating and threatens a sense of bodily integrity.

Bipolar children seem to be out of sync. Not only are they bothered tremendously by sensations, odors, and noises, but they seem to have great difficulty making shifts from one context to another. When the demand to do so is made—and it may only be a request to stop watching television and join the family in the kitchen for dinner—he or she may not be able to brook the transition and the change in the state of mood, attention, or motor response required. The child may become easily frustrated and irritable, and a repeated (or eventually heated) demand may provoke the child's angry outburst or rage.

The limbic system (the emotional brain) seems to be involved with the integration of sensory experience, and we will explore this more closely in Chapter 7.

## Problems with Peers

We asked parents in our survey to describe their child's relationship with friends. While some children were thought of as "charismatic," "very

generous to friends," and "extremely popular," the majority of the respon-
dents (77 percent) reported that their children were having tremendous
problems maintaining peer relationships. Some had never been invited to
a birthday party or had a sleepover. Many of the children were described
as "bossy," "intrusive," "has to have his or her own way or the game is
over," or "too overwhelming and aggressive." Sadly, these children want
very much to have friends, but they seem to miss the social clues or appreciate social boundaries.

## Temperature Dysregulation

In our research, we noticed that parents often mentioned how reactive
their children were to cold and heat. These children were often overheated
in winter and left the house wearing no coat or gloves. One child slept in
a house that was so cold the parents were burrowing under down quilts
even as their child kicked off the comforter, saying she was burning hot.
Many of these children take their clothes off as often as they can because
they are so heat intolerant. Some get red ears or red spots on their cheeks
when they make transitions from cold to warm environments. And all
foods—soups, teas, milk shakes—must be just the right temperature or
they are rejected. (Chapter 7 will also discuss some theories about this
pattern of temperature dysregulation.)

## Craving for Carbohydrates and Sweets

Another noted difference in children and adolescents with bipolar disorder is their insatiable appetite for carbohydrates and sweets. They may begin hoarding chocolate and cookies in their rooms and consume massive
amounts of pasta, potatoes, cereals, and bread. One mother referred to her
daughter as "the Carb Queen from way back"; another dubbed her daughter "Spud."

When we asked a young woman of twenty who had suffered bipolar
disorder since childhood if she ever craved carbohydrates or sweets, there
was a giggle at the other end of the phone. She asked, "Would you consider a gallon of Breyer's Mint Chocolate Chip every night a craving?"

She went on to tell us that her craving was so strong that she would
buy a half gallon and eat it in the car and then go back in the store and
buy another one. We asked if she had kept plastic spoons in the car. She
laughed out loud and said, "No, I would use my fingers. It was savage."

We know of other girls who pour sugar straight from the box down their throats, or teenagers who drive long distances to get powdered-sugar doughnuts that they consume by the dozen. Many of the girls suffer from co-occurring eating disorders and may become anorexic or bulimic (starving, gorging, and/or purging). Some of the girls (and a smaller percentage of boys) will begin periods of self-mutilation in their teenage years, where they rake their arms with razors, pins, or other sharp objects (see page 47 for more on this).

Children who have bipolar disorder typically have food aversions, sudden demands for certain foods to the exclusion of all others, or notable ingestion habits. A mother from Colorado referred to her son's eating patterns as "snaking" because "he barely eats for days and then devours ungodly amounts of pasta and other carbohydrate foods."

## Bedwetting and Soiling

Something also seems to be poorly regulated in the autonomic nervous system of these children. Many wet their beds for years throughout childhood. Other children may smear feces in the bathtub, on walls, or in closets. This enuresis (bedwetting) and encopresis (soiling) is poorly understood.

## Impending Mania

Some children cycle so quickly that it's hard to see the switch process from one mood to another; others have a more noticeable transition. At these times, the child may get very goal-oriented. One mother said:

> If he's getting manic, he starts looking for tools or unhooking the computer. If he wants to do something, watch out. Get out of his way, or he'll become very, very angry. You can't set limits. We'll see very up-up-up behavior. He quotes Ren and Stimpy, the cartoon characters, and screams "Happy, happy, joy, joy!" His voice gets louder and louder. He starts grabbing tools, playing loud music in his room. I don't know when it's going to end . . . could be tonight, could be in a couple of days.

Other parents describe periods of intense silliness—giddy and goofy behavior with a lot of mouthiness, grandiosity, and outrageous comments. The child's thoughts may race. One five-year-old boy told his mother: "My brain feels like it wants to go for a walk ten times . . . up the stairs and down the stairs . . . and again." When this youngster couldn't sleep, he explained: "My brain keeps kicking me out of bed." Dr. Barbara Geller speaks of a child who once told her, "I wish I had a button on my head so I could turn off all these thoughts."

In D. Jablow Hershman and Julien Lieb's book, *Manic Depression and Creativity,* Charles Dickens was described as quite manic in his early teenage years: "He became very sociable, was generally in a humorous mood, and was given to telling jokes and singing comic songs whenever the opportunity offered. His gaiety was so excessive at times as to embarrass school friends. His laughter would become uncontrollable, almost hysterical. He played pranks and acted the clown."

As the manic throttle is pushed, a child may become more and more grandiose. She may think she is the best, the brightest, able to do things no one else can. It may start simply when a student decides he or she can teach the class better than the teacher, or brag about how famous he is going to be someday. A little girl who drew a lot of pictures when she was hypomanic always placed a crown on her head, frequently picturing herself as a queen.

Accompanying this very "up" feeling may be an increased sexuality (hypersexuality). Some mothers report that their boys are always pinching the bottoms of women they meet in the store, or hugging and groping women they know. The phone bill may reveal a number of calls to 1-900 sex lines. A mother from Virginia who filled out our questionnaire commented that her daughter dresses in skimpy clothing when she becomes hypomanic and tries to sit on the laps of her older brother's friends who come over to the house.

Dr. Geller and her colleagues published an article in 2000 in which they looked at a group of ninety-three children and adolescents with bipolar disorder and found that 43 percent of this group who were manic were also hypersexual.

Often this hypersexuality is viewed by hospital personnel and Child Protective Services as a sign that sexual abuse is taking place inside the home, but it is a symptom of the mood disorder and is present in hypomanic and manic children, as well as hypomanic and manic adults. Dr. Geller reported that less than 1 percent of these hypersexual bipolar children had evidence of sexual abuse in the home environment.

Here is another description of a very hypomanic, hypersexual seven-year-old boy:

He got very silly after dinner—very affectionate with me, and hypersexual at bath time. He said, "I love you, Mommy," trying to kiss me. "Will you lay on top of me. I'm going to rub my penis, can you do it?" After his bath he jumped on top of me trying to give me "long kisses" and telling my husband that he knows a girl who would rub his penis.

The mood and behavior of a child who is becoming manic tends to be *labile*—it shifts dramatically and often. One day can be fairly uneventful; the next day hospitalization may seem imminent as psychotic symptoms appear and violent outbursts occur. This can be very confusing for the family members (and the child), who never know what to expect or how the day will unfold. The following fragments from a mother's journal illustrate this extreme lability of mood in her nine-year-old son.

### TWELVE DAYS IN MAY

5/11 Hypomanic, bizarre evening. "I hate me; kill me; Why am I like this?" Very rough with younger brother.

5/12 Good morning, dropped off well at school. Pretty good mood coming off bus, but more defiance in the afternoon. Uneventful evening. Went to bed well.

5/13 Up early, dressed well, good mood but problems on the bus. Kids teasing him. Teacher called and reported very bizarre behavior at school. She also reported a lot of ADHD symptoms—very fidgety, unable to remain seated in the afternoon, cruises around classroom, ran out of classroom, pestering other kids, unable to follow directions, not remaining on task or completing work.

5/14 Teacher reported a great day in school. Good mood after school.

5/15 Good A.M.—off to school well. Very defiant after school. Angered by new doctor. Got very angry in car—punching me, destructive to car, scribbling on dashboard, dumping over trash. Had to be restrained in office—punching, kicking, swearing—settled down at end of meeting and apologized.

5/16 Happy mood in A.M., but doing goofy, impulsive things—squirted water on dad's work shirt, squirted water on table and floor. Very aggressive after school—threatening me, hitting, increase in defiance. Aggressive toward other students.

5/17 Had a good time with grandparents. Crying a lot in the afternoon.

5/18 "Mixed," very irritable to hypomanic—increase in goal-directed activities, very easily frustrated and angered.

5/19 Good and uneventful day.

5/20 Very irritable in A.M.—threatened father—said: "I'm going to kill you someday." Manic after school—very goal-directed—taking all the tools out of the basement to use up in his room (hammer, sander, drill, staple gun). Very angry when I intervened—very loud, shouting, laughing, singing, dancing, "I don't feel good today. I want to kill myself. When I grow up, I am going to kill myself because being bipolar is bad." Hallucinating in afternoon—auditory and visual: goblin, clown, queen. "I hear the devil, I hear penises in your brain, Mom." Very hyperactive, and not rational. Gave him Risperdal and he went to sleep.

5/21 Hypomanic, happy in the afternoon.

5/22 Woke up laughing—found some needlepoint yarn and needles under the bed. "I'm giving myself a lab test"—trying to stick needles into his arm. Giddy, shouting "hubba, hubba, hubba, howdy, howdy" over and over again, very wound up. Settled down and watched some TV. Pleasant and more normal, but talkative in the afternoon. Easier to please. More irritable after dinner. Fascinated with knives, demonstrated how he would stab a wolf. Very quiet in my lap. He said: "I love you, Mom. You don't love me, you want me to die. I will if you want me to."

## Hallucinations

Not all bipolar children who get manic will suffer hallucinations, but many do. Often, if they don't vocalize their thoughts or act very bizarrely, the parents may not even know it is happening. Hallucinations do *not* mean the child is schizophrenic—they are very much a part of the bipolar picture, as we shall see in Chapter 2.

Auditory hallucinations, where the child hears voices or converses with people who are not visible to others, are the most common type of hallucination. The voices are experienced as real to the child and have extraordinary influence over him or her. There may be one voice, or several may be carrying on a conversation. They may simply be overheard by the child, or the voices may make direct statements to the child.

One young woman told us that she hears "hundreds of voices. I feel like my brain is being crushed by the voices." A mother wrote to us and described her daughter having a conversation with a grown man in the living room for about half an hour, and then she snapped out of it and realized no one was there. "She often hears voices of a group of people in the living room, having a conversation." (The girl, eighteen, has now admitted to her mother that she's been hearing these people since she was small but was afraid to tell anyone.)

Another mother wrote about her ten-year-old son's hearing voices and his unique way of making them disappear. She said:

> We have learned that an extra half a mg of Risperdal, given when the voices are present, will make them go away within ten minutes. On occasions where he could not take the Risperdal, the voices continue for hours. Derek sometimes says the voices don't want us to know about them. He is trying to work out his own cure. Sometimes he gets rid of the voices simply by telling them he is going to take a dose of Risperdal.

Many children also have visual hallucinations—they see things that others don't. One ten-year-old boy described a visual hallucination to his father. He said, "They are one-dimensional and appear flat and static. You cannot see through them, but a tossed pencil will travel through them. You see, Dad, you and the cat are three-dimensional and hallucinations are one-dimensional."

His father then wrote, "Earlier this week he saw one in our living room. It was a man with a knife. He was at first in shock and screaming. Then later he started playing and experimenting further with it to prove all his theories." The visual hallucinations often seem to include satanic figures. One girl was convinced she saw the devil sitting on the mantel of the fireplace in the living room. A boy who had been exhibiting very bizarre behavior began to hallucinate and told his mother that he felt that his head was going to fly off because the devil was hurting him.

Hallucinations are not only auditory and visual. They can involve any of the senses: There are tactile hallucinations (a child feels something touching her) and olfactory hallucinations (a child smells odors that others do not perceive).

## Suicidal Ideas

Long before the teenage years, children as young as four, five, six, and seven have suicidal thoughts and have been known to attempt to act on their impulses.

A mother from Texas wrote that her six-year-old son tried to jump out of the car while they were driving over a highway bridge. He said he was going to jump off the bridge and kill himself. Another little boy performed acts of self-mutilation that mimic suicide. He tried to cut his wrists with the wing of a metal toy airplane.

Parents don't know where these children are getting these ideas from. One woman wrote and said, "I was astounded to hear my four-year-old daughter, who had never seen a violent movie or even heard of the concept of suicide, sobbing through the bedroom door that she was going to 'make herself dead' during a horrible tantrum."

Sometimes the children don't make such bold gestures or statements but may ask curiously: "If I jumped off ten stories and opened an umbrella, would I fall?" or "Would you like me to go to heaven with Tucker [their dog] and watch out over all of you?"

A nine-year-old girl who was extremely creative started writing a book one evening. Chapter 6 is entitled "Death," and she says:

Maybe sometimes your child will say that they will kill themselves. This is something to take seriously. I have poked myself a few times because I get angry and stressed. Sometimes I just don't care about life anymore. I am also really scared.

If your child gets these thoughts, ask the doctor for medicine for them. If this situation ever happens, hold them still until they calm down and stop wanting to kill themselves. Hold them until they feel a part of this world.

A remarkable number of children are feeling these feelings and thinking these thoughts every day throughout the world. It is hard to fathom how they consolidate a core sense of self while struggling through days with moods that are careening from one pole to the other.

Unfortunately, researchers have reported that mood disorders seem to be increasing in incidence among the age group, or cohort, born since 1940. And the age of onset is shifting downward—younger people are being affected. Recently Dr. Raymond DePaulo's laboratory at Johns Hopkins University reported a ten-year earlier age of onset of bipolar illness in affected children compared with their bipolar parent. This trend was noted in the 1980s by Dr. Gerald Klerman, then at Yale, and by Dr. Elliot Gershon and his colleagues at the National Institute of Mental Health. They found that each successive generation of individuals born since World War II appears to have a higher incidence and earlier age of onset of both major depression and bipolar disorder. While there are many theories attempting to explain this "cohort phenomenon," little is actually understood.

Yet there is still cause for optimism.

- Today there are medications that can stabilize the moods of these children, effectively calm the irritability, and stop the raging and hallucinations. New treatments are in the pipeline.
- Research attention is finally being focused on this disorder of early childhood, and groups like the Stanley Medical Research Institute, the National Alliance for Research on Schizophrenia and Depression, and the Juvenile Bipolar Research Foundation are funding studies on the causes of and treatments for pediatric bipolar disorder. The Juvenile Bipolar Research Foundation's sole focus is the study of early-onset bipolar disorder.
- Great advances in the field of molecular genetics are accelerating our understanding of the biology of illness, as well as a person's susceptibility, and will soon improve diagnosis and treatment.
- Consumer advocacy organizations like the National Alliance for the Mentally Ill (NAMI) are using their members to change legislation and fight for equal insurance coverage, medical insurance

for the working poor, and better models of treatment for people with brain disorders.

- The Internet has become a vast source of information and support for parents who must deal with this illness and make critical decisions with the treating physicians. Thanks to the message boards and chat rooms of the Child and Adolescent Bipolar Foundation, no parent with a computer ever has to feel all alone with this illness ever again.

Diagnosed early, and treated appropriately, these children and their families can live infinitely more stable lives. The first step, then, is the diagnosis of the disorder, and it is to this that we turn next.

# The Diagnostic Dilemma

When we first met with publishers about this project, one editor listened intently and then asked the following pointed question: "But don't you think that parents will be reluctant to accept this diagnosis? Don't you think they will prefer that their child be labeled ADHD and adopt the 'ostrich syndrome'?"

"You mean bury their heads in the sand?" we replied.

"Yes" came the rejoinder.

It was a legitimate question. But the answers coming back to us on our survey and through our conversations with parents all over the country point to just the opposite reaction. These parents know that something more serious than attention-deficit disorder with hyperactivity is going on. Some who have the illness themselves recognize certain temperaments and behaviors because they either see early versions of themselves in their child, or they may remember all too well one of their family members showing similar traits of the illness. In fact, for many parents who recognize the traits, it is difficult to find a doctor even willing to *make* the diagnosis of bipolar disorder in a child.

The psychiatric profession's wariness about diagnosing early-onset bipolar disorder is a relatively modern phenomenon and requires some explaining. After all, in A.D. 150, Aretaeus of Cappadocia described manic-depressive illness in children younger than twelve; in 1854 the French alienist, Jean Etienne Dominique Esquirol, provided case reports of mania in preschool and prepubertal school-age children; and Emil Kraepelin—the paterfamilias of psychiatric diagnosis—reported mood disorders in children in his famous treatise *Manic-Depressive Insanity and Paranoia,* published in 1921.

But in the 1930s, the Freudian psychodynamic approach to the mind became predominant in the United States, and psychoanalytic theory took the position that a classical depressive syndrome could not occur in prepubertal children. As psychiatrists began to focus on the unconscious motivations of behavior, mood disorders in the young became a neglected issue. In fact, it wasn't until the 1975 National Institute of Mental Health Conference on Depression in Childhood that depression in children was even officially recognized in this country.

The idea that a child could ever suffer mania was almost completely buried, however, when two psychiatrists, E. James Anthony and Peter Scott, published a paper in 1960. In "Manic-Depressive Psychosis in Childhood," the authors detailed criteria for early-onset mania that were so stringent they literally guaranteed that the diagnosis of juvenile manic-depression would be a rare one indeed.

One of Anthony and Scott's criterion cautioned a clinician *not* to make the diagnosis of mania unless he or she found an illness so severe that it required "inpatient treatment, heavy sedation, or electroconvulsive therapy (ECT)." But they went even further: They reviewed the literature of reported cases of mania in children between the years 1884 and 1954, and, applying their criteria, they uncovered only twenty-eight cases of alleged manic-depression in young children. While this study was done quite some time ago, it contributed to the prevailing attitude that bipolar disorder was rare in childhood.

## DIFFICULTIES OF DIAGNOSIS

Diagnosis in psychiatry is a problem. After all, there are no lab tests that conclusively pinpoint a diagnosis, there are a host of overlapping symptoms (especially in children's disorders), and each person experiencing an illness expresses it through the unique filter of mind and temperament. The psychiatrist's main diagnostic instruments are the patient's report of symptoms, observable behavior, family history, and clinical course of the disorder.

Distinguishing between normal behaviors and pathological ones in a young child is even more challenging for a number of reasons: The span of time in a young life is insufficient to establish a course of illness; developmental factors are in full play; and a child's often nonstop motion, lack of impulse control, difficulty tolerating frustration, and vivid imagination are a part of the typical, everyday picture.

If you then consider that mood disorders in children *may* have a developmental evolution of symptoms—separation anxiety, night terrors, distractibility, poor attention, restlessness and hyperactivity followed by obsessions, defiant and contentious behaviors, finally culminating in a very rapid-cycling course with irritable or mixed mood states—it is no small wonder that children are often misdiagnosed, or plastered with a literal alphabet soup of diagnostic labels: attention-deficit disorder with hyperactivity (ADHD), obsessive-compulsive disorder (OCD), oppositional defiant disorder (ODD), conduct disorder (CD), generalized anxiety disorder (GAD), and so on.

Yet a correct diagnosis is vital to a child's well-being, for it is the proper diagnosis that guides the treatment and—equally important—prevents the child from being placed on medications that can considerably worsen the course of the disorder.

The most recent diagnostic criteria established by the American Psychiatric Association (APA) are delineated in the fourth edition of the *Diagnostic and Statistical Manual of Mental Disorders,* the *DSM-IV.* These criteria are used to determine psychiatric diagnoses in children and adults.

## What Does the *DSM-IV* Say About Children and Mood Disorders?

In the *DSM-IV,* mood disorders are divided into depressive disorders and bipolar disorders. Children are mentioned, but they are to be diagnosed basically according to the adult criteria. (And this is where the problem begins.) The criteria that must be met before a diagnosis of a major depressive episode can be made are as follows (our comments appear in italics).

CRITERIA FOR MAJOR DEPRESSIVE EPISODE
   A. Five (or more) of the following symptoms have been present during the same two-week period and represent a change from previous functioning; at least one of the symptoms is either (1) depressed mood, or (2) loss of interest or pleasure. Note: Do not include symp-

toms that are clearly due to a general medical condition, or moodin-congruent delusions or hallucinations.

1. Depressed mood most of the day, nearly every day, as indicated by either subjective report (e.g., feels sad or empty), or observation made by others (e.g., appears tearful). Note: In children and adolescents, can be irritable mood.

2. Markedly diminished interest or pleasure in all, or almost all, activities most of the day, nearly every day (as indicated by either subjective account or observation made by others).

3. Significant weight loss when not dieting or weight gain (e.g., a change of more than 5 percent of body weight in a month), or decrease or increase in appetite nearly every day. Note: In children, consider failure to make expected weight gains.

4. Insomnia or hypersomnia *(sleeping excessively)* nearly every day.

5. Psychomotor agitation or retardation nearly every day (observable by others, not merely subjective feelings of restlessness or being slowed down).

6. Fatigue or loss of energy nearly every day.

7. Feelings of worthlessness or excessive or inappropriate guilt (which may be delusional) nearly every day (not merely self-reproach or guilt about being sick).

8. Diminished ability to think or concentrate, or indecisiveness, nearly every day (either by subjective account or as observed by others).

9. Recurrent thoughts of death (not just fear of dying), recurrent suicidal ideation without a specific plan, or a suicide attempt or a specific plan for committing suicide.

B. The symptoms do not meet criteria for a Mixed State *(where a patient displays symptoms of mania and depression every day during at least a one-week period).*

C. The symptoms cause clinically significant distress or impairment in social, occupational, or other important areas of functioning.

D. The symptoms are not due to the direct physiological effects of a substance (e.g., a drug of abuse, a medication) or a general medical condition (e.g., hypothyroidism).

E. The symptoms are not better accounted for by bereavement; i.e., after the loss of a loved one, the symptoms persist for longer than two months, or are characterized by marked functional impairment, morbid preoccupation with worthlessness, suicidal ideation, psychotic symptoms, or psychomotor retardation.

The criteria that must be met before the diagnosis of a manic episode can be made are as follows:

CRITERIA FOR MANIC EPISODE

A. A distinct period of abnormally and persistently elevated, expansive, or irritable mood, lasting at least one week (or any duration if hospitalization is necessary).

B. During the period of mood disturbance, three (or more) of the following symptoms have persisted (four if the mood is only irritable) and have been present to a significant degree:

1. Inflated self-esteem or grandiosity.
2. Decreased need for sleep (e.g., feels rested after only three hours of sleep).
3. More talkative than usual or pressure to keep talking.
4. Flight of ideas or subjective experience that thoughts are racing.
5. Distractibility (i.e., attention too easily drawn to unimportant or irrelevant external stimuli).
6. Increase in goal-directed activity (either socially, at work or school, or sexually) or psychomotor agitation.
7. Excessive involvement in pleasurable activities that have a high potential for painful consequences (e.g., engaging in unrestrained buying sprees, sexual indiscretions, or foolish business investments).

C. The symptoms do not meet criteria for a Mixed State.

D. The mood disturbance is sufficiently severe to cause marked impairment in occupational functioning or in usual social activities or relationships with others, or to necessitate hospitalization to prevent harm to self or others, or there are psychotic features.

E. The symptoms are not due to the direct physiological effects of a substance (e.g., a drug of abuse, a medication, or other treatment), or a general medical condition (e.g., hyperthyroidism). Note: Maniclike episodes that are clearly caused by somatic antidepressant treatment (e.g., medication, electroconvulsive therapy, light therapy) should not count toward a diagnosis of Bipolar I Disorder.

Although the inclusion of childhood mood disorders in the *DSM-IV* could be seen as a major advance, thoughtful clinical investigators are beginning to realize that bipolar disorder in childhood presents in a very different pattern—one that often bears little resemblance to classical cycles of mania and depression as they are expressed in adulthood. For instance, children have more irritable moods with explosive outbursts, and their cycles of mania, hypomania, and depression are far more rapid than the typical adult presentation.

Which brings us to one of the major problems of the *DSM-IV* criteria as they apply to children: the fulfillment of the duration criteria. *DSM-IV* specifies that a mood episode (either manic or depressive) must last for a specified period of time. For instance, duration criteria for the diagnosis of a hypomanic episode requires a "distinct period of persistently elevated, expansive, or irritable mood lasting throughout *at least four days*" (italics ours). Yet a significant proportion of early-onset bipolar children (some estimates are as high as 70 percent) have a form of the condition that is marked by frequent mood and energy shifts that occur *several times within a day*.

For a depressive episode, the *DSM-IV* duration criterion is even more demanding: The manual requires at least a two-week period with five or more depressive symptoms. Therefore, by definition, an individual who has rapidly shifting mood states of less than the required duration cannot be formally diagnosed as having a bipolar disorder.

A separate and distinct category, code number 296.7—Bipolar Disorder Not Otherwise Specified (NOS)—was established to include disorders with bipolar features that do not meet full duration criteria. This category allows individuals who have a very rapid alternation of manic and depressive symptoms, but who do not meet minimal duration criteria, to be identified within the bipolar spectrum. While most children with bipolar disorder fit within this category, it still is not an accurate description of the condition as it presents in childhood.

It is becoming clear that bipolar disorder in children requires its own criteria. However, at this time, the APA has no plans to publish a revision until 2012.

This leaves researchers in an extremely difficult position: When they propose studies on children with bipolar disorder, either they cannot use *DSM-IV* criteria and must describe these children as having "manialike symptoms," or they must modify other diagnostic instruments in order to continue with their work.

It is hoped that new diagnostic instruments in future research studies will help to establish a more accurate picture of childhood-onset bipolar disorder. But, in the meantime, it is good for both clinicians and family members to keep in mind that the *Diagnostic and Statistical Manual* was not handed down at Sinai; it was always a tentative working system of classification that was intended to be changed and refined as it kept pace with new developments in psychiatry.

## MEDICAL CONDITIONS THAT CAN MIMIC MOOD DISORDERS

Even if the clinician begins to suspect a possible bipolar disorder, he or she must, as the *DSM-IV* cautions, rule out any medical conditions that can mimic or masquerade as depression or mania. The following list shows such conditions, which range from hormonal disorders and neurological syndromes to malignancies and diseases of the blood.

### HORMONAL AND METABOLIC DISORDERS
Cushing's disease
Diabetes
Hyperparathyroidism
Hyperthyroidism
Hypoglycemia
Hypothyroidism
Wilson's disease

### INFECTIOUS DISEASES
AIDS
Hepatitis
Influenzas

Mononucleosis
Syphilis
Viral pneumonias

NEUROLOGICAL DISORDERS
Kleine-Levin syndrome
Temporal lobe epilepsy

BLOOD DISEASES
Acute intermittent porphyria
Iron-deficiency anemia

METAL INTOXICATIONS
Manganese
Mercury
Thallium

NUTRITIONAL DISORDERS
Pellagra
Pernicious anemia

CANCERS
Central nervous system tumors

GENETIC DISORDERS
Asperger's syndrome (can be comorbid with bipolar disorder)
Velo-cardio-facial syndrome

OTHER DISEASES
Chronic fatigue syndrome
Lyme disease

Almost all of these medical conditions can be ruled in or out by physical examination coupled with appropriate clinical laboratory tests. Therefore, it is extremely important that the diagnosing physician take a personal patient and family medical history as well as request that the child have a complete physical exam and certain blood tests, including thyroid function studies. Only then should a primary mood disorder—one that is not secondary to or caused by a primary medical condition—be diagnosed.

Once a comprehensive medical workup has been done, the physician needs to elicit a complete family history of possible psychiatric illness and substance abuse. The substance abuse factor is an important piece of the puzzle because it has been shown that a significant number of individuals with bipolar disorder abuse alcohol and drugs. It is thought that many of these individuals are self-medicating (calming the agitation or sleep problems with alcohol or sustaining a high with cocaine), or that the two illnesses—bipolar disorder and substance abuse—are highly comorbid (they occur together). There is some thought now that a person with bipolar disorder is extremely vulnerable to addiction. In fact, studies have shown that comorbidity between bipolar disorder and alcoholism may exceed 40 percent.

Until definitive blood or other tests can confirm a psychiatric diagnosis, nothing can replace an informed diagnostician who understands how this illness manifests itself in childhood and who understands how important the family history is. (Chapter 3 discusses how to find a good physician.)

## THE FIRST DIAGNOSTIC DILEMMA: THE UNIPOLAR VERSUS BIPOLAR DISTINCTION

It is not uncommon for the initial episode of childhood-onset bipolar disorder to present as major depression. But as clinical investigators follow the course of the disorder in children, they have observed a significant rate of switching to bipolar symptoms.

In 1994 Dr. Geller published a study on a group of seventy-nine prepubertal patients suffering from depression. These children were followed for a two- to five-year period. Within two years, 32 percent of these children had switched into mania. In 2001, a follow-up study of seventy-two of the original seventy-nine prepubertal children was reported in the *American Journal of Psychiatry*. The mean age of these children was then about twenty, and 48.6 percent of them had been rediagnosed with some form of bipolar disorder. (If children with ADHD had not been excluded from the study, the rates would no doubt have been even higher.)

It may be that a depression manifested very early in life is the first salvo in the evolution of an illness that can progress to bipolar disorder, particularly after exposure to antidepressant medications.

Because it is a known fact that antidepressant treatment can induce hypomania, mania, rapid cycling, and mixed states—often accompanied by severe aggressive or violent behaviors in those who have as-yet-unexpressed predisposition to bipolar disorder—it is extremely important that all parents and physicians be alert to the possibility that the child may indeed be bipolar.

What are the possible predictors of a switch from a major depressive disorder to a manic-depressive disorder? In our survey, some of the common symptoms that preceded a bipolar course were depressions marked by a craving for sweets and carbohydrates, prolonged and aggressive temper tantrums, lethargy, oversleeping, separation anxiety, self-consciousness with others, and phobic anxiety.

Does this mean that a child should never be treated with an antidepressant? Even if a physician thinks there is a strong likelihood of a latent bipolar gene and is circumspect about initiating antidepressant treatment, the risk/benefit to the child needs to be considered. In Chapter 4, when we discuss medications, we'll outline some treatments and precautions for the child whose first episode is a depressive one.

## COMORBIDITIES: DISORDERS THAT CAN OCCUR SIMULTANEOUSLY WITH BIPOLAR DISORDER

Rarely does bipolar disorder in children occur as a pure entity by itself. Rather it is often accompanied by clusters of symptoms that—when observed at certain points in a child's life—suggest other psychiatric disorders, such as attention-deficit disorder with hyperactivity, obsessive-compulsive disorder, oppositional defiant disorder, conduct disorder, or Tourette's syndrome.

The questions researchers are attempting to resolve are:

1. Does bipolar disorder occur simultaneously with other psychiatric disorders, making it possible for a child actually to have three or four diagnoses?
2. Are these clusters of symptoms that suggest distinct disorders merely early precursors on a developmental continuum that eventually expresses itself as full-blown bipolar?
3. Are all these symptoms merely a more apt description of early-onset bipolar disorder?

The truth is no one knows for certain. And until research can provide clarification, parents are going to have to tolerate a great deal of diagnostic ambiguity, for surely they will come up against a few of the following comorbid diagnoses.

## The Great Debate: Does the Child Have ADHD, Bipolar Disorder, or Both?

Perhaps the greatest source of diagnostic confusion in childhood bipolar disorder is that its symptoms overlap with many of the symptoms of attention-deficit disorder with hyperactivity. At first glance, any child who can't sit still, who is impulsive, inattentive, easily distracted, or emotionally labile is more likely to receive a diagnosis of ADHD than bipolar disorder. (In our survey, 93 percent of the children met *DSM-IV* criteria for attention-deficit disorder with hyperactivity.)

The *DSM-IV* criteria for attention-deficit disorder with hyperactivity include:

DIAGNOSTIC CRITERIA FOR ATTENTION-DEFICIT DISORDER WITH HYPERACTIVITY

A. Either (1) or (2):

(1) Six (or more) of the following symptoms of inattention have persisted for at least six months to a degree that is maladaptive and inconsistent with developmental level:

*Inattention*

(a) Often fails to give close attention to details or makes careless mistakes in schoolwork, work, or other activities.

(b) Often has difficulty sustaining attention in tasks or play activities.

(c) Often does not seem to listen when spoken to directly.

(d) Often does not follow through on instructions and fails to finish schoolwork, chores, or duties in the workplace (not due to oppositional behavior or failure to understand instructions).

(e) Often has difficulty organizing tasks and activities.

(f) Often avoids, dislikes, or is reluctant to engage in tasks that require sustained mental effort (such as schoolwork or homework).

(g) Often loses things necessary for tasks or activities (e.g., toys, school assignments, pencils, books, or tools).

(h) Is often easily distracted by extraneous stimuli.

(i) Is often forgetful in daily activities.

(2) Six (or more) of the following symptoms of hyperactivity-impulsivity have persisted for at least six months to a degree that is maladaptive and inconsistent with developmental level:

*Hyperactivity*
(a) Often fidgets with hands or feet or squirms in seat.

(b) Often leaves seat in classroom or in other situations in which remaining seated is expected.

(c) Often runs about or climbs excessively in situations in which it is inappropriate (in adolescents or adults, may be limited to subjective feelings of restlessness).

(d) Often has difficulty playing or engaging in leisure activities quietly.

(e) Is often "on the go" or often acts as if "driven by a motor."

(f) Often talks excessively.


*Impulsivity*
(g) Often blurts out answers before questions have been completed.

(h) Often has difficulty awaiting turn.

(i) Often interrupts or intrudes on others (e.g., butts into conversations or games).

B. Some hyperactive-impulsive or inattentive symptoms that caused impairment were present before age seven years.

C. Some impairment from the symptoms is present in two or more settings (e.g., at school [or work] and at home).

D. There must be clear evidence of clinically significant impairment in social, academic, or occupational functioning.

E. The symptoms do not occur exclusively during the course of a pervasive developmental disorder, schizophrenia, or other psychotic disorder and are not better accounted for by another mental disorder (e.g., mood disorder, anxiety disorder, dissociative disorder, or a personality disorder).

Part of this bias toward making the ADHD diagnosis is the overlap of symptoms between the conditions. In fact, Drs. Janet Wozniak and Joseph Biederman of Harvard Medical School found that 94 percent of a sample of forty-three children with mania met *DSM-IIR* criteria for attention-deficit disorder with hyperactivity. Also, mindful of Anthony and Scott's incredibly stringent criteria for making the diagnosis of bipolar disorder, it just seemed sensible that "when one hears the clatter of hoofbeats on the roof, one looks for horses and not for zebras."

But now, realizing that there is a large population of children suffering with mood disorders, how would a clinician determine whether the problem is ADHD or a mood disorder?

According to Dr. Charles Popper, who has written about the issue of distinguishing between ADHD and bipolar disorders: "All of the features of ADHD can be seen in mood disorders at times, so *ADHD is a diagnosis reached only after ruling out a mood disorder.*" In his article entitled "Diagnosing Bipolar vs. ADHD: A Pharmacological Point of View," he lists several distinctions between the two diagnostic groups and brings great clarity to this diagnostic confusion. With permission, we quote them here:

1. Destructiveness may be seen in both disorders but differs in origin. Children who are ADHD often break things carelessly while playing ("non-angry destructiveness"), whereas the major destructiveness of children who are bipolar is not a result of carelessness but tends to occur in anger. Children who are bipolar may exhibit severe temper tantrums during which they release manic quantities of physical and emotional energy, sometimes with vio-

lence and physical property destruction. They may even exhibit openly sadistic impulses.

2. The duration and intensity of physical outbursts and temper tantrums differs in the two disorders. Children who are ADHD usually calm down in twenty to thirty minutes, whereas children who are bipolar may continue to feel and act angry for up to four hours.

3. The degree of "regression" during angry episodes is typically more severe for children who are bipolar. It is rare to see an angry child who is ADHD display disorganized thinking, language, and body position, all of which may be seen in angry bipolar children during a tantrum. Children who are bipolar may also lose memory of the tantrum.

4. The "trigger" for temper tantrums is also different. Children who have ADHD are typically triggered by sensory and emotional overstimulation, whereas children who have bipolar disorder typically react to limit-setting, such as a parental "no."

5. The moods of children who have ADHD or bipolar disorder may change quickly, but children with ADHD do not generally show dysphoria (depression) as a predominant symptom. Irritability is particularly prominent in children who are bipolar, especially in the morning on arousal. Children with ADHD tend to arouse quickly and attain alertness within minutes, but children with mood disorders may show overly slow arousal (including several hours of irritability or dysphoria, fuzzy thinking or "cobwebs," and somatic complaints such as stomachaches and headaches) upon awakening in the morning.

6. Disturbances during sleep in children with bipolar disorder include severe nightmares or night terrors, often with themes of explicit gore and bodily mutilation.

7. Children who are bipolar often show giftedness in certain cognitive functions, especially verbal and artistic skills (perhaps with verbal precocity and punning by age two to three years).

8. The misbehavior in children with ADHD is often accidental and usually caused by oblivious inattention, whereas children with bipolar disorders intentionally provoke or misbehave. Some bipolar children are described as "the bully on the playground."

9. The child with ADHD may engage in behavior that can lead to

harmful consequences without being aware of the danger, whereas the child with bipolar disorder is risk seeking.

10. Bipolar children tend to have a strong early sexual interest and behavior.

11. Children with ADHD usually do not exhibit psychotic symptoms or reveal a loss of contact with reality, whereas children with bipolar disorder may exhibit gross distortions in the perception of reality or in the interpretation of emotional events.

12. Lithium treatment generally improves bipolar disorder but has little or no effect on ADHD.

But the problem of diagnosis is even *more* complicated. Because many children meet full criteria for both disorders—ADHD and bipolar—some psychiatrists and researchers (but not all) have begun to talk about the two disorders as comorbid, or co-occurring. Indeed, in a recent study conducted by Drs. Wozniak and Biederman, they documented that in a subset of families the parents and siblings (the first-degree relatives) of manic children not only had increased risk for mania and ADHD but these two conditions occurred together in those same relatives. Their report of a 16 percent rate of bipolar disorder among relatives of bipolar-ADHD cases indicates that co-occurring bipolar-ADHD is highly familial.

Other researchers disagree strongly with the concept that these children have two co-occurring disorders. Still others think that attention-deficit disorder with hyperactivity may be, for many, an early stage on a developmental path that culminates in a full-blown bipolar disorder.

## Anxiety Disorders

Often unrecognized, and yet an insidious factor that severely impacts the children and adolescents who suffer with bipolar disorder, is a coexisting anxiety disorder. The *DSM-IV* devotes fifty-one pages to anxiety disorders, which broadly include generalized anxiety disorder (GAD), panic disorder, specific and social phobias, obsessive-compulsive disorder (discussed in the next section), post-traumatic stress disorder (PTSD), and, so commonly seen in children with bipolar disorder, the separation anxiety spoken about in Chapter 1.

The association between bipolar disorder and the anxiety disorders has been well documented. In 1995 Peter Lewinsohn and colleagues at the University of Oregon conducted a community study of high school students and found that anxious youths were seven times more likely to have a co-occurring bipolar disorder than students without any anxiety disorder. Other studies report that over 50 percent of children and adolescents diagnosed with bipolar disorder have multiple anxiety disorders. It is not uncommon for adolescents (particularly girls) to present with severe panic attacks initially and to be diagnosed with only that anxiety disorder. Yet the possibility of a coexisting bipolar disorder should be monitored carefully because the drugs often used to treat panic disorder, such as antidepressants, may worsen an underlying bipolar condition.

Conversely, in cases where the bipolar disorder is recognized, the primary focus of treatment becomes the stabilizing of the moods and the modulation of aggression, and the evaluation of residual anxiety is not high on the list of priorities. In many situations, anxiety is viewed as the least of the problem—more of a benign condition—and not the pernicious one that eats away at a child's feeling of safety and self-esteem. Dr. Ira Glovinsky, author of *Bipolar Patterns in Children,* told us that he worked with a child who described anxiety as "a tornado inside my body that my body just can't hold inside"; and "It's bigger than my body and it seeps out the side seams." Dr. Glovinsky added: "Many of these children are just hemorrhaging anxiety." It is easy to see how chronic anxiety would contribute to irritability, lack of concentration, and hyperactivity—all symptoms thought to belong in the realm of ADHD, but often missed as a coexisting condition of a mood disorder.

Sometimes, if the bipolar disorder is treated, the anxiety recedes; in some cases, however, once the mood disorder is treated, the anxiety moves front and center.

No studies direct a psychiatrist to which medications are best to treat anxiety in this population. Often benzodiazepines such as Klonopin (clonazepam), Ativan (lorazepam), and Valium (diazepam) are used as add-on medications, but these can cause paradoxical effects in younger children. It might be wise to choose a short-acting benzodiazepine, such as Ativan, at low doses, introduce it on a weekend, perhaps, and monitor any untoward reactions.

A study published in the March 2003 issue of the *Journal of Clinical Psychiatry* reported on 318 adult patients suffering with anxiety disorders and found that they did better on lithium than on anticonvulsants, but this has not been studied in the pediatric population.

New types of medications that target CRF (corticotropin-releasing factor) receptors and neuropeptides that participate in the generation of the stress response are in the pipelines of a number of pharmaceutical companies.

It is clear that children with bipolar disorder are predisposed to and suffer unduly from anxiety disorders (often more than one in their lifetime). This frequent comorbidity should be taken into consideration when a diagnosis is made so that the bipolar disorder is not missed and exacerbated by the wrong selection of medication. Anxious children with bipolar disorder should receive different medication from children whose problem is anxiety alone.

A clinician evaluating an adolescent girl presenting with panic attacks should rule out the possibility of a bipolar disorder before prescribing a selective serotonin reuptake inhibitor (SSRI) for the anxiety.

It is obvious that much needs to be learned about the strong, indisputable association between the anxiety disorders and bipolar disorder and that clinicians and researchers need to devote time and energy to this comorbidity.

## Obsessive-Compulsive Disorder

Many parents who answered our survey and a significant number of parents writing on the BPParents listserv note that their children have mood disorders as well as unambiguous symptoms of obsessive-compulsive disorder.

Children with OCD have recurrent and intrusive thoughts of impending harm that can be allayed only by some compulsive act. They feel compelled to perform repetitive acts or rituals to ward off the discomfort and anxiety they experience, but these acts can cause the child shame and embarrassment as well as make it hard to get out of the house and go about a typical kid's day.

Some examples of repetitive acts designed to reduce the anxiety and keep a dreaded event from occurring include: placing objects just right; touching things a self-specified number of times; checking behaviors, such as checking to see that the doors are locked over and over again; flicking the lights on and off; or turning the sink or shower faucets to the hot and cold settings a prescribed number of times. Some children count or repeat phrases over and over; other children compulsively pick at their skin.

Anyone who saw Jack Nicholson portray a man suffering with OCD in the film *As Good As It Gets* watched him turn the deadbolt on his front door

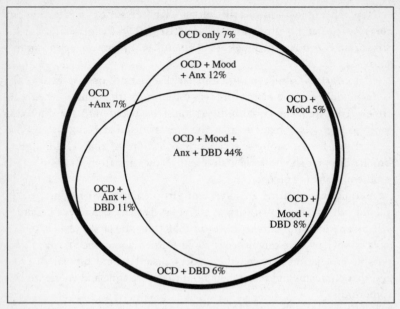

Comorbidity of Juvenile Obsessive-Compulsive Disorder. *Anx* (any non-OCD anxiety disorder); *DBD* (disruptive behavior disorder); *Mood* (mood disorder); *OCD* (obsessive-compulsive disorder).

to the left and to the right quickly and repetitively each time he entered his apartment and assiduously avoid cracks on the sidewalks of New York. He always carried plastic cutlery with him to avoid germs in restaurants.

Indeed, a majority of patients with OCD describe obsessions about dirt or contamination, and children as well as adults describe handwashing or showering rituals in which they wash their hands over eighty times a day or spend hours attempting to shower themselves clean.

Many children explain that they don't know why they do these rituals, that they know they are senseless. Still, they feel a sense of pressure, and the action partially relieves the anxiety.

In the diagram, one can see that juvenile OCD is highly comorbid with mood disorders, disruptive behavior disorder (hyperactivity oppositional defiant disorder), and anxiety disorders. Although this study of 217 children at the McLean Hospital/Massachusetts General Pediatric OCD Clinic focused on children with OCD, a full 69 percent of the study sample also carried diagnoses of mood disorders.

## Tourette's Syndrome

A percentage of children with bipolar disorder manifesting OCD symptoms also bear the diagnosis of Tourette's syndrome. This is almost certainly a physical disorder of the brain that causes involuntary movements (motor tics) and involuntary vocalizations (vocal tics). A child with motor tics may exhibit eye blinking, facial grimacing, nose scrunching, shoulder shrugging, head jerking, and hand movements. Common vocal tics include throat clearing, grunting, sniffing, making loud sounds, or saying words. A much smaller group of children exhibit copralalia—they use obscene or other socially inappropriate words. According to the *DSM-IV,* a child can be diagnosed with Tourette's only if "both multiple motor and one or more vocal tics have occurred at some time, but not necessarily at the same time."

An excellent book on this subject is edited by Tracy Haerle and is called *Children with Tourette Syndrome: A Parents' Guide.*


## Oppositional Defiant Disorder and Conduct Disorder

Many bipolar children also meet criteria for oppositional defiant disorder (ODD) and conduct disorder (CD), and vice versa. What do these behaviors look like?

### Oppositional Defiant Disorder
Oppositional defiant disorder as defined by the *DSM-IV:*

> A recurrent pattern of negativistic, disobedient, and hostile behavior toward authority figures that persists at least six months and is characterized by frequent occurrence of at least four of the following behaviors: arguing with adults, actively defying or refusing to comply with requests or rules of adults, deliberately doing things that will annoy other people, blaming others for his or her own mistakes or misbehavior, being touchy or easily annoyed by others, being angry and resentful, or being spiteful and vindictive.

One mother on the listserv wrote, "At one school my son went to this year, he had a list of the rules that he was taking back and forth with him. When I asked him why he was keeping them with him, he said he needed to make sure he broke them all!"

## Conduct Disorder

A child with ODD can infuriate adults; a child with conduct disorder is cause for great concern. Many clinical investigators have observed that some youngsters with bipolar disorder have expressed serious delinquent and antisocial behaviors, including burglary, stealing, and vandalism. Other behaviors may include bullying and intimidating people, intentionally destroying property, and using weapons such as baseball bats, broken bottles, knives, or guns with the intention of causing someone serious harm.

In 1989 Dr. Stan Kutcher and colleagues, who are now at Dalhousie University in Halifax, examined the comorbidity of conduct disorder in a group of ninety-six adolescent inpatients. Nineteen of this group had a primary diagnosis of bipolar disorder; the remaining seventy-seven individuals had been diagnosed with other primary psychiatric conditions. Dr. Kutcher and colleagues reported that while 27 percent of their entire sample had conduct disorder, 42 percent of the bipolar subgroup were also given a secondary diagnosis of conduct disorder.

In 1995 Dr. Maria Kovacs and Myrna Pollock, M.S.W., confirmed the strong association between bipolar disorder and conduct disorder in their study of twenty-six bipolar youths. In this group, eighteen were found to have had conduct disorder at some point in their lives, yielding a 69 percent lifetime comorbidity rate.

Some of the questions researchers are trying to answer are:

1. Are conduct disorder symptoms directly associated with bipolar disorder as a co-occurring diagnosis (therefore implying that they are inherited together)?
2. Are these defiant and oppositional behaviors expressed primarily during full episodes of mania or hypomania (implying that these behaviors are motivated by the mood disorder)?

Kovacs and Pollock found that more than half of their sample, or 54 percent of the entire bipolar group, had overlapping mania or hypomanic episodes with conduct disorder.

But apparently these conduct disorder behaviors can occur before or after the manifestation of bipolar symptoms. By determining the age of occurrence of conduct disorder in their bipolar subjects, Kovacs and Pollock found that, for eleven of the eighteen youths, conduct disorder appeared prior to the first episode; for seven subjects, conduct disorder occurred subsequent to the first episode of mania or hypomania. The study populations are too small to come to any definite conclusions, but it is clear that clinically these disorders are commonly linked.

To add to the confusion, both bipolar disorder and conduct disorder have been found to co-occur with ADHD. *Until we know more about the underlying causes of child psychiatric disorders, no diagnosis should be discounted because another disorder is present.*

Dr. Joseph Biederman, when speaking at the 1997 International Conference for Child and Adolescent Psychiatry in Toronto, said, "There is a group of children whose entire clinical picture of conduct disorder may evaporate if you treat the manic symptoms."

## Girls Who Binge and Cut: Bulimia and Borderline Personality Disorder

A subgroup of young women with bipolar disorder are diagnosed with co-morbid eating disorders, particularly bulimia, a condition in which one binges and then purges what one has eaten. In addition, substance abuse seems to be a part of the clinical picture, and a fair number of these adolescent girls have a history of cutting or scratching themselves with knives or razors.

These girls commonly report periods of unbearable agitation and irritability. Some of them attempt to calm themselves by using alcohol and drugs—they self-medicate; others attempt to stop this continuous state of depression and agitation by cutting or scratching their arms or legs with razors and knives, or burning their thighs with lighted cigarettes.

One young woman talked very openly about her self-mutilating behavior. She described it thus:

> I dig into my heels with my nails and rip layers and layers of skin off. While I'm doing it, I'm not thinking. I feel as though there's an animal rage inside me—it's like a super-electrically charged thing . . . like voltage. And when I see the blood, I stop feeling this horrible rage and come out of this state.

Chillingly, another girl described this feeling as "being trapped inside her body with a snarling and snapping wolf."

One theory about these self-mutilating behaviors is that a powerful impulse to discharge aggression is counterpoised against the individual's attempt to inhibit that impulse. The tension created by these conflicting forces builds to an unbearable pitch, and the tension is relieved by physical pain directed toward the self. This discharge of aggression and the concomitant activation of the pain pathways could act as a cathartic release, but no one really understands what exactly is happening and why hurting oneself resolves the problem temporarily.

Many doctors, upon hearing of self-mutilating behavior, begin to suspect a diagnosis of borderline personality disorder. Someone given this diagnosis typically has a history of unstable and tempestuous interpersonal relationships, impulsive behaviors, frequent displays of temper, marked shifts of mood with the moods lasting hours or days, identity confusion, feelings of emptiness, and "frantic efforts to avoid real or imagined abandonment."

Dr. Hagop Akiskal at the University of California at San Diego has always conceived borderline personality disorder as a part of the mood disorder spectrum. He feels it is closely linked to bipolar disorder, perhaps a subclinical manifestation. He and his colleagues, then at the University of Tennessee College of Medicine, reported a study of one hundred patients diagnosed as having borderline personality disorder. In this group, almost half (forty-five) were also found to have some form of mood disorder. Fifty-seven of these one hundred young women had substance abuse problems.

Follow-up data further supported the close kinship of borderline disorders to mood disorders. Of the one hundred patients, twenty-nine developed unmistakable major depression with melancholic symptoms, eleven had brief hypomanic episodes, four others had psychotic mania, and eight developed mixed states.

## Autistic Spectrum Disorders and Bipolar Disorder

There is a group of children who fit somewhere within the autistic spectrum, but if one looks closely, one can see a pattern of intense shifts in mood, irritability, and sleep loss. In many cases, the autistic behaviors are so dramatic that the possibility of a bipolar comorbidity is often overlooked.

The *DSM-IV* groups autistic disorder, Rett's disorder, childhood disintegrative disorder, Asperger's disorder, and pervasive development disorder not otherwise specified (NOS) under the umbrella category of Pervasive Developmental Disorders, or PDD. When the shorthand diagnostic label "PDD" is given to a child, it typically stands for PDD-NOS, not the general category of Pervasive Developmental Disorders.

The essential characteristics of a Pervasive Developmental Disorder are: impairments in social interaction, imaginative activity, verbal and nonverbal communication skills; and a limited number of interests and activities that tend to be repetitive.

Children diagnosed with autistic disorder have a moderate to severe range of communication, socialization, and behavioral problems. It is estimated that about 50 percent of children with autism have some kind of mental retardation, but there are also high-functioning autistic children.

Children diagnosed with Asperger's disorder have general language, but not social or reciprocal language. This means that they have adequate language skills in terms of vocabulary and grammar, but they fail to catch the subtleties of conversation, such as humor or irony, and their language does not mold and modify according to responses and cues from the person with whom they are conversing. These children also develop restrictive, repetitive patterns of behavior, interests, and activities, but it is not unusual for children diagnosed with Asperger's disorder to have average or above-average intelligence.

The inclusion of a diagnostic category of PDD-NOS within the *DSM-IV* complicates things because this is a diagnosis that is given when there is a "severe and pervasive impairment in the development of reciprocal social interaction or verbal and nonverbal communication skills, or when stereotyped behavior, interests, and activities are present, but the criteria are not met for a specific Pervasive Developmental Disorder. . . ." This description is not all that helpful, and it's difficult to grasp when a child has PDD-NOS or autistic disorder. No doubt the *DSM-IV* will change some of these categories and focus on the fact that this is a spectrum disorder, but a revision is not due to be published until 2012. In the meantime, the categories as they are presently defined are bound to confuse parents.

In 1988 George Robert DeLong, M.D., of Duke University, one of the first pediatric neurologists to study the interface between autistic spectrum disorders and bipolar disorder, published a paper in which he reported a very high incidence of mood disorders among family members of children with autistic spectrum disorders. He reported on the family histories of fifty-one children with autistic spectrum disorders and found that twenty-three of the fifty-one children had a family member with manic depression (first- and second-degree relatives were examined). The incidence of bipolar disorder was 4.2 percent, about fivefold greater than that expected in the general population, and the highest incidence was in the families of the children who had Asperger's syndrome. There could be some relationship between mood disorders and Asperger's syndrome.

In 1994 Dr. DeLong reported the results of another study of forty children with autistic spectrum disorders and examined their family histories. Twenty-nine of the families had a history of manic depression.

How common is it that a child diagnosed with one of the Pervasive Developmental Disorders is found to have a comorbid bipolar disorder? While there has been no formal study, Edwin H. Cook, M.D., Professor of Psychiatry and Pediatrics at the Department of Psychiatry at the University of Chicago, feels that "based on my experience, my best guess is that 10 percent of the children with autistic spectrum disorder have a bipolar comorbidity." Dr. DeLong feels this may eventually turn out to be higher (more in the 35 percent range).

Because several studies have shown that children in the autistic spectrum have benefited from antidepressant medications, it is important to look carefully at the family history of a child so diagnosed and also to look for any pattern of cycling, marked irritability, and disinhibition before prescribing these drugs. There is a high-potential risk for inducing increased cycling or switching in a child who may have both an autistic spectrum disorder and a bipolar vulnerability.

Dr. Cook reported that he sees a number of children who are on the autistic spectrum and have bipolar symptomatology and also obsessive-compulsive disorder. "These children are very hard to treat," he said, "because the use of antidepressants that would treat the OCD symptoms are so dicey."

Only family genetic studies that delineate specific subgroupings of autistic spectrum disorders will help us sort out this comorbidity. However, doctors and parents should know that this comorbidity exists (and perhaps in greater numbers than we know) and rule out the possibility of a comorbid bipolar disorder before initiating treatment with medications. In other words, it would be important to first treat a cycling disorder with mood stabilizers and perhaps an atypical antipsychotic and to be wary of antidepressant-induced cycling.

## Psychosis: The Schizophrenia Bugaboo

Psychotic symptoms—such as delusions (fixed irrational beliefs) and hallucinations (voices and visions)—*can occur during both phases of a bipolar disorder.*

The nature of delusional ideas may vary with the mood state. When manic, a child can exhibit grandiose delusions. The child may feel that he or she can teach better than any teacher in the school, or become convinced that he can "beat Michael Jordan at his game" following the first after-school basketball game. When depressed, a child's delusional ideas tend to bear more guilty or morbid content. For example, a young girl felt that she was so terrible and worthless that every time her mother answered the phone, she was sure it was the director of an orphanage making plans for her to be sent away. The delusions can be unshakable.

Auditory and visual hallucinations—hearing voices or seeing things that aren't there—are not uncommon in bipolar disorder. The nature of the auditory hallucinations may vary according to the mood state. For example, a six-year-old boy experiencing mania was prompted by a voice to fly from the top of the jungle gym. Sometimes the voices are threatening: A young woman told us that she used to hear the voice of a man telling her she would die at 6:30 in the morning. She would spend the nights up and alone, waiting until the hands of the clock swept past 6:34, signifying that she could let down her guard and start breathing calmly again.

Visual hallucinations can be interesting or terribly frightening. One teenage girl told her mother she saw cowboys in her room dressed in red. A young boy was very paranoid and saw one of his mother's porcelain figurines moving around the room and glaring at him. Quite a few other children report seeing bugs all over the room and desperately try to prove to their parents that the bugs really do exist.

In addition to auditory and visual hallucinations, children can experience olfactory hallucinations (they smell things that other people don't) and tactile hallucinations (they feel something touching their skin).

It is terrifying for a parent to watch reason fly from a young mind. The fear that a child is becoming "schizophrenic" looms large, and the specter of madness and locked asylums can leave a parent virtually paralyzed.

There is a long and tragic history to the assumption that anyone experiencing delusions or hallucinations is schizophrenic, and a discussion about this should help ground a parent or relative when dealing with a child who is delusional or hallucinating.

*The History of the Differential Diagnosis of Schizophrenia and Manic Depression*

In the beginning of the twentieth century, Emil Kraepelin drew strict boundaries between manic-depressive psychosis and dementia praecox (an early name for schizophrenia). But in 1911 the Swiss physician Eugen Bleuler reversed this line of thought and described a concept of schizophrenia that was so broad it diagnosed as schizophrenic a large group of patients that Kraepelin would have certainly called manic-depressive.

In 1960 a German psychiatrist named Kurt Schneider composed a list of symptoms that he felt strongly suggested a diagnosis of schizophrenia. His symptoms of "first rank" included auditory hallucinations, hallucinations of touch, the feeling that thoughts are being inserted into one's mind or that one's thoughts are being broadcast, and the feeling that all of one's actions are under the control of others. Accepting these criteria, psychiatrists—and particularly American psychiatrists—began to diagnose anyone experiencing even short-lasting delusional, bizarre, and psychotic thinking as schizophrenic.

But in 1973 Drs. Gabriele Carlson and Frederick Goodwin began to refute these diagnostic practices when they reported that there seemed to be three stages of mania. And in the third stage, the most extreme, patients did indeed experience hallucinations, bizarre beliefs, and paranoia. Drs. Carlson and Goodwin knew that these patients would have been diagnosed as schizophrenic if they hadn't appeared clearly manic both earlier in the course and later as the episode was resolving.

Dr. Harrison Pope of Harvard Medical School's McLean Hospital in Belmont, Massachusetts, also began to home in on this diagnostic problem. He reviewed twenty studies and found that so-called schizophrenic symptoms occurred among 20 to 50 percent of patients with extremely well-validated cases of manic-depressive illness.

In 1977 he and Dr. Joseph Lipinski joined forces to write what has become a landmark article in the psychiatric literature. It was titled "Diagnosis in Schizophrenia and Manic-Depressive Illness: A Reassessment of the Specificity of 'Schizophrenic' Symptoms in the Light of Current Research," and it argued forcefully that psychosis and schizophrenia are *not* synonymous. They cautioned psychiatrists to look first and foremost at the family history and to look at the patient's functioning before the onset of illness, his or her response to treatment, and the eventual outcome.

These illnesses tend to breed true. If the family history reveals manic depression, depression, or alcoholism, it is unlikely that the patient is schizophrenic. (Of course, a parent has to remember that Aunt Jane may have been labeled a paranoid schizophrenic because that was diagnostic tradition at the time. It was not necessarily the truth of her condition.)

Any teenager who is seen by the medical profession in a full psychotic episode may initially be suspected of drug use or of a schizophrenic break, because both of these causes of psychosis tend to appear first in that age group. Parents will need to understand the whole picture and gather any and all family history facts to ensure the correct diagnosis. (See the discussion about piecing together the family history in the next chapter.)

Parents with a child who is experiencing psychosis or extreme paranoia may also hear the term "schizoaffective" during the diagnostic evaluation. This is a term used when the patient seems to manifest a confusing mix of symptoms that straddle the boundaries of both schizophrenia and mood disorders. These children may meet the criteria for depression or mania, but their delusions and hallucinations are not related to the disordered mood—they are "mood incongruent," and they persist beyond the resolution of the mood disorder.

While the third revised edition of the *DSM (DSM-IIIR)* created an intermediate disease category for the schizoaffective diagnosis, *DSM-IV* returned schizoaffective disorder to the categories of schizophrenia and other psychotic disorders. It lists two subtypes, the bipolar type and the depressive type, and it requires that delusions and hallucinations last for a minimum of two weeks in the absence of prominent mood symptoms.

This remains a very controversial diagnosis. Whether schizoaffective disorder is a variant of schizophrenia, a variant of mood disorders, a mixture of the two, a transitional state between schizophrenia and a mood disorder, or a heterogeneous syndrome including different conditions is unknown at this time.

Still, many psychiatrists view schizoaffective disorder as a variant of mood disorders because the family studies of patients who meet criteria for schizoaffective disorder bipolar type reveal a higher incidence of bipolar disorder, almost identical to that of the families of pure bipolar patients.

## THE BIG PICTURE

It is obvious that the diagnosis of mood disorders in children is extremely complex. While the perplexing questions raised by the frequency of comorbid diagnoses cannot be resolved at this time, researchers have begun

to define a syndrome that encompasses symptoms of a number of childhood psychiatric disorders but also has unique features of its own.

Ranging from "very common" to "less common," the symptoms and
behavioral traits that have been consistently observed in children with
early-onset bipolar disorder include:

VERY COMMON
    Separation anxiety
    Rages and explosive temper tantrums
    Marked irritability
    Oppositional/defiant behavior
    Rapid cycling (frequent mood swings, occurring within an hour, a
        day, or several days) or mood lability
    Racing thoughts
    Aggressive behavior
    Distractibility
    Hyperactivity
    Impulsivity
    Restlessness/fidgetiness
    Risk-taking behaviors
    Elation as represented by periods of extremely silly, giddy, or goofy
        behavior
    Night terrors
    Difficulty getting to sleep
    Difficulty getting up in the morning (sleep inertia)
    Grandiosity
    Periods of low energy and withdrawal
    Low self-esteem
    Carbohydrate cravings
    Hoarding or avidly collecting objects or food
    Lying to avoid consequences of his or her actions
    Easily humiliated or shamed
    Complaints of body temperature extremes
    Hallucinations and delusions

COMMON
    Rapid or pressured speech
    Hypersexuality
    Obsessive behavior

Compulsive behavior
Excessive daydreaming
Learning disabilities
Poor working memory
Lack of organization
Fascination with gore or blood or morbid topics
Manipulative behavior
Extremely bossy behavior with friends/bullying
Self-mutilating behaviors
Destruction of property
Suicidal thoughts
Paranoia

LESS COMMON
Bedwetting
Bingeing/eating disorders
Motor and vocal tics
Cruelty to animals

A discussion recently took place over the Internet when a mother wrote that a child psychiatrist to whom she had taken her very young son was reluctant to make a diagnosis of bipolar disorder, despite the fact that the child had separation anxiety and periods of marked irritability and temper tantrums and was threatening to slice off his older sister's ears with a knife. In addition, the boy's father had been diagnosed with bipolar disorder.

The doctor did not want to "label" the child with a diagnosis of bipolar disorder until it was absolutely necessary. Instead, he focused on the boy's attentional difficulties, prescribed Ritalin, and advised a conservative "wait-and-see" approach.

Members of the BPParents listserv expressed a strong reaction to this psychiatrist's opinion and recommendations, and there were many postings in response. Our feelings lie closest to those of the mother who wrote in to vigorously protest this strategy and counseled:

You need the diagnosis because it explains so much of the emotional and behavioral experiences of the child, and it guides the appropriate treatment and helps avoid the use of medications that could worsen the course of the illness. An accurate and early diagnosis al-

lows the family to develop plans for the future, to make better decisions, and to obtain better services. It also helps families form relationships with other families who are experiencing the same
problems so that they don't feel so alone and so that they can share
information and solutions with each other.

The fact that the diagnosis even appears "optional" speaks to the complexity of this disorder in children, to its overlapping and evolving symptoms, and to its evanescent nature. (There are weeks and even months
when these children are, to quote one mother, "on a good roll," further
confounding the diagnostic investigation.)

But let us say this very clearly: *There are serious risks to delaying diagnosis and treatment.* We can't quite imagine what it must be like for a child
to experience overwhelming and almost atomic rage several times a day
triggered by a simple "no" from a parent or even by the loud chewing of
a sibling at a dinner table. We can only guess how a child responds inter-
nally to a sea of angry, disapproving faces surrounding him or her due to
out-of-control and oppositional or defiant behavior. And there is something known as kindling, or sensitization.

Some years ago Dr. Robert Post of the National Institute of Mental
Health advanced the idea that initial periods of cycling may begin with
an environmental stressor, but if the cycles continue to occur unchecked,
the brain becomes kindled or sensitized—pathways inside the central
nervous system are reinforced, so to speak—and future episodes of depression, hypomania, or mania will occur by themselves (independently of an
outside stimulus), with greater and greater frequency.

Perhaps the most important reason for early intervention and treatment is the fact that this can be a lethal illness. Suicide rates for bipolar
disorder have been estimated to be as high as 15 percent. Failed suicide
attempts are higher still.

Dr. Joseph Biederman made a plea for early diagnosis and intervention
when speaking to an overflowing audience at the 1998 National Alliance
for the Mentally Ill Conference in Washington, D.C.

He said:

In many cases, there is a ten-year gap between the onset of symptoms and intervention. Once you have ten years of anything
unchecked—from a car to your teeth, to some rampant psychopathology—I would propose this is the equivalent to having

metastatic disease ten years later. The problem could be different if the diagnosis were made at the beginning . . . and effective treatments were deployed. . . . It is possible that the prognosis could be very different than the one we see at the end of the line once these children reach adult psychiatry's shore.

Childhood is such a fleeting time and so much must be consolidated within a growing person: ego development, social and academic skills, biological and psychological maturation. . . . Every day counts. There is no time to waste.

Since the entire future of the child as well as the family rests on the proper diagnosis of the disorder and the extremely competent psychopharmacological management of it, we spend the next chapter exploring how one might go about finding a diagnostician/clinician who is adept at recognizing early-onset bipolar disorder and at initiating medication trials with the aim of stabilizing the child. In Chapter 4 we discuss the medications used to accomplish just such stabilization.

# How to Find
# Good Treatment

In our survey and in direct interviews, we asked parents how they initially understood their child's early symptoms and behavioral difficulties. The answers that came back to us were varied. Many parents blamed themselves and criticized their own parenting skills. "We thought we weren't firm enough," they wrote; or "Maybe we weren't always consistent." (Sadly, their relatives and even strangers in the street joined the chorus and gave plenty of unsolicited, often very hurtful advice.)

First-time parents, with no basis for comparison, were slower to recognize how atypical their child's behavior was. One woman said: "This was my first child and I assumed there are all different kinds of temperaments, but I thought: Wow! I got one on the other end of the spectrum. This is absolutely exhausting."

Over half of the parents thought their child was hyperactive. One mother joined a support group for parents of ADHD children, but soon noticed that her child's problems were of a completely different magnitude: "The more I talked with the other parents, the more I realized that they weren't dealing with the same behaviors I was," she told us. "Their kids weren't raging for hours a day, trying to strangle their parents, or experiencing such rapid mood shifts. Something more than ADHD was going on here."

Sooner or later, as the symptoms become more severe and disruptive, the family has to seek professional advice and find a name for the problem. And here's where things get complicated.

Ideally, a child psychiatrist should diagnose and treat a child or adolescent. A child psychiatrist is a medical doctor who has completed two or three years of an adult psychiatric residency and two additional years of a child psychiatry fellowship program.

But there is a nationwide shortage of child psychiatrists. Fewer than 6,500 practice in the United States, and locating a child psychiatrist in the states of Alaska, Arkansas, Idaho, Missouri, Mississippi, Montana, Nevada, Vermont, West Virginia, and Wyoming presents a particular problem: Each of those states has fewer than thirty child psychiatrists; Wyoming has just four.

Even if a parent is able to locate a child psychiatrist close to home, the treating clinician *must* have a view of childhood psychiatric diagnosis that is informed by the latest research findings in childhood bipolar disorder. If not, it is likely that the focus of attention will be on one of several potentially co-occurring or alternative diagnoses such as ADHD, obsessive-compulsive disorder, or oppositional defiant disorder, and the primary symptoms of bipolarity may be overlooked or misdiagnosed. And as we've mentioned in earlier chapters, trials of stimulants and antidepressant medications are likely to be prescribed, potentially complicating or worsening the course of the bipolar disorder.

In the event that a child psychiatrist (with expertise in mood disorders) is not available, an adult psychiatrist with a broad background in mood disorders and an interest in and history of treating children and adolescents may be a suitable alternative. A pediatric neurologist may also be suitable for the psychopharmacological treatment because pediatric neurologists have significant experience with the anticonvulsant medications that are fast becoming the first line of treatment for juvenile bipolar disorders.

Parents whose children had been seen by a number of child psychiatrists were very emphatic about what constituted a good doctor. They advise looking for someone who:

- Has an expertise in mood disorders, who is strong in psychopharmacology, and who keeps up with (or better yet, is involved in) the latest research with regard to bipolar disorder.
- Isn't convinced that he or she knows all the answers (too many variables with symptoms and meds at a young age).
- Communicates and does not talk over one's head, keeps the jargon

to a minimum while educating the child and family, responds to
questions openly, and has an empathic understanding of what the
family is going through.

- Listens well, takes subtleties into account, and returns phone calls
  in a timely manner.
- Is aggressive—taking too much time to give a diagnosis and initiate treatment hurts the child and the family—and is not afraid
  to initiate new medication trials to achieve stabilization.
- Wants to work along with the family, not blame them.
- Understands how traumatic a hospitalization is for the family and
  stays in close contact during this time. Even a message on the answering machine would be a big comfort.
- Is willing to wage a battle with the managed care companies to
  see to it that the child gets all the care he or she needs. Is also willing to speak with the school or come to the IEP meeting (see
  Chapter 9) to ensure that the child gets the proper modifications
  in the program and best education.
- Values parental input and has a good rapport with the child.

## HOW TO FIND A DOCTOR

Most pediatricians are familiar with the child psychiatrists in the area and
may be able to direct you to a good one. Or, if there is a university-
affiliated teaching hospital nearby, you can call the division of child psychiatry and ask to speak to the senior fellow, admissions director, or
clinical director, and then tell the person that you are looking for the
names of child psychiatrists who have an expertise in treating bipolar disorder in children and adolescents.

The Resources section on pages 437–440 includes the telephone numbers of the nation's two leading patient support groups. The patients and
family members who belong to these organizations have had firsthand experience with many of the psychiatrists in your area and are often in a
good position to steer you toward a competent physician. Naturally, if
you're enrolled in a managed care program, you will be referred to someone on its panel. (This does not ensure you a competent referral.)

The Internet may be your best ally in this quest. The Child and Adolescent Bipolar Foundation has message boards where parents often post
requests for "pdocs" (their term for child psychiatrists and psychologists)

in their geographical area, and two or three people always write back with details about the doctors with whom they are familiar. (The website is www.bpkids.org. Information there will also tell a parent how to subscribe to the listserv.)

Because the diagnosis is so critical, some parents seek out evaluations at major teaching hospitals that have clinics well known for their pioneering work in early-onset bipolar disorder. There are a handful of such clinics in the United States and Canada, and we've listed the most prominent ones, along with their medical directors:

**Boston, Massachusetts:** Massachusetts General Hospital, Pediatric Psychopharmacology Unit, Wang Building, Room 725, 15 Parkman St., Boston, MA 02114; (617) 726-2725; Dr. Joseph Biederman, director.

**Cambridge, MA:** The Child and Adolescent Neuropsychiatric Research Program, Cambridge Health Alliance/Mystic Center, 1493 Cambridge St., Cambridge, MA 02139; (718) 306-8630; Dr. Jean Frazier, director.

**Chicago, Illinois:** The Department of Psychiatry, The Section for Children and Adolescents, Rush University Medical Center, 1720 W. Polk St., Chicago, IL 60605; (312) 942-KIDS; Dr. Louis Kraus, director.

**Chicago, Illinois:** Pediatric Mood Disorders Clinic: Institute for Juvenile Research, University of Illinois, at Chicago, 1747 W. Roosevelt St., M/C 747, Chicago, IL 60612; (312) 996-7723; Dr. Mani N. Pavuluri, director.

**Cincinnati, Ohio:** Pediatric Bipolar Program at Children's Hospital Medical Center of Cincinnati, 3333 Barnet Ave., Cincinnati, OH 45229; (513) 636-4124; Drs. Robert A. Kowatch and Melissa DelBello, directors.

**Cleveland, Ohio:** The Stanley Research Center, Case Western Reserve University; University Hospitals of Cleveland, Department of Psychiatry, 11100 Euclid Ave., Cleveland, OH 44106; (216) 844-3881; Dr. Robert L. Findling, director.

**Columbus, Ohio:** Division of Child and Adolescent Psychiatry, The Ohio State University, 1670 Upham Dr., Columbus, OH 43210-1250; (614) 293-8235; Dr. Mary Fristad, director.

**Dallas, Texas:** Center for Pediatric Psychiatry at Children's Medical

Center, 6300 Harry Hines Blvd., Suite 900, Dallas, TX 75235; (214) 456-5937; Drs. Catherine Karni and Kirti Saxena, directors.

**Galveston, Texas:** The Mood and Anxiety Center, University of Texas Medical Branch, 1110 Nasa Parkway, Suite 400, Houston, TX 77058, (281) 333-3199; Dr. Karen Dineen Wagner, director.

**Halifax, Nova Scotia, Canada:** Mood Disorders Clinic, Department of Psychiatry, The IWK-Grace Health Sciences Center, Halifax, NS, Canada; (902) 428-8375; Dr. Stan Kutcher, director.

**Los Angeles, California:** Adolescent Mood Disorders Program, The Lynda and Stewart Resnick Neuropsychiatric Hospital at UCLA, 760 Westwood Plaza, Los Angeles, CA 90024; (310) 825-5730; Dr. Michael Strober, director.

**New Hyde Park, New York:** Long Island Jewish Medical Center of the Albert Einstein College of Medicine, 269–01 76th Ave., New Hyde Park, NY 11040; (718) 470-8444; Dr. Vivian Kafantaris, director.

**Philadelphia, Pennsylvania:** Children's Hospital of Philadelphia, Department of Child and Adolescent Psychiatry, 3400 Market St., Science Center, Suite 200, Philadelphia, PA 19104; (215) 590-7573; Dr. Elizabeth Weller, director.

**Pittsburgh, Pennsylvania:** Child and Adolescent Bipolar Services (CABS), 100 North Bellefield Ave., Bellefield Towers, #612, Pittsburgh, PA 15213; (412) 624-CABS or (877) 851-CABS; Drs. David Axelson and Boris Birmaher, directors.

**Richmond, Virginia:** Virginia Treatment Center for Children, Division of Child and Adolescent Psychiatry, Virginia Commonwealth University, 515 N. 10th St., Richmond, VA 23298; (804) 828-3129; Dr. Bela Sood, director.

**St. Louis, Missouri:** Washington University Child Psychiatry Clinic at Children's Hospital, Montclair Building, 24 South Kingsway, St. Louis, MO 63108; contact person: Rhonda Kidwell, (314) 286-1740; Dr. Barbara Geller, director.

**Stanford, California:** Stanford Pediatric Mood Disorders Clinic, Stanford University School of Medicine, 401 Quarry Rd., Stanford, CA 94305; (650) 723-5511; Dr. Kiki Chang, director.

**Stony Brook, New York:** Division of Child and Adolescent Psychiatry, State University of New York at Stony Brook, Putnam Hall-South Campus, Stony Brook, NY 11974; (631) 632-8850; Dr. Gabrielle Carlson, director.

After giving a diagnosis and initiating a trial of medications, the specialist may be willing to consult with a local child psychiatrist or pediatric neurologist and oversee the course of treatment by phone or e-mail.

## PARENTS' ROLE IN GETTING GOOD TREATMENT

The reality is that it can be difficult to get good treatment. There is confusion in the field of child psychiatry and no broad consensus about juvenile mood disorders. Thanks to the work of some pioneering researchers, the picture of bipolar disorder in early childhood is becoming clearer, but the diagnosis is by no means widely accepted.

Because the family history is one of the most important pieces of the puzzle, some knowledge of a parent's, grandparent's, aunt's, or uncle's temperament, behaviors, and reactions to life's events and psychiatric hospitalizations can contribute very useful information to the process of diagnosis.

It is incumbent on the mother and father of the ill child to search within his and her family of origin for evidence of bipolarity. This is not always easy. For one thing, diagnosis was not very accurate a generation or two ago; for another, stigma and shame forced families to hide a problem and present as normal a face as possible to the community. A parent may have to push hard against this reluctance to reveal the family psychiatric history and may even have to travel to interview family members who can help fill in the blanks.

Next, a few of the many possible behaviors, reactions to life events, or temperaments that may be suggestive of a bipolar illness in a family member:

- Your father's father was an alcoholic and seemed very withdrawn at times. But he was the life of the party and larger than life at other times.
- Aunt Sarah had a "nervous breakdown." She was hospitalized and received shock therapy.
- Uncle Mike was notorious for his temper. His family walked on eggshells around him.
- You remember your mother vacuuming at three o'clock in the morning and staying up all night cleaning the rest of the house. She was often irritable. She planned huge holiday parties and then spent a great deal of time in bed suffering an overwhelming fatigue and lassitude, "recuperating from her efforts."

- Your father crisscrossed the country with unrealistic ideas for making a lot of money. Multiple financial crises, even bankruptcies, may have been the result.
- You remember your mother spending a lot of time in bed after the birth of a baby. She cried a lot and found it difficult to get dressed, even months after the child was born.
- Two of your uncles were diagnosed "paranoid schizophrenic."
- Your mother's brother was a big gambler.
- There were suicides in the family.

Beyond the family history, the parents need to provide detailed information about the symptoms and behaviors of their own child. The Child Bipolar Questionnaire (CBQ) is a concise screening inventory developed by one of the authors.

We provide this screening instrument as an organizational aid in the assessment process only. Only an experienced diagnostician with a full understanding of the child's family history, as well as the symptoms and behaviors that the child exhibits, is qualified to make a diagnosis of bipolar disorder.

The questionnaire, completed by a parent, can be automatically scored online and submitted to the professional diagnosing the child. The questionnaire is available in English, Spanish, Portuguese, Polish, and French on the website of the Juvenile Bipolar Research Foundation (www.jbrf.org).

## THE CHILD BIPOLAR QUESTIONNAIRE — VERSION 2.0
©2002 Demitri F. Papolos, M.D. All rights reserved.

Instructions:
Your child has and/or had the following symptoms and/or behaviors. You may have noticed a behavior as far back as early childhood or you may have observed it more recently. In either case, estimate how frequently the behavior has occurred since you first noticed it. In other words, *please rate these symptoms and/or behaviors* as they *were at their most severe and/or prior to your child starting medication.* Then select a number in the "Frequency" column using the following key, to represent the frequency of occurrence:

| Never or hardly ever | Sometimes | Often | Very often or almost constantly |
|---|---|---|---|
| 1 | 2 | 3 | 4 |

## Symptom/Behavior

**Frequency**

| Symptom/Behavior | 1 | 2 | 3 | 4 |
|---|---|---|---|---|
| 1) displays excessive distress when separated from family | ○ | ○ | ○ | ○ |
| 2) exhibits excessive anxiety or worry | ○ | ○ | ○ | ○ |
| 3) has difficulty arising in the A.M. | ○ | ○ | ○ | ○ |
| 4) is hyperactive and easily excited in the P.M. | ○ | ○ | ○ | ○ |
| 5) has difficulty settling at night | ○ | ○ | ○ | ○ |
| 6) has difficulty getting to sleep | ○ | ○ | ○ | ○ |
| 7) sleeps fitfully and/or awakens in the middle of the night | ○ | ○ | ○ | ○ |
| 8) has night terrors and/or nightmares | ○ | ○ | ○ | ○ |
| 9) wets bed | ○ | ○ | ○ | ○ |
| 10) craves sweet-tasting foods | ○ | ○ | ○ | ○ |
| 11) is easily distracted by extraneous stimuli | ○ | ○ | ○ | ○ |
| 12) is easily distracted during repetitive chores & lessons | ○ | ○ | ○ | ○ |
| 13) demonstrates inability to concentrate at school | ○ | ○ | ○ | ○ |
| 14) attempts to avoid homework assignments | ○ | ○ | ○ | ○ |
| 15) able to focus intently on subjects of interest and yet at times is easily distractible | ○ | ○ | ○ | ○ |
| 16) has poor handwriting | ○ | ○ | ○ | ○ |
| 17) has difficulty organizing tasks | ○ | ○ | ○ | ○ |
| 18) has difficulty making transitions | ○ | ○ | ○ | ○ |
| 19) has difficulty estimating time | ○ | ○ | ○ | ○ |
| 20) has auditory processing or short-term memory deficit | ○ | ○ | ○ | ○ |
| 21) is extremely sensitive to textures of clothes, labels, and tightness of fit of socks or shoes | ○ | ○ | ○ | ○ |
| 22) exhibits extreme sensitivity to sound and noise | ○ | ○ | ○ | ○ |
| 23) complains of body temperature extremes or feeling hot despite neutral ambient temperature | ○ | ○ | ○ | ○ |

| Symptom/Behavior | Frequency | | | |
|---|---|---|---|---|
| | 1 | 2 | 3 | 4 |
| 24) is easily excitable | ○ | ○ | ○ | ○ |
| 25) has periods of high, frenetic energy and motor activation | ○ | ○ | ○ | ○ |
| 26) has many ideas at once | ○ | ○ | ○ | ○ |
| 27) interrupts or intrudes on others | ○ | ○ | ○ | ○ |
| 28) has periods of excessive and rapid speech | ○ | ○ | ○ | ○ |
| 29) has exaggerated ideas about self or abilities | ○ | ○ | ○ | ○ |
| 30) tells tall tales; embellishes or exaggerates | ○ | ○ | ○ | ○ |
| 31) displays abrupt, rapid mood swings | ○ | ○ | ○ | ○ |
| 32) has irritable mood states | ○ | ○ | ○ | ○ |
| 33) has elated or silly, goofy, giddy mood states | ○ | ○ | ○ | ○ |
| 34) displays precocious sexual curiosity | ○ | ○ | ○ | ○ |
| 35) exhibits inappropriate sexual behaviors, e.g., openly touches self or others' private parts | ○ | ○ | ○ | ○ |
| 36) takes excessive risks | ○ | ○ | ○ | ○ |
| 37) complains of being bored | ○ | ○ | ○ | ○ |
| 38) has periods of low energy and/or withdraws or isolates self | ○ | ○ | ○ | ○ |
| 39) has decreased initiative | ○ | ○ | ○ | ○ |
| 40) experiences periods of self-doubt and poor self-esteem | ○ | ○ | ○ | ○ |
| 41) feels easily criticized and/or rejected | ○ | ○ | ○ | ○ |
| 42) feels easily humiliated or shamed | ○ | ○ | ○ | ○ |
| 43) fidgets with hands or feet | ○ | ○ | ○ | ○ |
| 44) is intolerant of delays | ○ | ○ | ○ | ○ |
| 45) relentlessly pursues own needs and is demanding of others | ○ | ○ | ○ | ○ |

## Symptom/Behavior

**Frequency**

| Symptom/Behavior | 1 | 2 | 3 | 4 |
|---|---|---|---|---|
| 46) is willful and refuses to be subordinated by others | O | O | O | O |
| 47) argues with adults | O | O | O | O |
| 48) is bossy towards others | O | O | O | O |
| 49) defies or refuses to comply with rules | O | O | O | O |
| 50) blames others for his/her mistakes | O | O | O | O |
| 51) is easily angered in response to limit setting | O | O | O | O |
| 52) lies to avoid consequences of his/her actions | O | O | O | O |
| 53) has protracted, explosive temper tantrums | O | O | O | O |
| 54) has difficulty maintaining friendships | O | O | O | O |
| 55) displays aggressive behavior towards others | O | O | O | O |
| 56) has destroyed property intentionally | O | O | O | O |
| 57) curses viciously, uses foul language in anger | O | O | O | O |
| 58) makes moderate threats to others or self | O | O | O | O |
| 59) makes clear threats of violence to others or self | O | O | O | O |
| 60) has made clear threats of suicide | O | O | O | O |
| 61) is fascinated with gore, blood, or violent imagery | O | O | O | O |
| 62) has acknowledged experiencing auditory and/or visual hallucinations | O | O | O | O |
| 63) hoards or avidly seeks to collect objects or food | O | O | O | O |
| 64) has concern with dirt, germs, or contamination | O | O | O | O |
| 65) is very intuitive and/or very creative | O | O | O | O |

The Child Bipolar Questionnaire may be found online at the website of the Juvenile Bipolar Research Foundation, www.jbrf.org.

Also on the website of the Juvenile Bipolar Research Foundation (www.jbrf.org) is the Jeannie and Jeffrey Illustrated Interview for Children. This is a child-report version of the Child Bipolar Questionnaire, and it can be completed online by a child and automatically scored.

There are forty questions paired with illustrations for a girl (Jeannie) and forty for a boy (Jeffrey). The children can endorse a symptom or behavior that they, like Jeannie or Jeffrey, may be feeling but have no words to describe—and that even their closest observers may not realize. The Interview should be helpful to the evaluating physician, the therapist, and parents. A few sample items are included below.

## SAMPLE ITEMS OF THE JEANNIE AND JEFFREY ILLUSTRATED INTERVIEW FOR CHILDREN

### Mood Changes
After school, the way Jeffrey feels changes from being bored to cranky to really silly. When this happens, Jeffrey feels like he has a motor inside that's revving up really fast. How often do you feel like this in the afternoon or at night?

- ○ Never or hardly ever
- ○ Sometimes
- ○ Often
- ○ Very often or almost constantly

### Irritable
Today Jeannie is really cranky and angry at other people, even people she likes. How often do you feel like this?

- ○ Never or hardly ever
- ○ Sometimes
- ○ Often
- ○ Very often or almost constantly

### Grandiose
Jeffrey thinks that he is smarter and stronger than his friends or feels he is a very special and important person. How often do you feel like this?

- ○ Never or hardly ever
- ○ Sometimes
- ○ Often
- ○ Very often or almost constantly

**Anger**

When Jeannie's mom tells her that she can't go somewhere that she wants to go, she can get really angry and upset. How often do you feel like this?

○ Never or hardly ever

○ Sometimes

○ Often

○ Very often or almost constantly

Illustrations by Karl Gude.

Once you've received a referral to a physician, you simply make a phone call. Just give your name, mention the doctor or individual who referred you, and tell the psychiatrist you would like to schedule an appointment for him or her to see your child for a consultation. Unless the child psychiatrist asks you for it, this is not the time to go into great detail or have a lengthy conversation—all of that will be handled in the consultation session.

## HOW TO JUDGE A DOCTOR'S ABILITY TO DIAGNOSE AND TREAT BIPOLAR DISORDER IN CHILDREN

Family members have every right to inquire about the physician's orientation and clinical views, and questions such as "Do you strictly adhere to *DSM-IV* criteria?" or "Is it your observation that the symptoms of this illness differ from the adult form and can be diagnosed before puberty?" or "What is your view about the existence of comorbid conditions like ADHD, oppositional defiant disorder, and anxiety disorders with bipolar disorder?" will reveal the orientation and his or her level of knowledge and expertise.

If the doctor mentions that most children who have bipolar disorder cannot be diagnosed according to current diagnostic criteria, and he or she knows that the duration of cycling is much shorter in children, and then treats this form of the condition as a bipolar disorder anyway, the parents should breathe a sigh of relief. If there are comorbid syndromes such as ADHD, ODD, or OCD, and if the doctor views the treatment and stabilization of the bipolar disorder as the primary initial goal, the parents are halfway home.

Other clues into the doctor's experience level are how the doctor formulates a treatment plan when there are two coexisting conditions—one of them ultrarapid bipolar disorder and the other ADHD (stabilize the mood disorder first and then cautiously add low-dose stimulants); how experienced the doctor is in using mood stabilizers; how frequently the psychiatrist prescribes lithium, Depakote, Tegretol, Trileptal, or Lamictal; and how comfortable she or he is about trying newer medications. Naturally, the doctor should always explore the family history when making the diagnosis.

Parents should feel that the doctor welcomes an open dialogue and views the parents as collaborators on the treatment team. The doctor should want to teach the parents, should encourage them to chart their child's illness and course of treatment, and should not feel threatened when the parents do their own research. The parents should trust their gut instincts about a doctor.

## PSYCHOLOGICAL THERAPIES

Many families who recognize the need to address the psychological issues for the child and themselves seek out less expensive mental health professionals, such as psychologists, social workers, or nurse practitioners, to conduct the therapy. The child psychiatrist then manages the medical aspects of the treatment on a less frequent basis.

However, the professional who manages the psychotherapeutic part of the treatment must have a solid understanding of early-onset bipolar disorder, its course, and its medical treatment (and understand the side effects of the medications) in order not to misinterpret some of the child's behaviors. For example, a child's fatigue and phlegmatic behavior may be an early side effect of a medication rather than a symptom of depression, or both factors—depression and medication side effects—may be contributing to the picture. Granted, it's hard to tease apart moods and behaviors that arise from temperament and the flux of childhood life from those propelled by an impending episode of illness or its treatment (especially with children who have rapid mood shifts), but a child is best served when all things are considered, and this requires a comprehensive view of the child and the disorder.

Therapy for children with bipolar disorder is pretty much uncharted territory, but Dr. Nancy Austin, who practices in New York City, treats a number of bipolar children. We asked her to describe some of the particular ways she works with them. She told us:

First of all, a therapist has to understand the level of discomfort that is going on inside the bodies of these children. I tend to focus initially on the body experience of the child, because irritability and anger may be a response to this. Children often can't verbalize the internal experience of changing mood states, but I find they will symbolically represent it.

For instance, I had one little girl who repeatedly started each session by adding to a collection of rubber bands and attaching them to each other and to items in the room. The whole place looked like a spider's web. She showed me what it felt like to be inside her head: She couldn't get out. If she stepped there, she would fall through; if she stepped here she would be trapped. She was always "getting caught" in her weblike structure.

Dr. Austin knows that these kids are experiencing something terrifying for which they initially have no words, and therefore the shifting body experience can only be expressed in metaphor. In play or verbal expression via storytelling, Dr. Austin looks for the underlying mood state. She also focuses on the way the child takes in and expresses things. If the stimulation or demand is too great, the child and therapist adjust the therapy so the child's unique moment-to-moment experience of his or her world (in the therapy room) is shared by both.

Dr. Austin has adapted tools that were developed by Dr. John March from Duke University in his cognitive-behavioral approach to obsessive-compulsive disorder in children and adolescents. One tool that is particularly helpful is the image of a thermometer, which allows the child to indicate the intensity of an event that typically causes irritability and rage—such as frustration with homework, getting up and ready for the bus in the morning, dealing with shoelaces that are not tied tightly enough, or going into a store and not being allowed to buy every toy he or she wants.

"We discuss what upsets them," says Dr. Austin. "We talk about the temper tantrums." She and the child find ways of recognizing and then talking about the child's experience of shifting inner states. Only then can she help the child to recognize behaviors that scale back the intensity of a tantrum, and help him or her to deescalate. Once they've identified how to do that—and it may be deep breathing, quiet time, watching a familiar video, or taking a bath—she helps the parent-child team facilitate strategies that get the anger into a more manageable range.

Dr. Austin also helps the parent and child see how differently each of them is viewing a tantrum. For instance, on the scale from one to ten, a parent may experience his or her child as having a tantrum of incredible intensity: Often the parent views it as a "nine or a ten" and yet the child sees it as a "six or seven." "At this point the parents' nerves are shot," says Dr. Austin. "They experience something akin to a post-traumatic stress response, and they begin to assume that nothing will change. But when the parent successfully contributes to a scaleback, the parent begins to develop renewed hope about the enormously challenging task of parenting a bipolar child, and the parent is able to stay calmer and experience less anger and upset. I help the parent understand what the child is experiencing at the moment and intervene at the first sign of a tantrum. When there is improved attunement between parent and child, full-blown tantrums decrease."

A critical part of the therapy is working with the parents together and helping them to understand each other's actions. It is not uncommon to hear a husband complain to his wife: "You baby him. You indulge him in everything." But once the diagnosis is made, and it is understood what is going on inside the child, both parents may come to realize that the child needs this kind of attention and attunement. The father may come to realize that his wife is actually doing heroic parenting. Significant reduction of the tension and contention between parents is helpful to them and to all their children.

Dr. Austin also helps the parents identify which one is strong in which areas so that one can spot the other, support the other, but not ask the other to do what he or she does not do best. At some point, one of them will be so worn down that the other has to take over. When one spouse can help the other to stay calm, home life can be less traumatic. Parents can then regain their sense of competency as parents.

Dr. Austin feels strongly that the entire team—the parents, the prescribing physician, the school personnel, and the therapist—should be collaborating, and the therapist can facilitate an ongoing discussion.

It is not easy to find a therapist who has such an understanding of the internal states of a bipolar child. Trying to give a synopsis of all that goes on in such a complicated therapy is near impossible, but parents might be well served to think of elements that are present in Dr. Austin's work to ensure that a therapist is attuned to the rapidly shifting inner mood states of bipolar children and to the special problems they and their families face.

## Costs

How much would treatment with any of these different professionals cost? As of this writing, typical fees per session are:

| | |
|---|---|
| Psychiatrist | $180–$250 |
| Clinical psychologist | $100–$175 |
| Social worker | $90–$150 |

A comprehensive evaluation by a medical expert in child bipolar disorder may cost in the neighborhood of $1,000. Neuropsychological testing, which scores and defines the child's cognitive strengths and deficits, perceptual strengths and difficulties, and abstract reasoning abilities, with a full emotional functioning component may require up to nine hours of time and cost anywhere between $2,000 and $3,000. Parents should expect a detailed written report suitable for school and therapeutic purposes (some run from five to fifteen pages long) and a parent feedback session.

## Other Treatment Options

The National Institute of Mental Health (NIMH) and the Stanley Medical Research Institute (SMRI) are conducting research in the area of early-onset bipolar disorder, and they are funding a number of diagnostic studies and clinical trials that recruit volunteers from around the country. A call to the NIMH at (301) 443-4513 or to the SMRI at (305) 571-0760 will inform a parent of ongoing studies that may cost the family little or nothing for expert diagnosis and treatment. Another organization solely devoted to research into early-onset bipolar disorder is the Juvenile Bipolar Research Foundation. The foundation sponsors research that is conducted through a consortium of medical schools, notably Yale, Albert Einstein College of Medicine, Cornell, and Harvard. For information about ongoing studies, go to www.jbrf.org.

Some of the clinics mentioned earlier in this chapter may have an ongoing study that would accomplish the same thing, closer to home.

## PARENTS AS SHERLOCK HOLMES

In this chapter, we've tried to warn parents how difficult it is to obtain proper diagnosis and good treatment for a child with bipolar disorder. Parents are going to have to work hard to assemble as clear a family history as possible, take a close unvarnished look at their child's behaviors, become educated about this disorder so that they can discern which doctor they should trust for the diagnosis and treatment, and try hard to seek out a therapy that addresses the many issues that affect the child and the family members. If parents know what they need and want, they have a better chance of finding it and maximizing the benefits to their child and the family as a whole.

A few weeks before we sat down to work on this chapter, we got a call from a couple we had known for many years. Laura and Alan were living on the West Coast and had heard through other friends that we were writing this book. They had a young son named Matthew, who was living a tortured existence. Laura and Alan detailed the grim facts of Matthew's behaviors over the past few years. He had rages that went on for hours; he was very destructive, and though he was in a small therapeutic school, his parents kept receiving notes from the teacher reporting very disturbing events. Once Matthew tried to destroy the classroom and kicked a window out of its frame. Many days he was so out of control that Laura and Alan were called and asked to pick him up. Some days they kept him home because his behavior was just too erratic.

Laura and Alan trudged the route from doctor to doctor, and Matthew was finally diagnosed with ADHD. (Bipolar disorder was discussed, but Matthew was adopted and there was no family history. Also, one doctor told them that the diagnosis could not be made until Matthew reached puberty.) Matthew was put on a stimulant and an antidepressant, but within a few weeks he began experiencing visual hallucinations at night, begging Laura to see all the bugs and snakes that were crawling on his bed. He was about to be hospitalized when he was taken off these medications and actually had a few weeks on a good roll, his mother explained.

But the cycles continued, and "family life" was something that happened only for other families (or so they thought). Laura sent us her journals of these years, and they are extremely painful to read. In a series of telephone conversations, we discussed the importance of early diagnosis and intervention and mentioned that although Matthew was still young, the clock was ticking, and early childhood was coming to an end. Laura replied in a broken and grief-stricken voice: "This hasn't been a childhood, this has been a horror show." Demitri suggested a mood stabilizer, and their doctor on the West Coast initiated a medication trial.

And so, as we spent the week organizing this chapter, it seemed particularly meaningful that we received a letter in the mail from Laura. We held our breath as we sat down and opened it. Afterward, neither of us said anything for a minute or so. With Laura's and Alan's permission we reproduce part of it:

Dear Demitri and Janice:

Alan and I have been meaning to call to give you the miraculous details of Matthew's progress, and we will, but in the meantime, a short note to tell you what a fantastic change we are seeing in Matthew.

He is so much more even-keeled, so cheerful, cooperative, reasonable. His sense of humor has come out of hiding, and he actually jokes about things. The *darkness* is gone.

Of course he still tends to be impulsive and to overreact angrily to certain things, but these reflexes are fewer and he recovers much more quickly. For the first time we can see a real willingness and ability on Matthew's part to change his behavior. He's doing so well that we're even thinking of bringing him back to district school in the near future. It's just too good to be true . . .

Toward the end of the note, Laura repeated something her son, now nine years old, said to her after six weeks on a mood stabilizer and *off* stimulants and antidepressants: "Mommy, I'm going to ask God if he can please let me keep feeling this way."

It is possible for a child to be rescued from all that rage, aggression, and anxiety. There is, however, no way to know exactly which medication will work for any individual child. It is very much a trial-and-error procedure, and it may take multiple medication trials until the right drug or combination of drugs is found. (It is not uncommon for children with early-onset bipolar disorder to require a combination of two mood-stabilizing drugs to achieve stability.) All of the drugs have side effects—they will be detailed in the pages that follow. Many side effects are bothersome only in the beginning of treatment and disappear once the body grows accustomed to the medication. Some persist throughout the period the child is taking the drug. The hope is (and it is not an unreasonable one) that, as attention is paid to this disorder of early childhood, newer and safer drugs with fewer side effects will be coming through the pipeline.

Most of these medications have only recently begun to be used in children, and not many studies of their use in childhood exist. Many are not even approved by the U.S. Food and Drug Administration (FDA) for use in children, and double-blind placebo-controlled studies are only now being mounted or completed. Many psychiatrists are simply adapting what they know about the treatment of adults to the pediatric and adolescent population.

Foremost in a parent's mind must be the risk/benefit of any medication. While a few parents answered a question on our survey saying that they fought the use of drugs and that medicating a child made them "uneasy," the overwhelming majority of mothers and fathers said that they were relieved to know there was something that could help lift their child out of a "nightmare" and into a more naturally paced life.

In the pages that follow, we will explore all the psychiatric treatments for early-onset bipolar disorder. Before we do, however, we want to state bluntly, right up front, that *antidepressants and in many cases stimulants given without the benefit of a mood stabilizer (possibly even with the protection of a mood stabilizer) can cause havoc in a child suffering from a bipolar condition, increasing anxiety states, potentially inducing mania, more frequent cycling, and increases in aggressive outbursts and temper tantrums.* In our study, over 80 percent of the children given antidepressants of all kinds became agitated, or more aggressive, paranoid, or psychotic. Many were hospitalized.

Mood stabilizers are the mainstays of treatment of a bipolar disorder. People often ask if one mood stabilizer is better than another and how physicians make the choice for the first trial. The truth is, no studies have shown any of the medications to be superior to the others. In fact, lithium may be better in the maintenance part of treatment than any of the other drugs. Everything depends on the child's unique and individual reaction (and, of course, on the doctor's expertise in prescribing and titrating dosages).

Lithium, Tegretol, and Depakote are three mood stabilizers that require blood levels, and parents of needlephobic children can easily envision the struggle ahead with these medications. But one of these may work best for their child, and parents should know about a product developed in Israel called Emla. It is an anesthetic available by prescription that can be administered to a child's arm about an hour before the blood draw.

## Mood Stabilizers

### Lithium

Lithium is a naturally occurring alkaline substance that exists in trace amounts in the human body, in plants, and in mineral rocks. It has been used as a medication at different times throughout history. Over 1,800 years ago, the Greek physician Galen formulated a treatment for mania by bathing patients in alkaline springs and by having them drink the water. (It is thought that they were lithium springs.) In 1817 August Arfwedson, a young Swedish chemist, inserted lithium into the chemists' periodic table as the lightest of the alkali metals. He christened his new element lithium, from the Greek word for stone, *lithos*.

From the 1840s to the early 1900s, and for some years after that, lithium was touted as a cure for such maladies as gout, epilepsy, diabetes, sleeplessness, and even cancer. It was never all that effective, but something about the drug prompted its resurrection every few decades.

In the late 1940s, lithium chloride was prescribed as a salt substitute for patients with heart or kidney disease who required a low-sodium diet. And this time the use of lithium was a disaster. It was discovered—too late—that lithium exchanges for sodium in the body. If a person is salt-depleted, it competes with sodium and rises to toxic levels in the body and brain. Some people suffered lithium poisoning; several people died.

In what surely must be the worst timing in history, a psychiatrist named John Cade, far away in a primitive laboratory in Australia, stumbled on the true value of lithium. The year was 1948.

Dr. Cade had a hunch that people became manic when there was too much uric acid in their bodies. He decided to test out his hypothesis by injecting uric acid into guinea pigs. In order to control the potency of the uric acid, it had to be put into a soluble form so that it could be diluted. And what solution did he choose? Lithium salts.

The guinea pigs, notably excitable in the Cade laboratory, became extremely calm and impassive once they were injected with the solution. Perhaps the animals simply became toxic, but seeing their "calm," Dr. Cade ran upstairs to the ward and injected ten manic patients, six schizophrenic patients, and three patients diagnosed as melancholic with the lithium solution. In the *Medical Journal of Australia,* on September 3, 1949, John Cade reported:

> W.B., a male, aged fifty-one years, had been in a state of chronic manic excitement for five years, restless, dirty, destructive, mischievous, and interfering, had long been regarded as the most troublesome patient in the ward. His response was highly gratifying. From the start of treatment on March 29, 1948, with lithium citrate, he steadily settled down and was enjoying the unaccustomed surroundings of the convalescent ward. . . . He remained perfectly well and left the hospital on July 9, 1948, on indefinite leave with instructions to take a maintenance dose of lithium carbonate, five grains twice a day. . . . He was soon back working happily at his job. However, he became lackadaisical about his medicine and finally ceased taking it. His relatives reported that he had not had any for at least six weeks prior to readmission on January 30, 1949, and was becoming steadily more irritable and erratic. He ceased work just before Christmas. On readmission to hospital he was at once started on lithium carbonate, ten grains three times a day, and in a fortnight had again settled down to normal. . . . He is now (February 28, 1949) ready to return to home and work.

This seminal article reported ten case histories demonstrating the profound effect of lithium on manic patients, but Cade's monumental discovery failed to garner any attention. The lithium poisonings in America buried the medication under the weight of negative public opinion and government restrictions.

But a Danish psychiatrist named Mogens Schou, who became the world expert on the use of lithium in psychiatry, clearly understood the magnitude of its importance and was not about to let this drug retreat to the back shelves of the pharmacy. His brother apparently suffered severe mood swings for many years and yet became well stabilized on lithium. After studying more than 150 patients using double-blind study methods (neither the doctors evaluating the results of the "medicine" given nor

the patients taking the medicine know if the patients are taking a placebo
or the active drug), Schou was convinced that lithium worked not only
for the treatment of mania but also to prevent recurrence of the cycles in
either direction. He began to campaign for its use in 1957, and, slowly,
other countries began to use lithium for the treatment of manic depression. In America, however, the FDA restricted its use to small experiments only.

After many clinical studies and the determination of Drs. Samuel Gershon, Nathan Klein, and Ronald Fieve to reignite interest in a medication they saw as so lifesaving, the FDA partially lifted the nonapproved
status of lithium and allowed doctors to prescribe it for the treatment of
acute mania. But it was not until 1974 that the FDA finally approved its
status as a prophylactic medication—one that acted to prevent future
episodes of mania. To date, millions of people have lived normal lives
thanks to John Cade's serendipitous discovery.

## How Does Lithium Work?

While there are unequivocal data proving that lithium works in adults,
no one is sure how it exerts its effects, or why it works preventively in
both mania and depression. It is known that lithium affects a complex biological system called the phosphatidyl inositol cycle inside many types
of cells. This cycle is referred to as a "second messenger" system that relays and amplifies signals from neurotransmitters, hormones, and other
molecules. Apparently lithium inhibits or dampens down the activity of
the pathway, which may be overactive in both mania and depression, but
much remains unknown at present.

## How Well Does Lithium Work for Children?

In adults, lithium is considered to be the gold standard for the treatment
of bipolar or cyclic mood disorders. An estimated 70 to 80 percent of
bipolar patients have a positive therapeutic response to it. But the group
of patients who have been described as "rapid cyclers" (those who have
four or more cycles in a one-year period) were thought not to do as well
on lithium as they do on other mood stabilizers, such as Depakote or
Tegretol.

Since children typically have a rapid-cycling condition, and many children cycle several or more times in a twenty-four-hour period—they are
called *ultradian* cyclers—there was a question about lithium's effectiveness in the pediatric population. However, despite the rapid cycling,

many children do have an excellent response to the drug or to its use in combination with another mood stabilizer.

Very important, data from the research literature suggest that lithium has a strong and possibly unique effect against suicidal behavior in people with bipolar disorder. Apparently this is not true of the other mood stabilizers. According to Dr. Ross J. Baldessarini from Harvard Medical School, "If the antisuicidal effects of lithium are not shared with other mood-altering agents, this may be due to the cerebral serotonin-enhancing properties of lithium, properties that are not known to be associated with anticonvulsants."

Lithium has also been shown to be neuroprotective, and this will be discussed in some detail in Chapter 8.

## Determining Dosages

Before lithium can be prescribed for a child, a complete medical history is taken and a physical exam is performed. Some routine lab work, such as simple blood tests and a urinalysis, is ordered. Because lithium is almost entirely eliminated from the kidneys, tests of kidney function are done before the lithium therapy begins and at regular, approximately four- to six-month, intervals after that. A psychiatrist will also ask that tests of thyroid function be obtained, since lithium can occasionally cause goiter (a treatable and reversible enlargement of the thyroid gland) or a decrease in thyroid function (hypothyroidism). Blood tests of the levels of thyroid hormones (T3 and T4) and thyroid-stimulating hormone (TSH) are typically performed prior to initiation of treatment and annually thereafter.

Children will have to have periodic blood tests in order to determine the lithium concentrations in their blood. In order for lithium to be effective, its concentration in the blood must be held within a specific range: Too low a level is ineffective, but too high a level can be toxic. Maintenance therapeutic levels for children typically range from 0.8 to 1.2 mEq/liter.

At the beginning of lithium treatment, blood levels are monitored five to six days following each increase in dosage, but once the level of the drug has stabilized in the body, blood levels typically are obtained every four to six months.

The blood sample needs to be drawn approximately twelve hours after the last dose and before the child takes the next dose. Because a blood sample taken soon after a dose can be misleading, parents are going to have to time the trip to the lab carefully. (A new FDA-approved test,

called the Insta Read Lithium System, allows a physician in his or her office to check the level in minutes with just a finger stick.)

A liquid form of lithium citrate is available, which is helpful for young
children who can't swallow pills, and there are other choices of lithium
formulations. Most are 300 milligram immediate-release lithium carbonate tablets or capsules, but 150 and 600 milligram tablets and capsules
are available also. The drug is immediately absorbed and, as a result, can
produce relatively high peak blood levels. For this reason, a divided
dosage regimen is prescribed—often three or four times a day.

Several pharmaceutical companies produce different forms of release designed to minimize this sawtooth pattern of lithium levels in the blood.
For instance, Lithobid R is a slow-release form of lithium that flattens the
peak blood levels. The drug is released slowly enough that the blood level
peak occurs approximately four hours after ingesting the medicine.

Another of these release designs is Eskalith CR, a sustained release formulation. The lithium is embedded in a nondigestible carrier that delays
absorption even longer, as much as twelve hours after the child takes it.
This allows the drug to be given less frequently, perhaps only once a day,
but some children complain of lower abdominal cramps or diarrhea, perhaps because of this delayed absorption in the gut.

The following chart identifies a typical lithium-carbonate dosing
schedule for children under twelve years of age.

|                      | DOSAGE (MG) | | | |
| --- | --- | --- | --- | --- |
| WEIGHT (POUNDS) | 7 A.M. | 12 NOON | 6 P.M. | Total Daily Dose |
| Less than 55 | 150 | 150 | 300 | 600 |
| 55–88 | 300 | 300 | 300 | 900 |
| 88–110 | 300 | 300 | 600 | 1,200 |
| 110–132 | 600 | 300 | 600 | 1,500 |

*Source:* Adapted from "Lithium Dosage Guide for Prepubertal Children"
by Elizabeth B. Weller, Ronald A. Weller, and Mary A. Fristad, *Journal of
the American Academy of Child Psychiatry* 25 (1986): 92–95.

If a dose of lithium is missed, the next dose should *not* be doubled. It
is much safer to skip a dose than to double the next one.

Lithium is rapidly absorbed into the bloodstream and carried to all body and brain tissues. As mentioned, the medication is eliminated almost entirely by the kidneys. Sodium is also excreted by the kidneys in competition with lithium, and if there is sodium depletion in the body, lithium will be retained in its place. The possible buildup of lithium could result in toxicity. Therefore, a normal sodium balance is needed to ensure a reliable lithium balance. This means that patients must avoid taking diuretics and eating low-sodium diets, or the prescription should be adjusted downward. Also, parents should be aware that any severe loss of fluids, such as that caused by fevers, vomiting, and diarrhea, even dehydration on very hot days, can cause lithium levels to rise in the bloodstream to potentially toxic levels. In such situations, the doctor should be called and the child should be given fluids such as Pedialyte or Gatorade. Likely the doctor will request that a lithium level be taken and that the daily dose of lithium be lowered—perhaps even stopped—for the duration of the illness.

## Signs of Possible Lithium Toxicity

Elevated levels of lithium in the blood can be toxic, cause brain damage, or even be fatal. While long-term use of lithium does not damage the kidneys, toxic levels can. Parents should understand that what could be a subtherapeutic level for one child could be toxic for another. While rare, it has been reported that toxicity can occur at levels lower than 0.8mEq/liter. Therefore, parents should take careful note of the following signs of lithium toxicity:

| | |
|---|---|
| Fatigue | Coarse or worsening hand tremor |
| Sleepiness | Unsteady gait |
| Confusion | Tremor of the lower jaw |
| Muscle weakness | Muscle twitches |
| Heaviness of limbs | Nausea, stomachache, diarrhea |
| Slurred speech | Ringing in the ears (tinnitus) |

Some of these symptoms could be caused by other illnesses or, in adolescents, abuse of alcohol or street drugs. No matter what a parent suspects, the child should not be given any more lithium and the doctor should be contacted immediately. A blood test to check the lithium blood level should clarify the picture, and if necessary, the dosage can be adjusted.

## Side Effects of Lithium

Most young people tolerate lithium very well if it is carefully dosed and monitored. In fact, because their kidneys are so efficient, they excrete lithium quickly and often need doses similar to those prescribed for adults in order to maintain adequate levels in the blood for maintenance therapy.

Lithium is nonsedating and nonaddictive. Most of the side effects are both harmless and easily dealt with. The following side effects can occur as lithium therapy is instituted, but typically subside in a few days as the body adjusts to the medication:

EARLY SIDE EFFECTS
- Nausea, vomiting, diarrhea, abdominal distress
- Headache
- Excessive thirst (polydipsia) and frequent urination (polyuria), and bedwetting (nocturia)

These side effects usually can be dealt with by adjusting the dosage or raising the dosage more slowly, or changing the schedule of dosing.

OTHER SIDE EFFECTS
- *Hand tremor.* An active tremor of the hands is uncommon in children and adolescents taking lithium, but if it does occur, often it can be counteracted with small doses of propranolol (Inderal) or by lowering the dosage of lithium.
- *Weight gain.* Most children and adolescents will gain weight on lithium, probably five to ten pounds in the first year, sometimes even more. There is some speculation about lithium's anti-insulin effect on carbohydrate metabolism, but some weight gain can be attributed to the thirst that lithium can cause and a child's tendency to quench that thirst with soda or fruit juices, which are highly caloric. Low-calorie sodas or water will reduce the amount of weight gain. Many people in support groups have reported that increased exercise also can combat the problem of weight gain.
- *Acne.* Teens especially may experience the eruption or worsening of acne on the face, neck, shoulder, or back, but this can be treated with typical anti-acne therapies (but not Accutane, as this can cause depression).
- *Hypothyroidism.* This is a condition in which the thyroid gland becomes underactive and enlarges. Should a child report feeling cold, tired, slow, experience muscle aches, hair loss, menstrual changes, or an unusual weight gain, the doctor should be alerted and thyroid function studies be performed. Problems with the thyroid can be treated easily and effectively

with synthetic hormone replacement therapy, such as Synthroid or Levothroid. Selenium, such as that provided in a multivitamin like Centrum Silver, may help counteract any hair thinning or loss.

• *Cognitive problems.* Lithium has been reported to cause short-term memory problems; rarely, some children talk about feeling "spaced out." However, these problems seem to be dose-related.

### Are There Long-Term Side Effects to Lithium Therapy?

It is natural to think of the long-term side effects of any medication therapy that may continue for years. When lithium was first prescribed, there was some fear of kidney damage due to long-term treatment. But in 1984 the Consensus Development Conference of the National Institute of Mental Health concluded that, with the exception of possible thyroid problems, there are few significant permanent risks from long-term lithium therapy. However, in children it is wise to watch closely their kidney and calcium levels as well as their bone development.

Although lithium can be fatal in overdose, it is the only medication that has been proven to lower the risk of suicide. For this reason alone, lithium should be considered a potential first-line treatment for bipolar disorder in children and adolescents.

### Lithium Interactions with Other Drugs

The following chart details the interaction of lithium with other over-the-counter and prescription medications as well as with other psychotropic medications such as Tegretol, Depakote, and the antipsychotic drugs.

### INTERACTIONS OF LITHIUM WITH OTHER DRUGS

| LITHIUM MAY INTERACT WITH | RESULTING IN |
| --- | --- |
| *Nonsteroidal Anti-inflammatory Drugs* | |
| Ibuprofen (Advil) | |
| Indomethacin | |
| Ketorolac (Toradol) | Increased lithium level |
| Naproxen (Aleve, Naprosyn) | |
| Phenylbutazine | |

## INTERACTIONS OF LITHIUM WITH OTHER DRUGS

| LITHIUM MAY INTERACT WITH | RESULTING IN |
|---|---|
| *Antibiotics* | |
| Erythromycin | Increased lithium level |
| Metronidazole | |
| Spectinomycin | |
| Tetracycline | Reports conflict as to tetracycline's increasing or decreasing lithium levels |
| *Bronchodilators* | |
| Aminophylline | Significantly increased lithium excretion |
| Theophylline | |
| *Antihypertensives* | |
| Clonidine | Decreased antihypertensive effect |
| *Cardiac Medications* | |
| Ace inhibitors | Increased lithium level, increased potassium |
| Calcium channel blockers (verapamil, etc.) | Possible increased rate of lithium excretion |
| Quinidine | Decreased lithium effect, possible cardiac conduction effects may be potentiated by lithium |
| *Diuretics* | |
| Indapamide | Increased lithium level |
| Potassium-sparing agents (amiloride, etc.) | Increased lithium concentration |
| Thiazides | Increased lithium concentration, decreased potassium |
| *Insulin and Oral Hypoglycemics* | Increased glucose tolerance (careful monitoring of glucose levels is necessary) |

## INTERACTIONS OF LITHIUM WITH OTHER DRUGS

| LITHIUM MAY INTERACT WITH | RESULTING IN |
| --- | --- |
| *Anticonvulsants* | |
| Carbamazepine (Tegretol) | Increased carbamazepine toxicity unless doses of both drugs are modified |
| Divalproex (Depakote) | Possible decreased lithium level |
| *Neuroleptics* | Increased risk of neurotoxicity, tardive dyskinesia |
| *Sodium Bicarbonate* | Decreased lithium effect |

### *The Need for Caution When Discontinuing Lithium Therapy*

Lithium treatment is associated with an approximately sevenfold reduction of suicide attempts and fatalities in bipolar patients. However, Drs. Ross J. Baldessarini and Leonardo Tondo and colleagues recently reported that discontinuing lithium rapidly after long-term maintenance therapy led to sharp increases in suicidal risk. The risk increased twentyfold in the first twelve months than at later times, but was only half as great following slow discontinuation (fifteen to thirty days versus one to fourteen days). These researchers recommend gradually discontinuing mood-stabilizing medicines whenever possible, perhaps over several months.

Antidepressants should *not* be used during this time.

## OTHER MOOD STABILIZERS

In the 1970s, some studies conducted in Japan by Dr. Teruo Okuma showed that a drug introduced for the treatment of temporal lobe epilepsy, carbamazepine (Tegretol), can be an effective treatment for acute mania and work to prevent future episodes of bipolar illness. A team at the National Institute of Mental Health led by Drs. James Ballenger and Robert Post, using placebo-controlled double-blind conditions in a study of adult patients, reported data that supported these claims.

Shortly after that, studies about another anticonvulsant, valproic acid (Depakene), or its more commonly used salt form, divalproex sodium (Depakote), showed great promise in the treatment of patients who did not respond to lithium or who were in the difficult-to-stabilize categories of rapid-cycling or mixed states. More recent studies suggest that there are no large differences in effectiveness between lithium and Depakote in the long-term treatment of rapid-cycling bipolar disorder.

Today a number of anticonvulsant medications are being evaluated in the treatment of bipolar disorder: Tegretol, Depakote, Neurontin (gabapentin), Lamictal (lamotrigine), Topamax (topirimate), Gabitril (tiagabine), and Trileptal (oxcarbazepine). Of these, only Depakote and Tegretol have been FDA-approved for the treatment of mania in adults, and only Lamictal has been FDA-approved for the long-term maintenance of bipolar disorder. This renders the other anticonvulsants "off label." Although they are being used quite frequently in the treatment of bipolar disorder, they are not specifically approved for use as mood stabilizers at any age. And only lithium has been approved for the treatment of mania in children under sixteen. Parents should understand that paradoxical reactions have been observed with anticonvulsant mood stabilizers, particularly in very young children between the ages of two to seven. A paradoxical reaction is a reaction that is opposite of what the drug is expected to cause. For example, it may stimulate rather than calm.

We will list all drugs initially with their generic and brand names. Generic refers to the scientific, noncommercial name for the chemical compound and off-patent trade manufacturing; trade names are the names the drug companies choose for marketing purposes. We list both initially and then use whichever name is more commonly used by the lay public. (Beginning on page 142, we will discuss brand-name and generic versions of the same drug.)

## Depakote

We'll start with Depakote (divalproex sodium) because it's an antimanic anticonvulsant frequently prescribed for children.

### Getting Started on Depakote

Before a child is started on Depakote, he or she needs a medical examination to gauge liver function, blood cell and platelet counts, and serum iron concentration. These tests contribute to the safe use of Depakote and, when repeated, provide information to help the prescribing physician evaluate how the body systems are affected by the medication.

Depakote is supplied in 125, 250, and 500 milligram (mg) tablets or capsules (including a capsule that can be opened and sprinkled on ice cream or applesauce or some other food a child likes), and in a 250 and

500 mg extended-release preparation. There is also a red liquid syrup called Depakene.

Children can be started on a test dose of 125 mg and adolescents on 250 mg. The doses are gradually increased to obtain a daily target dose of between 1,000 and 1,200 mg. Once this is reached, a blood level is taken and the dosage increased until the serum levels are within the 70 to 100 microgram per milliliter of serum (mcg/ml) range. The blood levels should not be measured until the child has been on a stable dosage for about six days. It takes this long to ensure that a steady state has been achieved (when the amount of the drug ingested equals the amount excreted in a twenty-four-hour period). Many children respond best at levels between 80 to 90 mcg/ml, but some require levels of 100 to 125 or higher mcg/ml to achieve adequate symptom relief. It should be noted that the possibility of lowered platelet count increases significantly at valproate levels above 110 mcg/ml.

Never give a child a double dose of the drug if a dose is forgotten. If it is within four hours of the regular dosing time, the child should take the dose. If it is close to the hour of the next allotted dosing time, the forgotten dose should be skipped.

A parent should begin to see improvement in the child within two to three weeks of attaining a therapeutic serum level; the maximal clinical response may occur six to eight weeks after the steady-state serum levels are reached.

Blood tests should be taken in the morning, twelve hours after the last dose. Once an appropriate therapeutic level is attained, blood levels need to be taken every three or four months in the early stages of mood stabilization.

## Side Effects of Depakote

Many of the side effects of Depakote disappear as the body becomes adjusted to the medication. Drowsiness, indigestion, nausea, and vomiting sometimes occur, but these side effects may subside in a week or two. Taking Depakote with meals may diminish the nausea. A thinning or loss of hair has been reported, but usually resolves over time, and the use of a multivitamin with zinc (15 mg) and selenium (50 mcg) often can prevent this from happening.

Not all children gain weight on Depakote, but many do. Some children experience what is referred to as "Depakote hunger" for a few weeks after treatment starts; some continue eating (gorging, actually) at such fantastic rates that some mothers have made lists of the food consumed in a few hours. One log was particularly specific and included: five packets of instant oatmeal with tons of sugar on top, four potatoes, two cheeseburgers, two pieces of chicken, one hamburger bun, one piece of coffee cake, sixteen ounces of grape juice, and twenty ounces of Mountain Dew.

This hunger may be caused by a direct effect that Depakote has on the hypothalamic centers that regulate satiety. It does not happen to everyone, but it should be anticipated, and low-calorie snacks and drinks as well as an increased daily exercise schedule should be planned. Topamax, a newer anticonvulsant, used in low doses (25 to 75 mg) may counteract this ravenous appetite.

A very rare side effect of Depakote is liver toxicity. Most cases of this potentially fatal side effect involved children under the age of one who were taking the drug for a seizure disorder. Liver function studies should be done before treatment starts, several times over the first year of treatment, and annually thereafter. The signs of liver toxicity can be nausea, vomiting, fatigue, weakness, swelling in the ankles, jaundice (yellowing of the eyes or skin), or easy bruising. If these signs appear, the medication should be stopped and the parent should call the doctor immediately.

Another rare side effect, but one which all parents and caretakers should be alert to, is pancreatitis—an inflammation of the pancreas. In July 2000 the manufacturer of Depakote, Depakene, and Depacon added a black box warning to its labeling of this medication. To quote: "Parents and guardians should be warned that abdominal pain, nausea, vomiting, and/or anorexia can be symptoms of pancreatitis that require prompt medical evaluation." The abdominal pain is usually severe pain in the upper abdomen that moves to the back and is accompanied by nausea.

Should a parent note any of these symptoms, he or she should call the doctor immediately, state up front that the child is being treated with Depakote, and inquire about a possible case of pancreatitis. The doctor should order an ultrasound and/or computed tomography (CT) scan of the pancreas to determine if it is swollen or inflamed (a blood test of pancreatic enzymes is not totally predictive).

Pancreatitis caused by a medication typically resolves with the stopping of the drug, but a parent and a doctor must act quickly as it can rapidly progress to a lethal condition. Pancreatitis can develop early in treatment or after years of use.

*Depakote Interactions with Other Drugs*

Certain drugs should not be taken in combination with Depakote. They include:

Lamotrigine (Lamictal)
Carbamazepine (Tegretol)
Phenytoin (Dilantin)
Barbiturates
Phenobarbital
Alcohol (Depakote and alcohol may produce central nervous system depression)
*Note:* Caution is suggested with aspirin because the interaction of aspirin and Depakote may cause higher Depakote levels.

Parents of girls prescribed Depakote will hear about (and need to know the entire story of) the reports of polycystic ovary disease in young epileptic women treated with Depakote before the age of twenty. In 1993 Dr. Jouko Isojärvi in Finland studied menstrual disturbances in 238 young women treated with anticonvulsants—either Depakote or Tegretol—for epilepsy before the age of twenty. Of the twenty-nine women taking Depakote, twenty-three were followed, and ten (or 43 percent) of the twenty-three developed polycystic ovary disease. At first it looked like the culprit was the anticonvulsant, but after following these patients for three years, some new facts came to light.

It seems as if the majority of these young women were severely obese. And because obesity can lead to increased insulin levels, and high levels of insulin promote the ovarian production of testosterone, and testosterone can produce polycystic ovary disease, it seems more likely that the problem begins with severe obesity. No nonobese women taking Depakote developed polycystic ovary disease.

If parents are at all worried about this, their daughters could have a yearly gynecological exam to ensure that all is well.

## Tegretol

Another anticonvulsant, Tegretol (carbamazepine), has acute antimanic effects and also acts to prevent future episodes of illness in bipolar adults. Moreover, Tegretol has been established to have anti-aggressive properties, something that might make it particularly useful for children with frequent rage attacks.

In 1992 an open pilot study conducted by Dr. Vivian Kafantaris and her colleagues at Long Island Jewish Hospital treated ten children between the ages of five and ten who had symptoms of explosive aggressiveness. Five of the ten had taken lithium and it had not been effective, but on Tegretol, nine of the ten experienced a significant reduction in explosiveness and aggressiveness. The European literature has many reports of the use of Tegretol to treat children and adolescents, but there are no placebo-controlled studies.

Despite the fact that there are no controlled studies in children, almost twenty nonblinded studies and five double-blind placebo-controlled studies in *adults* showed Tegretol to be effective in acute mania. (Seventy percent of all the patients had an excellent response.) So, clinically, Tegretol is often considered as an alternative to lithium in the younger population who need mood stabilization.

### Getting Started on Tegretol
Before starting on Tegretol, a child needs a medical evaluation and blood tests to evaluate liver function, blood cell and platelet counts, and iron concentration. A child between the ages of six and twelve is typically started on a dose of 100 mg twice daily (or 50 mg four times daily if the liquid is used). The dose may be increased weekly by increments of 100 mg, with a daily target dose of 400 to 800 mg and a blood level of 6 to 12 mcg/ml.

Patients older than twelve years usually start treatment with doses of 200 mg twice daily; the dose is increased weekly by increments of 200 mg. The usual daily maintenance dose is 800 to 1,200 mg, with the same therapeutic blood levels established for adults with epilepsy. The drug is supplied in 200 mg tablets, 100 mg chewable tablets, a liquid suspension, and in an extended-release form, Tegretol XR.

Because Tegretol activates certain enzymes in the liver, and this causes the drug itself and many others to be metabolized faster, the serum Tegretol level may drop somewhat after the first month of treatment, requiring increased doses based on blood levels. Blood tests are needed more frequently in the beginning of treatment and every three months or so afterward. The blood should be drawn twelve to fourteen hours after the child's last dose, usually in the morning before the first dose of the day.

If a dose is forgotten, and less than three hours have elapsed since the dosage time, the child should take it. If more than three hours have elapsed, the child should skip that dose and resume taking the medication at the next regularly scheduled time. In other words, do *not* double the dose.

Always store this medication away from sources of heat and out of direct sunlight, and never store it in a bathroom cabinet because humidity may cause it to lose one-third or more of its effectiveness. The tablets can absorb the moisture, harden, and become less soluble and less well absorbed when taken. The Food and Drug Administration recommends that during humid weather, Tegretol be dispensed in limited amounts and in moisture-proof containers.

## Side Effects

The most common side effects of Tegretol are dizziness, drowsiness, unsteadiness of gait, nausea, headaches, rash, double vision, and confusion. Many of these side effects—if they occur—don't last beyond the first week or so of treatment, and can be curtailed by lowering the dose. If the treatment is begun at low doses and the doses are raised in small increments, many of them may not occur at all.

There have been some reports of bone marrow suppression (aplastic anemia) with Tegretol. While very rare, this is a life-threatening condition. Therefore, it is good medical practice to have a red blood cell count weekly at first and again if the patient starts to develop any bruisability or chronic infections.

What are the signs of aplastic anemia? Photosensitivity (the skin's extreme sensitivity to sunlight), easy bruising, fever, sore throat, and purple spots on the skin. Should *any* of these symptoms appear, the Tegretol should be stopped immediately and the doctor called. After the first few months on Tegretol, the risk of aplastic anemia is reduced.

## Tegretol Interactions with Other Drugs

Tegretol interacts adversely with some other drugs, as shown in the list below.

INTERACTIONS OF TEGRETOL WITH OTHER DRUGS

*Increased Tegretol Levels and Toxicity Produced by:*
Diltiazem
Erythromycin (and similar agents)

Fluoxetine (Prozac)
Fluvoxamine (Luvox)
Isoniazid
Nefazodone (Serzone)
Propoxyphene (Darvon and others)
Sertraline (Zoloft)
Triacetyloleandomycin
Verapamil
Viloxazine

*Decreased Tegretol Levels Produced by:*
Phenobarbital
Phenytoin (Dilantin and others)
Primidone (Mysoline)

*Tegretol Diminishes Effects of:*
Barbiturates
Benzodiazepines
Corticosteroids (decreases levels and therapeutic response to
   steroids)
Dexamethasone
Dicumarol
Ethosuximide (Zarontin)
Neuroleptics (decreases blood level)
Oral contraceptives
Phenytoin (decreases levels of both drugs)
Pregnancy tests
Theophylline
Thyroid hormone (decreases thyroid levels)
Tricyclic antidepressants
Valproate (Depakote)
Warfarin

Young women taking birth control pills should understand that Tegretol interferes with the contraceptive ability of the pills. (It accelerates their normal breakdown and makes them less reliable.)

In the past few years, other anticonvulsants have been used as mood stabilizers in adults, and studies are now beginning in the pediatric population. While controlled clinical trials are only in the early stages, these novel anticonvulsants are being used clinically in adolescents and in children. So, without the benefit of substantial data, we'll discuss what is known about Trileptal (oxcarbazepine), Neurontin (gabapentin), Lamictal (lamotrigine), Topamax (topiramate), and Gabitril (tiagabine).

## Trileptal

Trileptal (oxcarbazepine) is an anticonvulsant launched in this country in February 2000 (but used in the European pediatric epilepsy population since 1990). Its use in bipolar children is just being evaluated, but it seems to be quite effective for some children, it requires no systematic blood draws, and it does not cause weight gain, liver toxicity, or aplastic anemia.

Trileptal is an analogue of Tegretol (carbamazepine). An analogue is structurally similar to another compound, but differs slightly in its composition (such as replacing one atom with another atom of a different element).

Someone in the Ciba-Geigy labs in Switzerland played around with the Tegretol compound and added one oxygen atom to the top of the middle structure. What a difference an oxygen atom can make: Whereas Tegretol oxidizes in the body into an active metabolite called 10/11 epoxide, Trileptal rapidly converts in the body to 10-monohydroxide derivative (MHD). Tegretol is a very effective mood stabilizer for bipolar disorder, but it seems that the 10/11 epoxide metabolite is responsible for some of the major problems that can occur with the drug, most notably the activation of certain enzymes in the liver that cause the Tegretol itself to be metabolized faster so that the serum Tegretol level may drop during treatment.

In contrast, the principal metabolite of Trileptal—MHD—has little effect on liver enzymes, so that its own serum levels remain fairly constant. Moreover, unlike Tegretol, it is less likely to increase the elimination of many other drugs.

Because of its different metabolism, Trileptal is much less likely to cause the rare cases of aplastic anemia we referred to in the Tegretol section. In addition, liver toxicity occurs rarely with Tegretol, but is unknown with Trileptal.

*How Well Does Trileptal Work in Bipolar Disorder?*

Several studies have evaluated the effectiveness of Trileptal in acute mania. In 1983 Dr. Hinderk M. Emrich of the Max Planck Institute in Munich performed a double-blind placebo-controlled study in adults using oxcarbazepine and found an average change of 50 percent in the mania scales was achieved by this medication. As a consequence of these findings, Ciba-Geigy of Basel organized two multicenter studies using the drug. One compared oxcarbazepine with the antipsychotic drug haloperidol (Haldol). After two weeks, both treatments (haloperidol and oxcarbazepine) were about equally effective in the fifty-eight-patient study, on the basis of decreasing mania-scale scores.

Another international study compared the antimanic effects of oxcarbazepine to lithium. Again, after a two-week period, the drugs were found to have about equal efficacy for the treatment of acute mania.

In May 2001, at the American Psychiatric Association's annual conference, Dr. Michael Reinstein of Rush Medical Center in Chicago presented a poster in which he compared Trileptal to Depakote in the treatment of mania in adults and found them to be indistinguishable in both efficacy and tolerability of side effects.

How well does Trileptal work as a maintenance medication? To date, no drug but lithium has been approved for the prevention of episodes of mania in bipolar disorder, and none is approved for preventing episodes of bipolar depression specifically. Nevertheless, Tegretol and Depakote are used routinely for these purposes and often do the job well. We have only anecdotal information about prevention of episodes and future stability with the use of Trileptal, and more studies are needed to assess the medication—especially for children.

*Getting Started on Trileptal*

Before starting on Trileptal, it is wise for a child to have baseline blood tests and serum electrolyte panels. Because a drop in sodium blood levels (hyponatremia) can occur in 3 percent of those taking Trileptal, a baseline lab test should be done on all patients before the drug is started, and children with sodium levels below 135 mEq/liter should be watched more closely. Hyponatremia is rare in children, but teenagers who may ingest diuretics surreptitiously for weight loss are at risk and this should be explained to them at the beginning of treatment.

Symptoms of hyponatremia include ankle swelling, headache, confusion, tiredness, a reduction in urination, and, if very severe, seizures and coma. Hyponatremia can be treated easily. It is recommended as a general practice that every fourth drink should be a sodium-containing one, such as milk or Gatorade. Milk has 125 grams of sodium in an eight-ounce glass, and Gatorade has 115 mg of sodium in an 8.45-ounce juice box.

After the intial lab work, no blood levels need to be done when taking Trileptal (a great boon for needlephobic children and their parents). A blood level can monitor the serum level of MHD, but the clinical value of this measurement is uncertain. At this point the blood test might be useful to ensure that an adolescent is taking the medication—more of a measurement of compliance. Dosing is better guided by clinical response and tolerability by individuals.

Trileptal is supplied in 150, 300, and 600 mg tablets, scored so that they can be cut in half. In addition, there is a lemon-flavored oral suspension for children who have difficulty swallowing tablets. The liquid preparation must be shaken well before being given to a child. It is supplied at a concentration of 60 mg/ml, or 300 mg per 5 ml teaspoon.

Children are typically started at 300 mg per day in divided doses— 150 mg in the morning, 150 mg approximately twelve hours later. The dosage is then raised every six or seven days in increments of 300 mg (again, the 300 mg increases are best divided into two-a-day half doses) with a target dose of approximately 900 to 1,200 mg (some children may require as much as 1,500 to 2,400 mg).

The drug reaches a steady state, or stable, concentration in the bloodstream after about four doses or within two days. One mother whose eleven-year-old was cycling wildly throughout the day—despite his being on Clozaril and Zyprexa—wrote of her son's experience with Trileptal: "At about three weeks, as his dose was 900 mg, we began to see the amplitude of his mood swings diminish. At six weeks and 1,200 mg, the cycling practically stopped. Since no other medication was added at this time, we're sure the Trileptal smoothed out the cycling pattern."

This young man had been on the medication for a few months, as of this writing, and continues to do well, but only time will tell if the drug is effective as a long-term mood stabilizer.

## Side Effects
The most common side effects that may occur early in treatment with Trileptal are sleepiness (somnolence), headache, dizziness, double vision, ataxia (unsteadiness), vomiting, rash, and abdominal pain. Most of these side effects—should they occur—recede as the body adjusts to the drug

in a few weeks. We have heard of a case of sun sensitivity caused by the drug (not surprising because Tegretol can cause this also). Trileptal causes little if any weight gain.

Trileptal's manufacturer, Novartis, alerted health-care professionals of the very rare possibility of serious skin conditions such as Stevens-Johnson syndrome and toxic epidermal necrolysis as a result of the medication. (We discuss these potentially life-threatening conditions in the section on Lamictal.) There have also been a dozen reports of multi-organ sensitivity reactions.

Parents should not be alarmed, merely watchful, and should a child or adolescent taking this medication develop a rash or fever, the doctor should be notified immediately.

### Interactions of Trileptal with Other Drugs

Although Trileptal has less risk of drug-to-drug interaction than Tegretol, it can increase the rate of elimination, and reduce the effectiveness of some drugs—notably oral contraceptives and one calcium channel blocker, Felodipine. Trileptal may be safely combined with Lamictal, Depakote, and lithium, as well as with antipsychotic and antidepressant medications.

## Neurontin

Neurontin (gabapentin) is an anticonvulsant drug that seems to have few side effects except for some fatigue, dizziness, ataxia (unsteady gait), and tremor, and it can be used safely with other medications often needed by a patient with bipolar disorder. It does not cause weight gain. Studies in adults have found Neurontin to be ineffective as a mood stabilizer, but it is useful as an anti-anxiety agent.

A therapeutic dose seems to be between 900 and 1,800 mg a day, and it must be given in divided doses, three times a day using 300 to 400 mg capsules.

There have been reports of Neurontin-induced mania in the psychiatric and epilepsy literature, and a number of children have become activated and aggressive on the medication (but this paradoxical reaction can happen with any of the drugs).

## Lamictal

Lamictal (lamotrigine) is an anticonvulsant medication that seems to have several advantages: It is frequently effective for controlling rapid-cycling and mixed bipolar states, and it seems to work in the depressed phase of bipolar disorder. (The other mood stabilizers work against acute mania and prevent future episodes of mania and depression but are less effective against current depression.)

Studies to confirm this antidepressant effect of the drug are going on now at medical centers across this nation and abroad. The first report of a double-blind placebo-controlled study was published by Dr. Joseph Calabrese at Case Western Reserve University and his colleagues in February 1999. This multicenter study evaluated Lamictal treatment of Bipolar I depression and found that 200 mg a day in adult patients was significantly effective against the depression.

A second study by Dr. Calabrese and his group published in November 2000 concluded that Lamictal was effective as a monotherapy over a six-month period, particularly for patients who had the Bipolar II form of the disorder.

Most people tolerate the drug very well, but the side effect profile includes gait disturbances, dizziness, headaches, nausea, blurred vision, and sleepiness. A patient is most likely to experience these side effects for a few days after a dosage increase, but they tend to disappear as the body adjusts. The drug does not cause weight gain.

Perhaps the side effect of greatest concern is rash. The risk of rash is greatest in the first eight weeks of treatment. A rash is also more likely to develop when the dosing schedule starts too high or is increased too rapidly (start low and go slow is the pertinent phrase here), or when Lamictal is prescribed with Depakote, a practice that was common early on until the problem became apparent. There have been many reports of people breaking out with mild rashes—similar to a slight sunburn—or with a total body rash that resembles a severe case of poison ivy. If a rash occurs, the doctor *must* be notified immediately. Usually the rash clears up after ceasing to take the drug (and a patient can even resume the drug later and no rash will occur), but in rare instances the rash is associated with a life-threatening syndrome known as Stevens-Johnson syndrome or the more deadly toxic epidermal necrolysis. These are severe and sometimes fatal allergic reactions to an infectious disease or a drug. Stevens-

Johnson syndrome is typically an abrupt onset of rash accompanied by high fever and complete exhaustion (prostration). The eyes may become puffy and blisters may appear around the mouth. It is often misdiagnosed as chicken pox; toxic epidermal necrolysis resembles more of an extensive burn with painful lesions.

Stevens-Johnson syndrome can also be caused by sulfa drugs, penicillin, and anticonvulsants—especially Dilantin (phenytoin). The syndrome seems more likely when Lamictal is given with Depakote or Depakene, which can double Lamictal blood levels. This particular combination of drugs may produce the vulnerability for Stevens-Johnson syndrome. Currently the FDA has ordered the manufacturer of Lamictal to place a strong warning on the package insert of the drug: It is not to be given to children under the age of sixteen.

However, new reports confirm that starting Lamictal at lower doses and titrating the doses with more gradual increments significantly decrease the risk of rash. Dr. N. Earl and his colleagues examined a database of more than 10,000 adult patients with epilepsy or bipolar disorder who were treated with Lamictal. Twenty-eight percent of this group had serious rashes, of which eleven (0.10 percent) had Stevens-Johnson syndrome and none had toxic epidermal necrolysis. When the researchers looked at the 5,798 patients who were treated with the more conservative dosing guidelines now recommended by the manufacturer, the incidence of Stevens-Johnson syndrome was 0.05 percent. This study indicates that—with conservative dosing—more patients should be able to use Lamictal, with a decreased likelihood of a serious problem.

We spoke to the mother of a sixteen-year-old girl who had asked her daughter's doctor to initiate treatment with Lamictal. He was wary and warned her of the dire side effect of Stevens-Johnson syndrome. This mother was a registered nurse, had read the literature on the drug, and knew her daughter, Mariana, had been on every class of medication except the monoamine oxidase (MAO) inhibitors (a type of antidepressant). She also knew that Mariana had been suicidal all summer and was in a very fragile state. Time was running out. Her child's life was in the balance, and the threat of death by suicide was infinitely greater than the chances of a problem with Lamictal. The mother's last update informed us that Mariana had been stable on the drug for eight months. While she is still experiencing some activation in the early evenings, her mother told us that the drug has been a miracle for her. "She's the best she's ever been," she reported.

Lamictal is supplied in 25, 100, 150, and 200 mg tablets. It is also available in 5 and 25 mg chewable tablets for children.

If Lamictal is prescribed for an adolescent, it is started at 12.5 mg once a day (usually in the morning) and *very slowly* raised—every 6 to 7 days—by 12.5 mg. A target dose of 75 to 100 mg a day may be effective, but sometimes as much as 250–300 mg is required.

Some patients feel the antidepressant or antimanic effects early in treatment, but a significant improvement usually takes about three or four weeks.

Because of Lamictal's antidepressant effects, the dosage may need to be reduced in the spring (any time between mid-February and late April) in order to avert manic or hypomanic symptoms during this period of heightened vulnerability. Seasonal changes in mood must be considered carefully in the fall also. If depression is an issue, the dosage of Lamictal may need to be raised prior to the period of vulnerability.

The following table lists Lamictal's interactions with other drugs and alcohol.

## LAMICTAL INTERACTIONS WITH OTHER DRUGS AND ALCOHOL

| LAMICTAL MAY INTERACT WITH | RESULTING IN |
| --- | --- |
| Depakote (divalproex sodium) Depakene (valproic acid) | A doubling of the plasma level of Lamictal. In some patients, the level of Depakote is decreased. |
| Tegretol (carbamazepine) | Increased plasma level of Tegretol and its metabolites. In turn, Tegretol lowers the concentration of Lamictal in the blood. |
| Zoloft (sertraline) | Increased plasma level of Lamictal. |
| Phenobarbital and Primadone | A significant lowering of the plasma level of Lamictal (approximately 40 percent). |
| Alcohol | An increase in the severity of Lamictal side effects. |
| Oral contraceptives | Decreased effectiveness in both the Lamictal and the oral contraceptive. |

## Topamax

Topamax (topiramate) is an anticonvulsant drug chemically unrelated to any other anticonvulsant or mood-stabilizing medication. It seems to work to control rapid-cycling and mixed bipolar states in some patients who have not responded well to lithium, Trileptal, Tegretol, or Depakote, but because it was approved in this country only in the last week of 1996, it is not yet established whether the drug offers long-term prevention from cycling. No studies of the drug's use in children have been reported, but it is being prescribed for young people nevertheless.

What makes this drug of particular interest is that it causes no weight gain (in fact, some people lose weight on the drug).

An initial dose of 25 mg is given once or twice a day and increased by 25 to 50 mg every week. When Topamax is prescribed as an add-on drug with other anticonvulsants, a target dose of 150 to 200 mg is often enough for mood stabilization, but some children will require higher doses, even up to 400 mg a day.

The side effect profile includes: sleepiness (for many people it is simply too sedating), fatigue, dizziness, vision problems, speech problems, unsteadiness, nervousness, nausea, memory problems, and cognitive dulling in an estimated 20 percent of patients. Clinical experience suggests that increasing the drug slowly can reduce the likelihood of cognitive blunting. Many of these side effects are most noticeable the few days after a dosage increase and then often fade away as the body adjusts. Some people notice the antidepressant or antimanic effects early in treatment, but significant improvement may take up to four weeks.

While no interaction between Topamax and lithium has been noted, Topamax may increase the blood levels of phenytoin (Dilantin) and decrease the effectiveness of birth control pills. Depakote and especially Tegretol have the ability to lower the blood levels of Topamax.

In the fall of 2001 the FDA and the manufacturer strengthened the label of Topamax, warning of the possibility of eye problems—specifically secondary angle closure glaucoma in pediatric and adult patients taking the drug. The signs of the condition would be ocular pain or decreased vision. The treatment would be discontinuation of the medication. As of August 2001 there were twenty-three reported cases—mostly with adults—but children should have periodic eye checkups with a screening for glaucoma.

## Gabitril

The anticonvulsant Gabitril (tiagabine) has been FDA-approved for the treatment of convulsive disorder in adolescents but is now being used in patients with bipolar disorder as well. Not a great deal is known about its effectiveness yet, but anecdotal reports show it to work for some children who have not responded to the other mood stabilizers.

The maximum recommended daily dose of Gabitril is 32 mg, and, again, the medication should be started at low doses and increased slowly—only weekly—until a good response is noted or the dose reaches 32 mg.

The side effect profile may include dizziness, fatigue, and an unstable gait. Like Topamax, there may be drug-to-drug interactions, and no medications should be taken without checking with the child's doctor.

### What Constitutes an Adequate Trial of a Mood Stabilizer? At What Point Do You Move on to the Next?

In attempting to tackle these questions, we need to point out several things:

1. Reports from many clinical researchers indicate that a combination of two mood stabilizers is often necessary to achieve symptom remission. Therefore, partial response does not mean that the first drug tried is of no value.
2. If antidepressants have been administered prior to the trial of a mood stabilizer (between one week and three months), or are prescribed at the same time, it will be difficult to judge the effectiveness of the mood stabilizer. Antidepressants are destabilizing for the majority of children with bipolar disorder. While some clinicians believe that high doses of mood stabilizers will buffer the activating effects of antidepressants, this still needs to be established by clinical trials.

Now the question becomes: How long should a child be kept on a mood stabilizer before it is determined that another choice might better be instituted? Although it has not been objectively established, a reasonable time period to continue a mood stabilizer once a high therapeutic level has been established (and this can take weeks to months) would be between five and six weeks.

A physician, the parents, and the child have to decide if the drug has any beneficial effects. If so, it might be wise to add another mood stabilizer for increased stability. If not, the drug should be tapered slowly and another trial should be initiated.

## ANTIPSYCHOTIC MEDICATIONS

Despite the wide use of mood stabilizers, antipsychotic drugs play a significant role in the treatment of bipolar disorder. They may be prescribed periodically for some children during manic states, particularly when they may be experiencing severe aggressive behaviors, delusions, or hallucinations and when rapid control of mania is needed; or they may be a long-term component in the maintenance treatment of children or adolescents. Emerging evidence suggests that a combination of a mood stabilizer and one of the newer "atypical" antipsychotic medications may be required for adequate mood stabilization and to control rage and aggression, as well as any psychotic symptoms. They are often prescribed for children to treat the symptoms of Tourette's syndrome.

Listed below are the traditional as well as the newer antipsychotic drugs. Although the newer antipsychotic drugs such as Risperdal (risperidone), Zyprexa (olanzapine), Clozaril (clozapine), Seroquel (quetiapine), Geodon (ziprasidone), and Abilify (aripiprazole) produce fewer motoric side effects than the traditional antipsychotics, the newer drugs are expensive (some may cost thousands of dollars a year), have other potential side effects, and may not work for every child. We discuss the traditional antipsychotic drugs and their side-effect profiles first.

### COMMON ANTIPSYCHOTIC MEDICATIONS

| GENERIC | BRAND NAME |
| --- | --- |
| *Traditional Antipsychotics* | |
| chlorpromazine | Thorazine |
| fluphenazine | Prolixin |
| haloperidol | Haldol |
| molindone | Moban |
| perphenazine | Trilafon |
| thioridazine | Mellaril |

| | |
|---|---|
| thiothixene | Navane |
| trifluoperazine | Stelazine |

*Newer Antipsychotics*

| | |
|---|---|
| clozapine | Clozaril |
| olanzapine | Zyprexa |

## COMMON ANTIPSYCHOTIC MEDICATIONS

| GENERIC | BRAND NAME |
|---|---|
| quetiapine | Seroquel |
| risperidone | Risperdal |
| ziprasidone | Geodon |
| aripiprazole | Abilify |

Children seem to be more sensitive to the movement disorder side effects we discuss below, and they may need lower mg/kg doses than adults do. As with the anticonvulsant medications, paradoxical reactions have been observed with antipsychotic medications in some young children.

## Side Effects of Traditional Antipsychotic Drugs

Dr. Ross J. Baldessarini from Harvard Medical School, one of the foremost experts on psychotropic medications, says that "the antipsychotic agents are among the safest drugs available in medicine." This is not to say that they don't cause side effects and that some of the side effects aren't upsetting and uncomfortable. Early side effects of an antipsychotic drug are constipation, blurring of vision, drowsiness, nasal congestion, and dry mouth. These typically fade as the child adjusts to the medication.

### Movement Disorders
Also common (but terribly upsetting to a child experiencing them and a parent observing them) are the movement disorders: dystonic reactions and akathisia. These are known as *extrapyramidal* effects, and they are more commonly seen with the high-potency antipsychotics such as Thorazine, Haldol, and Navane. These movement disorders are treatable and reversible, and are defined as follows:

• *Dystonic reactions.* These are involuntary muscle contractions that cause uncontrolled and alarming movements of the face, neck, tongue, and back and an uncontrolled rolling of the eyes. Boys are at greater risk for dystonic reactions. All of this can be counteracted in minutes with an anti-Parkinson's drug such as Cogentin (benzotropine) or Artane (trihexyphenidyl).

• *Akathisia.* This is a feeling of internal and external restlessness. A child may be incapable of sitting still and may feel a sensation of discomfort akin to anxiety or agitation. This side effect is often mistaken for anxiety or agitation or an increasing aggressiveness rather than a side effect of the medication, but a parent should listen carefully to the child describe how he or she is feeling and call the doctor. Inderal (propranolol) or clonidine sometimes helps counteract this truly horrible feeling.

These two movement disorders can be dealt with in a number of ways: The dose of the antipsychotic can be lowered, an anti-Parkinson's drug can be added to the drug regimen prophylactically (some doctors prescribe Cogentin, Artane, or Benadryl along with the antipsychotic drug to prevent or treat dystonia), or the child can be switched to another class of antipsychotic drug. Generally, the more sedation an antipsychotic causes, the less chance that the child will be bothered by movement abnormalities. And, as we mentioned, the newer antipsychotic drugs cause less of this.

• *Akinesia.* This is characterized by stiffness and diminished spontaneity of gestures, physical movement, and speech. Again, Cogentin and Artane counteract this.

• *Tardive dyskinesia.* Another worrisome side effect of antipsychotic drugs is "late-appearing abnormal movements" called tardive dyskinesia. TD, as it is called, is more typically a problem in elderly patients taking traditional antipsychotics continuously for many years, but it is characterized by involuntary facial grimacing, lip-smacking, chewing and sucking movements, cheek puffing, and wormlike movements of the tongue and fingers and toes. The patient may also experience sudden and purposeless movements of the arms and legs or writhing movements of the body. (This is seen more often in boys.) TD is not painful but is disfiguring, and a spontaneous remission is most likely in children once the child is no longer taking the medication. Parents should *not* just discontinue the antipsychotic abruptly, however. They should consult with the psychiatrist and perhaps even a neurologist specializing in movement disorders.

Although children seem to be less vulnerable to tardive dyskinesia than elderly patients, there are ways to minimize the risk. A child should be put on the lowest dose necessary to control the psychotic symptoms, and the doctor should regularly attempt to reduce the dose. The child should be closely watched for any signs of TD.

While there are little data available, the antipsychotic drug Moban (molindone) seems to cause fewer movement disorders than some other antipsychotics.

### Other Side Effects

• *Menstrual changes* in young women have been reported, as have *breast discharge* and the swelling of breasts in both sexes as well as a diminished sex drive.

• *Weight gain.* Children and adolescents can gain a great deal of weight on antipsychotic medications (especially young women, and this is a major factor in noncompliance). The only antipsychotic that doesn't seem to cause weight gain is molindone (Moban), and this drug may be particularly helpful for a bipolar child because, in small doses, it seems helpful in treating conduct disorder.

• *Sun sensitivity.* Parents need to know that a child is likely to develop a sensitivity to the sun while taking antipsychotic medications (especially low-potency ones). Children may burn very easily. Therefore, children's activities in full sun should be limited, and a sunscreen with a high SPF—15 or higher—and with protection against UVF and UVB light—should be applied and reapplied often.

• *Neuroleptic malignant syndrome.* Neuroleptic malignant syndrome is a now-rare but life-threatening side effect of antipsychotic medications that is poorly understood. The patient can become severely rigid and may have a high fever, rapid heart rate, labored breathing, and sweating, and a blood test may show irregularities.

This syndrome constitutes a true medical emergency. The medication should be stopped immediately at home, and the child should be admitted to the hospital. There cardiac monitoring, fever control, and fluid maintenance will be administered, and Dantrium (dantrolene) or Parlodel (bromocriptine) will be given.

Many people might ask: Who would expose their child to such a symptom profile? Well, it all goes back to risk/benefit. The chances are that the movement disorders and TD may not appear, but certainly psychosis, severe rage, and mania are malignant for a child. Psychosis untreated gravely imperils a child.

Fortunately, the newer antipsychotic medications seem less likely to produce tardive dyskinesia and the acute movement disorders.

## Newer Atypical Antipsychotic Medications

Since 1990 newer antipsychotic medications have begun to be used in this country, in both adults and children. They are clozapine (Clozaril), risperidone (Risperdal), olanzapine (Zyprexa), quetiapine (Seroquel), ziprasidone (Geodon), and aripiprazole (Abilify).

They are considered "atypical" because they have relatively lower risks of acute extrapyramidal symptoms (the movement disorders spoken of on pages 105–106 and tardive dyskinesia).

Clinical experience with childhood bipolar disorder patients suggests that the atypical antipsychotic agents may accomplish things and target symptoms the mood stabilizers don't. The atypicals may benefit children who have prolonged rage attacks, psychotic symptoms, mixed-irritable moods, and possibly very rapidly cycling mood, all of which are commonly associated with early-onset bipolar disorder and may require different forms of treatment than are usual in adults.

### Clozaril

Clozaril (clozapine), the first atypical neuroleptic to be marketed, was hailed as revolutionary because it produced no dystonia, little akathisia or Parkinsonian syndrome movement symptoms—the extrapyramidal symptoms we described earlier. Its ability to produce tardive dyskinesia or neuroleptic malignant syndrome is very low. Clozaril can, however, cause sedation, profound weight gain, seizures in a small percentage of patients, diabetes, and drooling or excessive salivation.

In the first years of prescribing Clozaril, doctors thought it produced agranulocytosis—a disease in which the bone marrow stops producing neutrophilic white blood cells. With biweekly monitoring of the blood, however, there have been fewer than ten cases in the United States. If the white blood cell count begins to drop and the medication is stopped, the patient's blood returns to normal.

This frequent taking of blood makes Clozaril somewhat less than ideal as a treatment for children. Today, children with early-onset bipolar disorder who require antipsychotic medication are more commonly prescribed Risperdal (risperidone) and Zyprexa (olanzapine).

### Risperdal

Risperdal (risperidone) is prescribed for a number of reasons. It not only treats psychotic symptoms, but—very important—the drug seems to calm the rages these children often experience. And it works rather quickly, sometimes within hours.

Very low doses of this medication are somewhat less likely to produce the extrapyramidal side effects that the more traditional antipsychotics can cause. Risperdal does have side effects, however. Sedation can be a problem, and weight gain can be extremely troubling: One nine-year-old girl gained thirty-five pounds in four months, but children have been known to gain even greater amounts of weight. We've heard parents complain of drooling and urinary incontinence (a leaking of urine, actually). Less common side effects include nausea, dizziness, headache, and a runny nose, and the swelling of breasts and the oozing of milk from nipples (for males as well as females). The possible counteraction of these side effects with the drug Abilify is discussed on pages 111–113.

A child is typically started on a dosage of 0.5 mg, increasing the dose until symptom relief is achieved, or until the onset of sedation. Many children do well on 1 to 2 mg a day; some children experiencing acute mania require higher doses.

### Zyprexa

Zyprexa (olanzapine) was introduced in 1996. It is effective for psychotic symptoms and may decrease them within hours of taking the drug, but the full benefit usually takes several weeks. Zyprexa has been approved by the FDA to treat both acute mania and as a maintenance drug for bipolar disorder.

The main side effect is weight gain, and it too can be considerable. Zyprexa can cause tardive dyskinesia, but the risk is lower than with most traditional antipsychotic drugs.

Children usually take 5 to 15 mg of Zyprexa in an acute manic state. As a maintenance drug, 2.5 mg to 5 mg is often sufficient.

### Seroquel

Seroquel (quetiapine) may prove especially useful since it appears to produce far less weight gain at lower dosage ranges (50–150 mg) than its cousins Clozaril, Risperdal, and Zyprexa. It is also possible that Seroquel reduces depressive symptoms and suicidal thoughts in adolescents with or at familial risk for bipolar disorder. In a poster presented at the Sixth International Conference on Bipolar Disorders in 2005, Dr. Melissa DelBello and colleagues reported on 132 adolescents suffering bipolar depression. Some were administered a combination of Seroquel plus Depakote; the others were treated with Seroquel alone for varying periods of time.

The investigators concluded that Seroquel alone, or in combination with Depakote, reduced depressive symptoms and suicidal ideation in this sample.

Seroquel is supplied in 25, 100, 150, 200, and 300 mg tablets. A child is typically started on an initial dose of 12.5 to 25 mg a day and increased to a target dose of 100 to 200 mg given two or three times a day. Some children may require higher doses. The adolescents in the study above were prescribed up to 600 mg a day.

Although there was some initial concern about cataracts and high-dose Seroquel treatment, there is less so now. Still, it is prudent to have baseline and follow-up eye examinations if long-term usage is contemplated.

## Geodon

Geodon (ziprasidone) was of particular interest to parents of bipolar children because it causes little if any weight gain. The medication can induce an odd kind of overarousal (this may be seen at lower doses and not higher doses; however, a number of parents have written to us about anxiety and maniclike reactions to the drug).

Geodon's major risk is that it has at least weak direct cardiac depressant effects (seen in the electrocardiogram [EKG] as a prolonging of the electrical recovery time of the heart QTc interval, potentially increasing the risk of arrythmia). This cardiac depressant effect is not unlike that of some of the older tricyclic antidepressants and even the antipsychotic drug Mellaril, all of which were more dangerous in this regard. Good medical practice would follow EKGs in children throughout the time spent on Geodon. A baseline measurement of serum potassium and magnesium would also be wise.

The most common side effects are sleepiness and nausea, orthostatic hypotension (dizziness when rising from a prone position), and rash.

Geodon is supplied in 20, 40, 60, and 80 mg capsules. A child is typically started on an initial daily dose of 20 mg twice a day and increased every few days to a level of 80 mg twice a day (160 mg daily). Some patients in clinical trials have taken as much as 200 mg a day, and some experts believe that at least 80 mg a day is required for an antipsychotic benefit.

## Abilify

Abilify (aripiprazole), launched in this country in late 2002, is the newest atypical antipsychotic medication on the market. It is considered a "next-generation" atypical antipsychotic, as it is chemically different from other atypical antipsychotic agents, and it is also believed to have unique pharmacological actions.

Abilify acts as a weak stimulator (so-called partial agonist) at dopamine $D_2$ receptors, with the potential for exerting either inhibitory (antagonistic) or stimulating (agonistic) effects, depending on the sensitivity of the receptors and availability of dopamine—its natural agonist in the brain. The drug also has similar actions at serotonin $5\text{-}HT_{2A}$ receptors.

In somewhat simpler terms, partial agonism means the ability of the drug to block a receptor if it is overstimulated or in competition with a natural agonist, such as dopamine or serotonin, but also to stimulate a receptor when the natural agonist is unavailable.

Promising research studies have been conducted with adults suffering with bipolar disorder. A multicenter double-blind, randomized, placebo-controlled trial included 262 adult patients diagnosed with acute mania or mixed mania states. By day four of treatment, Abilify was significantly better than placebo in reducing acute manic symptoms, including elevated mood, irritability, disturbed thinking, and disruptive-aggressive behavior.

There are no studies published regarding children yet, but the findings just described have prompted adult and child psychiatrists to prescribe Abilify for both indicated and off-label applications, including early-onset bipolar disorder in children and adolescents.

### ADVANTAGES OF ABILIFY

Like other atypical antipsychotics, Abilify has a lower risk of producing extrapyramidal symptoms (EPS)—the disorders of posture and movement that some patients experience with the older neuroleptic-type antipsychotics, such as chlorpromazine (Thorazine) and haloperidol (Haldol). Typical EPS include early and later muscle contractions (dystonia), slowed movements (akinesia, or parkinsonism), motor restlessness often accompanied by severe anxiety (akathisia), and later-emerging tardive dyskinesia. Low does not mean never, however. Both doctors and parents have reported a number of children suffering motor restlessness (akathisia) as well as involuntary muscle contractions (see page 106 to read more about these reactions).

Later in this chapter we sound some concerns about a series of general medical or metabolic problems that were being increasingly reported in association with the atypical antipsychotic medications, such as Clozaril, Zyprexa, Risperdal, and Seroquel. These include new-onset, type II (noninsulin-dependent) diabetes mellitus, changes in lipid metabolism and blood concentrations, sometimes severe and persistent elevation of prolactin and other hormonal imbalances (milk oozes from children's nipples), and a range of adverse cardiovascular effects that include low blood pressure and abnormal functioning of the heart. The long-term implications of such adverse effects are not known, particularly for youngsters who may require such medications for decades.

Studies conducted with Abilify show that most—but not all—patients gain little if any weight; and the drug seems to cause no changes in the plasma glucose levels that might suggest risk of diabetes. Nor does it seem to increase serum cholesterol or other lipids. Also, the drug does not increase prolactin levels; in fact, some clinicians use Abilify to counteract the increase of blood levels of prolactin that may be produced by other antipsychotic medications. There have been no reports of heart rhythm abnormalities (such as a prolonging of the electrical recovery time of the heart [QTc interval] in the EKG), hematological changes, serum chemistry changes, or thyroid problems.

## GETTING STARTED ON ABILIFY

Abilify is supplied in 5, 10, 15, 20, and 30 mg tablets. Tablets can be cut into halves or even quarters. (A crushed tablet will not oxidize and retains 100 percent of its bioavailability.) An oral solution recently came on the market.

Children typically are started on low doses of the medication. Youngsters weighing less than 110 pounds might start at 2.5 mg and those over 110 pounds at 5 mg initially to avoid nausea. The dose may be doubled within a week if it is tolerated. Further dose increases usually are not made for another week or two as steady state, or stable, tissue concentrations are achieved. The target dose differs for each youngster, depending on age, tolerability of the drug, and drug response.

## SIDE EFFECTS

The most common adverse side effects reported include headache, agitation, anxiety, insomnia, nausea, sleepiness, internal restlessness (akathisia), vomiting, and constipation.

It is a good idea to give the medication in the morning with a meal or some food in order to minimize risk of nausea and insomnia, which are among Abilify's most common side effects. Also, parents should ensure that the child eats fruit and vegetables, or high-fiber cereals, and drinks plenty of fluids in order to prevent constipation.

## INTERACTIONS OF ABILIFY WITH OTHER DRUGS

The anticonvulsant Tegretol can increase the ability of the body to eliminate Abilify and so *decrease* Abilify's concentration in the blood. If both drugs are taken at the same time, the dose of Abilify will have to be increased somewhat by the physician.

Antidepressants, such as fluoxetine (Prozac), fluvoxamine (Luvox), and paroxetine (Paxil), can slow the body's ability to eliminate Abilify by inhibiting certain liver enzymes, and so increasing blood levels of the drug. The treating physician will need to reduce the Abilify—sometimes by half—if any of the selective serotonin reuptake inhibitors are prescribed.

## Atypical Antipsychotics as the Only Treatment for a Bipolar Child?

The popularity of the newer atypical antipsychotics for childhood bipolar disorder is growing rapidly, and some clinicians are beginning to prescribe one of these medications as an initial treatment choice without a concurrent mood stabilizer.

One mother whose son's psychiatrist placed him on Zyprexa (olanzapine) as a monotherapy for his newly diagnosed bipolar disorder wrote us and asked: "Is my child being used as a guinea pig?"

Some thoughtful and experienced clinicians are using this approach, and find that it can be quite helpful for some young patients in certain situations. Dr. Maurizio Tohen and his team at Eli Lilly laboratories have been studying Zyprexa and have reported on its mood stabilizing effect. When we spoke with him, he said that Zyprexa not only worked on the manic and psychotic symptoms, but was also effective on the depressive symptoms of mixed states or the depressive aspects of acute mania. That statement may be a bit bewildering, but manic states are not just a constant high with grandiose and activated thought, speech, and behavior. Often in adults, and very commonly in children, mania is interlaced with a rapidly shifting mood (mood lability), irritability, sadness, sleeplessness, anxiety, and agitation.

In 1995 Drs. Gianni Faedda and Ross Baldessarini and their colleagues published an important review, entitled "Pediatric-Onset Bipolar Disorder: A Neglected Clinical and Public Health Problem." In it they made a strong point that juvenile mania often includes psychotic features and a good deal of agitation and aggression, possibly more so than in adolescent or adult forms of the illness. They also emphasized evidence of the tendency toward an admixture of manic and depressive-dysphoric-irritable elements in children—more than in adults—and a common lack of a clean, episodic course, or very rapid fluctuations of mood and behavior in bipolar children.

Since agitation is a principal component of mixed manic-depressive states, it should come as no surprise that the atypical antipsychotic medications have a special place in the treatment of pediatric bipolar disorder. Risperdal, Zyprexa, Seroquel, and Abilify can calm the agitation, anxiety, rage, and hostility, as well as diminish psychotic symptoms such as hallucinations and delusions.

So there is some rhyme and reason here, based on the nature of juvenile bipolar illness for some doctors to use these medications as a first line of treatment. They are easy to administer, and blood drawing to determine serum levels of the drugs is not necessary.

But—ease aside—do these treatments do the job and are there any negatives associated with them?

## Some Negatives

As with lithium and with some anticonvulsants, two words come to mind when discussing the downside of most of the atypical antipsychotics: weight gain. Not every child gains weight on these medications, but many do, particularly with Clozaril, Zyprexa, and Risperdal. And when they do, the amount can be astonishing. The mother whose son was placed on Zyprexa wrote this to us: "He has put on eight pounds since Friday and it's continuing." Since we received her e-mail on Tuesday, we wrote back to make sure we were talking about a four-day period. "Yes," she shot back through cyberspace. That's two pounds a day and climbing.

The atypical antipsychotics cause more weight gain than most of the conventional antipsychotic medications. Dr. Tohen told us that the weight gain seems to be greater in children than in adults and that the younger the child, the greater the risk, but it is unclear why. Since weight gain usually appears right away in children, as it did in the boy mentioned above, one can assume it will continue and consider alternative treatments. It is unknown why people gain weight (and so much of it), but it is hypothesized that the drugs' effects on the part of the hypothalamus that regulates satiety may be the root cause. Some clinicians will mix Zyprexa with Risperdal and particularly with Seroquel in order to limit weight gain, and there are promising observations of a weight-limiting effect of the novel anticonvulsant Topamax. The dose range for the appetite-suppressant effects of Topamax is usually between 50 to 75 mg, and this is best administered at night, given the drug's secondary sedating properties.

The histamine receptor blocker Axid (nizatidine), whose primary indication is for the treatment of stomach and intestinal ulcers, has been found to counter weight gain associated with Zyprexa. A sixteen-week study of 132 patients treated with Zyprexa taking 300 mg twice daily of Axid gained significantly less weight (6.08 pounds) than a control group taking a placebo (12.5 pounds).

Some clinicians report that the potential benefit of this countermeasure occurs only when Axid is administered at the beginning of treatment with the atypical antipsychotic (and some child psychiatrists report using 150 mg twice a day). Studies will have to be done to shed real light on the benefits and risks of the use of Axid.

All hopes have been on Geodon for its weight-neutral property, but clinical reports of its effectiveness in children with bipolar disorder are equivocal at best, and anecdotal reports suggest that Geodon carries a greater risk for activation of these children than the other atypicals.

## Side Effects Beyond Weight Gain

There is anecdotal evidence and a few case reports in adults that Risperdal and Zyprexa have been associated with the induction of mania or mixed states. This may be because the atypical antipsychotics have an antiserotonin (5-HT2) receptor-blocking effect and thus are mood elevating. (We have seen and heard of an induction of mania in children and a few adolescents, and it is something parents should be aware of. This tends to happen more frequently in children younger than eight.)

Finally, a series of general medical, metabolic problems is being increasingly reported in association with clozapine as well as the newer antipsychotics. These include new-onset, type II (noninsulin-dependent) diabetes mellitus, changes in lipid metabolism and blood concentrations, sometimes severe and persistent elevations of prolactin and other hormonal imbalances, and a range of adverse cardiovascular effects that include low blood pressure and abnormal functioning of the heart. The long-term implications of such adverse effects are not known, particularly for youngsters who may need to remain on such medication for decades to come. We are just starting to be concerned about the potential individual and public health implications of such effects, which threaten to be at least as problematic as tardive dyskinesia and the extrapyramidal symptoms of the older drugs.

It is recommended that prior to the institution of treatment with any atypical neuroleptic—particularly if long-term use is contemplated—a set of baseline measures should be taken. These include measurements of weight, fasting blood glucose, glycosylated alpha 1c hemoglobin, and blood lipids. Children should be retested periodically (every four to six months) during treatment, and those children who experience significant weight gain or have a family history of diabetes should be monitored especially closely.

In general, children tend to break down and eliminate most drugs more rapidly and efficiently than adults and elderly persons. That tends to protect them from drug side effects. However, there is both laboratory and clinical evidence that children are more sensitive to antipsychotic drugs than adults, and require much smaller doses. As the optimal dosing with the newer antipsychotic drugs is worked out, it is wise to start with low doses in children. For example, daily doses of Risperdal of 0.25 to 2.5 mg, 2.5 to 5 mg of Zyprexa, and less than 200 mg of Seroquel may suffice. It is hoped that such doses may also limit side effect risks.

It is obvious that the safety and efficacy of atypical antipsychotics in the maintenance phases of treatment require further investigation. Lithium and perhaps other anticonvulsant mood stabilizers have been found to provide a neuroprotective effect in the brain, as they increase gray matter. Dr. Ross J. Baldessarini and colleagues have found that lithium treatment results in major reductions in suicide attempts and completed suicides in the depressive and mixed phases of bipolar disorder.

Not all children can tolerate lithium treatment, nor is it effective for all children, but its therapeutic benefits should encourage careful evaluation when considering an atypical antipsychotic as the only medication used in the long-term treatment of children and adolescents with bipolar disorder.

## Seasonal Adjustments of Mood-Stabilizing and Antipsychotic Medications

Many children and adolescents with bipolar disorder are extremely vulnerable to seasonal change: They suffer depressive slides as the days shorten in autumn and begin to be activated as the photoperiod lengthens in February or March. In fact, parents have wryly dubbed this springtime phenomenon "March madness."

It is important for clinicians and parents to document these vulnerable periods and preempt breakthrough mania or depression before it threatens stability. Often the change in mood repeats itself, sometimes to within a week year to year. Treatment strategies may need to be revised prior to these seasonal perturbations.

If a youngster is becoming activated in early spring, perhaps the level of lithium or another mood stabilizer should be raised, and the addition or the raising of an atypical antipsychotic should be considered.

Parents whose children are taking Lamictal should understand that the drug's robust antidepressant effects, so helpful in the depressive phase of the disorder, can produce activation in the springtime. Thus, the dose of Lamictal may need to be lowered in advance of the shift of season in order not to induce or exacerbate breakthrough agitation and irritability that accompany a resurgence of hypomanic or manic symptoms. A reduction of only 5 to 10 mg may suffice, but some children may require a larger decrease in their daily dose.

Clinically, a similar phenomenon has also been observed with bright light treatment (discussed on page 126). A reduction in exposure to light by even ten minutes may avert activation.

Conversely, before a troublesome autumn, light therapy might be initiated. If Lamictal is considered, it must be prescribed well in advance of that vulnerable period, as it must be started at low doses and titrated slowly upward.

## BENZODIAZEPINES AND OTHER MEDICATIONS FOR SLEEP AND MANIA

### Benzodiazepines

There is a definite place for the benzodiazepines, such as Klonopin (clonazepam), Ativan (lorazepam), and Valium (diazepam), in the treatment of adults with bipolar disorder. These drugs help to put a brake on acute mania or hypomania. In addition, the benzodiazepines decrease activity in brain arousal systems and can diminish anxiety, agitation, and activity and promote standard sleep. Benzodiazepines are used most commonly as adjuncts to mood stabilizers and antipsychotic medications in acute mania.

In prepubertal children, it has been observed that this class of drugs can produce paradoxical effects—they can be disinhibiting rather than calming. Therefore, their use may be more limited in this population. Nevertheless, the low threshold for anxiety these children have and their commonly comorbid anxiety disorders make these drugs useful under certain circumstances. If a decision is made to use benzodiazepines, good medical practice would be to start with low doses of a short-acting benzodiazepine, such as Ativan, perhaps on a weekend, and watch carefully for any signs of disinhibition.

Because there is often a daily pattern in mood and energy (particularly in children who cycle within the day), it is not uncommon for a child to experience increased activity, agitation, anxiety, irritability, and aggressive behavior from the late-afternoon hours well into the evening. Their thoughts may race, they may become distractible and have difficulty concentrating (thus, complicating any completion of homework), and they may find it nearly impossible to settle down. A benzodiazepine given in the late afternoon may preemptively stop this arousal from reaching a certain pitch.

Benzodiazepines not only reduce the number of awakenings these children experience throughout a night, but they also exert an effect on the architecture of sleep. They can decrease the time spent in stages 3 and 4 of slow-wave sleep. This may be particularly advantageous to children who are bipolar; a decrease in stage 4 sleep is accompanied by a reduction in the night terrors commonly experienced by these children.

Despite the benzodiazepine's shortening of stage 4 sleep and rapid-eye movement (REM) sleep, the net effect is usually an increase in total sleep time. And it is recognized that enhanced sleep can improve mania.

The question that arises about the benzodiazepines is: Do they cause dependency? There is always the risk, and there are definitely withdrawal effects, so a child should always be tapered off the drug slowly.

Which of the benzodiazepines should be prescribed and when? If the child is experiencing increased activation and restlessness and racing thoughts that begin and escalate from early evening to bedtime, and the child has difficulty going to sleep (but once asleep, sleeps through the night), Ativan might be prescribed just prior to the period of activation and again shortly before sleep. If on the other hand the child has trouble getting to sleep and is also experiencing interrupted sleep, Restoril forty-five minutes before bedtime would be a better choice.

The side effects of the benzodiazepines include sedation, drowsiness, and decreased mental acuity.

## Clonidine

Clonidine (Catapres) is used to treat high blood pressure in adults but is often used to treat children with tic disorders, ADHD, pervasive developmental disorders, and aggression. It is often prescribed for bipolar children who have comorbid ADHD or Tourette's syndrome, who are aggressive, or who have difficulty sleeping at night. Although clonidine is an excellent hypnotic agent, there have been anecdotal reports of this medication causing depression in children. Therefore, children with bipolar disorder who are prescribed clonidine should be watched very carefully for this adverse effect.

Clonidine is supplied in 0.1, 0.2, and 0.3 mg tablets, as well as in transdermal patches that are applied to the skin.

## Tenex

Tenex (guanfacine) is another adult blood pressure medication that appears to be less sedating than clonidine and to have more of an effect on attentional difficulties.

Tenex is supplied in 1 and 2 mg tablets, and most children are started on one-half a tablet twice a day. The side-effect profile includes irritability, fatigue, confusion at higher doses, and, rarely, agitation. Because clonidine can cause mood swings in bipolar children, there is speculation as to whether Tenex does as well, as they are in the same class of drugs. If a child seems unstable or irritable and he or she is taking Tenex, its use should be examined. Like clonidine, it should never be discontinued abruptly because of the risk of rebound hypertension.

## Omega-3 Fatty Acids

Ever since Dr. Andrew Stoll and his colleagues at Harvard University published provocative findings about the greater stabilization of rapidly cycling adult bipolar patients with the supplementary use of high doses of fish oils (the majority of patients were on traditional mood stabilizers), a large percentage of parents have opted to add omega-3s to their children's regimens of pills and capsules.

Omega-3 fatty acids are essential fatty acids. They are called that because although they are crucial for growth and development, they cannot be manufactured in the body, but must be consumed through the diet we eat or from the supplements we swallow.

There are two families of essential fatty acids: omega-6 fatty acids and omega-3 fatty acids. The omega-6s are found in common vegetable oils such as corn, safflower, sunflower, and cottonseed; omega-3 fatty acids are found in the tissues of oily fish such as mackerel, anchovies, herring, and salmon, and in green leafy vegetables, canola oil, flaxseed, and walnuts.

While omega-6 fatty acids are distributed throughout the body, the omega-3 fatty acids are needed in the brain to an extraordinary degree. In fact, the major structural component of the brain and its cells is fat and water. The dry weight of the brain is 60 percent fat.

### A Closer Look at Omega-3s

There are three important omega-3 fatty acids:

> LNA—alpha-linolenic acid
> EPA—eicosapentanoic acid (pronounced EE-ko-sa-pehn-ta-NO-ic acid)
> DHA—docosahexaenoic acid (pronounced do-ko-sa-HEX-eh-noic acid)

LNA is a shorter chain omega-3 that comes from walnuts, flaxseed, canola oil, and other green leafy vegetables. LNA can be converted— sometimes inefficiently—into the longer chain EPA and DHA molecules.

EPA and DHA, the longer chain essential fatty acids, come primarily from the tissues of certain fish, and the fish get them—in the wild—by eating the chloroplasts of plants. Only the chloroplasts of marine and freshwater algae produce high quantities of long-chain omega-3 fatty acids. These are eaten by small aquatic animals and shrimp, which are in turn eaten by larger fish, which are in turn eaten by humans (if they eat fish!). Only wild fish, not farmed fish, have large quantities of essential fatty acids in their tissues.

## The Fish Connection to the Increasing Rates of Depression and Bipolar Disorder

Something has been going on since 1945: The rates of depression have increased worldwide, and the age of onset is shifting downward—younger people are being affected. This trend, called "the cohort phenomenon," was noted in the 1980s by Drs. Gerald Klerman, Myrna Weissman, and Elliot Gershon, who found that each successive generation of individuals born since World War II appears to have a higher incidence and earlier age of onset of both major depression and bipolar disorder.

While there are many theories attempting to explain this striking increase, one of them points to the increase in our diets of sources of omega-6 oils (corn and soy as two examples) and the corresponding marked decrease in omega-3 fats. (This has not been proven, however.)

The association between depression and the types of fats we consume was made when Joseph R. Hibbeln of the National Institutes of Health examined the consumption rate of omega-3 in countries around the world. In an important paper published in 1998 in the British journal *The Lancet,* he reported that the rates of depression were lower in countries that consumed a lot of fish. He found that the rates of depression could actually be predicted based on fish consumption.

A year after this association had been established, Dr. Andrew Stoll and his colleagues published the first double-blind placebo study that examined what happens when bipolar patients had their medications supplemented with high doses of fish oils (it should be noted that eight of the thirty were not on medications of any kind).

The thirty patients were divided into two groups, and one group got a placebo of olive oil capsules; the other, nine grams of pharmaceutical-quality EPA and DHA fatty acids. While the study was designed for a nine-month period, a preplanned preliminary analysis of the data found a significant discrepancy between the placebo control group and the omega-3 fatty acid group; the patients on the placebo relapsed or failed to improve, while the patients taking the omega-3 supplements experienced dramatic recoveries.

Why might this be? To paraphrase Dr. Stoll in his book *The Omega Connection*: When a neurotransmitter binds to a receptor, the receptor sets in motion within the cell a series of chemical processes known as signal transduction, amplifying the original signal and ultimately altering the activity of the cell. We know that mood stabilizers inhibit signal transduction.

Dr. Stoll goes on to write that "inhibiting signal transduction in bipolar disorder would be analogous to building a dam across a raging river, quieting the downstream waters."

Lithium and the anticonvulsants inhibit signal transduction; so too do omega-3 fatty acids.

## A Host of Questions

Since the Stoll findings were published and received a lot of media attention, a number of parents have placed their children suffering with bipolar disorder on fish oil supplements. Some parents report a difference in their children's behaviors: They seem less explosive, calmer, and their moods appear more stable. One mother whose very young child was given only omega-3s said: "He went from a ten in severity to a two."

Another mother wrote that her daughter was stabilized on lithium, but at age thirteen she began taking 1 gram of an enriched EPA omega-3 product in addition to the lithium. "She's gained a higher level of stability than we've ever seen before," the mother reported.

But questions about this treatment abound: How many grams of omega-3s a day must a child ingest (in addition to many pills and capsules of prescription medications)? Which brand should children take? And (most confusing), what ratio of EPA to DHA is optimal?

Unfortunately, there are no conclusive data to suggest that one ratio of EPA to DHA is more effective than another for children. There is, however, some clinical consensus that EPA in the range of 1,000 mg may be an effective target dose. We do know that each child responds differently to different brands and different EPA and DHA ratios, so it behooves a parent to try more than one brand if the first produces little effect.

## So What's a Parent to Buy?

Omega-3 supplements abound in every health food store and even in supermarkets. We will direct parents to a few companies that manufacture pharmaceutical-grade omega-3 fatty acids. When looking to choose a brand, always look at the source of fish oil. Those made from anchovies and sardines are less likely to incorporate mercury and other contaminants, such as PCBs, as they are lower on the food chain. Parents should also understand that a 500 mg capsule is much smaller than a 1,000 mg capsule. This is important to know if a child has difficulty swallowing pills. In alphabetical order, some brands to examine are:

COROMEGA takes fish oils and delivers them in a creamy, pudding-like orange-flavored emulsion that is packaged in a squeeze pak (think Go-Yurt). There are no pills to swallow, and when blended with orange juice it's almost like a smoothie.

Each packet contains: EPA: 350 mg; DHA: 230 mg; plus vitamins C and E and folic acid. Three packets would give a child over a gram of EPA (although we still don't know what a child needs). Sold at Stop and Shops across the country; go to www.coromega.com for more information.

NORDIC NATURALS' Pro DHA is a 500 mg capsule that is strawberry flavored. Each capsule provides 250 mg of DHA and 150 mg of EPA, with small amounts of vitamins E and C for freshness. The Pro EPA is a lemon-flavored 1,000 mg capsule that provides 450 mg of EPA and 100 mg of DHA. Go to www.nordicnaturals.com for more information, or call 1-800-662-2544.

OMEGABRITE offers 500 mg capsules. Three capsules provide 1,125 mg of EPA and 100 mg of DHA. Go to www.omegabrite.com, or call 1-800-383-2030.

In addition, the website www.consumerlabs.com reviews brands of Omega-3s, analyzes their purity and freshness, and lists their EPA/DHA ratios.

## What Are the Downsides of Omega-3 Supplements?

There seems to be the smallest possibility of mania induced by omega-3 supplements. We have read of six cases to date. Interestingly, five of the six occurred with EPA-enriched products (much higher doses of EPA than DHA), but researchers have the impression that mania would more likely occur with a DHA-enriched product. Again, there are many questions and very few answers.

Fish oils should not be used by people allergic to iodine or those who are using blood thinners or anticipating surgery. It is recommended that fish oils be taken with supplements of antioxidants to prevent the oxidation of the extra omega-3 oils going into the body; 400 IU (international units) vitamin E and 600 mg vitamin C should take care of this.

Parents should understand that flaxseed oil is not equivalent to omega-3, and some patients have experienced hypomania on it.

## ANTIDEPRESSANT THERAPIES

While antidepressant medications, and in particular the SSRIs such as Prozac, Zoloft, Paxil, Celexa, and Lexapro, and the atypical antidepressant Wellbutrin (bupropion), have found widespread and popular acceptance for the treatment of unipolar depression, anxiety, and panic disorders, their use in children and adolescents has been established only recently.

The SSRIs, Wellbutrin, and the older tricyclic antidepressants can be miracle drugs for children suffering from nonbipolar depression, incapacitating obsessive-compulsive disorder, and anxiety disorders, but for those children who carry an inherited vulnerability for bipolar disorder, the rose can hide thorns.

Reports from both the adult and child literature document that individuals with bipolar disorder who have been treated with antidepressants during depressive episodes may have a significant risk of switching into mania or hypomania. In addition, antidepressants have been reported to increase the frequency of cycling. There is considerable concern in the field that the introduction of antidepressants may cause an earlier onset and possibly more virulent course of the illness. In 1998 Demitri Papolos, M.D., and his colleagues reported on twenty-five adult ultrarapid and ultra-ultrarapid cycling patients, as well as patients who cycled four or more times a year—all of whom had had childhood or adolescent-onset bipolar disorder. Of these patients, over 90 percent retrospectively reported increased cycling on exposure to all classes of antidepressants.

In addition, our survey of 120 children revealed that over 80 percent of those who were taking an antidepressant switched into mania or psychosis or became very activated, aggressive, and even violent.

Some did well for weeks or even months before a deterioration in behavior became evident. ("It seemed like a miracle, he was so happy," said one mother of an eight-year-old boy. "Then he began to think that he could fly and flew off the playground's jungle gym and broke his hand." After trying to smash his younger sister in the head with his casted hand a week later, he was hospitalized in a psychotic state.)

We have heard of and seen variations of this story with hundreds of children who are bipolar. Even Wellbutrin, a mild stimulant antidepressant unrelated to the SSRIs and thought to be less likely to induce hypomania or mania in adults, can produce both mania and increased cycling.

Therefore, the use of antidepressants for children with known bipolar disorder, or even for children who initially show symptoms of depression only (but who may have a family history of bipolar disorder), must be considered highly risky and potentially harmful.

For children who are currently being treated with an antidepressant, parents and physicians should ask themselves: Has the child been *unstable*—despite the protection of a mood stabilizer? If the answer is yes, then the use of an antidepressant should be suspect and perhaps the child should be slowly withdrawn from it.

And this is where doctors and parents find themselves between a rock and a hard place. While many children cycle through depressed states very rapidly, for some children depression is the predominant pole of the illness, and they linger in depressed states for agonizing periods of time. Some retreat to their rooms, or move from the bed to the sofa and back. All outside activity ceases. This behavior is excruciating not only for the child but for the parents watching him or her as well. There is also the risk of suicide.

It is so tempting to want to use an antidepressant and watch that child's life take shape again. But if antidepressant medications are ultimately so destabilizing, the price may be very high. So then the questions become: What do you do about the depressions, and are there any other options?

There may be several:

- If the child is over sixteen, Lamictal (lamotrigine) is a unique mood stabilizer that has robust antidepressant properties.
- If the depressive episodes have a seasonal component, or if, as is often the case, the child is manifesting an increased need for sleep, low energy, and a marked craving for sweets and carbohydrates, then phototherapy (treatment with bright lights) may be a useful adjunct to mood stabilizers.

- Despite all negative media connotations, electroconvulsive therapy (ECT) may be the most beneficial alternative in the battle against depression and mood instability. Later in the chapter we'll discuss a study that showed that young people who had ECT had had beneficial results from the treatment. ECT should not be overlooked as a treatment option.

So, would you ever want to use antidepressant medications? In some instances, where comorbid obsessive-compulsive symptoms interfere significantly with the child's daily functioning (and behavioral treatments have failed) and mood stabilizers and antianxiety drugs or behavioral desensitization approaches do not produce relief, an appropriate approach to treatment may be low doses of an SSRI such as Luvox (fluvoxamine) plus increased levels of the mood stabilizer.

If an SSRI *is* used, a rule of thumb is that once the medication produces an antidepressant effect that is sustained for several weeks, attempts should be made to *slowly* reduce and discontinue the drug. To put it another way: The less exposure a bipolar child has to antidepressant treatment, the better.

For all these reasons, we start the discussion of antidepressant therapies with nondrug interventions, such as light therapy and electroconvulsive therapy, mention the new and experimental therapy of repeated transcranial magnetic stimulation (r-TMS), and finally move on to the SSRIs, such as Prozac, Zoloft, Paxil, the atypical drug Wellbutrin, and others.

## Light Therapy

Light therapy (phototherapy) was originally studied for its effects on seasonal affective disorder (SAD). This syndrome was characterized by Dr. Norman Rosenthal and his colleagues at the National Institute of Mental Health (NIMH) when their studies revealed that some patients became very sluggish, irritable, and depressed as the days grew shorter in the fall. They began to sleep excessively, binge on carbohydrates, and withdraw from social activities. But come spring and the lengthening of the photoperiod (the hours of light in the day), these patients experienced new energy and found their moods returning to normal or slightly elevated levels. (It is now pretty well accepted that these patients are bipolar with seasonal depressions and hypomanias.)

Dr. Rosenthal found that sitting these patients in front of a bank of high-intensity, full-spectrum (all wavelengths—like sunlight) lights for certain periods of time in the morning or the evening lifted the depressive symptoms, and most of the patients felt better. When the light treatments were stopped, a number of patients relapsed.

Today it is understood that the pineal gland—the gland that secretes melatonin—receives information about light from special nerve pathways, and the secretion of melatonin may provide the link with depression. Melatonin is a sleep-inducing hormone, produced in the dark. Melatonin secretion is at its highest levels in the winter. Serotonin (long associated with depression and suicide) is actually a precursor of melatonin.

It seems that the timing of circadian rhythms varies in relation to mood in a predictable way in rapid-cycling patients. Specifically, the phase of temperature, the excretion of a metabolite of norepinephrine (MHPG), and melatonin secretion all occur earlier in the day in a hypomanic state than in the depressed state. Bright light can shift the phase of circadian rhythms, with morning light shifting the rhythms to an earlier time and evening light delaying them. Manipulating these phase shifts could treat the depressed phase of the illness.

Dr. Ellen Leibenluft and her colleagues at the NIMH conducted a small pilot study on nine rapid-cycling patients and found that midday light—between the hours of 12:00 and 3:00 P.M.—improved the symptoms of a number of the patients. There is reason to believe that midday light treatment may prevent phase shifts in the normal nightly rhythm of melatonin release. Midday light seems to increase the potency of the signal that melatonin gives to areas in the central nervous system. By increasing the amount of melatonin released *at a particular time,* you make it more difficult for other influences to delay or advance the rhythm of melatonin secretion.

Studies in rapid-cycling children are now being conducted, and we spoke with Dr. Norman Rosenthal about the administration of light therapy in children and adolescents. We started discussing the light boxes that a parent can purchase to begin light treatment.

According to Dr. Rosenthal, "A suitable light box is usually a metal fixture approximately two feet long and one and a half feet high. It contains ordinary white fluorescent lightbulbs set behind a plastic diffusing screen, which houses a film that filters out most of the ultraviolet [UV] rays from the bulbs."

Typically, the light emitted from these boxes is 10,000 lux in intensity, but Dr. Rosenthal mentioned that the eyes of children under the age of eight have greater sensitivity to light; thus, for them, less intense light sources should be used—for example, 2,500 lux. (Lux is a unit used to measure the intensity of light. Indoor light levels range from 200 to 700 lux; outdoor light levels on a sunny spring day range from 2,000 to well beyond 10,000 lux.)

A box that can be angled is best so that the light fixture can be positioned at an angle toward the eye and more light can enter. A child should sit approximately one to two feet from the light source and look up for a few seconds to the light every several minutes or so. A child can play video games in front of the light, watch television, or read. The treatment may take twenty to thirty minutes a day, and if there is any activation or hypomania, this timing can be scaled back. Dr. Rosenthal said it would take approximately two weeks to see a full response to the lights.

But how is a rapidly cycling child going to receive fifteen minutes of treatment between the hours of 12:00 and 3:00 P.M. on a school day? Well, this depends on how much a parent wants to keep this noninvasive intervention going (and whether the parent can afford two light boxes). One can be stationed at home for weekends and nonschool days, and one might be placed in a resource room or some area of the school where the child could go for fifteen minutes and do schoolwork while glancing into the light. (Since 3 to 4 percent of school-age children may suffer from SAD, the school might be willing to purchase a light box, or several parents could buy one together for their children's treatments.)

Dr. Rosenthal and Dr. Susan Swedo at the NIMH and Drs. Martin Teicher and Carol Glod at McLean Hospital in Massachusetts studied light therapy and dawn simulation together and found that the combined treatment worked well to reverse the depressive symptoms *and* helped the children get up in the morning.

Parents of a child with bipolar disorder can tell you how terribly difficult it is to awaken his or her child in the mornings for school. The children seem almost in an anesthetized state (the sleep inertia we will discuss in Chapter 8), and no amount of coaxing, noisemaking, or screaming can get them up. One boy actually asked his mother to throw a pitcher of ice water on him in the morning. Then he instructed his mother to just jiggle the pitcher with the ice on the following mornings and his Pavlovian fear reaction would make him get out of bed. (The thought of a mass of wet bedding did not appeal to her, and she found the icy water treatment a bit sadistic, so we can't report if this self-styled method works or not.)

Dawn simulators seem much kinder and perhaps more scientific. This is a small electronic timer that can be plugged into an ordinary bedside lamp with a 60- to 100-watt-intensity bulb. It can be programmed to create an artificial dawn lasting between sixty to ninety minutes. In other words, if your child has to get up at 6:30 to make the school bus, the timer should be set at 5:00 or 5:30 A.M.

How does this work if the eyes are closed? we asked Dr. Rosenthal. "No one is really sure, but it may be that the eyes are particularly sensitive during the predawn hours and may be capable of responding to even the very small amounts of light that are transmitted through the child's closed eyelids." He added: "It may be that some phase-shifting is going on also."

There are quite a few light box manufacturers, and we will mention three here:

Apollo Light Systems Inc.
Orem, Utah
1-800-545-9667
www.apollolight.com

Northern Light Technologies
Montreal, Canada
1-800-263-0066
www.northernlight-tech.com

The SunBox Company sells both sunboxes and dawn simulators
Gaithersburg, Maryland
1-800 LITE-YOU (548-3968)
www.sunboxco.com

Light boxes cost between $160 and $300. A dawn simulator costs approximately $160. Some companies will rent you the box to see if it works and, if you buy it, deduct the rental fee from the total cost. Also, insurance companies may pay for the box if the child's doctor writes a letter detailing its medical necessity.

## Melatonin for the Promotion of Better Sleep

Children and adolescents with bipolar disorder often have irregularities in their thermoregulatory systems. They overheat—even when the ambient temperature feels cold (often very cold) to everyone else. Parents struggle constantly to get them to wear jackets in the winter. It is not uncommon to see the ears turn beet red. (The pinna, or outer cartilage, of the ears is one of the areas through which the body dissipates heat.)

Scientists have found that the rapid onset of sleep occurs when the blood vessels in the skin of the hands and feet dilate and cause heat loss at the extremities. This causes the core body temperature to lower. A group of researchers—Drs. Kurt Krauchi, Christian Cajochen, and Anna Wirz-Justice—noted this functional relationship between core body temperature and sleepiness, and hypothesized that the opposite would also be true: The *constriction* of blood vessels would raise the core body temperature, and the human being would come to a state of wakefulness. (Think colder at night and the onset of sleepiness, and warmer in the morning and the onset of wakefulness.)

There is a close correlation between the timing of the endogenous increase in melatonin in the evening and vasodilation, an effect that is mimicked by pharmacological doses of melatonin.

As we mentioned in the light therapy section, the phase shifts commonly seen in bipolar disorder can alter the nightly rhythm of melatonin release. Could irregularities in the timing of the release of melatonin—a peptide known to reduce core body temperature and induce sleep—be a factor in the increased activity level seen at night and the marked sleep inertia seen in the morning? Since melatonin is known to lower core body temperature, this may explain one of its effects on the regulation of the sleep/wake cycle.

Some clinicians are finding that a trial of pharmaceutical-grade melatonin may enhance an earlier onset of sleep, promote a more restorative sleep, and even abolish sleep-arousal disorders such as night terrors. For some children, a dosage between 1.5 and 3 mg melatonin given twenty minutes before bedtime is effective, although 6 mg may be necessary for others.

Another effective method for preventing the body from overheating and causing sleep disturbances is to place a fan close to an uncovered area of the skin. Parents who have used this method have reported that their children have a more restorative sleep.

## Electroconvulsive Therapy for Children

It's hard to imagine that a treatment that involves the distressing image of an electrical current passed through one or both hemispheres of the brain could result in a dramatic change in mood and energy, but, in fact, ECT as a treatment for depression, psychosis, suicidal impulses, and intractable mania is unsurpassed by any other treatment in psychiatry. It has evolved into a safe option, one that works. And it bears little resemblance to the way it was performed in the 1940s, from which came sadistic fictional characters such as Nurse Ratched in Ken Kesey's *One Flew Over the Cuckoo's Nest.*

In fact, ECT is especially safe for pregnant women who probably should not take drugs for depression or mania throughout the gestation period. But is it a safe option for children and adolescents? Won't the seizures "damage" a developing brain? According to case reports and reviews, apparently not. In 1990 Drs. Mark W. Bertagnoli and Carrie M. Borchardt published a review of the use of ECT in 151 children and adolescents ages five to nineteen years in which 67 percent of the children improved.

ECT is usually given to a child or adolescent three times the first week and twice each week thereafter for a total of six to nine or fifteen to twenty completely painless treatments. The number of treatments depends, of course, on the clinical response.

The child is put to sleep with a very short-acting barbiturate, and then the drug succinylcholine is administered. This medication temporarily paralyzes the muscles so that they do not contract during treatment and cause fractures. An electrode is then placed above the temple of the nondominant (usually right) side of the head, and a second is placed in the middle of the forehead (this is called unilateral ECT); or one electrode is placed above each temple (this is called bilateral ECT). A very small current of electricity is passed through the brain, causing a seizure. The child breathes pure oxygen through a mask, and the heart is monitored by an electrocardiogram (EKG) while the seizure activity is monitored by an electroencephalogram (EEG).

Since seizure thresholds in adolescents are notoriously low, the first treatment should be given at the minimum energy level; only if the seizure is not adequate should the energy be increased. Adolescents develop tolerance quickly, and the third or fourth treatment may call for increased energy. The child wakes up ten to fifteen minutes after treatment.

It is not unusual for a child to have a headache upon awakening, some muscle aches, confusion, and disorientation, and perhaps some nausea, but these side effects typically clear up within an hour or so of the treatment. The child will probably have no memory of the period surrounding the treatment, and studies in adults have found that experiences up to three weeks prior to the first treatment may not be consolidated in memory. We do know that unilateral ECT causes less immediate memory impairment than bilateral placement. With unilateral treatment, the individual usually experiences less confusion and disorientation after the seizure. However, there remains a question as to whether unilateral is as effective as bilateral treatment. Experts agree that in adults, memory losses may persist for up to several months posttreatment.

### How Does ECT Work?

To this day, no one is sure how ECT works. Animal research shows that it enhances dopamine sensitivity, reduces the uptake of serotonin, and activates the systems in the brain that use norepinephrine. It definitely seems to increase the amount of the major inhibitory neurotransmitter, gamma-aminobutyric acid (GABA), and thereby to increase inhibitory tone in the central nervous system. But much remains unclear about ECT's mechanism of action.

### How Do Patients Feel About ECT?

A study done in England almost twenty years ago reported on interviews with seventy-two consecutive adult patients treated with ECT. Some of the questions asked were: "Were you frightened by the procedure?" "Were you angered by the experience?" "Would you ever have ECT again?"

Fifty-four percent of the sample said they considered a trip to the dentist more distressing. Many praised the treatment, and 81 percent said they would have ECT again.

## Repeated Transcranial Magnetic Stimulation (r-TMS)

Researchers at the NIMH wondered if magnetic waves could be used to speed up the motor nerve pathways in patients suffering with Parkinson's disease and found that some of the patients became less depressed.

Naturally there is great enthusiasm for a treatment that seems to have few side effects beyond an occasional headache, does not require anesthesia, and causes little or no discomfort, but much remains to be learned about this experimental therapy.

The treatment involves a patient sitting in a lounge chair while a small but powerful coiled electromagnet is placed on the scalp. This creates a strong magnetic field that passes through the skull. When this rapidly changing magnetic field encounters the brain's nerve cells, it causes an electric current that depolarizes them—in other words, the nerve cells fire.

The eight-inch coils in the electromagnet must be water-cooled because the electricity generates heat; and the patient wears ear protection because the treatment is noisy.

The patient receives forty stimulations in two seconds, and this is repeated twenty times. One patient described it as painless but a little like "having Woody Woodpecker on your head."

Dr. Mark George at the Medical University of South Carolina has transferred his research from the NIMH and is completing studies that show the treatment to be safe and effective.

Apparently, some of the bipolar adult patients had excellent responses to r-TMS—it reduced their depression, and only one of the nine became slightly hypomanic. No mania was induced in any of the bipolar adult patients.

## Newer Antidepressant Drugs

Imipramine was discovered in the late 1950s, and it and other tricyclic antidepressants are named after their three-ring chemical structure. These drugs are effective against depression, but they have largely been displaced by the newer selective serotonin release inhibitors (the SSRIs), and atypical drugs such as bupropion (Wellbutrin), venlafaxine (Effexor), mirtazapine (Remeron), and duloxetine (Cymbalta), which have a more benign side effect profile and are extremely difficult for patients to overdose on. The SSRIs and the other newer antidepressants are just as effective against depression as the tricyclic antidepressants, but their common side effects include:

- Sleepiness
- Insomnia
- Agitation
- Nausea

- Diarrhea
- Dry mouth
- Sexual dysfunction (Wellbutrin and Remeron do not cause this)

All SSRIs—Prozac, Zoloft, Paxil, Luvox, Celexa, and Lexapro—can produce withdrawal hypomania, agitation, and aggression, and therefore need to be tapered slowly during the discontinuation period. For instance, if a child is taking 20 mg of Paxil, then perhaps the medication should be reduced by 5 mg every five to ten days. If agitation, panic, or sleep problems follow the reduction, the tapering process should be lengthened and perhaps a benzodiazepine should be prescribed for that period of time. This is especially important with Paxil, Luvox, and Effexor because of their shorter half-lives.

## Tricyclic Antidepressants (TCAs)
Tricylic medications are still prescribed, and side effects of these drugs include:

- Sedation (drowsiness or sleepiness)
- Anticholinergic effects (dry mouth, blurred vision, constipation, difficulty urinating, increased heart rate, delirium)
- Orthostatic hypotension (light-headedness or dizziness when rising quickly from a sitting or lying position)
- Weight gain

The less commonly reported side effects of the tricyclic antidepressants are:

- Skin rash
- Sweating
- Tremor
- Altered orgasmic function

It is important to bear in mind that these side effects may decrease as the body adjusts to the medications.

## When Should a Child Be Treated with an Antidepressant?

We thought it might be a good idea to explore several scenarios illustrating when and if a child with bipolar disorder should be exposed to an antidepressant.

A nine-year-old child is brought by her parents to a psychiatrist's office. She appears withdrawn, melancholic, and complains of feeling tired. She has been oversleeping and has sweet and carbohydrate cravings. The family history reveals that her alcoholic father has an explosive temper, and her maternal grandmother had been treated with ECT.

Since a high preponderance of bipolar adolescents and adults have a similar profile of "atypical symptoms" (fatigue, oversleeping, and carbohydrate cravings) when they become depressed, this triad should be considered a risk factor for a bipolar vulnerability.

Given the risk factors on both maternal and paternal sides of the family and the "atypical" symptoms of depression that are classically found in bipolar disorder, and based on our current state of knowledge, this child would have a high risk of mania and the onset of rapid cycling if exposed to antidepressant treatment.

*Prescription:* The first intervention might be to start bright light treatment in the morning or midday coupled with a dawn simulator set an hour in advance of the usual time of current morning awakening. If the depressive symptoms are unabated after two to three weeks of treatment, what are the options? Because ECT is not typically used in nine-year-olds, it is an unlikely choice. Therefore, in preparation for the likelihood of starting the child on antidepressant treatment, a mood stabilizer such as lithium, Trileptal, or Depakote should be introduced until a therapeutic level is reached, at which point an antidepressant medication such as bupropion (Wellbutrin) can be prescribed. If Wellbutrin is deemed necessary, it should be started at a low dose—either 18.25 mg or 37.5 mg—and then the doctor and parents should wait seven to ten days to observe whether this low dose has an effect, or whether it is activating. If it is neither activating nor effective at that dose, it should be raised incrementally by 18.25 mg every seven to ten days.

This is not the standard method of dosing in the field, however. Generally it is common practice to start treatment as high as 100 mg and increase the dose to 200 or 300 mg over a three-week period. But clinical experience in treating children with bipolar disorder has suggested that this higher dosing pattern is more likely to induce such adverse effects as manic induction, increased cycling, and even psychosis, despite the presence of a mood stabilizer.

The parents of a ten-year-old boy take him to a psychiatrist for an evaluation because they are concerned about their son's severe obsessive-compulsive symptoms, hand washing, and showering. He washes his hands approximately fifty times a day, and they are chafed and reddened. He has had several previous episodes of depression and has been increasingly irritable with pronounced temper tantrums, racing thoughts, and difficulty sleeping at night. He says that unless he goes to sleep with a radio or television turned on in his room, he becomes extremely fearful. His mind is filled with thoughts that something terrible will happen to his parents as well as to him.

The boy tells the doctor that in the past few months his mood goes up and down. Sometimes he's happy; sometimes he's sad. Some days he awakes filled with energy and feels really good. Then he gets really down on himself and doesn't know why.

His father has been diagnosed with bipolar disorder and his mother with recurrent depressions. She has had periods of bulimia. The boy had been diagnosed with obsessive-compulsive disorder and separation anxiety disorder.

Although the OCD symptoms are the primary concern of the boy and his parents, the fact that the father has a bipolar disorder and the mother a recurrent mood disorder, coupled with the boy's current mood and anxiety symptoms, should raise concerns about the likelihood of a bipolar disorder evolving.

*Prescription:* Beginning treatment with a mood stabilizer would be a prudent first step in the treatment plan.

Once adequate therapeutic levels have been reached, and the boy reports feeling more even-keeled and his sleep has improved, it is important to reassess the nature and intensity of the OCD symptoms. If they persist, behavioral treatments that can reduce obsessive-compulsive symptoms, especially with the addition of an antianxiety medication such as gabapentin (Neurontin) or clonazepam (Klonopin), might be the next step.

If these treatments fail to bring relief, adding an SSRI such as Luvox (fluvoxamine) may be the next most likely treatment.

A fifteen-year-old young woman comes to a psychiatrist's office with her parents and complains of a loss of energy, depressed mood, and wanting to sleep long hours. She also tells the doctor that she has been consuming large quantities of mint chocolate chip ice cream every day and cannot stop herself.

These symptoms began in early September, and she recalled that the same set of symptoms had occurred in each of the previous two years in late autumn and continued through the early spring. In fact, she typically experienced improvements in energy and mood throughout the spring and summer months. Then, in mid-August of this year, she became extremely active, stayed out late at night, and grew argumentative and oppositional when her parents tried to set a curfew.

As mentioned, many individuals with bipolar disorder commonly experience regular seasonal episodes. The pattern of fall depressions and spring-summer hypomania is one of the most common and has been termed seasonal affective disorder (SAD).

*Prescription:* This fifteen-year-old would be best treated with bright light therapy during the fall and winter months. Her behavior, activity level, sleep/wake cycle, and mood state in the summer months should be monitored for hypomania. If this pattern continues, a mood stabilizer such as lithium carbonate or Tegretol should be considered.

## Riluzole, Pramipexole, and Agomelatine: Potential New Medications for Bipolar Depression?

Riluzole (Rilotek) was originally developed to slow the progression of amyotrophic lateral sclerosis (Lou Gehrig's disease), but a recent study in adults with bipolar depression found it effective—when added to lithium—for treatment-resistant depression with no switches into mania.

Like Lamictal, riluzole is an inhibitor of glutamate release (glutamate is the most widely distributed excitatory transmitter in the central nervous system). Preclinical and clinical evidence indicate that the glutamatergic system may play a role in the pathophysiology of mood disorders.

Because Lamictal has demonstrated effectiveness in bipolar depression, researchers at the National Institute of Mental Health undertook a trial of riluzole with lithium and found it had a significant effect against depression.

The trial had a small number of subjects, and there are no data on riluzole's use in children or adolescents. Still, this drug and other drugs that block glutamate release are worth watching, as bipolar depression is so difficult to treat without triggering hypomanic or manic episodes. This drug is extraordinarily expensive at the present time, however.

Pramipexole (Mirapex) is a dopiminergic medication that is FDA-approved for the treatment of Parkinson's disease. Based on early pilot studies, the National Institute of Mental Health and the Stanley Medical Research Institute are currently supporting clinical trials to determine if this medication will fight the depression of bipolar disorder. If so, pramipexole comes with the added benefit of being neuroprotective—it protects nerve cells in the brain and may promote nerve-cell growth and regeneration.

Agomelatine (Valdoxan) is an investigational drug being studied for its possible role in managing bipolar depression. It is a melatonin agonist that seems not only to improve depressive symptoms but also to improve disturbances of the sleep-wake patterns so often seen in depression. The hope is that the drug will not induce hypomania or mania or rapid cycling in patients with bipolar disorder.

## STIMULANTS

Attention-deficit disorder with hyperactivity (ADHD) is a behavioral disorder that appears to have a strong genetic component and to involve dysregulation of the norepinephrine and dopamine neurotransmitter systems. ADHD is characterized by inattention, impulsiveness, and hyperactivity. These behaviors, which may appear at home, at school, or in other social situations, are generally worse in situations requiring sustained attention; as a result, academic underachievement is a frequently associated problem.

Although the onset of ADHD usually occurs before the age of four, it is most commonly diagnosed when a child enters school. Four percent of school-age children are said to be affected, and it occurs six times more often in boys than girls.

The majority of individuals who have pure ADHD respond to an adequate trial of one of the four available stimulants: dextroamphetamine sulphate (Dexedrine), methylphenidate hydrochloride (Ritalin), and pemoline (Cylert), and a combination of dextroamphetamine and levoamphetamine (Adderall). An extended-release methylphenidate (Concerta) is also available.

But a child who has bipolar disorder will also manifest the cardinal symptoms of ADHD (inattention, impulsiveness, and hyperactivity). And as we discussed in Chapter 2, it is not unusual for these symptoms to be early manifestations of bipolar disorder or for a child to carry a dual diagnosis: It appears as if he or she has both disorders concomitantly.

Distinguishing whether a child has pure ADHD, bipolar disorder, or both is complicated. (See Chapter 2 for a complete discussion of the differential diagnosis.)

One might ask: How could a simple trial of a drug that is so commonly prescribed and that wears off in a number of hours be detrimental to a child's well-being? Out of seventy-three children in our study who were diagnosed initially with ADHD and subsequently treated with stimulant medications, 65 percent were thrown into manic or depressed states or became psychotic on these drugs.

A recent report by Dr. Melissa DelBello and her colleagues at the University of Cincinnati College of Medicine evaluated thirty-four adolescents who were hospitalized for mania. Using a retrospective chart review and interviews with the parents and the adolescents themselves, the researchers systematically determined the age of onset of the bipolar disorder and the pharmacological treatment history.

Although this was a small sample, they found that the adolescents with bipolar disorder who had a history of stimulant exposure prior to the onset of the bipolar disorder manifested the bipolar illness at an earlier age than those without prior stimulant exposure. Additionally, bipolar adolescents treated with at least two stimulant medications had a younger age of onset compared with those who were treated with only one stimulant medication.

Why might this be so? Stimulants directly increase the release of the neurotransmitters dopamine and norepinephrine. Both of these neurotransmitters have long been implicated as associated with bipolar disorder. Indeed, one theory with a significant body of evidence suggests that an increase in dopamine and norepinephrine transynaptically results in a switch into mania. Therefore, the use of stimulants on a daily basis, potentiating an excess release of these neurotransmitters, could interact with a genetic predisposition for bipolar disorder, perhaps precipitating an earlier onset of the illness.

While stimulants may positively address attentional issues, they may also negatively affect other areas of the brain, such as the amygdala. Dopamine pathways in the amygdala have been known to directly influence the modulation of aggression.

As yet, there is no consensus in the field and no established guidelines in the pediatric psychopharmacology literature regarding either the use or withholding of stimulant drugs. However, the following clinical scenarios should give families pause before pursuing treatment with stimulant drugs:

- There is a strong family history of bipolar disorder.
- Prolonged temper tantrums and mood swings are present along with symptoms of inattention, impulsiveness, and hyperactivity.
- The child is oppositional and defiant.
- The child appears to have better behavior at school and a marked deterioration of behavior in the home.
- The child is explosive and manifests aggressive behavior toward parents and siblings.
- The child has severe separation anxiety, night terrors, and a fascination with gore and mayhem.

When some children who appear to have both bipolar disorder and attention-deficit disorder with hyperactivity are treated with a mood stabilizer, they suffer much less distractibility, inattention, impulsive behaviors, and hyperactivity. (In these cases, it would seem that the "ADHD" symptoms were merely part of the bipolar disorder.) However, other children experience mood stabilization yet continue to have attentional problems. Now the question becomes: Is it safe to give them stimulant medication after a therapeutic level of a mood stabilizer has been achieved?

A number of clinical investigators have reported anecdotally that the addition of stimulant medication to a regimen of one or more mood stabilizers, for the purpose of treating residual attentional problems, can be effective. However, recent private conversations with other investigators who are engaged in treatment trials in bipolar children and adolescents have raised concerns about this practice, particularly with high doses of stimulants. The children *seem* to tolerate lower doses without untoward effects. However, long-term studies have not been conducted that would allow any conclusions about long-term stimulant use in bipolar children.

Many hopes were raised when Strattera (atomoxetine), the first non-stimulant medication for ADHD, came on the market. Unfortunately, it has proved to be a problem for many children and adolescents with bipolar disorder as it can trigger mania or mixed episodes and can increase cycling patterns.

Based on a review of earlier clinical trials, it seems that the drug can increase suicidal thoughts in children and adolescents, and the FDA has asked the drug's manufacturer, Eli Lily, to add a "black box" warning on its prescribing information.

For now, the clinical treatment of the ADHD aspect of bipolar disorder remains unclear.

## NEW GENETIC TESTS TO DETERMINE DRUG RESPONSE AND DOSAGE

A physician treating juveniles with bipolar disorder has little dosing guidance from clinical studies, and the children and families often are forced to suffer much trial and error as medications and dosages are tweaked and changed.

Recent and exciting breakthroughs in the field of pharmacogenomics, however, will take some of the guesswork out of prescribing certain of the drugs that we've discussed in this chapter: those that are metabolized predominantly by two key regions encoding the enzymes of the cytochrome P450 complex—the CY2D6 genes and the CY2C19 genes. These genes produce enzymes in the liver that metabolize certain classes of medications. The 2D6 gene metabolizes drugs including antipsychotics (Risperdal is one), antidepressants, Strattera, and pain medications; the 2C19 is involved in the metabolism of other classes of medications, including anticonvulsants and benzodiazepines.

The genotype of each individual and which variants of the genes he or she has determines how that individual will metabolize a drug from the above classes of medications. A "normal" metabolizer has two effective copies of the gene; an intermediate metabolizer has one effective copy of the gene and one defective copy; a poor metabolizer has two defective copies of the gene. An individual with three or more effective copies of the gene, due to uneven crossovers during meiosis, is an ultrarapid metabolizer.

Poor metabolizers are at high risk for developing adverse side effects and toxic levels of medications; ultrarapid metabolizers will often fail to achieve therapeutic blood levels within the ordinary dosage range.

How will a doctor know who is more likely to metabolize a drug normally, too slowly, or too quickly? A new AmpliChip CYP450 test powered by Affymetrix technology is now available from Roche Molecular Systems. The results of the test—the first one to be approved by the FDA—will help guide the prescribing of any drugs that are metabolized primarily by these enzymes. (We discuss this new technology in greater detail in the next chapter.)

It is important to note that this test does not indicate whether a child will respond to a medication, only the rates at which he or she will metabolize those that are in the classes of medications listed. Moreover, other factors affect dosing, including age and coadministered medications.

As of this writing, the test is available at Quest Diagnostics, LabCorp, Specialty Labs, and Spectrum Laboratory Network but will soon be widely available.

## ARE GENERICS JUST AS GOOD?

Once the doctor and the parents agree to try a child on a medication or a combination of medications, the physician writes the prescription(s) and the parent troops off to the pharmacy to have them filled. But the first question the pharmacist will ask is: "Do you want the generic or brand-name version of the drug?"

In the cases of Depakote (divalproex sodium), Neurontin (gabapentin), Lamictal (lamotrigine), Risperdal (risperidone), Zyprexa (olanzapine), and others, there is no generic version. They are all under patent. But for many older drugs, including Tegretol (carbamazepine), Klonopin (clonazepam), Haldol (haloperidol), Mellaril (thioridazine), and others, there are generic equivalents that are usually much cheaper, and managed care companies would prefer you to use the generic formulations.

Most people assume that a generic version of a drug is identical to a brand-name drug, merely minus all the exorbitant advertising in glossy magazines and trade journals. They also reason that the generic companies don't have the enormous expense of maintaining the huge sales staff known as detail men (many of them are women) who visit doctors at their offices and attempt to get them to dispense their drugs.

But while generic versions are cheaper to produce (after all, the generic company did not spend the $800 million it takes to develop a drug today), the FDA does not require generic drugs to be carbon copies of the brand-name drugs.

The active chemical ingredients must be the same, and the strength, the route of administration, and the dosage form (tablet versus capsule) must be identical. But the FDA allows other variations: The inert ingredients, such as binders, fillers, color, and flavoring, can differ, and often the manufacturing process itself is distinct from that of the brand-name drug. However, the generics must be shown to be "bioequivalent" to the brand-name drug. They must deliver the same amount of active ingredients into the patient's bloodstream in the same amount of time as the brand-name medication. (Incidentally, brand-name drugs are subject to the same bioequivalency tests as generics when their manufacturers reformulate them.)

Parents should know that many brand-name manufacturers package their own brand-name drugs as generics so as not to lose market share to their generic competitors and that almost 80 percent of the U.S. generic drug production is done by brand-name firms in modern manufacturing plants.

When possible, should a parent opt for the generic or the brand name?

The major problem with generic prescriptions is that a pharmacy may buy from different suppliers from time to time (or a parent may fill a prescription at a different pharmacy whose drugs are supplied from a different manufacturer). Since no two drugs can be superimposed perfectly (nor are they supposed to be), blood levels may change, behavior and side effects may change, and all of this will be problematic for the child and the family. If the child is switched from a brand-name to a generic drug, or from one generic to another, and the parents note adverse effects or behavioral changes, it's a good idea to check the blood levels about two weeks after the change is made to ensure that proper levels are maintained.

Of course, a patient may have no choice about generic versus brand-name decisions if the managed care company decides that a drug is too expensive and does not list it on the company's formulary (its list of approved drugs). In such cases, the parent can pay for the brand-name drug him- or herself or agree to try one of the drugs that is covered. (These tend to be the older, cheaper medications.) All parents should check their insurance company's drug formulary and dicuss its latitude with the psychiatrist before a decision is made about prescriptions.

So, understanding all of this, let us close this section by pointing out that everyone should comparison shop for medications. The same medication in three drugstores in the same neighborhood can have three very different prices. Also, purchase the largest-size tablet or capsule available, consistent with the dosage prescribed. A patient taking 1,000 mg Depakote a day would pay less for two 500 mg tablets than for four 250 mg tablets.

Sometimes a child needs half of a tablet for his or her dosing regimen, and parents spend a lot of time with pills flying through the air as they try to cut them. One mother cleverly joked that she is "preparing for her next life as a diamond cutter in Amsterdam." Inexpensive cutters are available that catch all the pieces, and some pharmacies will compound the smaller doses in tablet or capsule form (to the specifications of the prescribing physician) and ship them overnight, anywhere in the country. Naturally, this will be more expensive. Check with your local pharmacy for a referral.

## What If a Family Can't Afford Prescription Medications?

Many psychotropic drugs are extremely expensive, and many of the pharmaceutical companies have special programs to assist parents who can't afford the medications their children need. The treating physician typically has to fill out a form to apply for free medications, but the website called www.NeedyMeds.com lists most of the meds and gives the manufacturers' contact numbers, program guidelines (including how much a family can earn in a year and still qualify for the program), and directions for the doctors initiating the enrollment.

## HOW TO GET A CHILD TO TAKE A MEDICATION

All of us have stories about our attempts to give balky children medication, and some of us still have stains on rugs and furniture where the medicine was spit out or the spoon was knocked out of a frustrated parental hand. So, how, we wondered, do you get a medication into a child who is smack in the middle of a rage or who refuses to take it?

We asked this question of many parents and got a variety of answers. Some parents bribed their child if he or she was not raging. The toy-for-spoonful trade can be effective but quite expensive. One mother told us that she simply said to her child: "You have a choice: You can take this now or we can go to the hospital where they can give you a shot." She said that usually earns her more cooperation.

One mother on the BPParents listserv wrote: "He is on 1,000 mg now and doing much better, especially with the rages! He must be able to tell a difference, because he doesn't give me a hard time about taking his meds anymore."

We were quite taken with one father's idea: He and his wife take their vitamins, blood pressure pills, and other medications together when their daughter takes her medications so she doesn't feel she's doing anything out of the ordinary.

In Chapter 11 we discuss the particular problem of teens on medications and how to deal with it.

## THE ART OF PILL SWALLOWING

Getting a child to "go along with the program" is one thing; teaching a child the skill of swallowing pills and capsules is another. Here are some tips that might make the mastery of this skill easy, and even interesting.

- Purchase a bag of M&Ms (the minis are a good choice) and ask the child to swallow one with some milk. This teaches the child the sensation and sequence of swallowing something pill-like. If it doesn't happen the first time, just give the candy to the child and try another day.
- Use a thicker liquid, such as a milkshake or yogurt drink. Thick drinks slow down swallowing and move the pill along with the liquid so they don't separate.
- Try a straw. Have the child place the pill on the tongue and suck three gulps of a chosen liquid (the thicker the better) through the straw. This method keeps the pill from floating around the mouth.
- Use the soda pop method. Have the child choose a soda or juice in a bottle and place the pill in her mouth. Now, pursing the lips on the bottle and never losing contact with the bottle opening, have her gulp the pill down. (This method reduces the tendency to gag.)
- Serve up the pill or tablet in peanut butter, pudding, or applesauce.

Please check with your pharmacist as to whether there are any food or drink interactions with the prescribed medication. For instance, grapefruit juice can increase the absorption of Tegretol, Valium, Buspar, Sonata, Trazedone, Anafranil, and several of the calcium channel blockers. This increased absorption can cause the drug to overshoot its desired effect and potentially produce problems and increase the risk of side effects.

Also, certain extended-release tablets or capsules should not be split, crushed, or mixed with food, as the crushing and mixing can interfere with the extended-release mechanism.

## DRUGS TO BE AVOIDED BY CHILDREN WITH BIPOLAR DISORDER

The following prescription and over-the-counter drugs and even herbs can cause hypomania, mania, mixed states, rapid cycling, or increased aggression in children who are bipolar:

- Beta blockers (such as propranolol). These drugs can induce depression. (Sometimes they are needed with an antipsychotic medication, however.)
- Caffeine. It acts on certain second messenger systems that may contribute to activation and arousal. (See the section on cyclic AMP, pages 225–226, in Chapter 7.)
- Imipramine or desipramine used to treat bedwetting. (The nasal spray desmopressin [DDAVP] seems to be safe.)
- Nitrous oxide (laughing gas used at dentists' offices).
- Steroids, particularly cortisol derivatives. Even topically applied agents, such as hydrocortisone 1 percent, if applied to richly vascularized areas such as the scalp, the hands, or the face, have been known to induce hypomania. Parents should try to ensure that their child has reduced exposure to poison ivy, oak, and the like—any rash necessitating the use of steroids. (However, steroid use for the treatment of severe asthma may be essential as asthma is a life-threatening illness. The pediatrician and psychiatrist should be in close communication during the time of steroid treatment and during the weaning-off period.)
- St. John's wort. St. John's wort has several active ingredients that can activate a bipolar child.
- Sudafed (or any medication with pseudoephedrine). It acts on the noradrenergic system, increasing norepinephrine and therefore increasing arousal and anxiety states.

## DEALING WITH THE DISILLUSIONMENT OF A FAILED MEDICATION TRIAL

It is highly unlikely that the doctor will hit upon the right drug and dose right away for every child. What works for one child may fail miserably for another or produce intolerable side effects. Unfortunately, psychopharmacology is still very much of a guessing game, guided by experience and perhaps good luck. Many, many parents have had to deal with their hopes being dashed when their child doesn't respond, responds poorly, or is unable to tolerate the side effects of the medication or medications. During the search period (which can last quite a while), the child and the family become deeply distressed and demoralized. As one mother graphically put it, "I think if all of us at once flushed all the medications that didn't work or caused too many side effects, we would back up the sewer systems."

Therefore, we thought it might be helpful to quote from parents who've been through many medication trials and who have finally happened upon the right regimen for their child.

I won't go through the gory details, but suffice it to say "been there, done that." We tried over ten different medications in varying combinations with zero luck. Then last spring we were put in a study for the drug _____.

Within four weeks my son was a different person. Actually, he was coming back to being the kid we always thought he could be. I'm happy to report that he is back in public school and though we still have our "moments," we are actually getting to the point where we get angry at him for all the normal stuff (like: "Get your feet off the sofa!") without feeling like we are taking our lives in our hands.

The medication part can take some time. Doctors throw the dice, come up with some combination, and finally see some results. For example, the Depakote helped Alicia, but when the lithium was added, it helped a bit more, and so on and so on. She has been on nine meds. Then when you start doing combos, sometimes you don't know what has worked and what you might possibly remove. Some things put them on the ceiling; some on the floor. Finding the middle ground takes time. Just when you think you have found it, your kid grows a few inches, puts on a few pounds, etc. Hang in there!

Everyone responds so differently to meds. I believe you have to keep trying and "turning over all the stones" with the meds. I have found it helpful to keep a journal, especially when trying new meds, to note behaviors, etc. I have also compiled a list of all the meds he has been on and the doses, the effects, and so on. We are up to twenty-four meds in three years! The list is very helpful to look back on.

Fortunately, we found a combination of meds and he is doing quite well now.

We thought it appropriate to close this chapter in much the way we opened it: with one more story of a child who feels and behaves well now, who is once again capable of smiling and participating in life, in family life, *and in her childhood*—all due to treatment with the proper medication.

After years of tantrums and misbehaviors that only another parent of a child with bipolar disorder could understand, Micaela has finally been placed on medication that is making a huge difference.

A while ago, my husband went to Micaela's weekly doctor appointment. He said to the doctor: "We can't stand it anymore. We can't live with her. You have to do something. It's been five years. You have to help us."

His upset was so great that the doctor finally agreed to try something different. (She hadn't, to this point, agreed with the diagnosis of bipolar disorder that two previous psychiatrists had given.) She tapered the existing med (an SSRI) and then started Micaela on Lithobid a week later.

The first week on Lithobid was awful. The SSRI had finally left her system and the lithium hadn't kicked in. Then a powerful change began to take place.

The child was transformed. She can wait for things now. We can say "no" to her. She can accept disappointment. She has stopped teasing and tormenting her sibs. She has been getting along with her sister. They even asked to go back to sharing a room. A month ago her sister Anna (age nine) was saying that she wished she lived with another family because she hated Micaela so much she would give up living with the rest of us just to get away from her.

Micaela is sweet and loving and funny. She asked me yesterday if she could help me fold the laundry. She came home an hour early last night from a neighbor's house because it got to be "too much" for her (the noise, excitement), and she was attuned to herself enough to know she couldn't take it anymore.

Her behaviors were *not* part of her personality. She was *not* suffering from "middle-child syndrome." She was *not* trying to get more attention focused on herself. My husband and I are *not* bad parents. She was ill, and after many years, countless hours of anguish, many lost friendships, months of lost learning and schoolwork, a lifetime of heartache, she is better.

It's not perfect. She wigs out a little at night. We also have her on risperidone, and we moved the dosing time from bedtime to 5:00 P.M., which helps. We're thrilled with the 80 to 85 percent that we have her "normal." We'll gladly take the small percentage of time when she's her "old" self. She has no side effects to the medications. She remains bubbly and chipper.

I am so grateful for what has happened. I will take it as it comes and not dare hope that this will last a lifetime. But I now have hope and I now have proof that I have a wonderful child who was trapped in a prison of her illness. Seeing her like this makes it all worthwhile, and I am so thankful that we never gave up as we were tempted to so many times.

I hope this will give a lift to someone who may be struggling at this point and wondering if there will ever be an end in sight. Don't give up the fight!

# The Genetic Aspects of Bipolar Disorder

Rarely does a person speak of only one family member with depression or manic depression. More often two or more relatives are affected, as these illnesses tend to run in families. That these illnesses are passed down through the generations was recognized long before we understood the nature of genes and the genetic code. Among the first to remark on this heritable tendency was Emil Kraepelin, the father of modern psychiatry. Kraepelin was a German physician who spent countless hours with the mentally ill, carefully noting their symptoms and the course of their illness. He observed that of his patients who suffered from manic depression, over 80 percent had positive family histories. In 1921 Kraepelin reported on nine hundred patients and found that the greatest frequency of initial attacks of the illness occurred between the ages of fifteen and twenty.

Today, children with bipolar disorder tend to experience the first episode of illness ten years earlier than their parents. Several studies have confirmed that in every generation following World War II, there is a higher incidence and earlier age of onset of both bipolar and recurrent depressive illness. And it is anticipated that in the coming decades, a lifetime hazard of a broad spectrum of mood disorders will occur that is greatly in excess of the rates observed in previous generations.

## The Amish Studies

Dr. Janice Egeland of the University of Miami School of Medicine has been conducting an important and imaginative study with a group of people who dress in plain clothes and live much as they did when they first came to America in the eighteenth century.

In many ways the Amish community provides a living laboratory for all genetic research. They are a well-defined, closed population, numbering some twelve thousand people, with little migration into or out of the community. They are able to trace their ancestry back to thirty original progenitors, and they keep extensive geneologic records. Very important, the couples marry young in life and the community encourages a very high birth rate, thereby allowing genetic researchers to study large and multigenerational families.

Because of a long-standing trusting relationship with Dr. Egeland, the Amish have been extremely cooperative with her and colleagues from several universities and the National Institute of Mental Health (NIMH). These scientists have been engaged in a longitudinal study on the genetic basis of bipolar disorder.

Readers will be especially interested in one aspect of the study in which the children of Bipolar I parents are being observed over time. The researchers have made a surprisingly discordant finding: Data from the first completed interviews of two hundred at-risk children suggest a different symptom presentation from the one depicted by recent research findings in the non-Amish population at large.

First of all, few Amish children who go on to develop bipolar disorder are reported to have the same early comorbid conditions. For example, separation anxiety, symptoms of attention-deficit disorder with hyperactivity, and oppositional defiant behaviors are uncommon. While anger dyscontrol and bossiness are frequently present in the Amish bipolar children, the degree and intensity of these symptoms seem markedly tempered in comparison with children diagnosed with the disorder in the general population.

The regularity and simplicity of the Amish lifestyle, characterized by consistent social values, a philosophy of nonviolence, strong family and community kinship structures, and a proscribed daily, weekly, and monthly schedule centering around the church provide focus and structure to the social world. The absence of electricity weds the Amish to the natural daily and seasonal light/dark cycles, and—in comparison to the ordinary American child—introduces a complete buffer to overstimulation.

These social and environmental buffers may modify many behaviors that could reach their extreme pitch in families that do not have such defined social and religious values and cannot provide such consistent boundaries.

## NATURE VERSUS NURTURE

So this brings us to the age-old question: What part does the inheritance of genetic material ("nature") contribute to early-onset bipolar disorder, and what part does the environment ("nurture") play in this form of the illness? In order to disentangle the subtle strands of heredity from environmental influence, scientists turned to the classic methods of examining the nature/nurture controversy—twin and adoption studies.

Monozygotic (identical) twins share the same genes, whereas dizygotic (fraternal) twins share 50 percent of their genes, the same as any set of siblings. By looking at the frequency with which monozygotic and dizygotic twins share the same illness (the so-called concordance rate), scientists can get an idea of the genetic and environmental contributions to a problem. If a trait is wholly genetic and one partner of an identical-twin pair develops an illness, then the other twin will develop it also. Their concordance rate—the rate of similarity—would be 100 percent. For a simple genetic disorder, monozygotic twins will usually have close to a 100 percent concordance, whereas the concordance for dizygotic twins will be anywhere from 25 percent to 50 percent, depending on how many copies (one or two) of the abnormal gene are needed in order for the disease to occur.

Seven twin studies gathered from five countries examined the rates of mood disorders for identical twins and pegged the combined concordance rates at 76 percent. However, nearly all these twin pairs were raised in the same homes, so the issue of nature versus nurture remained unresolved.

Scientific researchers then looked at identical twins raised apart from each other. They examined twelve pairs of identical twins adopted away from each other at birth and found that eight of the twelve pairs—or 67 percent—were concordant for major depressive or bipolar disorders. These data suggest that there is indeed a genetic component at play but that the disorder is not wholly genetic. Environmental factors must be interacting with the genetic trait in some way.

## BIPOLAR DISORDER AND ALCOHOLISM

Perhaps the differences in the presentation of the illness early on in the Amish and non-Amish children may be accounted for by more than simply the "gentler" way of life and greater social structure that exists in the Amish community.

Alcoholism and substance abuse are rare conditions in the Amish. In comparison, alcoholism in combination with bipolar disorder in the general population seems to be quite common—particularly where early-onset bipolar disorder is concerned.

Dr. Richard Todd and colleagues at Washington University in St. Louis found increased rates of mood disorders and alcoholism among the adult relatives of seventy-six prepubertal children who were initially diagnosed with major depressive disorder. All of these children were followed over two to five years by Dr. Barbara Geller. Within this period, almost 30 percent of these children progressed from depressive to Bipolar I or Bipolar II disorders. The rates of alcoholism were higher in adult relatives of bipolar children (20.3 percent) than in relatives of those children diagnosed with depression only (12.3 percent). Follow-up studies in this latter group of children now being conducted by Dr. Geller will likely yield important information.

As we transferred information from our questionnaires to coding sheets to enter the findings in a database, we were struck by a consistently recurring pattern: In the majority of the children who had been diagnosed with bipolar disorder before the onset of puberty, the family histories revealed mood disorders and/or alcoholism coming down both the maternal *and* paternal sides. Analysis of the data showed that over 80 percent had this unique "bilineal transmission."

Now that the bipolar/alcoholism link is being studied in the families of children with early-onset bipolar disorder, the question arises: Could the same heritable tendencies predispose one family member to bipolar disorder, another to alcoholism, and a third to the combination of the two? And, if this is so, does environmental influence play a presiding role in the frequency of expression of these different manifestations of the illness in the general population? Does some other genetic variable play a modifying role? Is it the combination of nature shaping the expression of certain biologically based temperamental traits that modify and are modified by experience—traits that may bias the way an individual registers, elicits, and reacts to stimuli from the environment or, alternatively, influences choices about mate selection?

Individuals who share temperamental and behavioral traits are often attracted to others with similar predispositions. *Assortative mating,* the tendency for individuals with similar phenotypes to mate more frequently than expected by chance, has been reported for a variety of complex traits, including mood disorders. Evidence from a number of controlled studies suggests that the degree of assortative mating is higher for individuals with bipolar disorder than for those with major depression. One study by Drs. Kathleen Merinkangas and David Spiker found a high degree of diagnostic concordance between the patients and spouses for both affective illness and alcoholism, again with a higher degree of assortative mating among bipolar patients than among unipolar patients.

## GENETICS 101

The completion of the Human Genome Project in 2003 and the developments in the field of biotechnology are increasing our knowledge of behavioral genetics at breakneck speed. Having established that the familial loading for bipolar disorder is primarily due to genes, the next step, of course, is to try to find those genes.

When scientists declare their intention to find the gene for a disease, they do not mean that there is a specific gene for that problem. Everyone, for all intents and purposes, is born with the same set of genes, except for those found on the sex chromosomes (X and Y); men have genes on the Y-chromosome that are not found in women, and women have two X-chromosomes while men have only one. Consequently, women have twice as many X-chromosome-linked genes as men. However, women inactivate half of the genes on their X-chromosomes, so, in effect, the number of active genes is the same for both sexes.

Otherwise, we all share the same basic genetic structure—some 25,000 genes in all—arranged in the same order in everyone, from chromosome number 1 to chromosome number 22. The phrase "finding a gene for a disease" actually means finding a DNA mutation in a particular gene. There are no bipolar genes, per se; rather, there are genes found throughout humanity that are altered—mutated in some fashion—in patients with bipolar disorder.

## DNA: The Stuff of Life

Genes are made of DNA, which, in turn, is constructed from chemical units called nucleotides, the letters of the DNA alphabet. There are four nucleotides in the kingdom of animals: adenine, thymine, guanine, and cytosine (A, T, G, and C in scientific shorthand), as well as in the plant and bacterial kingdoms, repeated over and over again. The entire complement of DNA found in an organism is referred to as a *genome*. The human genome contains more than three billion nucleotides, about the same number found in the genomes of mice and rats.

Genes contain the instruction, in a coding message based on the order of nucleotides, for generating a protein. Proteins, in turn, are the major workhorses of cells. They are used, along with lipids, to construct the membranes that surround cells—the scaffolding that holds them together—and the enzymes, receptors, and chemical transporters needed for cells to function properly. If DNA is the blueprint of life, proteins are the bricks and mortar.

However, the genes that generate proteins are not the same in every individual. If they were, we would all look alike and, to some extent, behave in identical ways. DNA is slightly different from individual to individual—about 0.1 percent different. The genetic differences between humans are due to variations in genes caused by mutations in DNA that have arisen randomly in the course of evolution.

The term *mutation* usually refers to a single nucleotide change in a gene's blueprint that results in some alteration in the protein coded by that gene. That alteration could be quantitative, resulting in either an increase or a decrease in the efficiency with which the protein is synthesized. Alternatively, the blueprint alteration caused by mutation can change the genetic code, resulting in the synthesis of a protein whose structure and function are defective (the sickle-cell anemia mutation is an example).

Mutation is not the only factor that is capable of changing the DNA blueprint; pieces of genes can break off, turn around, or move from one chromosome to another. The same fundamental problem occurs—the protein encoded by that dysfunctional gene will be affected in some manner, sometimes with dire consequences, as seen in some inherited disorders and in the development of cancer. However, most variations in the genome have no effect on the organism, because they occur in the vast wasteland of DNA. More than 95 percent of the genome does not contain genes.

## GENETIC VARIATION AND ENVIRONMENTAL INFLUENCE

But how do these changes in DNA lead to the kinds of symptoms that we see in bipolar disorder? For some genetic disorders, changes in DNA can affect someone in subtle ways: by increasing susceptibility to conditions that arise later in life, for example, or by interacting with an environmental factor that exposes an underlying inherited flaw. Someone born with the genetic predisposition to develop blood clots in their veins may not have any manifestation of the problem until they develop a leg vein thrombosis during a period of prolonged immobility such as a long plane ride.

Bipolar disorder and several other psychiatric problems may occur in this manner. Children are born with a few susceptibility genes, but the disease may not emerge until adolescence, if at all.

The environmental factors that may trigger the development of bipolar disorder in a genetically susceptible person are not yet clear, but arousal disorders of sleep, such as night terrors, sleep deprivation, sensitivity to seasonal change, the social stresses of adolescence, being away at school, and experimentation with drugs and alcohol could all be contributing factors. We know that bipolar disorder is sensitive to the environmental influence in general and, specifically, to the effect of seasonal change, and that alterations in the timing of sleep may trigger the onset or offset of episodes of depression and mania.

Peak episodes of mania and depression have long been observed to occur in the fall and the spring. Seasonal changes, sleep duration, and the preference for a time to go to sleep and a time to get up (known as *morningness-eveningness*) differ significantly among twins with bipolar disorder compared to twins without the disorder. This "night owl" phenomenon—increased activity in the evening hours—is a common diurnal variation reported by parents of children with bipolar disorder.

Morningness-eveningness is influenced by the circadian system and is specifically determined by circadian-clock-relevant genes. Bipolar twins also have greater seasonal changes in sleep duration and mood. Sunny days have been found to have a greater positive effect on well-being in the bipolar twins compared to non-bipolar twins.

These individual differences are potentially shaped by genes that influence sleep timing, and the way children respond to light/dark cycle transitions and seasonal variations can have important behavioral consequences. Genetic variation may predispose to the tendency to develop symptoms such as sleep/wake reversals (common in children diagnosed with bipolar disorder and thought to be a major trigger for episodes of mood instability during seasonal change). It is in this way that multiple genes, in combination with environmental stressors, may be at play.

## GENETIC VARIATION AND TEMPERAMENT

Temperament and the individual differences associated with it are thought of as the behavioral style of an individual—the behavioral phenotype. To talk of a child's temperament is to refer to his or her mode of emotional response. It is a difficult concept to capture in words. Dr. Richard Allport (Baba Ram Das), formerly a professor of psychology at Harvard University, describes temperament as "the characteristic phenomenon of an individual's emotional nature, including the susceptibility to emotional stimulation, his customary speed of response to stimuli, and the quality of his prevailing mood."

To some extent, temperament is genetic and heritable. Emerging clinical research suggests that bipolar children inherit a basic set of temperamental traits, such as easy arousal, over-reactivity to stress, poor modulation of impulses, behavioral inhibition, and fear of harm. All these temperamental traits could contribute to the development of many clinical features such as mood deregulation, rejection sensitivity, avoidant and oppositional behaviors, and co-morbid anxiety disorders.

Individual differences in the way children respond to environmental stimuli can have important consequences for their ability to pay attention and learn to adapt to the environment as well as for how they navigate interpersonal relationships. For example, there is strong evidence to support the existence of a specific temperament type in infancy that involves heightened distress to novel and unfamiliar stimuli. These infants tend to develop into children who avoid people, objects, and situations that are novel or unfamiliar. Infants who exhibit this temperament are likely, as they get older, to display behavioral inhibition-wariness and heightened vigilance of the unfamiliar, particularly in social situations.

Behavioral and physiological features of this temperament, termed *behavioral inhibition,* are moderately stable from infancy into early adolescence. The underlying biology of this temperament has been linked to neural systems supporting fear responses in animals.

Dr. Carl Schwartz and his colleagues at Harvard Medical School found that adults who had been categorized at age two as inhibited, compared with those previously categorized as uninhibited, showed greater functional MRI signal response within the amygdala to novel versus familiar faces. These findings led investigators to suggest that this temperament is, in part, due to variation in amygdalar responses to novelty.

## Temperament and Psychiatric Illness

One important line of inquiry has been to ask this question: To what degree does temperament correlate with a predisposition to psychiatric illness?

Behavioral inhibition has been found to be a familial and developmental risk factor for panic and phobic anxiety, or social withdrawal disorders. Co-morbid anxiety disorders are common clinical manifestations in juvenile-onset bipolar disorder. A newly defined behavioral phenotype for juvenile-onset bipolar disorder known as the Core Phenotype has been found to be strongly correlated with a behavioral trait marker Fear of Harm, found to be highly concordant in a study of 465 sibling pairs. (This will be discussed in the next chapter.)

Evidence is already emerging that mood and anxiety disorders result from partially common causative factors—a combination of genetic vulnerability and experience. Temperamental dimensions such as behavioral inhibition and Fear of Harm are complex traits, potentially associated with various psychiatric disorders, and they are already a focus of DNA analysis.

By combining quantitative genetics and molecular genetic strategies with new methods in the study of animal behavior, researchers are now increasingly able to explore the genetic basis of these conditions that broach the interface between nature and nurture.

## MOLECULAR GENETIC APPROACHES TO GENE DISCOVERY

It's sobering to think that somewhere in the three billion nucleotides that make up the human genome a few tiny changes may exist—perhaps in two or three genes that generate proteins expressed in the brain—that may cause a child to develop bipolar disorder later in life, perhaps only awaiting a trigger.

A few letter changes in an otherwise normal three-billion-nucleotide genome is the equivalent of a couple of spelling errors in 5,000 two-hundred-page books. The challenge is to find the genetic spelling mistakes. With this information, scientists will better understand the neurobiology of bipolar disorder and, one hopes, determine more effective ways to prevent or treat the problem.

## Chromosomal Damage: An Eye into the Storm

One method that human geneticists use to identify genes responsible for disease is to analyze a person's chromosomes to look for signs of breakage or damage. Chromosomes are sometimes damaged during meiosis, the process that generates eggs and sperm. Chromosomal injury can disrupt genes, altering their function in some capacity, usually destroying the ability of the damaged gene to instruct cells to produce its encoded protein. Chromosomal damage occurs spontaneously; it's an intrinsic property of DNA. So, two otherwise normal parents can conceive a child with a chromosome abnormality not present in either one of them. However, if a damaged chromosome does not affect survival or reproductive fitness, it can be passed down to children.

After many years of carrying out studies designed to detect chromosomal damage in psychiatric disorders, two very promising, albeit very rare, findings have emerged. One involves a condition called Velocardiofacial Syndrome (VCFS), a congenital disorder that occurs in about one in every 2,000 to 5,000 live births. The other finding is an extremely rare abnormality found in one family in Scotland; this abnormality is not named, only assigned the cryptic genetic designation *translocation* (1;11) (q42.1;q14.3). Translocation is the movement of a specific gene fragment from one chromosomal location to another, which often alters or abolishes expression of the gene.

## VELOCARDIOFACIAL SYNDROME (VCFS)

In VCFS, a piece of chromosome 22 containing some two dozen genes has been lost. The loss of so many genes can cause severe problems: children with VCFS have congenital heart disease, cleft palate, learning disabilities, and an assortment of other ailments. The condition was first discovered in the 1970s by a speech pathologist specializing in genetic disorders of communication, Dr. Robert Shprintzen, who was then at the Albert Einstein College of Medicine. Children and adults with VCFS were also found to suffer from a variety of psychiatric problems, including ultrarapid cycling bipolar disorder, schizophrenia, ADHD, and OCD. Although the gene responsible for the most important physical problems found in VCFS has been identified, scientists still haven't determined which others cause the many psychiatric problems.

Translocation caused schizophrenia and bipolar disorder in members of the Scottish family mentioned above, the only family known as yet to have this defect. Three genes are affected by the disrupted chromosome, but the one on which scientists have focused is DISCI (an acronym for *disrupted in schizophrenia*). Although investigators are just now learning how DISCI works, early evidence shows that the protein for which it encodes is involved in the migration of neurons during development. This process is critical for the formation of the cerebral cortex, the part of the brain that makes humans, well, human.

Although the (1;11)(q42.1;q14.3) translocation is rare, this "experiment of nature" has provided a key to understanding how schizophrenia and bipolar disorder may emerge. Studying DISCI function has provided scientists with a target gene to study in other patients with bipolar disorder and schizophrenia. If chromosomal damage involving DISCI can cause psychiatric problems, perhaps more subtle types of abnormalities can do the same. Recently, investigators at the Johns Hopkins School of Medicine identified a DISCI mutation that seems to be responsible for causing schizophrenia and schizoaffective disorder in one family. Other mutations are likely to be found when the DISCI gene is analyzed more extensively.

While no one really knows precisely how many genes are involved in bipolar disorder, dozens may ultimately be found. That is not to say that any one person with bipolar disorder needs to inherit dozens of different genetic variants. In reality, combinations of any two or three could likely cause the onset. Indeed, there are dozens of susceptibility genes, and only a few are needed for bipolar disorder to emerge. The implication is that different combinations of problematic genes will be found in patients who seemingly have the same clinical problem. It is this "heterogeneity" that has complicated the discovery of bipolar genes.

Since the overwhelming majority of patients with bipolar disorder do not harbor visible chromosomal defects, another strategy has to be used to identify the genetic culprits. How can we locate problem genes in a three-billion-nucleotide genome when there are no clues that signal their whereabouts?

## LINKAGE ANALYSIS: A METHOD FOR FINDING HIDDEN GENES

Remarkably, human geneticists do have a method for finding hidden genes, and it's called *linkage analysis*. Simply put (and by no means is this a simple process), linkage analysis is a technique used by geneticists to identify the chromosomal position of genes through their association with other genes whose chromosomal positions have already been established.

As we mentioned earlier, each human has two copies of every chromosome, one inherited from each parent, except for the sex chromosomes. During meiosis, the chromosome pairs separate so that only a single copy is found in each germ cell. During fertilization, chromosome pairs—one from the mother and one from the father—are reunited in the newly formed embryo. If one parent transmits two genetic traits located on different chromosomes, the probability of passing them both down to a child (assuming that only a single copy of the gene causing the trait is sufficient) is one in four. This is similar to getting heads on two consecutive coin tosses. However, if both traits are located close together on the same chromosome, they will both be transmitted together as a unit. The probability of their both ending up in the same germ cell becomes one in two. In other words, linked genes are co-inherited (there are complicated caveats to this idealized version of linkage, which for the sake of simplicity will not be discussed here).

Geneticists carry out this "coin toss" scenario—linkage analysis—using many markers evenly dispersed on every chromosome, to determine if the disease under investigation is co-inherited with any particular marker. Typically, about four hundred markers are needed to scan the entire genome in initial experiments. These studies are usually carried out in large families with a genetic illness in at least three generations of living relatives. When a marker and the disease under investigation are not co-inherited, they are assumed to be located on different chromosomes. That would be expected to be the case for the overwhelming majority of markers. However, when a marker is consistently inherited in every member of a family with the illness under investigation, it suggests that the gene responsible for the disease and the marker are located close together on the same chromosome.

So, if a marker is known to be located at a specific chromosomal position, say somewhere near the tip of one end of chromosome 11, and that marker is consistently co-inherited with a disease, then the gene responsible for the disease must be on the tip of chromosome 11 also. In essence, linkage is guilt by association.

Linkage analysis, mapping the chromosomal position of an unknown gene, is a strategy geneticists have used since the early twentieth century, from the very beginning of genetics as a scientific discipline. Scientists used this method to successfully map the chromosomal position of the genes responsible for cystic fibrosis, Huntington's disease, and most other simple genetic disorders.

However, mapping is just the beginning of the process. The mapped position may be quite extensive, spanning a region containing millions of nucleotides and dozens of different genes. Much more work has to be carried out before the actual gene and its disease-causing mutation are identified.

## THE HUMAN GENOME PROJECT

The situation for geneticists has improved significantly ever since the early 1990s, when the Huntington's disease gene was identified. Today, scientists have the information collected from the human genome project at their disposal. The entire human genome, all three billion nucleotides of it, has been decoded. Special computer algorithms have been designed to fish out the small percentage of the genome—approximately 5 percent—that contains genes that actually code for proteins. A map of the entire sequence of the human genome and the 25,000 gene blueprints it contains can be viewed by anyone with Internet access.

In the past, millions of dollars and many years of laboratory work were needed to find a gene whose general location had been mapped by linkage analysis. Now, with a few clicks on a computer mouse, investigators can identify the likely candidate genes for the problem being investigated while they drink their morning coffee! There is still work to be done to identify the mutation responsible in those genes, but most of the painstaking labor has been done courtesy of the hundreds of scientists involved in the two competing initiatives that resulted in the decoding of the human genome.

We asked Herb Lachman, M.D., a psychiatric geneticist at the Albert Einstein College of Medicine in New York City, why, if linkage analysis is so straightforward, it has proven so difficult to identify the genes for bipolar disorder. He replied:

> Linkage analysis in its original design cannot be used to map complicated genetic problems, a category that certainly applies to inherited psychiatric disorders. There are too many genes to sort out. Even in individual families, there may be several different genes to consider, any combination of which could cause illness in affected family members. Linkage analysis falls apart when you can't establish a consistent connection between the disease and a single set of markers. . . .
>
> Fortunately, psychiatric geneticists were introduced to a new form of linkage analysis, invented by a few very clever statisticians, which provided investigators with the necessary mathematical and computational tools needed to map complicated genetic disorders. The novel solution to the problem involved increasing the number of subjects in the primary analysis. Instead of a few large family pedigrees, hundreds or thousands of subjects needed to be recruited, and new statistical programs to assess the genetics data in a novel manner had to be created.
>
> Armed with these tools, investigators from all over the world have mapped a number of different regions of the genome in psychiatric disorders. Schizophrenia has been the most thoroughly investigated, with bipolar disorder lagging behind. The findings show that discrete regions on chromosomes 1, 4, 6, 8, 13, 15, 18, 21 and 22, to name a few, harbor schizophrenia and bipolar susceptibility genes.

## TECHNOLOGICAL BREAKTHROUGHS: THE DISCOVERY OF NEW DNA MARKERS AND THE INVENTION OF DNA CHIPS

Simply mapping a gene to a specific chromosomal region is a big first step, but more work has to be done to find the actual gene and the responsible mutations. In complex traits such as bipolar disorder, the mapped region is usually fairly wide, extending tens of millions of nucleotides, each containing fifty to a hundred genes. Choosing the correct one for a more comprehensive analysis is difficult. Scientists, therefore, have to use a more refined form of genetic analysis to more precisely pinpoint the locations of the responsible genes. Refined analysis translates into using more genetic markers—many more. In fact, so many markers need to be analyzed to precisely map a complex trait that, with a few notable exceptions, entire new technologies had to be developed before it could even be attempted.

The two most important technological breakthroughs in the field of molecular genetics have been the discovery of DNA markers called SNPs (pronounced "snips") and the invention of DNA chips.

## Single Nucleotide Polymorphisms (SNPs)

A SNP is the most common type of genetic variant in the human genome, occurring on average once in every one thousand nucleotides of DNA. Tens of millions exist in the human genome. Several million have already been discovered in the course of the Human Genome Project and by savvy biotech companies who invested tens of millions of dollars in SNP discovery efforts. The analysis of SNPs holds the key to tackling complex traits and improving human health.

The simplest way to understand SNPs is that they create a detailed map of the human genome at its most ultimate level of resolution. Whereas the older generation of genetic markers generated a map equivalent to a geographical map of the United States displaying the outline of every county, the layout of the genome organized by SNPs is more like a map displaying every street in every city in America.

A SNP is similar to the binary code used in computer logic. Imagine each SNP as a light switch: when in the ON position, the SNP has a certain DNA pattern or sequence; when in the OFF position, the SNP is in the form of its mutant partner. The DNA sequence ATATATGATATTT-GGCAAAATAAAGATACA on a region of chromosome 8 is found in 65 percent of Caucasians and about 87 percent of African Americans. However, at the bolded C nucleotide is a SNP, a mutation. Instead of a C, a T is found in 35 percent of Caucasians and 13 percent of African Americans. Similarly, farther down the DNA road on chromosome 8 about 800 nucleotides away is another SNP (a C to T change) found at a certain frequency in the population; and another 500 nucleotides farther, an A to G change, and so on through the entire genome.

## Haplotypes

Consecutive SNPs form a structure geneticists call a *haplotype*. So, one individual may have a haplotype on one of his or her chromosomes number 8 consisting of C-C-A, depending on which versions of the three SNPs described above were passed down from a parent. This same haplotype pattern is shared by a certain percentage of the population. The other chromosome from the other parent could contain the same or a different haplotype. For argument's sake, let's assume it's different, say, C-T-A. Someone else may have a T-T-G haplotype on one chromosome 8 and a C-C-G on the other. These haplotypes are used as maps by geneticists, as they can identify the location of disease-causing mutation by determining whether a particular haplotype is co-inherited with a disease.

For example, by analyzing haplotypes throughout the human genome, or within a region targeted by linkage analysis in large numbers of patients and a large number of controls, geneticists can determine if one particular haplotype is found more commonly in patients than in a control group. If true, then the disease-causing mutation has to be very close to the haplotype, and, since haplotypes are generated by SNPs that are close together, the sought-after mutation must be nearby as well.

Here is Dr. Lachman's analogy for the actual process of identifying genes through haplotyping: If someone (the disease-causing mutation) is waiting for you on an unnamed street, but she tells you it is one block east of Main, Elm, and Spruce streets (the haplotype), you will have no problem finding her. If the only information you had was that she was sitting on an unnamed street in Orange County, California (corresponding to a less detailed genome map), you would have great difficulty finding her.

The problem with a detailed map is that the number of markers one has to analyze is much greater than with crude maps. To map a gene with SNPs and SNP haplotypes, thousands, perhaps hundreds of thousands, need to be analyzed. With so many different markers requiring analysis, it is virtually impossible to carry out such studies using standard genetic techniques. The biotech industry came to the rescue with an innovative new tool called the gene chip.

## Gene Chips (Microarrays)

Developed by a biotech company called Affymetrix, gene chips are glass slides or silicone chips that contain thousands of DNA molecules. Each specific DNA molecule is firmly attached at a designated site on the chip, an address, if you will. Some chips are fabricated with DNA molecules that have first been synthesized in bacteria or in a test tube and then spotted onto the chip; others contain DNA molecules that have been synthesized directly onto the chip.

When Dr. Lachman explains microarray technology, it's like standing with him in a laboratory. He asks one to picture a one-inch-square slide divided into one hundred evenly spaced rows and columns of tiny dots. Each dot contains a large quantity of a specific DNA molecule, 10,000 dots (100 × 100). Each set of DNA molecules has the ability to attach to DNA molecules introduced by the investigator that are similar in sequence. So, for example, let's say that the dot located at row 90, column 16, corresponds to the gene for the serotonin transporter (which codes for the protein that is targeted by Prozac and several other antidepressants). If an investigator introduces to that chip DNA from a test sample, the serotonin transporter gene sequences present in the sample will bind to the spot at row 90, column 16, and nowhere else. If the test DNA is labeled with a sensitive dye (a fluorescent chemical is usually used), the spot will, in essence, light up like a firefly's belly.

The fluorescent signal is then measured by a photo detector, and the data are recorded onto a computer file. In an actual experiment, all or most of the dots will light up as each DNA molecule on the chip captures its corresponding partner in the test sample. The dots on the chip will light up in a seemingly chaotic display of signals of various intensities, corresponding to the amount of partner DNA each dot captured.

These DNA marker chips contain the sequences that correspond to the ON–OFF signals of tens of thousands of SNPs. If someone has two copies of a particular SNP, either the ON dot *or* the OFF dot will light up. Someone else, with one copy of each, will generate a signal in *both* the ON and OFF dots. This pattern is repeated for each of the thousands of SNPs loaded onto the chip. Only a computer is capable of making sense of the varying intensity of fluorescent-light signals.

Dr. Lachman summed up the exciting work that he and his colleagues are doing in laboratories across the world and how fast things are moving. He likened the speed in invention to Moore's law in computer design:

Gordon Moore postulated, correctly it turns out, that every 18 months, the number of transistors and resistors that could be placed onto a computer chip would double because of technological advances.

The number of dots fabricated onto a DNA chip is also doubling at a fantastic rate. The biotech company Perlegen, which spun off from Affymetrix a couple of years ago, is a pioneer in chip manufacturing, and has developed a chip capable of analyzing 100,000 SNPs all at once.

## The "HapMap": A Detailed Haplotype Map of the Human Genome

Making sense of all the possible haplotypes generated by researchers posed a considerable problem. However, in 2005 an international team of investigators from more than forty academic centers and private companies, including Perlegen, analyzed millions of SNPs and constructed a "HapMap," a detailed haplotype map of the human genome. This map will make it easier for investigators to identify the location of genes responsible for complex traits. In addition, the map will be used by investigators to identify markers associated with adverse responses to medications and environmental pollutants, as well as to predict which patients will respond to a particular class of medications. With the exception of the AmpliChip, discussed in Chapter 4, and the rates of metabolism it reveals about a few medications, psychiatrists can use only clinical observation to determine whether a medication is having a therapeutic effect, and, in most instances, they can only wait for side effects to occur before realizing that the dosing or medication may need adjusting or changing.

## Personalized Medicine: Genetic Variation and the Identification of Disease Vulnerability

In addition to its use as a research tool that will uncover the genes involved in bipolar disorder, DNA chip analysis will one day be ordered as a routine clinical test to help determine disease susceptibility (so that appropriate preventive measures can be instituted), which medications should be tried, and which medications should be avoided.

The era of personalized medicine will be enormously beneficial to people, but it must be accompanied by strict privacy laws so that disease susceptibility cannot be factored into insurance or employment opportunities.

## "WHAT ARE THE CHANCES THAT OUR NEXT CHILD COULD HAVE THE ILLNESS?"

Advances in molecular biology will no doubt shed much light on the causes of early-onset bipolar disorder, but parents of these children are desperate for answers to some more immediate concerns. They want to know: "If we have the risk factors [the positive family history, perhaps linked to alcoholism], what are the chances that any of our other [or future] children will develop the illness?" This is an extremely difficult question to answer.

The likelihood of developing bipolar disorder is many times greater in relatives of patients with mood disorders than in the general public (although the illness can, and often does, skip a generation). Overall, researchers have observed that a first-degree relative (parents, siblings, or children) of a bipolar patient has a 13 to 35 percent risk of developing a mood disorder of any type. The offspring of two ill parents have at least double the risk for mood disorders in comparison with the offspring of one affected parent. Likewise, it has been consistently reported that the risk for an individual to develop mood disorders increases significantly if both a parent and a sibling are ill, in contrast to an individual with *either* an ill parent or sibling.

The chart that follows is merely a general guide for the risk to various relatives. It is important to remember that there is considerable variation in reported risk figures among investigators as a result of differences in methods and diagnostic criteria used in the various studies. In addition, the chart does not include the influence of alcoholism, which, as discussed earlier, appears to confer a greater risk for early-onset forms of bipolar disorder.

| RELATIVE | BIPOLAR PATIENT (%) |
|---|---|
| Identical twin | 70 |
| Fraternal twin | 15–25 |
| Offspring of one ill parent | 15–30 |
| Offspring of two ill parents | 50–75 |
| Sibling | 15–25 |

Second-degree relative            3–7
General population                1

## In Conclusion

This chapter has shown that there is strong evidence for a genetic component in the susceptibility to develop bipolar disorder. But we need to point out again that multiple genes probably are involved in the disorder, each with an addictive effect.

If parents are aware of the existence of genetic risks, they can observe thoughtfully and be ready to intervene early in the life of their child. They also can ensure that their child is not placed on antidepressants without mood stabilizers and attempt to establish regular sleep/wake patterns and social structure in their households. It is hoped that the time is coming soon when a better understanding of what is happening on the level of the genes will bring new and better medications targeted at the primary biological dysfunction and producing minimal side effects.

PART II

# Inside the Brain and Mind

# The Psychological Dimensions

When Melissa and her husband discovered she was pregnant, they were overjoyed about having their first child. As she began to feel the frequent kicks and movements within, Melissa would chuckle to herself and talk about the "Ninja Baby," a nickname that would come to haunt her as Eric grew older.

"The doctor did not need to give him a tap on the bottom, because he was delivered screaming like a banshee," Melissa recalled. "On the night the nurse first brought him to me, he howled so loudly that he woke up every newborn on the wing, and after that he never seemed to be able to get to sleep easily."

Melissa was sure that the bright lights and the activity level in the nursery were overstimulating him, and once she got him home, she would be able to settle him. Eric took to nursing with a voracious suckling instinct, yet he was hard to satisfy and unusually fussy. He was also extremely colicky and a poor and erratic sleeper. Rarely able to sleep for more than four hours, he seemed to have no schedule and did not sleep through the night until he was fourteen months old. When Melissa would try to put him down, or if her husband Tom offered to take him, Eric would struggle so much against leaving her chest, his nails would dig into her skin.

By the time he was a toddler, Melissa began to notice that everything in the house ended up in pieces on the floor. Regardless of where he was or who he was with, Eric always seemed to take up the whole room. At nine months, a very embarrassed nursery school director took Melissa aside to ask if she and her husband would mind if he were moved up to the toddler nursery, as he was bulldozing over all the other children in the room. When he started nursery school, he was easily the most difficult child in the class. Melissa and Tom would share their concerns with friends, family, or the pediatrician, but the usual response was to pass remarks on the difference between boys and girls.

In preschool the problems became even worse, as Eric had a hard time staying in his seat and remaining attentive to his work. Shortly after the family moved to Delaware, Eric started kindergarten. He seemed all right at first, but the problems of staying in his seat and remaining focused continued. Outside of school, the behavioral problems increased. One day, after Melissa refused to buy him candy, Eric ran out of the grocery store and attempted to run across the street. A few times he attacked her— hitting, kicking, and biting. Once, when sent to his room for a time-out, he opened the second-story window, knocked out the screen, and threatened to jump. Later he told his mother that he thought he could fly.

## EARLY SYMPTOMS AND BEHAVIORS

Melissa's story of Eric's early development underscores a number of the most commonly reported early features of children who are later diagnosed with bipolar disorder. From the beginning of her account, we are struck by the high levels of motor activity, the high state of arousal, the volubility of his crying, the sleep disturbance, and the pronounced difficulties in separating from his mother. Also obvious is Eric's impulsiveness, aggressiveness, and grandiosity.

From its earliest manifestation in infancy, often long before the advent of what are considered the cardinal symptoms of mood swings, certain temperamental features and common behavioral responses to environmental triggers arise as precursors in a significant number of children. These temperamental features interact with social experience to shape the child's ability to be and engage in the world and to form behavioral responses, thereby influencing nearly every aspect of the child's development.

If we define these early symptoms and behavioral traits that appear to persist over time, we will be better able to explore the likely impact of their interaction with the major developmental stages of childhood and to learn how these factors may shape the formation of enduring personality characteristics.

Because of the continuing controversy over how early-onset bipolar disorder is defined by the fields of child psychiatry and psychology, and because, until recently, it was thought that the condition was exceedingly rare in childhood, no longitudinal studies that examine the early evolution of symptoms and behaviors have been available to clinicians.

## CHILDREN WHO ARE EASILY STARTLED AND AROUSED

Many children who have bipolar disorder are highly excitable, have problems integrating sensory experience, and clearly have difficulties regulating their level of mental and physical arousal. They have difficulty getting to sleep at night, experience an unusual degree of motor restlessness, and have rapid and prolonged periods of emotional excitability as well as high rates of anxiety symptoms. Frequent bouts of anxiety can be abruptly triggered by any number of stimuli or demands. In early childhood, thunder and lightning, vacuum cleaners—almost any sound that threatens to break or dominate sensory and attentional focus—can induce high levels of arousal and anxiety. By any current definition, these traits are examples of a tendency toward high arousability.

## AROUSAL STATES IN INFANCY

A great deal happens in the first year of the life of an infant, and emotional development starts at the beginning. Through constant interaction with the mother, early social responses and behaviors begin to evolve. We now know that the influence of a select set of experiences in the first year extend far into the future and alter, in some mysterious way, the structures and processes that will emerge in the three-, four-, and five-year-old. To understand the potential behavioral disturbances of early childhood and the evolution of the personality, the defining events of the first weeks and months of infancy must be understood.

Of primary importance is the capacity to manage frustration and to settle into calm states that allow for easy transitions between the several stages of an infant's sleep and arousal states. Recently studies have found that the degree of control an infant has over the range and variation of these states is the best predictor of cognitive and social performance at eighteen months.

An infant progresses through various states of consciousness linked to different levels of central nervous system arousal during the day and night, ranging from deep and light sleep states, to semiconsciousness, then to a very alert state, on to fussy, and then to inconsolable crying. Aroused, alert, and active to quiescent, inattentive, and passive—an infant's early existence consists of transitions back and forth between these states.

The length of sleep cycles (rapid-eye movement [REM] active and non-REM deep sleep) typically changes with maturation. In a full-term infant, sleep and waking occur approximately in four-hour cycles. Within these cycles a baby is in deep sleep for forty-five to fifty minutes and then rouses to become active but remains in light sleep. After a certain period, the infant settles back down into deep sleep. A lack of regularity in these cycles may signal problems in the maturation of the nervous system, particularly in those components that regulate shifts from one state of arousal to another and the timing functions of the transitions from sleep to wakefulness.

Learning to sleep for longer than a four-hour period involves learning how to cope with transitions from REM-active into non-REM deep sleep. It is a complex process that requires the capacity to reach a state of calm and remain in that state for an extended period. For this to happen, the infant's nervous system must be mature enough to tune out stimuli from the environment without waking up. In order to sleep beyond these three- or four-hour cycles, babies must develop reliable behavioral patterns that serve to comfort them when they are trying to move from light sleep into a deeper sleep. Babies who are able to manage these transitions for themselves when frustrated or overstimulated during the day are also more likely to learn patterns necessary for nighttime sleep.

A hereditary predisposition to become aroused easily, leading to internal states that produce motor restlessness (fidgetiness), would certainly tend to counter this natural developmental process. We have already noted the frequent reports of difficulty settling and the irregular and shortened sleep patterns in children who later develop bipolar disorder. The sensitivity to sensory stimulation and overreactive startle responses in these children may be related to the difficulty they seem to have in keeping themselves from falling off to sleep and also waking at short intervals each time they come up to REM sleep. Many of these children have "restless leg syndrome," in which their legs flail around during sleep.

## Arousal and Relaxation

Seen from the outside, the newborn appears to move from a state of relative calm and well-being to intense distress, to the ready intake of milk with blissful satisfaction, to the ebbing of distress, and a return to ease, calm, and well-being. In hunger, the distress soon becomes a generalized discomfort that overtakes the whole body with crying and thrashing about. With nursing the whole body relaxes. It is these states of generalized arousal and heightened anxiety, followed by relief, that characterize the diffuse pleasure and anxious distress of the newborn.

Rooting and sucking are the most reliable activities of newborn babies. When the mother offers a breast or bottle and touches a newborn's cheek, the baby will turn his or her head repeatedly, then gobble the nipple firmly in the mouth. Infants have been observed to suck in a regular pattern of bursts and pauses. Bursts seem to be sequenced in groupings of five to twenty-four sucks per burst. The interval between bursts is a time of rest and recovery as well as a time in which information is processed. Dr. T. Berry Brazelton, founder of the Child Development Unit at Boston Children's Hospital, has suggested that these pauses are important in the early mother-child relationship, since mothers use them to stimulate the infant to return to sucking.

Dr. Brazelton has noted that mothers tend to look down to talk to and jiggle their babies when they pause between bursts of sucking. Infants, in turn, come to anticipate these responses, and over time, the mothers' shaking of the breast actually prolongs the pause as the infants become alert yet relaxed and attend to the signals given by their mothers.

In exchange for these regular pleasurable interactions with the mother, the infant begins to postpone the immediate need to satisfy hunger and perhaps takes the first steps toward acquiring the capacity to regulate need and manage frustration. This patterning may provide one of the earliest experiences of self-other boundary formation and the development of an internal stimulus barrier, foreshadowing the capacity to postpone immediate gratification and to take turns in exchange for the pleasures of social contact with others.

Many mothers of bipolar children commented in their descriptions of early infancy that rooting and suckling behaviors were intense, persistent, and often brooked no interruption. Clearly such patterning, lacking rest and recovery pauses, might displace one of the earliest and most fundamental aspects of bonding and affiliative behavior between mother and child and could contribute to the difficulty in the maturation of natural strategies for managing overaroused states and to subsequent difficulties in initiating social interaction.

## HABITUATION: MANAGING THE SENSORY WORLD

The infant's waking life centers around continuous attempts to achieve sensory and emotional homeostasis. Habituation—the ability to appropriately modulate arousal induced by internal or external sensory experience—is a protective response, a closing down of the nervous system against too much stimulation from the outside. It is essential to newborns' capacity for survival, helping them deal with potentially overwhelming demands on their immature sensory systems. The steady hum of an air conditioner eventually fades away and is lost, until it is switched off and the hum suddenly becomes conspicuous by its absence. Infant studies have found that when presented with a series of bright lights, babies first startle, then gradually respond less and less. The motor responses eventually cease. The increases in heart and respiratory rate that occur after the initial bright light stimulus eventually decreases. The infants begin to breathe deeply and steadily until they appear to go into a deep sleep.

The habituation response can be initiated by auditory, visual, or tactile stimuli. A balance between the capacity to become alert, and evaluate and assess a new stimulus, and the capacity to withdraw interest through inhibition of sensory systems is a critical regulatory function for human survival, and one that may be poorly modulated in children with bipolar disorder.

Studies of an infant's behavioral responses to stimulation—for example, the degree to which a newborn turns away or approaches a stimulus—have found that these early coping responses can evolve into defensive styles, such as psychological avoidance, denial, or confrontational modes in later years. An abundant literature on startle and fear responses in animals confirms the biological and hence genetic basis for these temperamental differences.

## NIGHT TERRORS IN BIPOLAR CHILDREN

A significant number of parents in our survey for the first edition of this book reported wakening in the night with bloodcurdling screams. One mother wrote to us and described her toddler's sleeping hours thus: "My son gets up many times throughout the night, crying, screaming, and thrashing his body. Sometimes his eyes are closed and you can't wake him due to a hypnotic-like state he seems to be in."

When a child is experiencing a night terror and actually remembers it, he or she later reports dreams that are extremely threatening. The content has to do with some predatory person or animal chasing them, or terrible fears of abandonment, such as a parent being killed. Some adults who suffer them and seem to have greater recall speak of ceilings and walls pushing down on them, and others report snakes and spiders slithering and crawling all over the bed or room.

Since other features of bipolar disorder indicate that these children have very low thresholds for arousal (they are easily provoked to anger, are easily excited, have low thresholds for anxiety, and are easily overstimulated by external and internal stimuli), it is not surprising that they experience these physiological states of overarousal during sleep.

In fact, in a study of the relationship between parasomnias (night terrors), sleepwalking, confusional arousals, restless leg syndrome, bedwetting (enuresis), teeth grinding (bruxism), and psychiatric illness in a very large sample of adults, Dr. Maurice Ohayon and his colleagues at the Phillipe Pinel Research Center in Montreal reported a strong association between the adults who experienced night terrors and those diagnosed with bipolar disorder and depression comorbid with anxiety.

In order to discuss night terrors, we need to explain the architecture of sleep and the way night terrors differ from nightmares, for night terrors are not happening during the dreaming period of sleep—rapid-eye-movement sleep—but apparently in the deepest stage of non-REM sleep, or in some transitory state in between.

## THE TYPICAL ARCHITECTURE OF SLEEP

Normally throughout the night a person experiences two kinds of sleep that alternate rhythmically. One is called rapid-eye movement (REM) sleep, during which most dreaming takes place; the other (not surprisingly) is called non-REM. Non-REM sleep has a four-stage development plan as revealed by electroencephalogram (EEG) sleep studies. Stage 1 is the light sleep that begins the night and from which a sleeper may be easily awakened. The brain waves are small and fast. After about a half an hour, the sleeper slips deeper into sleep as stages 2, 3, and 4 of non-REM sleep progress. EEGs of stage 3 reveal larger and slower brain waves. Stage 4 brain waves are large, slow, and regular. This is the deepest period of sleep.

After approximately ninety minutes have passed, a brief period of REM sleep appears (the eyeballs can be observed moving rapidly beneath the eyelids), only to be followed by one of the non-REM stages. A pattern develops in which the REM and non-REM sleep phases alternate with each other, cycling back and forth in a remarkably periodic ebb and flow. Later on in the night, REM sleep asserts itself for longer periods of time. Apparently the sleep cycle oscillates on a ninety-minute time frame. The first ninety-minute cycle might consist of eighty-five minutes of non-REM sleep and five minutes of REM; by the time the fourth cycle rolls around, it might consist of sixty minutes of non-REM and thirty minutes of REM.

But all is not always so regular. As Drs. Mark W. Mahowald and Carlos H. Schenck of the Minnesota Regional Sleep Disorders Center at the University of Minnesota Medical School have written: "The rapid oscillation of states or the inappropriate intrusion of elements of one state into another may result in the appearance of parasomnias, which are particularly apt to occur during the transition periods from one state to another. Given the large number of neural networks, neurotransmitters, and other state-determining substances that must be recruited synchronously, and given the frequent transition among the three states of being, it is surprising that parasomnias do not occur more frequently."

Although people dream during the REM stage of sleep and can usually remember a nightmare or bad dream if it occurs at that time, a child or adult experiences a night terror commonly in stage 4 (and possibly 3) of the non-REM period. It has been supposed that the mind is void during the deeper stages of non-REM sleep, but this may not be true. A person having a night terror will moan, cry, scream, and bolt upright in apparent terror. The heartbeat can be as fast as 160 to 170 beats per minute, which is excessively fast. These rates are similar to those seen in severe panic attacks.

A night terror can last anywhere from five to twenty minutes and though the child's eyes may be open, he or she is still asleep and—typically—inconsolable. A parent should not yell at the child and startle him or her, but make reassuring and soothing sounds and make sure that no glass objects are anywhere near the bed area. Also, halogen or hot lamps could be dangerous with a panicky child thrashing about, so keep the light low and away from the child's body and bedding. Take care to lock or blockade windows that are near the bed (but ensure that another window exit is available in the event of fire).

One mother wrote to us and chillingly described her five-year-old daughter's night terrors. Note the child's degree of panic as well as the imagery of blood and dismemberment:

> In the last few months she had had some very upsetting dreams, with details of children in the school playground that have been stabbed, and seas of blood on the ground. She came into my bedroom to tell me this, dripping with sweat and heart racing. I struggled to calm her down and didn't succeed as she got so worked up she vomited on the bed.
>
> Other dreams include a decapitated man with blood coming from his neck and his head lying on the floor talking to her. We've heard about giant moles rumbling under the ground of her classroom, and apparently this mole was choosing which table of kids he was going to come up and gobble up.

This may explain why children with bipolar disorder seem fixated on blood and knives and always seem under threat. Something is overaroused in the amygdala—the part of the brain that governs "fight or flight." While researchers such as Jonathan Winson, author of *Brain and Psyche: The Biology of the Unconscious,* have suggested that REM sleep preparations were for the formulation of strategies for dealing with local predators (to rehearse and ready the system), this primitive survival mechanism is overstimulated in these children, and, trapped in transitory states from one stage of sleep to another, they are suffering horribly. Is it any wonder that these children are so often in combative and irritable modes and that they are terrified of going to sleep at night?

We are concerned about the effects such parasomnias are having on the psychological development of these children. The rate and frequency of night terrors and nightmares and the nature of the highly disturbing content, which seems referable to fight-or-flight mechanisms, seem coupled with many of the behavioral problems these children have. Many of the behaviors are congruent with "fight": oppositional, defiant, argumentative, defensive behaviors; while other behaviors are more consonant with "fright": anxious, fearful, withdrawn, and phobic. The disturbances in sleep may be contributing to the disturbances within the psyche or reinforcing them on a nightly basis.

## SEPARATION DISTRESS

Our study of 120 children with early-onset bipolar disorder revealed that over 60 percent had some pronounced degree of separation distress, often preceding any other diagnosable psychiatric symptoms. These children expressed great fearfulness and anxiety about the loss of their parents, exaggerated worries about harm befalling their parents, and excessive anxiety when separated from family members.

Many had extreme clinging behaviors. Mothers have told us that they felt as if they and their child were "joined at the hip." They often had to clean the house carrying the child in a sling. One woman said, "If he could crawl back into the womb, he would."

Anxiety and separation distress along with easy arousability, hyperactivity, and distractibility and an exaggerated tendency to overreact to situationally related stress make these children more likely to express avoidant and oppositional behaviors. Taken together, these features represent some of the most pervasive and enduring psychological determinants of the condition.

## SENSORY PROCESSING DEFICITS AND OBJECT CONSTANCY

In bipolar children, well-modulated sensory processing that would provide for fluid transitions between varying states of attention and arousal seems to be lacking. A child who is unable to adequately buffer environmental stimuli will often experience overstimulation. For such a child, it would be quite difficult to sustain attentional focus.

In order for a young child to separate successfully from the mother, an image of the mother must be internalized. "Object constancy" is a term applied to describe the mental process of holding an image of another in conscious awareness long enough to endow it with emotional meaning and to sustain the idea and feeling of a positive, protective source of comfort. It may be that in the bipolar child, the deficits mentioned earlier produce a developmental delay in this psychological function of object constancy. This delay may combine with other factors to set off a reverberating alarm, signaling an almost primal fear at the times of separation from the mother as well as during transitions to unfamiliar settings. Being able to sustain the image of the mother when physically separated from her could become a herculean task.

Dr. Margaret Mahler, the person most associated with a full exploration of infant-mother differentiation, observed that in the progression from a so-called symbiotic phase, where the child is totally dependent on the mother for nutrients and nurturance, to separate functioning, the toddler seems to show two modes or poles of self-orientation. Interest and curiosity about his own body and its functions represent the landmarks of one pole; interest in the mother represents the other.

In infancy, a child's states of well-being and discomfort center more around the presence or absence of the mother. The child psychoanalyst and pediatrician D. W. Winnicott counsels that "at this stage, it is necessary to think of the infant not just as a person who gets hungry, and whose instinctual drives may be met or frustrated, but rather as an immature being who is all the time on the brink of 'unthinkable anxiety.' " For a newborn, this kind of "unthinkable anxiety" is kept at bay by the vitally important function of the mother and her capacity to empathize with her baby—to know what her baby needs and to calm states of high arousal.

This "unthinkable anxiety" is well illustrated by a night terror that occurred over and over again between the ages of four and eight, described by a twelve-year-old boy who had recently been diagnosed with bipolar disorder. He recalled: "I was in a space suit, and I would start floating out there all by myself, and all of a sudden, I would start screaming at the top of my lungs, but no one is there to hear me."

This dream imagery of being locked in a space suit in the vastness of the universe, with no experience of external boundaries, with no possibility of human contact, and the terror of absolute isolation and abandonment, clearly captures the fear of annihilation that many children with this disorder report.

Like newborns, who do not easily or consistently distinguish the experience of inner and outer self and other, children with bipolar disorder often have self and other boundary issues, which—for many—seem to persist long into adolescence and adulthood.

## STAGES OF RAPPROCHEMENT

The period that extends from about the ninth to about the eighteenth month and coincides with what psychoanalyst Phyllis Greenacre termed the child's "love affair with the world" is a primary stage of ego development. The child begins to acquire upright, free locomotion as well as what the pioneer in child development, Jean Piaget, regarded as the beginning of representational intelligence. During this period of rapid development of motor skills and cognitive development, most children have major periods of exhilaration or at least relative elation. These functions absorb so much of the child's energy and attention that the junior toddler appears for a while relatively independent of the mother. But as the child achieves success in these areas, an increasing awareness of separateness develops, and the need for mother's acceptance and renewed participation reasserts itself as the so-called rapprochement stage begins.

How does the child's sense of self-awareness and independence from the mother develop? The child's expanding awareness of the mother as a different entity creates the necessity for him to begin to establish a new form of relationship with her and to negotiate the loss of the familiar symbiotic relationship. It is at this critical juncture that separation anxiety arises, signaling that the child has developed a concept of a separate and differentiated self and that a new developmental pathway has been established. The child then begins to move in two directions, with halting steps forward toward autonomy and regressive pulls backward toward dependency.

What if the development of some critical physiological function, such as habituation, lags behind its normal developmental trajectory? And what if this lag produces a tendency to overrespond to novel stimuli? With the age-appropriate demands for independent functioning, the child would no longer be protected by the mother's capacity to dampen arousal states, and deficits in habituation responses likely would pose a significant and terribly upsetting problem for the child.

The type of emotional response provided by parents of children with such deficits—whether generous, supportive, empathic, and accepting, or refusing, rejecting, withholding, demanding, critical, and punitive—will exert a significant modifying influence on future emotional development.

Mahler suggests that during the rapprochement stage, the main forces that need to be balanced are the child's wishes for continued gratification through contact and reunion and his knowledge of and anxiety over repeated brief separations from the mother. Two typical patterns of behavior—closely following or shadowing the mother and then fleeing from her with the expectation of being chased and enfolded in her arms—indicate the toddler's desire for reunion. Side by side with this wish is a fear of being reingulfed. How this critical phase of establishing a sense of separateness from the mother is negotiated is thought to be of enormous consequence for future psychological and emotional development. According to Mahler, it is a mainspring in humans' eternal struggle against

fusion and isolation—the beginning stage of establishing boundaries between self and others.

Could this natural stage of psychological and emotional development
be impinged upon by some genetically endowed physiological traits that
shape sensory experience? For example, how would a child's emotional
and psychological development be affected by an extreme sensitivity to
stimulation, and/or low threshold for anxiety and arousal, or early, excessive motor activity? The answers to these questions could have far-
reaching implications for our understanding of the psychological features
and treatment needs of children with bipolar disorder and may also point
to specific forms of intervention that might have special value in the early
treatment of the condition.


Thus it appears that children with bipolar disorder have a behavioral predisposition that leads to a greater tendency to startle as well as difficulties
settling as infants. Some progress to pronounced separation anxiety during
the rapprochement stage, and most—if not all—experience a heightened
response to stress. Later, establishing and sustaining peer relationships in
childhood becomes a major obstacle in emotional development, as shy-
ness, social withdrawal, or oppositional behaviors begin to emerge in full
force. Social avoidance, social phobia, and panic attacks, all frequently associated with bipolar disorder throughout life, may be predictable outcomes as these children reach the shores of adolescence and adulthood.

## HIDDEN REGULATORS OF ATTACHMENT AND
## SEPARATION BEHAVIOR

Dr. Myron Hofer and his colleagues at Columbia University in New York
City performed a compelling series of experiments using a well-
established experimental model: the separation paradigm in animals.
They began to focus on a change in behavior that occurred in rat pups after four to eight hours of separation from their mothers. The rat pups became hyperactive.

To explore the regulatory processes of the mother-infant interaction,
they attempted to selectively supply aspects of the mother's presence. For
example, they found that by simulating the body temperature of the
mother, her touch, or olfactory cues, the level of motor activity after separation from the mother lessened substantially. This led the researchers to

propose that the mother herself provides a combination of signals that act together to exert a long-term control over infant behavioral responsiveness. Furthermore, since much evidence exists that the neurotransmitters norepinephrine and dopamine may mediate generalized behavioral activity in animals, and since these neurotransmitter systems are most involved with motor activity and attention, they asked whether, by her presence, the mother was directly regulating specific brain neurotransmitter systems and thereby affecting the pups' levels of behavioral arousal and motor activity.

The researchers then decided to see if drugs that prevent the accumulation of norepinephrine and dopamine would prevent the development of hyperactivity in separated pups. And that is precisely what they found. A small dose of reserpine given at the time of separation entirely prevented the development of hyperactivity during the ensuing hours of maternal deprivation. Since reserpine is known to prevent the accumulation of these neurotransmitters at nerve terminals in the brain, the researchers concluded that sustained interaction with the mother normally depletes norepinephrine and dopamine to a moderate degree in rat pups. The loss of interaction with the mother would cause the concentration of these neurotransmitters to rise in the brain, and the pups would become behaviorally hyperresponsive.

From the work of Hofer and others we now know that in animals, the regulatory interactions with the mother serve to maintain high levels of physiological functions in the infants' systems during normal conditions. For example, interaction maintains the infants' heart rate and oxygen consumption at ordinary levels. In addition, interaction with the mother dampens other activities: behavioral reactivity, arousals during sleep, and suckling. See infant separation responses on chart below.

INFANT SEPARATION RESPONSES

| BEHAVIOR | PHYSIOLOGY |
| --- | --- |
| *Acute ("protest" phase, lasting minutes to hours)* | |
| Agitation | Increased heart rate |
| Vocalization | Increased cortisol |
| Searching, inactivity | Increased catecholamines |

*Chronic (slow-developing "despair" phase, lasting hours to days)*

| | |
|---|---|
| Decreased social interaction, play | Decreased body weight |
| Mouthing, rocking | Sleep disturbance |
| Hyporesponsiveness or hyperresponsiveness | Decreased rapid-eye movement, increased arousals |
| Decreased or variable food intake | Metabolic |
| Postures and facial expressions of sadness | Decreased core temperature |
| | Decreased oxygen consumption |
| | Cardiovascular |
| |   Decreased cardiac rate, increased vascular resistance |
| |   Increased ectopic beats |
| | Endocrine |
| |   Decreased growth hormone |
| | Immunologic |
| |   Decreased T-cell activity |

*Source:* Reference for each response is given in Hofer, 1984. (Reproduced with permission from *Psychosomatic Medicine* [1975], 37, 245–264. Baltimore: Lippincott, Williams & Wilkins.)

Persistent and severe separation anxiety in a child is a signal that successful negotiation and completion of this critical phase of psychological and emotional development are in jeopardy and that perhaps some underlying biological process is impaired. While individual variability does occur, the broad outline and even some of the details are surprisingly similar for different species. It is tempting to think that since proximity to the mother is a clear emotional regulator that produces varying degrees of arousal and separation distress in all mammalian species studied, warmth provided by her body may be one of the important links to emotional arousal in infancy.

As Hofer has suggested, this early postnatal period might be considered as "extrauterine gestation," in that the infant's heart rate, respiratory rate, and endocrine status are under subtle but pervasive maternal control. What is of particular interest about this model is the implication that the way in which maternal behavior and infant physiology interact is reciprocal and largely dependent on the infant's stage of development.

## WHAT TO DO ABOUT SEPARATION ANXIETY

In almost all instances, the mother is most affected by the child's powerful attachment demands; but as the child's exclusive desire for her companionship begins to rule the roost, others in the family also will be affected. Some fathers may be entirely excluded from this intense relationship and viewed by the children as intruders. Mothers who remain identified with the role of satisfying the child's needs are easily drawn into perpetual motherhood. They too find it hard to separate, particularly if they have inherited a bipolar disorder or temperament and their own fears of separation and abandonment fuse with those of the child.

There are no formulas for dealing with these particular problems, but it is abundantly clear that managing the separation anxiety in the child and becoming aware of its effects on the family should become a primary therapeutic goal in the clinical treatment of the condition. Each mother and each family will handle this problem differently. Their reactions will be shaped in large measure by their experiences as children, parented by mothers who may or may not have had the illness themselves.

Crucial is helping the child who experiences this level of fear and terror to understand that the sense of imminent loss of control (by becoming isolated from the mother) is not based on reality. But how do you do this? Again, there are no formulas. Mothers have always cuddled, swathed, swaddled, and rocked their babies to quiet and calm their distress, and mothers of bipolar children find themselves engaged in these efforts, working overtime. They need to help the verbal child to grasp the range and intensity of his or her feelings—anxiety and anger as well as elation and depression—and to express these feelings openly on a regular basis. Any exercise that helps a child to label feelings and talk about them in play gives order, definition, and a feeling of self-control that would counter the prevailing tendency to believe that feelings are overwhelming and unmanageable—a tendency likely to impede emotional growth and maturation.

## EFFECTS OF GENETIC PREDISPOSITION ON BEHAVIOR

If applied to humans, Hofer's model of a continuous dynamic interaction between infant and mother that itself acts as a modifying influence or buffer on the infant's central nervous system arousal functions is intriguing. It leads us to focus not only on the importance of mothers' parenting styles with children but to wonder how genetic influences that may confer a decreased capacity to break down brain catecholamines might influence the early developmental stages of ego maturation during the separation and individuation phase.

Could this commonly observed tendency of behavioral hyperresponsiveness to separation from the mother in animals and in humans be affected by a diminished capacity to break down brain catecholamines, such as in those individuals who inherit two copies of the low-activity catechol-O-methyltransferase (COMT) gene.

Interestingly, several recent studies have confirmed that the inheritance of two copies of the COMT low-activity gene, which confers a three- to fourfold lower level of activity on the enzyme, is strongly associated with ultra-ultrarapid cycling, the most common form of cycling in childhood-onset bipolar disorder.

How might such an inherited predisposition manifest itself developmentally? If being apart from the mother produces an expectable increase in the release of norepinephrine and dopamine (as per Hofer's animal model), but the child's genetic endowment leaves him or her with a diminished ability to break down the rising brain levels of these neurotransmitters, susceptibility for pronounced and prolonged separation distress could result.

Increased motor activity and restlessness as well as pronounced separation anxiety are frequently reported as early-occurring features of childhood-onset bipolar disorder. In fact, Margaret Mahler's observations of human mothers and infants led her to propose that if the maturational spurt of locomotor activity takes place simultaneously with a lag in the child's emotional readiness to function separately from the mother, "organismic panic" may result. This state of panic would not be readily discernible because the preverbal child cannot communicate it. If each attempt at separation and reattachment is suffused by high degrees of fearfulness, increased arousal, and high states of anxiety—all disruptive states—and these are relieved only by continuing close proximity to the mother, an intense emotional attachment will likely ensue.

The normal phenomenon of active wooing and pleasure in sharing with the mother could turn into a repetitive, coercive, aggressive pattern of manipulation. Shadowing of the mother then becomes a desperate appeal to ward off the anticipated anxiety of overstimulation. In this state, toddlers have been observed to aggressively exclude any other goal-directed activity or substitute comforting by any person other than the mother. Clearly, a sense of mastery and autonomy could not develop if such anxiety were to persist. Thus a critically important transitional phase of individual social development would be arrested. And it would not be surprising that interactive play, sharing, and the acquisition of the language of interpersonal experience would be delayed. Each of these features was commonly reported in our survey of parents of children with early-onset bipolar disorder.

## WILLIAM'S STORY

We have spent a good deal of time examining and trying to underscore some of the earliest behaviors and tendencies in children with bipolar disorder, and have speculated on some of the possible consequences on psychological development. The following account of William further illustrates the impact of the condition on the development of psychological defense mechanisms that evolve in these children.

William, age twelve, was referred by his psychotherapist for a diagnostic consultation. He was described as a gifted young boy who had an exceptional talent for mathematics and science and a strong self-esteem regarding these abilities. He was an avid reader who demonstrated intense and prolonged concentration playing computer games. While he loved to read and was enthused by science and mathematics, he was also very distractible, would lose his school equipment, and would overreact when teased by classmates. If he perceived their teasing as an insult, his mother said, "He would go to war, couldn't let it go, and would force a conflict." At these times he became quite volatile. Yet at other times he could be quite charming and often mischievous.

At age seven, William's social studies teacher reported that he was often squirming and fidgeting in his seat as well as disrespectful of rules and to authority figures at school. She viewed him as not achieving up to his potential and noted that he was melancholic, became easily bored, or lacked motivation. Yet at other times he could be a cheerful and engaging youngster who was excited by classroom discussions. These latter moods could easily escalate, and he would begin talking loudly and in a boisterous manner, sometimes using funny voices or offering nonsensical responses. On these occasions William appeared to think he was smarter than the other students and refused to share the same assignments, regarding himself as special and entitled to a more individualized program of study.

William's oldest sister had been diagnosed at age twenty-five with rapid-cycling bipolar disorder and had periodic rage attacks. William's maternal grandmother had been hospitalized and treated with electroconvulsive therapy, and two paternal uncles were in treatment programs for alcoholism.

William had met all the normal milestones for motor and language development. While he toilet trained on time, he had a history of bedwetting and daytime wetting and soiling, which continued until the age of nine. He also experienced night terrors and had severe separation anxiety during early childhood until the age of nine.

He was noted by his teachers to have trouble reading social cues and was often in physical fights. William's parents reported that his oppositional behavior began to escalate during the first-grade year, whereas before that time he was viewed as being an "easy kid." His mother reported that he began to refuse to stop playing computer games at night and then would get to sleep late and have trouble waking up for school the next morning.

Concerned about these changes in their son's behavior, William's parents arranged for psychological testing, which revealed confusion about his emotional life and intense aggressive impulses. William's need to develop rigid defenses to ward off constant perceived threats from the environment (anything that portended of bodily harm or emotional abandonment) had become a predominant feature of his mental life. William's responses on the Children's Thematic Apperception Test (see Chapter 10) were particularly disturbing. Eight of the nine stories he created involved death and dying and were filled with bizarre and gruesome content. They revealed anxious fantasies about losing his parents and were heavily laden with sadistic, aggressive elements as well as fears of bodily harm, physical mutilation, and emotional separation and loss.

William scored poorly on tests that used familiar pictures of real-life social situations and required careful attention to visual detail to find missing features in pictures, suggesting significant problems in the ability to decode social cues.

During a psychiatric evaluation he recounted many times of being picked on and fighting with older siblings and peers. He described feeling in a state of almost constant fearfulness—always threatened and feeling vulnerable to outside attack. Because he had difficulty distinguishing social cues, he would often misinterpret social advances for hostile intrusions into his private space, especially when outside of familiar contexts where he otherwise might feel secure or protected.

During the evaluation William described two personas that evolved over time to respond to his experience of an ever-threatening environment:

It's like I have two minds, one for living and one for fighting—like two different organisms with two different sets of logic, and they seem to have no connection to each other. When my fighting self, William Fight, takes over, he is unscarable, invulnerable. No bully can scare him. When I feel frightened, William Fight takes over and immediately begins to consider strategic options and the appropriate weapons of choice.

He described an encounter with a peer at school, who, according to William, brandished a knife. William Fight immediately chose an X-Acto knife and prepared to throw it.

William was also afraid of being either physically or sexually abused at night, while asleep, and slept with a long stick at his bedside, saying, "If anyone intrudes in my space, I wake up immediately, alert, and prepared to do battle." When in "Fight" mode, William would experience a lot of energy and imagined fighting four or five other kids simultaneously. During these periods, he stated, "I get a rush of energy and I think really clearly."

William Fight was also, he thought, the source of his creative ideas. Says William, "He'll give me thoughts about medical technologies, antiterrorist activities, guns, missiles, space ships, and computer games."

He first recalls experiencing these intense aggressive feelings at around age seven, interestingly when the oppositional defiant behavior was originally observed by parents and teachers. At age twelve he described becoming easily fearful, then angry and volatile, sometimes four to five times within a day. Typically this would occur when he perceived others as picking on him or when surprised by some new situation or event. His sensitivity to social rejection, humiliation, disappointment, and loss was profound.

At other times when not feeling threatened, William would switch over to his second self, William Live. He explained that William Fight lets William Live do only things that have to do with happiness and that William Live is very optimistic. "He even thinks I still may be able to go back to being normal."

During these periods William described feeling silly, goofy, giddy, and elated, and would become mischievous, develop fast, pressured, and loud speech, often saying things that were nonsensical and that others found odd. These periods, like the irritable, angry periods, could last for minutes or hours, and would occur many times within a day. William also volunteered that he had a very high level of energy and was often able to do with four to five hours of sleep on a regular basis. Although he would sleep deeply ("I'm able to sleep through fire alarms"), when he arose in the morning he was fully alert and aroused.

It is obvious that William has the common developmental sequence of signs, behaviors, and symptoms that are consistent with the diagnosis of early-onset bipolar disorder: separation anxiety; bedwetting and soiling; rapidly shifting irritable moods alternating with periods of elation; avoidant and oppositional behaviors; distractibility; angry aggressive rages; and, alternatively, a grandiose and self-deprecatory self-image; an abbreviated sleep cycle; and morbid concerns of death, dying, and mutilation.

Profound fears of loss and separation, the difficulty in adequately modulating intense emotions of elation, irritability, and the aggressive and sadistic impulses, coupled with discrete deficits in visual-motor integration (in the area of attention and executive memory and in the capacity to decode social cues accurately), have placed significant obstacles in the way of the maturation of more adaptive coping skills that would lead to autonomous self-esteem regulation and the possibility of positive and sustaining peer relationships.

To cope with these intense impulses, emotions, and fears of abandonment and bodily harm, which can become magnified by the accumulated experience of the "perceived sense" of constant danger and threat from the environment, an inflexible, rigid defensive style often develops.

William's two personas, then, can be viewed as efforts to organize in thought, feeling, and behavior the intense mood and energy states—the hallmarks of untreated childhood bipolar disorder—that dominated his mental life. The irritable, angry, aggressive, and sadistic impulses that occur periodically throughout the day—often induced by perceived threat or slights—and the silly, goofy, giddy periods of elation are also a function of the ultra-ultrarapid cycling pattern typical of the condition.

## Fear of Harm

As one reads through William's story, it is not difficult to sense that the world around and within him is very threatening and that he is in almost perpetual fear that he will be harmed by others or that he will lose control of his own aggressive impulses.

William's experience is not unique. A 2005 study that examined parent reports of over 1,500 children and adolescents assigned a community diagnosis or at risk for bipolar disorder found a similar profile in these youngsters when compared to a control group. Reported in the *Journal of Affective Disorders,* Demitri Papolos, M.D., and colleagues examined objective behavioral measures of obsessive fears of harm and aggression using two well-validated instruments—the Yale-Brown Obsessive Compulsive Scale (YBOCS) and the Overt Aggression Scale (OAS). While the field of psychiatry has been focused primarily on symptoms of mania and irritability and co-occurring diagnoses as a central feature of the condition, these investigators looked at measures of aggressive obsessions and overt aggression directed at others and self.

By dividing the sample into high-frequency and low-frequency subgroups on these measures, and contrasting the high-fear-of-harm group with the low-fear-of-harm group, the authors of the study found that the children with a high fear of harm were more likely to be more aggressive toward themselves and others. In fact, they were eight times more likely to engage in injurious acts directed toward others and were at a thirtyfold higher risk of committing self-injurious acts. (This seems counterintuitive, but it is what the data revealed.)

This pairing of clinical symptoms (aggressive obsessions and poor modulation of aggressive impulses) may help clinicians distinguish bipolar disorder from other more commonly diagnosed psychiatric disorders with which it is commonly confused.

Moreover, the prescription of SSRI antidepressants, otherwise appropriate for the treatment of obsessive fears, should be considered carefully when the obsessive fears occur in the context of severe aggression directed toward self and others.

Many children like William are profoundly affected by the difficulty they have in modulating aggressive impulses, and this intense fearfulness can come to dominate their inner world. They tend to attribute negative meaning to events and perceive others as threatening, hostile, or judgmental, which may not be the case at all. These youngsters may become avoidant and fearful of getting too close to others, and they may expend an inordinate amount of energy trying to dampen down intense feelings of anger, fearfulness, anxiety, and irritability. This may lead to great difficulty expressing feelings and experiencing pleasure.

A psychological therapy that explores these obsessional, aggressive fears that many of the children suffer is of great importance.

## OPPOSITIONAL BEHAVIOR AND DEFIANT ATTITUDES

Just as William displayed oppositional behaviors toward authority figures, our survey revealed that oppositional behavior and defiant attitudes toward parents were high on the list of associated features of early-onset bipolar disorder. Confirmation of this observation comes from preliminary findings reported by the Stanley Foundation Childhood-Onset Bipolar Disorder Consortium, showing that 80 percent of the children and adolescents they studied met *DSM-IV* criteria for oppositional defiant disorder.

Usually appearing between the ages of six and eight, this aspect of the condition poses significant challenges for parents and educators who must contend with the unreasonable demands, refusals, and unprovoked rigidity that commonly occur in these children.

Psychological theory suggests that oppositional behavior is defensive in nature and arises out of an attempt to maintain control when stressful experience threatens personal autonomy or judgment. Children who are striving to feel safe when the world around them feels threatening, who are distractible, who have difficulty switching from one activity to another, who are easily aroused by novel stimuli, or who frequently misrepresent the intentions of others are prime candidates to use oppositional behavior to protect themselves and establish some semblance of control in the world. They try to accomplish this by constantly standing their ground—admitting no new stimuli, no changes, and no transitions—with absolute resolve.

Such intensity of conviction might be tolerated if it were attached to some important value, but a struggle of this proportion can ensue over a parent's request to come to the dinner table. The combination of intensity and inflexibility that these children bring to social interactions cannot help but produce conflict with parents, siblings, friends, and educators. But from the point of view of a bipolar child, this is an adaptive response. Any request to change or to transition from one place to another is perceived as a stressor and then quickly transformed into a threat. Anxiety levels rise, and when the parent persists and reinforces some necessary priority, such as "You've got to get up now so you have enough time to get dressed and have breakfast before the school bus arrives," anxiety over this regular daily separation arises and tips the scales toward stubborn opposition.

It is as if these children are responding to a pressing inner emotional directive that is signaling red alert and whose switch is easily triggered. Since the children have little capacity to stop, reflect, and interrupt this alarm, they meet change with oppositional and defiant behaviors that eventually can crystallize as formidable defensive postures. Resistance from the outside simply raises the pitch.

The constant exercise of oppositional and stubbornly defiant behaviors in interactions with others, while personally and socially maladaptive, serves the greater goal of preserving self-identity. Ultimately, however, the continuation of this behavior draws greater and greater negative attention, further isolating these children from others, narrowing their social experience, and limiting the possibilities for healthy interactions that might serve to provide a greater sense of mastery, self-control, and self-esteem.

Over time, children who constantly dig in their heels and refuse to listen to parents and whose behavior alienates potential friends feel negatively about themselves and are more isolated and more fearful. In adolescence these behavioral tendencies can consolidate as defense mechanisms and gradually become enduring features of the personality. Such behaviors, typically experienced as disobedience and disrespect, elicit consistent negative responses from parents and the larger social world, further eroding an already fragile sense of self-esteem. Oppositional behavior and defiant attitudes combine with a strong inclination to take risks and easy addictability to psychoactive drugs, such as marijuana and cocaine, rendering adolescence a minefield waiting to detonate the illness.

When children feel threatened by something they cannot contain or control, opposition to the source of that feeling can provide a sense of immediate relief that some pressing need will not be extinguished or forever lost. Frequent refusals to accept the legitimacy of a parental "no" can be viewed as the bipolar child's inadequate effort to establish some absolute boundary—some anchor that holds time still and everything else constant.

## ANXIETY, NEGATIVE EMOTIONS, AND THE FEAR OF LOSS OF CONTROL

Current developments in cognitive and emotion theory suggest that anxiety plays a central role in negative emotions, such as anger, rage, and irritability. Growing evidence indicates that early experience with diminished control may foster a mind-set likely to interpret or process events as out of one's control. Persistent anxiety of imminently losing an attachment to the mother, easy distractibility, motor restlessness, and bedwetting are common in boys with childhood-onset bipolar disorder. Such a set of symptoms occurring daily in the life of a child could be expected to cause high levels of anxiety; over time, the child could tend to interpret events as being out of control. When combined with frequent misrepresentations of the intentions of others, anger, rage, and irritability in a child might be a final common behavioral pathway.

When children continuously experience aggressive and explosive outbursts and prolonged temper tantrums, they are certain to feel even more of a loss of control. This leads to a poor sense of mastery over a host of cognitive, bodily, and emotional functions. In these children arousal, attention, motor behavior, and emotional responses are all subject to erratic regulation, which reinforces a feeling of threat to personal autonomy and self-integrity.

## IMPULSIVE BEHAVIOR

As children mature, they become increasingly capable of manipulating objects and events symbolically, thereby becoming free of concrete dependency on them. Jean Piaget spoke of the development of intelligence as always moving toward increased spatial and temporal distance between the individual and the environment. And although young children cannot inhibit impulse expression very well, over time they become increasingly capable of interposing thought and reflection between impulse and action, which allows them to delay action and attune to the demands or requirements of the social situation.

Children with bipolar disorder have difficulty postponing gratification, taking turns, waiting on others, or holding back an impulse to talk first or have it all. This sets the stage for frequent conflict with others, sadly restricting the possibilities for the adaptive and maturing experiences of sharing, appreciation, and empathy.

## DISTRACTIBILITY AND INATTENTION

All of the behaviors and symptoms that occur in attention-deficit disorder with hyperactivity were also reported in our survey of early-onset bipolar disorder—at very high rates. A significant majority of children have five or more of the primary symptoms, including difficulty sustaining attention and effort (distractibility), lack of attention to details, difficulty following through on tasks or instructions, motor restlessness, difficulty waiting one's turn, and interrupting or intruding on others. Children with early-onset bipolar disorder have deficits in a crucial set of thinking skills that are most often referred to as "executive functions."

Specifically, executive functions include cognitive skills such as the ability to shift efficiently from one mind-set to another and the ability to organize and plan strategically. This kind of planning includes the anticipation of problems and the formulation of goals in response to problems. Deficits in working memory—information stored and accessible in short-term memory—and the ability to separate one's emotions from one's thoughts interfere with these executive functions.

The ordinary demands of the child's life are fraught with the constant perceived dangers of loss of emotional control and anxiety over change. We know from recent research studies that the capacity to assess information, plan reactions smoothly, adhere to social rules, and evaluate what is and what is not a threat varies with the degree of individual control over arousal and its effects on attention and social memory (reflection on past experience). If a child who is easily aroused has difficulty separating emotion from thought, cannot regulate angry impulses, and selectively feels the need to defend against a perceived threat or rejection, there are few behavioral alternatives available; these imperatives dictate an expectable response, such as opposition, anger, or rage.

## CONCLUSION

During early development, human beings learn to substitute the exclusive caring that is provided by parental figures with attachment to others.

Gradually humans attempt to establish mastery over the environment, developing varying and unique styles of adaptation that provide in adult life the individual distinction we call character or personality.

Along the way a child must meet a variety of developmental challenges; he or she learns how to walk, to modulate emotion and response to stress, to organize memory, to establish psychological defenses. Each stage has its issues, however, and many things can go awry. Whether it is the separation-individuation stage of infancy, the learning and peer-relatedness of childhood, or the struggles over dependence and autonomy that come to prominence in adolescence, the individual temperament of the child plays a large role in how each stage is negotiated.

As we have described, children with bipolar disorder appear to have pronounced deficits in modulating arousal states and sensory responses to the environment from an early age. Not surprisingly, their reactions to stressful or novel stimuli lead to high levels of anxiety and deficits in negotiating social boundaries as well as to problems with separation and attachment and to persistent difficulties in sustaining stable peer relationships.

Because of the high degree of arousability and sensitivity to physical and environmental stimuli, these children may need to make more dramatic and often more extreme adaptations to social contexts. They tend to be more rigid and inflexible in response to parental rules and requests—their reactions may be driven primarily by natural attempts to safeguard themselves from overstimulation and to protect against a pervasive fear of losing control. Yet, paradoxically, they may also be bold, adventurous, and uninhibited—driven toward the pursuit of stimulation that brings physical pleasure and/or intellectual or creative satisfaction. These latter tendencies, when channeled appropriately and with sufficient discipline, have produced some of the greatest scientific and artistic achievements in the history of humankind.

All of these states of increasing or diminishing arousal are regulated by central nervous system processes in reaction to bodily and environmental demands. Since neuroscience has delineated the basic characteristics of the arousal system, disturbances in levels of arousal can be reliably traced to particular regions of the brain, innervated by known neurotransmitter and neuropeptide pathways. It is to these systems that we turn next.

# What Causes
# This Condition?

Parents watching a child smile one minute, turn tyrannical the next, then hurl obscene phrases at family members, and finally escalate into explosive tantrums may look to appease the child for a time and feel tremendous anger and confusion. Sooner or later, after relentlessly examining their own parenting skills and attending class after class to improve them, these parents are going to ask themselves: "What on earth could be going on inside this child's brain?"

What indeed.

To address this question, we begin by focusing on brain/behavior relationships that seem most relevant to the clinical description of the illness. We explore the most recent findings from psychiatric and behavioral neuroscience research, and we provide the background information necessary to examine the hypotheses being advanced to explain the underlying biological basis of the condition.

We believe that genetic information inherent in our cells unfolds in the context of the internal and external environment and that certain vulnerability genes predispose to disturbances in the regulations of emotion and behavior.

In this chapter we also examine the overall workings of the brain and its multiple circuits and their interactions and how these interactions play into behavior. And we examine the neurotransmitter and neuropeptide systems that influence arousal, anxiety, stress, fear, aggression, attention, reward, sleep, and body temperature regulation, and the biological timing functions of these systems. In addition, we look at the interacting functions of the limbic and neuroendocrine systems and their known effects on the organization of behavior.

## THE DEVELOPMENT OF NEW DIAGNOSTIC CRITERIA FOR JUVENILE-ONSET BIPOLAR DISORDER

Although there is continuing debate over the validity of the diagnosis of mania in children, a number of studies have begun to shed light on the presentation and naturalistic course of early-onset bipolar disorder, suggesting a developmentally different presentation in young children as compared to adults. Adult-onset and juvenile-onset forms of bipolar disorder have certain similar features and comorbidities in common, but in the juvenile form of the disorder, the frequent overlap of symptoms with other disorders that are far more commonly diagnosed in childhood has for years had a confounding effect on clinical diagnostic practice.

In 2001 the National Institute of Mental Health Roundtable on prepubertal bipolar disorder convened a panel of experts to review the growing literature on the prevalence and clinical presentation of pediatric bipolar disorder and to develop recommendations for future research. Members of the roundtable proposed behavioral phenotypes for two groups of children: those who met the adult *DSM-IV* criteria for mania/hypomania and those who did not. Members of the latter group presented differently from adults but were severely impaired by symptoms of mood instability.

These experts also recommended that the *DSM-IV* diagnosis Bipolar Not Otherwise Specified *(BP-NOS)* serves as a "working diagnosis" to categorize such children for further study, with the caveat that the dimensions of their impairment, such as attentional deficits, anxiety symptoms, aggression, thought disorder, cognitive impairment, disruptive behaviors, and substance abuse, be investigated using multiple rating instruments.

In 2003 the Juvenile Bipolar Research Foundation developed an Internet-based acquisition program utilizing the Child Bipolar Questionnaire (see page 464) and other well-validated diagnostic instruments. The assembled database of over five thousand children and adolescents diagnosed with, or at risk for, bipolar disorder provided a rich opportunity for the development of a fine-grained profile of the illness.

The "core" phenotype places the *DSM-IV* manic or mixed episode in a broader framework of specific functional impairments directly related to the regulation of affect, drives, attention, arousal, and circadian rhythms. These impairments are linked to defined neurobehavioral systems, reflecting a neurobiological model informed by recent research.

A newer definition of juvenile-onset bipolar disorder that builds on earlier views, but is further informed by more recent clinical and family genetic studies, might be:

MUST MEET CRITERIA A–D FOR DIAGNOSIS

A. Episodic and abrupt transitions in mood states accompanied by rapid alternations in levels of arousal, emotional excitability, sensory sensitivity, and motor activity. Variable mood states are characterized by the following features: manic/hypomanic (mirthful, silly, goofy giddy, elated, euphoric, overly optimistic, self-aggrandizing, grandiose); depressed (withdrawn, bored/anhedonic, irritable, sad, dysphoric, or overly pessimistic, self-critical).

Episodes are defined by *DSM-IV* symptom criteria but not by *DSM-IV* duration criteria; manic/hypomanic or mixed episode required for diagnosis:

1. Manic or hypomanic episodes are associated with elated/euphoric (silly-goofy-giddy) or angry/irritable mood states and 3 of the following symptoms and behaviors (4 if irritable mood only): more talkative than usual; pressured speech; flight of ideas; subjective experience of thoughts racing; distractibility; diminished need for sleep; increase in goal-directed activity; heightened interest, enjoyment, and enthusiasm for usual activities; excessive involvement in pleasurable activities that had a high potential for painful consequences; overestimation of resources and capacities; overvaluation of self and others; more argumentative than usual; overbearing, bossy, in pursuit of personal needs or agenda.

2. Depressive episodes are associated with dysphoric/sad/irritable or anxious/fearful mood states, with loss of interest and pleasure in previously enjoyed activities often resulting in expressions of boredom and excessive stimulus-seeking behaviors; in addition to depressed mood or anhedonia, 4 or more of the following symptoms are present: decreased sense of self-esteem; slowed speech; paucity of thought; increased need for sleep or disrupted sleep;

loss or increase in appetite; decrease or loss of energy; difficulty sustaining attention; diminished ability to concentrate or indecisiveness; psychomotor retardation; loss of initiative and motivation; underestimation of resources and capacities; devaluation of self and others; negative interpretation of events and misattribution of other's behaviors; recurrent thoughts of death, recurrent suicidal ideation.

3. Mixed episodes are associated with overlapping features of the primary mood states (manic/hypomanic, angry, depressed, anxious) accompanied by other associated symptoms of manic/hypomanic and depressive mood states. The presentation may include irritability, agitation, insomnia, appetite dysregulation, poor control over aggressive impulses, in addition to course modifiers such as aggression directed against self or others (e.g., suicidal thinking or attempts, aggressive displays, rages) or psychotic features. Mixed episodes may be due to the direct effect of exposure to antidepressants, stimulant medication, electroconvulsive or light therapy, or other medical treatments (e.g., corticosteroids, sympathomimetic agents).

B. Poor modulation of drives (aggressive, sexual, appetitive, acquisitive) resulting in behaviors that are excessive for age and/or context. This regulatory disturbance is associated with excessive aggressive/fight-based behaviors (critical, sarcastic, demanding, oppositional, overbearing "bossy," easily enraged, prone to violent outbursts), and/or self-directed aggression (head-banging, skin-picking, cutting, suicide) as well as premature and intense sexual feelings and behaviors (precocious curiosity about and sex premature expression of sexual impulses as well as inappropriate public displays), appetite dysregulation (excessive craving for carbohydrates and sweets, binge eating, purging, and anorexia), and poor control over acquisitive impulses (relentless pursuit of needs, buying excessively and hoarding).

Episodic and abrupt transitions in mood states and poor modulation of drive are currently present most days and have been present for at least the past 12 months without any symptom-free periods exceeding 2 months in duration, and cause functional impairment in 1 or more settings (e.g., significant behavioral problems at home but not necessarily in the school setting).

C. Four (or more) of the following disturbances have been present during the same 12-month period:

4. Excessive anger and oppositional/aggressive responses to situations that elicit frustration. Compared to his/her peers, the child exhibits difficulties in the postponement of immediate gratification, when parents set limits. In particular, when answered "no" to expressed wishes, when having to wait his/her turn, or when there are changes in planned activities or routines, this deficit results in maladaptive responses, such as seeming not to listen (purposeful), the display of disruptive, intrusive and overbearing behaviors, or, in the extreme, temper tantrums and aggressive attacks, often followed by sullen withdrawal and expressions of remorse.

5. Poor self-esteem regulation. At times is overly optimistic, defiant, arrogant, filled with bravado, and prone to self-aggrandizement, exaggeration of abilities, and has feelings of omnipotence, or, alternatively, is overly pessimistic, self-critical, and overly sensitive to criticism or rejection, often responding to criticism with intense feelings of humiliation and shame. The child often expresses feelings of insecurity, worthlessness, and is capable of rapid and intense idealization and/or devaluation of self and others.

6. Sleep/wake cycle disturbances; at least 1 of the following: (1) Sleep discontinuity (initial insomnia, middle insomnia, early-morning awakening, hypersomnia), (2) Sleep arousal disorders (sleep inertia, night terrors and nightmares—often containing images of gore and mutilation, and themes of pursuit, bodily threat and parental abandonment, sleepwalking, confusional arousals, bruxism, and enuresis); (3) Sleep/wake reversals (a tendency toward periodic lengthening or shortening of sleep duration, often dependent on circadian and circannual changes in light/dark and temperature cycles as well as the availability of regular social time givers).

7. Low threshold for anxiety. A tendency to react with excessive anxiety and fearfulness in response to novel or stressful situations; transitions of context, loss, separation, or the anticipation of loss/separation from attachment objects or loss of social status. Anxiety often arises from fear of harm to self in the form of anger, re-

jection, criticism, ostracism, or, alternatively, from the fear that he/she will harm others or self. This deficit can predispose to behavioral inhibition or flight-based behaviors, such as separation anxiety disorder, social phobias, and other anxiety disorders, including panic disorder, obsessive-compulsive and post-traumatic stress syndrome.

8. Disturbance in the capacity to habituate to sensory stimuli often when exposed to novel, repetitive, or monotonous sensory stimulation. A tendency to overreact to environmental stimuli and to become overaroused, easily excited, irritated, angry, anxious, or fearful when exposed to novel sensory experiences, e.g., crowds, loud or unexpected sounds (e.g., vacuum cleaners, ticking clocks, thunder and lightning) and dissonant sensations (e.g., shirt tags, fit of clothes or shoes, perceived foul odors).

9. Executive function deficits; 1 of more of the following: Mental inflexibility—difficulty shifting cognitive set, planning ahead, planning strategically as seen in unrealistic estimates of energy resources and time requirements for the accomplishment of tasks (e.g., difficulty adjusting to changes in plans for the day, such as planned trips and changes in venue); difficulty giving up an idea or desire, no matter how unrealistic or unfeasible; difficulty starting and completing school assignments without a great deal of prompting, often getting caught up in small details of an assignment and missing the larger picture. This executive dysfunction is often associated with working memory deficits, problems making transitions from one context to another, poor organizational skills, distractibility, excessive daydreaming, and performance deficits in school, particularly in the organization of thought for written expression.

10. Emotional inflexibility—impulsive, acts before thinking. Overreacts to small events, rapidly shifts emotional states, can demonstrate sudden anger, resentment, and/or rage for longer than 15 minutes that is unresponsive to reason, discussion, or soothing, can become progressively unrestrained or silly, and does not appear to gain pleasure from mastering a skill

11. Inflexibility of motor activity—the initiation of movement directed at the accomplishment of motor tasks is effortful (e.g., has difficulty starting activities in the morning and requires help in initiating any activity), is often restless and fidgety. Handwrit-

ing is poor, and has trouble initiating and completing written assignments.

12. A family history of recurrent mood disorder and/or alcoholism as well as other bipolar spectrum disorders. A history of bilineal familial transmission is commonly observed.

D. Symptoms are not due to a general medical condition (e.g., hypothyroidism).

Could a common frame of reference encompass these seemingly disparate symptoms—exaggerated startle and stress responses, separation distress, sleep/wake disturbances, heightened and inhibited sensory states, elation/irritability and depression, high- and low-energy states, and poor control of impulses, particularly seen in the tendency for aggressive rages? Can biological differences attributable to a genetic predisposition and environmental interactions explain this unusual combination of symptoms and behaviors?

To answer these questions, we need to understand the architecture of the brain and the processes by which it communicates with the body and the world around it.

## INSIDE THE BRAIN: THE LIMBIC DIENCEPHALON

The human brain is the most complex structure on earth. Its three and a half pounds of gray and white matter compressed into a structure no larger than a grapefruit sits above our bony spines. Packed into this space are perhaps 100 billion brain cells. Each of these cells may make thousands of connections with adjoining or distant cells. There are likely to be more than 100 trillion possible interconnections. A final measure of the brain's complexity is its dynamic nature: It changes constantly and undergoes continuous modification in response to environmental stimuli.

A major task of the nervous system is to maintain the regularity of the internal environment—homeostasis—and to integrate and modulate incoming information from our senses. Although virtually the whole brain is involved in maintaining homeostasis, neurons that control the internal environment are concentrated in the hypothalamus, a set of nuclei located in a small area in the center of the brain called the diencephalon. The hypothalamus interacts with the limbic cortex—the emotional brain—and the cerebral neocortex—the thinking brain—via hormonal, neuropep-

**Figure 7.1 The Limbic Diencephalon**

tide, and neurotransmitter systems. The hypothalamus and closely linked structures in the limbic system keep the internal environment constant by regulating four related functions: hormonal secretions, the autonomic nervous system, the emotions and drives, and body temperature (see Figure 7.1).

## Autonomic Nervous System

The autonomic nervous system automatically controls glands and structures such as the lungs, heart, blood vessels, and pupils of the eyes. Linked with the brain's hypothalamus and spinal cord (which carries information from our senses), this system is influenced by the central nervous system but is responsible for activities over which we have no conscious control. In fact, the autonomic nervous system harks back to our reptilian ancestors.

The autonomic nervous system consists of two subsystems—the parasympathetic and sympathetic systems—that act more or less in opposition to balance each other. The sympathetic-system nerves work as a unit and deal particularly with the body's reaction to emergency. In times of physical danger or stress, they cause sweating, increase blood pressure, and mobilize the organism for fight or flight. The lack of a properly functioning sympathetic nervous system becomes evident under circumstances of stress. Body temperature cannot be regulated when environmental temperature varies; the concentration of blood glucose does not rise in response to urgent need; instinctive reactions to fright and danger are lost; and a host of other serious deficiencies occur in the protective forces of the body.

In direct contrast to the sympathetic nervous system, the parasympathetic system puts a brake on the heart rate, contracts the pupils, and feeds blood away from brain and muscles to the intestines. Normally, these two opposing systems maintain a balance in the body. Under stress, the sympathetic system dominates; during relaxation, the parasympathetic system takes over (see Figure 7.2).

Different patterns of activity of the autonomic nervous system can produce different emotional states. Acting through different parts of the limbic-hypothalamic system, the autonomic nervous system elicits different types of emotional behaviors, such as the stress, startle, and rage responses. Importantly, all of these responses are clearly magnified and/or poorly modulated in children with bipolar disorders.

## The Brain and the Limbic-Diencephalic System

Over millions of years of evolution, the human brain has developed from the bottom up, with higher centers developing as elaborations of more primitive parts. Near the center of the brain is the area on which most mood disorder researchers focus—the limbic-diencephalic system. This is composed of the limbic system, the hypothalamus, and the brain stem. In addition to its involvement in emotion, memory, and motivated behavior, the limbic system influences all parts of the body's endocrine system by controlling the release of hypothalamic hormones that regulate behavioral reactions to environmental events.

### Limbic System
The term "limbic" was originally an anatomical designation given by Pierre Paul Broca in 1876 to a ring of brain tissue containing a group of

structures closely connected to the hypothalamus. These structures contain the hippocampus, the amygdala, and the septum. They form a border (limbus) around a ventricle, or fluid-filled cavity, in the center of the brain that bathes many of the structures of the limbic system with chemical messengers from the adjacent hypothalamus. The hippocampus and the amygdala are the two key parts of the primitive brain that, during evolution, gave rise to the cortex and then the neocortex (the thinking brain).

The brain, excluding the brain stem, could be viewed as two concentric shells surrounding this central ventricle. The inner shell, or limbic lobe, contains the amygdala, hippocampus, and septum as well as other important regions that receive, integrate, and interpret information from the senses and regulate emotion and modulate its expression. The structures of the limbic system are connected by a complex series of circuits that employ neurotransmitters and neuropeptides as information messengers and respond to hormonal, temperature, and other sensory influences. Within the network of limbic circuitry, internal as well as external sensory states and the imprint of experience is superimposed and remembered.

*From Sensation to Feeling*
The limbic system (see Figure 7.3) appears to act as a central information-processing system, channeling the sensory input, regulating the motor output pathways of the brain, and imbuing the processes with emotional meaning. The structures within the limbic system do not receive any sensory input directly; rather, they interact and exchange information with the neocortex, the hypothalamus, and the autonomic nervous system. As the mediator, so to speak, of human feelings, the limbic system receives, regulates, and assembles highly organized information derived from sensations, momentary events, memories of events, and emotions associated with those events. The limbic forebrain acts as a filter for the sensory receiving areas of the brain prior to the assignment of emotional meaning to an event or experience. Additionally, through its reciprocal relationship with the hypothalamus, it governs sexual desire and hunger and thirst as well as the response to fear and the self-protective mechanism of fight or flight. It is no wonder that researchers in the field of bipolar disorder focus on this region of the brain.

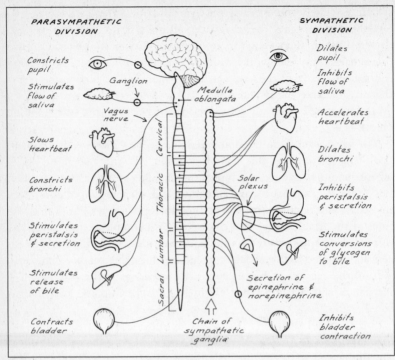

**Figure 7.2 The Autonomic Nervous System**
The sympathetic and parasympathetic divisions of the autonomic nervous system and the organs and glands that are stimulated or inhibited by their mutually opposing effects.

*Startle Response—An Overresponsive Early-Warning System*
When presented with a series of bright lights, babies first startle, then gradually respond less and less. The increase in heart and respiratory rates seen after the initial startle gradually diminish. "Habituation" is the term used to describe this protective response of closing down the nervous system.

Many bipolar children have a marked tendency to experience more intense startle responses from a very early age.

The startle reflex evolved to protect animals from blows or predatory attacks by quickly stiffening the limbs, body, and neck muscles before the decision to flee or fight. So it is directly linked to the biological "equipment" that generates the stress, or fight-or-flight, response.

We now know that these pathways involve the flow of information from sensory neurons in the body traveling via neurochemical pathways to the cerebral cortex and amygdala, a structure that resides within the temporal lobes of the limbic system and is directly connected to the hippocampus.

## The Amygdala

The amygdala is the brain structure that commandeers rational response and leads to the expression of powerful and unmodulated emotion in full-scale rage attacks.

In the brain's architecture, the almond-shape amygdala is poised like an emotional sentinel or alarm center and is involved in fear responses and in initiating the first stages of the assembly of emotional memories (see Figure 7.4). The amygdala receives signals that are of potential danger: (1) Signals from the eyes and ears travel first to the sensory thalamus (2), which transmits partial information about the stimulus to the amygdala (3), allowing a more rapid response well before centers in the visual cortex, or thinking brain (4), have fully assessed the complete nature of the signal. A primitive emotion such as rage takes this route to the amygdala, causing a response that is totally raw and unvarnished. Most of the signal, however, is delivered to the visual cortex, where it is analyzed and assessed for meaning and appropriate response. If this more measured response of the signal confirms that it indeed poses a threat, the fight-or-flight response is triggered in the amygdala.

The amygdala is not the bad guy of the brain. If ears register a growl and eyes perceive an animal that looks like a lion, the amygdala provides a rapid and perhaps lifesaving response.

Studies in humans, using new functional magnetic resonance neuroimaging techniques that allow brief time-elapsed observations of the brain, have shown that the amygdala is activated in response to the sight of frightening faces. Other reports describe individuals with complete destruction of the amygdala who cannot form accurate social judgments based on facial expression.

Incomplete or confusing stimuli from the sense organs signal the amygdala to scan the environment for danger. Bipolar children and those with learning and attentional deficits have significant problems with the integration of sensory information. Such disturbances may cause bipolar children to misinterpret a casual touch as a threatening gesture or to over-

**Figure 7.3 The Limbic-Hypothalamic-Pituitary Axis**
An overview of some of the connections among the limbic system, hypothalamus, and autonomic nervous system. A proposed neural circuit underlying emotional expression starts with the mammillary body of the
hypothalamus as the site of output for expression of the emotions
through its projections to the midbrain (not shown). The cingulate gyrus
that projects to the hippocampus is considered to be the receptive field
for emotional information in the cortex. The hippocampus combines this
and other inputs and organizes the information to be transmitted to the
mammillary bodies in the hypothalamus, thus completing the circuit.

react to normal social verbal cues. These children can become hypervigi-
lant and show paranoid tendencies as well as express severe and prolonged
defensive reactions. For instance, they can become oppositional or aggressive, or they can withdraw. These overreactions could derive, in part, from
the isolated activity of the amygdala, cut off from the modulating influences and accumulated wisdom of the higher cortical centers, through
which attention and motor behavior are coordinated. Or perhaps some
sensory-perceptual disturbance provides a confusing signal to the brain,
or both.

**Figure 7.4 Neuronal Pathways of the Fight-or-Flight Response**

## *The Hippocampus*

The hippocampus looks like a wishbone that fits snugly against the inner wall of the neocortex. It is the gateway from the neocortex to the rest of the limbic system, and it plays a central role in processing and distributing information from the cortex to other parts of the limbic system. In effect, the neocortex and the sensory nervous system feed information to the hippocampus, and the hippocampus then returns the processed information back to the neocortex. Somehow, within this loop of nervous tissue, sensory information is analyzed and brought together to register an event, imbue it with emotional meaning, and store it in memory. But just how is sensory information from the environment registered in the brain?

*The Hippocampal Theta Rhythm: A Signal of the Processing of Sensory Information*

In 1953 John Green and Arnaldo Arduini at the University of California at Los Angeles placed electrodes in the hippocampus and neocortex of rabbits, trying to record the electrical activity of both structures simultaneously. They found that brain waves oscillating at about four to seven times per second, called theta waves, were the most prominent electrical signal recorded from the hippocampus.

Neuroscientist Dr. Jonathan Winson of New York University has proposed that the theta rhythm in lower animals is a signal of the neuronal processing of sensory information that may have evolved originally to coordinate all sensory input with cycles of scanning and exploration of the environment. Such focused attentional responses are likely to have evolved in direct relationship with efforts to rapidly distinguish between predator or prey and therefore represent important survival behaviors that are closely linked to fight-or-flight behaviors.

Alternations in theta rhythm might act like a gating mechanism, switching the path of information flow through the hippocampus during different states of "fearful" arousal stimulated by the amygdala. A "state" refers to the degree of attentiveness, the variation in mood or motor responsiveness. So, the theta rhythm could be seen as a reflection of an important brain mechanism that enhances or withdraws attention from external or internal stimuli. It may operate as a selective filter that either prolongs our attentional focus or habituates to a signal from the environment.

When brain functions are balanced, people can make smooth transitions from one state to another. They are able to switch gears from inattention to attention, from fear to receptivity, from drowsiness to alertness, from relaxation to readiness to action. A modulation process balances the flow of sensory information coming into the central nervous system. Poorly modulated arousal systems would predispose to emotional imbalance and distractibility of attention. Bipolar children seem to experience almost any transition that requires shifting the focus of attention or giving up stimuli that they are focusing on as threatening and unmanageable.

Sometimes the brain of the bipolar child appears to register sensory experiences too intensely; at other times, events are registered barely at all, with wide variations. When overaroused by sensations (internal or external), the child reacts as if the sensations are irritating, annoying, or even threatening. Thus, the child may be extremely distractible because he or she is attending to too many stimuli and is unable to discriminate between those that are useful and those that are irrelevant. Such a deficit in sensory equilibrium could contribute to the extreme expression of the two poles of the stress response—fight-oppose or flight-avoid. This disequilibrium could result in behaviors that are negative, defiant, oppositional, aggressive, or alternatively fearful, anxious, or cautious—socially maladaptive behaviors commonly seen in early-onset bipolar disorder.

### Bursts of Rage and the Theta Rhythm

Irrational rage attacks are the most disturbing behavior of children with bipolar disorder, and certainly the one that most disrupts family life and sours relationships. Psychological explanations clearly do not do justice to these overwhelming assaults on the ordinary boundaries of self-control. The amygdala may be one area of the limbic system involved in the expression of unmodified emotion; the septum is another.

For many years researchers have known that electrical stimulation or surgical destruction of the septum (the source of the hippocampal theta rhythm) produces profound effects on the expression of emotional behaviors. The term "septal rage" has been coined to describe the marked hyperemotionality and hyperactivity seen in animals after lesions have been made in this important area of the limbic system. Distractibility, hyperalertness to approaching movement, explosive startle reactions to auditory and tactile stimulation, and vicious attacks coupled with loud vocalizations are among the many behavioral aberrations associated with septal rage in primates.

In many ways the intense emotionality and reactivity to sensory stimulation that seem to provoke the septal-rage syndrome are indistinguishable from the long-lasting rage attacks so commonly reported in children with bipolar disorder.

Neurotransmitter and neuropeptide pathways that influence the capacity to inhibit theta rhythm in animals may be directly related to dampening or enhancing the effect or intensity of sensory stimuli. Thereby they may affect the degree of behavioral responsiveness in situations of high alertness and general emotional arousal.

## CIRCUIT OF EMOTION

The interconnections among the various limbic centers, the hypothalamus, and the neocortex led neuroanatomist James Papez to propose in 1937 that this anatomical circuit is the neuronal substrate of emotion. He claimed that these structures formed a circuit that permitted emotion to arise through neuronal activity in the limbic system and noted that the lesions of the rabies virus principally attack the hippocampus. The intense behavioral and emotional symptoms that occur in the early stages of the disease—insomnia, irritability, and restlessness—typically usher in a stage of excitement and profound mood lability as well as excruciating sensitivity to all forms of stimuli, such as light and sound. All of these rabies-related behavioral, sensory, and mood changes are similar to the signs and symptoms experienced by patients with bipolar disorder.

When adults with bipolar disorder describe the heightened sensory awareness that often accompanies hypomania and mania, they describe this awareness as initially pleasurable; however, as the mania escalates, people lose the capacity to halt the incessant barrage of sensory stimulation or to modulate the sensory overload, and the mood turns irritable as mental faculties are overwhelmed.

With the hippocampus no longer able to filter sensory experiences, the world is extremely overstimulating and threatening. Individuals in this state experience intense panic and paranoia and often end-of-the-world annihilation delusions. The famous and often-reproduced woodcut *The Scream,* by the Norwegian artist Edvard Munch, who himself suffered from manic-depressive illness, perhaps best captures this state of unending overstimulation.

## Panic, Dread, and a Sense of Impending Doom

Patients in the throes of a panic attack experience a sense of impending doom—each moment is filled with dread and a sense of imminent danger from an unseen, imagined source. Physical symptoms, such as a racing heart, sweating, and short, uneven, and rapid breathing that accompany this fearful state, are driven by the autonomic nervous system, presumably activated by limbic sources. A disturbance in the neuronal activity of the limbic system could produce difficulties in registering emotional meaning and cause children to be overalert to stimuli. This disturbance might lead children to display extremes of attentional focus (hypervigilance), emotional arousal, and an overactive startle response. Such children might overreact to environmental stressors and are more likely to experience anxiety and have a tendency to panic. Interestingly, recent population studies have found that over 30 percent of adult patients with bipolar disorder have recurrent episodes of panic attacks. In our survey, high rates of panic symptoms were also observed in children diagnosed with bipolar disorder.

Eli Robbins and his colleagues at Washington University in St. Louis used positron emission tomography (PET)—a scanning procedure that allows visualization of cerebral blood flow and metabolic changes in the brain—on patients with panic disorder. These researchers discovered a circumscribed abnormality in the right parahippocampal gyrus of the limbic system, a region of the hippocampus that lies near the amygdala. In these patients, blood flow to this area is abnormally higher than that in the corresponding area in the left hemisphere.

Also using PET, Dr. Wayne Drevets and colleagues at the University of Pittsburgh School of Medicine recently reported finding abnormalities in patients diagnosed with bipolar disorder who had positive family histories for the disorder. These researchers localized an area of abnormally decreased activity in the prefrontal cortex. Other studies have implicated this area in autonomic responses to stressful and emotionally provocative stimuli. The prefrontal cortex seems to respond when a person is fearful or enraged, and it stifles or controls the feeling in order to deal more effectively with the situation at hand. This area of the neocortex receives the largest sensory projection from the thalamus, possibly for taking in and making sense of perceptions and planning responses.

## Hypothalamus

A whole constellation of nuclei participate in the expression of emotion. The hypothalamus works with the limbic system in the genesis of emotion, and together they are involved in the control of hormone secretion and the regulation of the autonomic nervous system. Functionally, this interaction allows coordination between emotional and motivational states and the regulation of visceral functions, such as blood pressure, heart rate, body temperature, and size of the eye's pupil.

Many of the clinical features of depression and mania as well as the physiological findings suggest some dysfunction in the limbic-hypothalamic circuit. One consistently replicated finding is that the interval between sleep onset and the beginning of the first period of rapid-eye movement sleep (REM) is shortened. This shortening of the first REM period is called "shortened REM latency." Another finding, particularly true of bipolar patients who have seasonal cycles, is a seasonal disturbance in body temperature regulation—a difficulty dissipating a heat load in the summer months. Preliminary findings from our own pilot study suggest that childhood-onset bipolar patients run persistently low body temperatures ranging from 96.5° to 97.4°F.

REM sleep and body temperature regulation are closely related. Mammals become essentially cold-blooded during REM sleep, when the primary heat loss mechanisms are practically unresponsive to changes in the ambient temperature. The onset of sleep is usually preceded by a dramatic descent in body temperature. During the first part of sleep the temperature continues to fall, and this is associated with increased heat loss, a relatively high percentage of stages 3 and 4 sleep, and a high percentage of REM sleep. Heat retention, through decreased sweating and blood vessel constriction, appears to be closely linked to REM sleep. These thermoregulatory changes, governed, in part, by warm-sensitive and cold-sensitive nerve cells in the hypothalamus, together with the close temporal relationship of REM onset to the body temperature minimum, suggest that the circadian rhythm of REM propensity is one of the major oscillating systems involved in body temperature regulation. Clinical reports of profuse sweating during sleep and heat intolerance in patients with childhood-onset bipolar disorder may be related to some disturbance in thermoregulation that is associated with sleep/wake disturbances.

## The Hypothalamic-Pituitary-Adrenal Axis: Stress and Defense Responses

The four-gram, walnut-size hypothalamus is arguably the most important structure of the limbic system. This "brain" within the brain regulates a host of human processes, including appetite, thirst, sleep, sexual desire, energy metabolism, and body temperature, as well as the timing of many other basic behavioral functions on an hour-by-hour or daily basis. The hypothalamus regulates the master gland of the brain—the pituitary— and the pineal gland, a major part of the daily and seasonal timing system of the brain. The pituitary releases adrenocorticotropic hormone (ACTH), which activates the adrenal gland to release cortisol, setting off the so-called stress response. The pineal gland receives light/dark signals from the environment through another hypothalamic nucleus with the tongue-twisting name suprachiasmatic—the master clock of the nervous system.

*The Stress Response/The Defense Response*

Stress prompts a series of marked physiological changes. For humans, many times stress results from a change in meaning of a given experience or changes in sensory responses to the environment. As we have seen, the attachment of emotional meaning to remembered events is mediated through the interaction of limbic system and neocortex. A response is then transmitted via limbic connections to the hypothalamus, where it is evaluated in the cortex and then transmitted through the sympathetic nervous system to coordinate the fight-or-flight response.

The release of adrenal glucocorticoids represents the end result of the activation of the hypothalamic-pituitary-adrenal (HPA-limbic) axis. Under most circumstances, this response occurs as a result of the release of specific neuropeptides from specialized neurons in the hypothalamus. In the face of danger, this short-lived reaction helps individuals survive. However, if the stress response is regularly tripped for the wrong reasons, or alternatively, if it cannot be turned off, it can have the opposite effect. Excessive stress can also cause developmental abnormalities, unhealthy weight gain, heart disease, hypertension, diabetes, depression, and immune suppression.

## What Activates the Stress Response?

The major stimulators of arousal and stress appear to be pain, novelty, uncertainty, and conflict. The response to novelty, for example, requires a comparison between patterns and features of the particular stimulus and the remembered characteristics of the stimulus recorded in long-term memory. The greater the difference or dissonance between the pattern evoked by the immediate stimulus and the prior experience, the greater the degree of the adrenocortical stress response.

When adrenal steroids such as cortisol are released into the circulatory system, they reach the brain and influence central nervous system functions by attaching to glucocorticoid receptors—the receptors for cortisol—located in specialized regions in the brain. An intricate feedback loop regulates the availability of these receptors in the dentate gyrus of the hippocampus. Changes in receptor number can alter the degree to which a hormonal signal is "heard" by the cell and how rapidly the stress response can be stopped.

Laboratory studies have shown that the reduction of glucocorticoid receptors in the dentate gyrus, due to exposure to stress or to persistently high blood levels of glucocorticoids, is associated with a reduced capacity to shut off the adrenal stress response. For example, rats that are subjected to stress produced by daily handling shortly after birth develop lifelong changes in the number of hippocampal glucocorticoid receptors and exhibit lower resting cortisol levels and greater sensitivity to cortisol in comparison to unstressed control animals.

Since glucocorticoid receptors regulate gene expression, it is likely that stressors experienced early in life can produce long-lasting effects on the HPA-hippocampal axis. Even transient stress may affect the nerve cells containing glucocorticoid receptors at the DNA level, resulting in changes that strongly influence nerve excitability and perhaps individual capacity to regulate the response to stress. In effect, early experience in combination with genetic predisposition has been shown to set the sensitivity of an individual's stress response.

Individuals with bipolar disorder seem to carry genetic vulnerabilities and sensitivities that predispose them to a low threshold of response to stressful events. But animal studies also have shown that an active nurturing environment can buffer the effects of this vulnerability.

## Social Factors That Determine the Intensity of the Stress Response
Although all infants respond to separation with increases in circulating levels of cortisol, the magnitude of these changes largely depends on the degree of social support available during the separation period. The most dramatic elevations occur when infants are completely isolated in a novel environment during separation. By contrast, separated infants who remain in familiar surroundings with other mothers and their infants show minimal signs of distress and minimal increases in adrenocortical activity.

In an elegantly designed series of experiments, Dr. Seymour Levine and colleagues at the Stanford University School of Medicine in Palo Alto, California, chose a naturalistic fearful stimulus—visual exposure to a live caged snake—to test the hypothesis that the presence of familiar social companions buffer stress-induced elevations in cortisol. When exposed, individually or in pairs, to a live boa constrictor contained in a box that prevented direct physical contact, monkeys showed increased levels of vigilance, agitation, and avoidance of the snake, along with high stress-activated cortisol levels when tested individually as well as in pairs. However, when monkeys were exposed to the fearful stimulus in a group, an increase in adrenocortical activity did not occur.

These studies make it abundantly clear that the same stimuli do not act in identical ways and that social relationships can modify fearful situations that activate the stress response. Bipolar children who react fearfully to situations can buffer the greater degree of stress they will likely experience if not isolated and withdrawn from figures of social support.

In addition to heritable vulnerabilities, an individual's susceptibility to undue stress seems to reflect, in part, the effects of early life experiences. Michael Meaney and his colleagues at the Douglas Hospital Research Center in Montreal examined levels of the stress hormone corticotropin-releasing factor (CRF) in infant rats. They found that when mother rats lick their offspring often, the pups produce less CRF. According to these studies, the amount of maternal licking during the first ten days of life is highly correlated with the production of CRF in the hypothalamus of the brain of the adult offspring. In addition, compared with isolated or orphaned pups, licked rats develop more glucocorticoid receptors in the hippocampus. These receptors, when activated, inhibit the production of CRF in the hypothalamus and thus dampen the stress response. Licked rats also produce more receptors for the CRF-inhibiting neurotransmitter GABA in both the amygdala and locus coeruleus, brain regions associated with fear, vigilance, and response to novel environmental stimuli.

## Corticotropin-Releasing Hormone Potentiates the Startle Response

Corticotropin-releasing hormone is a neuropeptide that participates in the generation of the stress response. Through its actions at the level of the HPA-limbic axis, CRF also plays a key role in the control of neuronal activity in the central nucleus of the amygdala. CRF fibers that pass from the central nucleus of the amygdala directly connect with nerve cells in the forebrain and affect a wide population of brain cells. These same CRF fibers also reach out to norepinephrine-containing nerve cells in the brain stem that regulate emotional arousal and to those that influence autonomic nervous system activity.

This dual regulation pathway calibrates and integrates hormonal response and neurotransmitter release, bringing together the combined emotional and sensory information processed within the limbic system and the vital response of the hypothalamus. Therefore, CRF plays an important role in fear-related processes, notably in the enhancement and inhibition of the startle and stress responses.

## INTERCELLULAR COMMUNICATION

In higher animals, the two major pathways of intercellular communication are the endocrine system (the glandular system of the body) and the nervous system. In the endocrine system, specialized cells secrete hormones that are carried in the bloodstream and through the cerebrospinal fluid via an elegant system of connecting chambers to distant parts of the body and influence the activity of specifically responsive target cells.

### Hormonal Messages

Neurotransmitters trigger the activity of the hormone neurosecretory cells that reside in the hypothalamus, adrenal, thyroid, and pineal glands. Because of their capacity to translate neuronal activity into hormonal output, they have been called transducer cells.

Most hormones exert their effects in two stages. Initially, the hormone receptor promotes the transcription of a small number of genes. This effect usually occurs within thirty minutes and is known as a primary hormonal response. However, since many of the genes that are transcribed during this initial phase are themselves capable of inducing transcription, these newly synthesized proteins activate additional genes in a delayed or secondary response. A single hormone, therefore, can initiate a complex pattern of gene expression.

### Neurons

The other major pathways of intercellular communication in the nervous system are composed of interconnecting cells called neurons. A neuron, the basic cell of the nervous system, consists of a cell body, a long, thin tube jutting from the cell body (the axon), and a set of shorter fibers (dendrites) that branch and reach out to receive impulses from other nerve cells. A nerve impulse travels electrically down the axon until it cannot continue because of a tiny gap—the synaptic cleft—that separates it from other cells. Little sacs or vesicles at the end of the axon spill out chemical transmitter molecules that ferry the impulse across the gap and attach to the cell membrane on the other side (see Figure 7.5).

Each of these neurotransmitters has a certain shape and seeks out a molecule, or receptor, on the adjacent cell membrane into which it fits— like a key and its complementary keyhole. In these cells, the back-and-forth movement of ions, such as calcium, sodium, potassium, and chloride, through the cell membrane is responsible for their excitability and also endows them with rhythmic electrical properties. Chemical and electrical contacts between these neurons permit them to fire in unison as a network. The firing rates of these "pacemaker" nuclei signal light/dark transitions, temperature variations in the environment and within the body, and shape attention. They also provide appropriate timing in motor coordination, adjust levels of arousal throughout the sleep/wake cycle, and even modulate the perception of pain. Is it possible that some dysregulation of pacemaker function exists in bipolar disorder?

## Neurotransmitter Signaling Systems

The monoamines, which include norepinephrine, serotonin, and dopamine, are a special class of neurotransmitters. Each of these neurotransmitter systems consists of a small number of neurons that originate in the brain stem and connect to many regions of the brain, each with its own set of targets. They all prominently connect to the limbic system.

### Norepinephrine System

Norepinephrine-containing cells in the brain stem originate in a small cluster of cells called the locus coeruleus. The norepinephrine system may serve to bring an individual to an alert state in order to prepare the brain to deal effectively with a novel environmental situation. The studies of Drs. Floyd Bloom and Gary Ashton-Jones and colleagues at the Salk Institute in La Jolla, California, suggest that sensory neurons in the neocortex may decrease their random firing and respond more strongly to outside sensory stimuli due to increased input from norepinephrine neurons during the alert state. Therefore, norepinephrine firing rates in the locus coeruleus provide an appropriate tuning or modulation of the sensory systems as an individual awakes from sleep or is otherwise aroused into an alert state, enabling the person to mount a response to some novel environmental challenge.

The firing rate of these neurons is variable across the sleep/wake cycle and plays a critical role in regulating the transitions between REM and non-REM sleep stages. Almost totally silent during REM sleep, these neurons fire slowly during slow-wave sleep and fire at their maximum rate (four to five times per second) during periods of alertness.

While the locus coeruleus sends its nerve terminals widely throughout

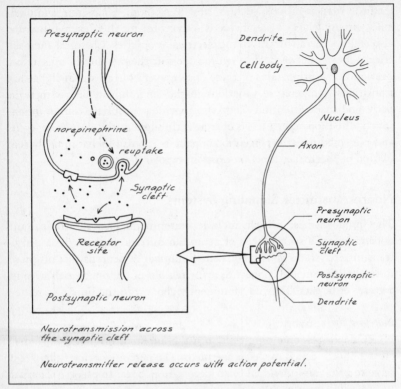

**Figure 7.5 Neurotransmitter Release at the Synaptic Cleft**
The presynaptic and postsynaptic neurons that release and receive the neurotransmitter norepinephrine across the synaptic cleft. Norepinephrine is released from the presynaptic neuron and attaches to receptors in the membrane of postsynaptic neurons. It is then taken back up into the presynaptic neuron by a process called reuptake.

the brain, only a few brain regions connect to it; the bulk of connecting fibers arise from two other brain stem nuclei. One projection arising from the brain center that uses the neurotransmitter acetylcholine—the giant tegmental cell nucleus—provides a potent inhibitory influence that acts on norepinephrine receptors in the locus coeruleus. The firing rates of these two pacemakers alternate from rapid crackling volleys to complete silence throughout the sleep cycle, mirroring the transitions from REM to non-REM sleep.

Alterations in the firing rate of the locus coeruleus neurons are responsible for activation of aspects of the stress response as well, and are thought to play a role in anxiety and panic states. Distractibility and the disruption of attentional focus, commonly experienced symptoms of bipolar disorder and ADHD, may be related to disturbances in this system that affect the ability to sustain attention and mental effort. Stimulant drugs that enhance attentional focus, such as Ritalin, all increase norepinephrine release. Drugs that increase central norepinephrine transmission, such as tricyclic antidepressants, as well as drugs that enhance dopamine transmission, such as stimulants, have been found to induce hypomania or mania and increase the frequency of cycling.

The neurons that make up the locus coeruleus contain several different neuropeptide receptors, such as neuropeptide Y (NPY), CRF, and the μu opiate receptor, activated by morphine and the naturally occurring opiates. All of these neuropeptides share a common regulatory function with the alpha-2 norepinephrine receptors: They activate a second messenger that resides within the cell, cyclic adenosine monophosphate (cAMP).

This second messenger, cAMP, plays a critical role in cell signaling processes that determine the firing rate of locus coeruleus neurons; therefore, its level of activity directly influences behavioral alerting responses and sleep/wake transitions between REM and non-REM stages.

## Dopamine Neurotransmitter System

Dopamine is the principal neurotransmitter responsible for physical movement, reward-motivated behaviors, and body temperature regulation. There are three principal dopamine-producing systems in the brain, and at least two of them are likely to be involved with mood disorders— the nucleus accumbens and the arcuate nucleus. The nucleus accumbens is located at the interface of limbic projections from the amygdala and the hippocampus. It sends fibers to dopamine neurons in midbrain centers that activate motor behavior, and it is well situated to form the circuitry that mediates the behavioral and mood-activating properties of several stimulant drugs, such as Dexedrine and Ritalin, known to enhance both dopamine and norepinephrine transmission.

Dopamine-releasing cells in the arcuate nucleus, like similar cells in the locus coeruleus, contain the receptors of neuropeptides such as NPY and μu opiates—the brain's naturally occurring morphine. These receptors interact with the cyclic AMP (cAMP) second messenger signaling system to prolong and/or enhance the effects of dopamine. Activation of these circuits by positive-reinforcing environmental stimuli may influence mood, appetite, and other reward-motivated behaviors. Indeed, a wealth of research on animals leaves little question that the dopaminergic system mediates some of the rewarding properties of stimulants (amphetamines), opiate drugs (morphine and heroin), and cocaine and marijuana. Antidepressant drugs of all classes appear to enhance the function of this reward system.

Antipsychotic drugs that block dopamine receptors and inhibit adenylate cyclase (the enzyme that activates the second messenger cAMP) in the limbic system are extremely effective treatments for the core symptoms of mania.

Abnormal variations in the activity of the dopamine system may affect self-esteem; may contribute to abnormal mood states, such as elation and melancholia; and may result in marked variations in activity/hyperactivity and pressured speech seen in mania and hypomania.

## Serotonergic Neurotransmitter System

The serotonergic system consists of a diverse group of neurons whose cell bodies are located in the raphe nuclei and some regions of the reticular-activating system—the brain's arousal system. Its terminals fan out to virtually all regions of the central nervous system. Antidepressant drugs such as Prozac, Zoloft, and Paxil act to enhance serotonin availability in the brain.

The midbrain raphe nucleus provides a dense input of serotonin-containing terminals to the suprachiasmatic nucleus, the master clock of the circadian system. Disruption of raphe activity may interfere with the adaptive changes in circadian rhythms generated by the suprachiasmatic nucleus. Surgical lesions of the raphe nucleus in animals have been found to disrupt rhythmicity in running activity and to result in the loss of the circadian cortisol rhythm. Chronic treatment with the antidepressant imipramine (Tofranil) was found to produce a significant increase in the sensitivity of nerve cells in the suprachiasmatic nucleus. Such an effect could be related to the high frequency of antidepressant-induced switching that has been reported in bipolar disorder.

Sleep disorders have been commonly described in children with bipolar disorders. The normal slow-wave sleep of stage 4 depends on serotonin function. Night terrors and sleepwalking, both commonly observed early symptoms in bipolar children, also occur during stage 4 sleep. Adults with depressive disorders have been found to have persistent disturbances in stage 4 slow-wave sleep even after clinical symptoms of depression have subsided. There are reports of a subgroup of patients with bipolar disorder who have persistently low levels of the major breakdown product of serotonin in their cerebrospinal fluid, even after recovery.

Blood and cerebrospinal fluid levels of serotonin and its metabolites have been found to vary seasonally in an inverse relationship with the pineal hormone melatonin. A number of investigators have reported clear seasonal variations with peaks in April and September. Interestingly, there is a robust correlation between the monthly occurrence of homicides and violent suicides and the observed seasonal rhythms of serotonin.

## G-Proteins and Second Messengers

A class of membrane-based proteins known as G-proteins is among the first to respond when a neuronal cell receives a neurotransmitter signal. They are called G-proteins because, in their active state, the protein grasps a cell molecule known as guanosine triphosphate (GTP). In this GTP-bound form, the G-protein activates the next step in a chain of events that leads eventually to a cellular response. Often the signal activates an enzyme like cAMP in such a way that, by adding a phosphorus atom, it can change the enzyme's activity level or allow a protein to bind to the cell's DNA and thereby have a direct effect on the kinds or amounts of proteins the cell manufactures.

So far we have described how certain neurotransmitters, by binding to a specific receptor, stimulate the production of enzymes such as cAMP within the cell that receives the neurotransmitter signal. The question remains: How does an activation of this pathway translate the neurotransmitter's message into some physiological action?

The phosphoinositides, a group of phospholipid molecules that lend structure to the cell membrane, appear to play a central role in signal transmission for a wide variety of neurotransmitters and hormones. When cells are stimulated, a phospholipid called phosphatidylinositol-bis-phosphate (PIP2) is broken down into two compounds: diacylglycerol (DAG) and inositol triphosphate (IP3), both of which act as second messengers capable of igniting great changes within the cell. IP3 provokes the release of calcium from tiny storage pockets in the cytoplasm; the calcium then begins to trigger a number of enzymes. At the same time, DAG sparks the enzyme protein kinase C, which excites yet another string of cellular enzymes. Eventually all this activity reaches the nucleus of the cell.

Both lithium and omega-3 fish oils may exert their therapeutic effect in this crucial part of the signal transduction pathway. As we mentioned, this cycle is a second messenger system that relays and amplifies signals from the neurotransmitters, hormones, and other molecules. Lithium and omega-3 fish oils apparently inhibit or throttle down the activity of this pathway. Dr. Michael Berridge of the Baraban Institute in Cambridge, England, was the first to propose that lithium's antimanic and antidepressant effects worked on this cellular pathway. Subsequently, James Allison and William Sherman at the Washington University School of Medicine in St. Louis found that lithium ions inhibit the enzyme that removes the final phosphate group in this degradation pathway. Paul Worley and Jay Baraban from Johns Hopkins have shown that when cells in a slice of the brain taken from the hippocampus are treated with low levels of lithium, their response to neurotransmitters that cause either excitation or inhibition is dampened. Other investigators have suggested that the target of lithium's effect on cells may be via cyclic nucleotide metabolism. For example, in animals it has been reported that therapeutic concentrations of lithium inhibit the ordinary stimulation of adenylate cyclase, an enzyme that induces cAMP. Sophia Avissar and colleagues of Ben Gurion University in Beersheba, Israel, have found that lithium blocks GTP binding induced by the neurotransmitter acetylcholine. Since this effect is a measure of the degree of activation of the important G-proteins, these investigators and others hypothesize that lithium reduces cAMP responsiveness via its inhibition of a G-protein that is known to regulate adenylate cyclase.

It has become more and more appreciated that the long-term treatment of complex neuropsychiatric disorders such as bipolar disorder involves the strategic regulation of signaling pathways in the brain and alterations in the expression of specific genes in critical neuronal circuits. Studies over the last decade have sought to identify specific changes in gene expression as a potential source of lithium's therapeutic effect. Indeed, in cell and animal studies, the expression of different genes has been found to be markedly altered by both short-term and chronic lithium administration.

One of the first studies to demonstrate the short-term effects of lithium salts on gene expression was reported in 1991 by Drs. Elyse Weiner, Vasundhara Kalasapudi, Demitri Papolos, and Herb Lachman of the Program in Behavioral Genetics at the Albert Einstein College of Medicine. These researchers observed that lithium has a dramatic augmenting effect on expression of the immediate early gene activator, *fos*, in the animal brain. *Fos* induction, mediated by a muscarinic receptor that activates the enzyme protein kinase C, was found to be exquisitely sensitive to the effect of lithium.

Excessive cell stimulation by gene activators can trigger a prolonged wave of immediate early gene transcription that can lead to degeneration and nerve cell demise. Prolonged immediate early gene transcription serves as a marker of traumatic brain injury and may play a role in neurodegeneration. Degeneration and neuronal death—apoptosis—is the fundamental process responsible for the clinical manifestations of many different neurological disorders of aging, incuding Alzheimer's disease, Parkinson's disease, and stroke.

Considerable evidence from brain imaging and postmortem studies also demonstrates that significant reductions in the number of neurons in specific regions of the brain are associated with mood disorders. Preliminary studies of adolescent and young adult twins suggest a strong correspondence between genetic influence, early-onset depression, and deficits of regional brain volume.

Most recently, chronic lithium treatment has been shown to exert neuroprotective effects against a variety of experimentally induced insults to the brain that lead to neuronal death or apoptosis. Specifically, the work of Dr. Husseini Manji and colleagues from the Cellular and Clinical Neurobiology Program at Wayne State University School of Medicine found that chronic lithium treatment of rats resulted in doubling of the levels of Bcl-2 in the frontal cortex. A neuroprotective role for Bcl-2 has been well established, and expression of high levels of this protein has been found to enhance the survival of cells when exposed to adverse stimuli. These findings raise the intriguing possibility that lithium may exert some of its long-term beneficial effects in the treatment of mood disorders via underappreciated neurotrophic and neuroprotective influences. The robust increase in Bcl-2 levels in the frontal lobe is of particular importance, as emerging evidence is beginning to suggest that deficits in this region of the brain may play a key role in the development of many of the symptoms that are observed in childhood-onset bipolar disorder (see Chapter 10).

## NEUROPEPTIDES THAT AFFECT BEHAVIORAL RESPONSE

The effects of neuropeptides, such as substance P, NPY, and CRF, are fundamental to our understanding of the neurochemical organization of the central nervous system and how it integrates and responds to environmental signals. These chemical messengers all have important influences on the systems that regulate arousal, stress, sleep/wake transitions, appetite, activity, energy production, and the experience of pleasure and pain. The actions of neuropeptides, no matter where they are released, tend to be enduring and to serve a modulating function, controlling neuronal excitability and the effectiveness or stability of neurotransmission.

Many of these neuropeptide-containing neurons innervate structures of the limbic system. The abundance of neuropeptides and their complex pattern within the amygdala, which acts as a focus for a number of peptide pathways and incoming catecholamine pathways, implies that they act to regulate endocrine responses to stressful events and/or to alter emotional responses to fearful stimuli.

Neuropeptides frequently coexist with one another or with monoamine neurotransmitters, such as norepinephrine, dopamine, and serotonin, with as many as three biologically active substances residing within a single neuron. This arrangement greatly increases the possible number of different chemical signals that a neuron can use in communicating with its neighbors.

### Substance P

The delicate balance between our experiencing too much or too little pain is largely controlled by substance P, a neuropeptide found virtually wherever primary pain fibers extend. Substance P causes an increased level of excitation at sensory nerve terminals that bring information from the skin and salivary glands and light/dark information from the retina. Recent studies suggest that it also contributes to the degree of stress we experience.

Because substance P is also located in a region of the brain that coordinates the stress response—the amygdala—and because repeated administration of antidepressant drugs causes a decrease of substance P synthesis in the brain, researchers suspected that substance P inhibitors might have psychotherapeutic properties. Indeed, recent trials of various forms of substance P inhibitors have found antidepressant effects in patients with moderate to severe depression.

Many sites within the brain might account for the antidepressant effects of substance P inhibitors. Substance P provides a powerful input from the amygdala to the hypothalamic region that is important for the expression of defensive rage in animals. When researchers injected substance P inhibitors into the hypothalamus of cats, they were able to block the effects of the amygdaloid stimulation that elicits this defensive rage response.

Although the precise mechanism of the antidepressant effects of substance P inhibition is not as yet known, current research suggests that psychological stress causes the release of substance P in the amygdala. Therefore, substance P inhibitors may enhance integration of emotional responses to stress. If this theory is borne out by further research, and substance P inhibitors do not cause an increase in cycle frequency or induce mania, these drugs could become important new treatment options for childhood and adult forms of bipolar disorder.

## Neuropeptide Y and Its Effects on Behavior

Over the past decade animal studies have found that NPY has specific effects that are closely linked to behaviors associated with bipolar disorder. NPY has specific effects in the regulation of anxiety, stress, carbohydrate craving, and energy production and on the ability to shift circadian rhythms.

NPY neurons are found in high density in the "master clock" that regulates circadian rhythms, the suprachiasmatic nucleus. The suprachiasmatic nucleus is a receiving station for the flow of information coming from the eyes to the hypothalamus, a nerve pathway that carries information about environmental conditions of light and darkness to the brain.

Several lines of evidence indicate that NPY plays a role in the modulation of the HPA-limbic axis and is a principal part of the signaling system for the chain of activities that allows an individual to respond to stress. In an attempt to understand the long-term effects of NPY on the central nervous system, Dr. A. Inui and colleagues at Kobe University School of Medicine in Japan raised a group of mice that were genetically engineered to produce increased levels of NPY in the brain (about 15 percent above levels in control animals). These mice displayed marked behavioral signs of anxiety and substantial increases in the size of the region in the adrenal gland that produces corticosterone. The anxiety-like behaviors of the mice could be reversed by the administration into the brain of a neuropeptide that specifically blocks the action of CRF, suggesting that NPY and CRF may interact to regulate the level of anxiety in response to stress.

## CRF and NPY

As we have described, corticotropin-releasing factor appears to have activating properties on behavior and to coordinate responses to stress. Direct administration of CRF into the central nervous system produces activation; however, the profile of the behavioral actions of CRF changes dramatically when animals are exposed to a prior stressor. The same dose that produces activation in a familiar environment suppresses exploration in a novel, and presumably stressful, environment. And CRF, in this context, can enhance the reactions of animals subjected to noxious stimuli or averse psychological states.

Thus behavioral activation produced by CRF injected into unstressed animals is transformed into a behaviorally inhibiting effect under stressful conditions. Could CRF, through its interaction with neuropeptide Y, and substance P coordinate coping responses to stress that are dependent on other factors, such as degree of arousal or prior levels of fearfulness and anxiety?

Clinically, stress has long been linked to overeating and bingeing on sweets and carbohydrates. This behavior is the most common symptom of appetite dysregulation during the depressive, low-energy periods of bipolar disorder. In addition to their actions on the stress response, both NPY and CRF are known to have potent effects on appetite, energy storage, and energy expenditure. After being injected into the hypothalamus, NPY markedly stimulates carbohydrate craving and hormone secretion.

Although bipolar disorder is primarily identified by extreme mood swings, a wide variation in energy levels is also a cardinal feature of the condition. Among the most well-studied actions of CRF in animals is its influence on energy balance. CRF treatment blunts energy storage (energy balance) by simultaneously reducing food intake and augmenting energy expenditure, features commonly reported by individuals experiencing hypomanic and manic episodes.

In contrast to the effects of CRF, NPY promotes energy storage through an increase in appetite and reduction in energy expenditure. Circulating blood levels of cortisol dramatically affect both systems. An imbalance between CRF and NPY systems produced by disturbances in cortisol levels due to protracted stress responses could be fundamental in the alteration of energy balance observed in bipolar disorder.

## CLOCKS THAT TIME US

While the various interconnected brain nuclei and their multiple neurotransmitter, neuropeptide, and hormonal circuits keep us grounded in three-dimensional space, alerting us and assessing danger, remembering adaptive responses to environmental and social cues, what biological mechanisms anchor us to the passage of time, and how do they influence our behavior? Human-made clocks divide the day into seconds, minutes, and hours. Inside, our bodies keep time quite differently. Cycles may last mere fractions of a second or take hours to complete.

The timing of events within the central nervous system is at least as important as the spatial arrangements of the centers of neuronal activity in the brain. Neurotransmitters, neuropeptides, and hormones must not only lock into their corresponding receptor keyhole, but they must act with appropriate timing—in relation to one other and to periodic events in the environment. Genes with names like Tick Tock or ICER are the gears of the biological clockworks whose role is to coordinate the apparent stable functions of the brain and body that are poised on the paradox of continuous but well-regulated change. Temperature, blood pressure, hormonal secretions, blood sugar, and dozens of other aspects of bodily activity continuously wax and wane according to varying schedules.

### Ultradian Clocks

Our inner clocks prefer certain periods for their cycles. Ultradian clocks keep time in units shorter than a day. Our swiftest-running clocks, the ultradian rhythms, do the work of the nervous system. When we are resting, an electroencephalogram shows the brain's electrical rhythms averaging from eight to twelve cycles per second. During the morning, our brain waves cycle at the slow end of this range. They speed up when darkness falls and cycle most quickly when we are asleep. The ultradian rhythm perhaps most familiar to us is the beating of our own hearts.

For our brains, a day may be marked by sixteen cycles alternating at ninety-minute intervals. Other rhythms may be only milliseconds long, like the cycle in which certain neuronal cells fire, or a few minutes or hours long, like the ninety-minute sleep cycle alternating between REM and non-REM stages.

Quick-cycling rhythms are built into all living systems at the genetic level. Short-cycle ultradian clocks, such as the REM/non-REM sleep cycle, must be remarkably small, perhaps even smaller than a single gene. Subtle disturbances in the clock mechanism or other external factors that perturb the rhythms set by these clocks could very likely contribute to the ultra-ultrarapid cycles of mood, energy, sleep, and activity that characterize early-onset bipolar disorder.

## Circadian Clocks

For some hormonal rhythms, the clock may be set to produce cycles of sixty minutes each. A second type of clock measures time in periods about twenty-four hours long. These circadian clocks generate rhythms of REM sleep propensity, body temperature, and daily activity as well as subtler rhythms of when we are most sensitive to pain, how well we estimate the passage of time, or when our bodies are most affected by alcohol.

All human beings have established sleep and activity cycles as well as periods of hunger and satiety, but many other regular cycles take place below the level of conscious awareness, most notably the secretions of the endocrine system—hormones such as CRF, ACTH, cortisol, and melatonin. Interestingly, there are also regular variations in the production of many neurotransmitters, including norepinephrine and serotonin, as well as in the numbers of receptor sites that receive these neurotransmitters.

The various rhythms play an intricate counterpoint, reaching their peaks (acrophases) and troughs (nadirs) at different phases of the circadian day. At given times of the day, month, or year a particular biological or behavioral activity is either necessarily restricted or appropriately undertaken. For example, REM sleep must alternate with non-REM sleep at specific times and in a regular pattern.

Circadian rhythms are described by their period (cycle length) and their phase (relative position in time). If the organization of rhythmicity falters, some rhythms will desynchronize from others. This alteration in the relative coordination of mutually timed events could cause a breakdown in internal temporal order. As a result, oversensitized or desensitized physiological systems that normally prime one another would fail to do so, perhaps leading to many other physiological functions not being switched on or off at the appropriate times.

## Circadian Dysregulation or Desynchronization

Alterations in the timing functions of the circadian system have been postulated to play a key role in the causes of bipolar disorder. If you examine the course of bipolar disorder, you find that many people have a pattern of recurrence: The cycles come and go, sometimes at the same time of year.

In childhood-onset bipolar disorder, rapid daily cycles of mood and energy are commonplace. In fact, the majority of children experience an ultra-ultrarapid or ultradian (many cycles within a day) form of cycling, most often characterized by difficulty awakening from sleep in the morning with low energy on arising that then switches at midafternoon or evening to high activity and high levels of energy. These rhythmic disturbances point to the possibility that bipolar disorder is a temporal one in which the timing of biological rhythms is pathologically altered.

A major question posed by researchers is: What deficit in biological systems might lead to a disturbance in circadian or ultradian timing that could account for the rapid shifts of mood and energy states, sleep/wake reversals, and the high rates of ultra-ultrarapid and seasonal cycling patterns that have been observed clinically? Could the same or a similar vulnerability of physiological timing account for the recent finding that the rate of interhemispheric switching is slow in patients with bipolar disorder? Could sensitivity to light and its effects on melatonin release from the pineal gland, alterations in the circadian body temperature rhythms, and the shortened REM latency found in bipolar patients also be related to the same dysfunction of biological timing?

## A "Sticky" Hemispheric Switch

Drs. John Pettigrew and Steven Miller from the Vision Touch and Hearing Research Center at the University of Queensland in Brisbane, Australia, have reported intriguing new findings in a group of bipolar patients who were studied while in normal mood states. To study the interhemispheric switching process in these subjects, they examined a high-level attentional process known as binocular rivalry: that is, the alternating perceptual states that arise when viewing different images presented separately to each eye.

Because the cerebral hemispheres can function independently of each other during perceptual and attentional tasks, Pettigrew and Miller hypothesized that the resolution of the conflicting visual stimuli in binocular rivalry might occur by alternating hemispheric activation and that competition for awareness during binocular rivalry occurs between rather than within hemispheres. They have reported preliminary evidence that two unilateral hemisphere-stimulating techniques, caloric vestibular stimulation and transcranial magnetic stimulation, can alter the rate of interhemispheric switching. Interestingly, both techniques have been found to reverse depressive and manic periods in bipolar patients. In their study bipolar patients showed a dramatically slower rate of perceptual switches between left and right hemispheres when presented with a task that measures binocular rivalry.

Other recent studies have reported that perceptual transitions experienced during binocular rivalry involve both the visual and prefrontal cortex. These findings were obtained by measuring brain activity with functional magnetic resonance imaging (FMRI) in humans. In fact, a wide variety of evidence supports hemispheric asymmetries of mood. Imaging studies suggest that there is a greater relative right prefrontal activation in depression. Activation asymmetries favoring the left hemisphere have been reported in mania. In keeping with these activation asymmetries, transcranial magnetic stimulation administered to the left cerebral hemisphere of the prefrontal cortex has been found therapeutic for depression.

The pacemaker for binocular rivalry targets regions at high stages of visual processing in the temporal-parietal cortex. An interhemispheric switch for cognitive style and mood would likely engage both frontal and limbic regions of the brain and have a rhythm similar to that of the ultradian rhythms of cerebral dominance. To explain this, Pettigrew and Miller have suggested that a slowing of the pacemaker for the temporal-parietal cortex also might be accompanied by a proportionate slowing of a pacemaker that governs interhemispheric switching in other regions of the brain, such as the prefrontal cortex, that govern emotional response.

Since pacemakers with different rates have been found coupled genetically in some organisms, a genetic mutation that affected the timing rates of one or more of these pacemakers might account for many of the cognitive and behavioral features of bipolar disorder. But specifically which pacemakers and what functions are disturbed? Could some perturbation in biological timing functions result in the attentional problems and the sleep disturbances as well as the ultra-ultrarapid mood and energy swings so common in childhood-onset bipolar disorder?

## Ultradian Cycles of REM–Non-REM Sleep and Waking Performance

Research indicates that the quality of the performance of some mental tasks, such as alertness, varies in cycles whose period is approximately ninety minutes, remarkably like the period of the REM—non-REM sleep cycle. This matches the adult daily sleep/wakefulness cycle, which, as we have seen, develops from briefer sleep/wake cycles evident in infants. As the adult sleep cycle evolves, the basic period progressively lengthens from fifty to sixty minutes to eighty to one hundred minutes. One of the earliest sleep researchers, Dr. Nathaniel Kleitman of the University of Chicago, predicted that the human basic rest-activity rhythm (BRAC) developed from a more primitive rhythm in digestive function that was adjusted to an individual's nutritional needs and that this basic cycle, which appears in sleep as the REM and non-REM cycles, would be manifest during the waking hours in periodic fluctuations in alertness. Indeed, ultradian rhythms have been found in human waking performance and psychophysiological measures attributable to alertness or attention as well as in a number of ingestive, digestive, and excretory functions.

Circadian rhythms also are known to shape human performance efficiency as well as physiological processes such as body temperature, rest activity, and sensitivity to light. These latter rhythms can modify the performance of mental functions. Other research has found that ninety-minute alternations in the relative efficiency of verbal (left hemisphere) and spatial (right hemisphere) matching tasks are 180 degrees out of phase, lending support to the notion of alternating rhythms of cerebral dominance. Taken together, research suggests that some aspects of the basic rest/activity rhythm are associated with reciprocal alternations in the activation of the two cerebral hemispheres.

## Subjective Alertness, Mental Performance, and Body Temperature Rhythms

Until the mid-1970s, it was believed that there was a strong parallel between the circadian body temperature rhythm and "all" performance rhythms. Then Dr. S. Folkard's groundbreaking studies of time-of-day effects on complex memory tasks, such as verbal reasoning, revealed that there was no single performance rhythm but many and that while a parallel with body temperature did exist, it was not uniform.

We now know that the capacity to perform different mental tasks is associated with different time-of-day functions, adjusting at different rates to a change in schedule and under the unified control of several biological clocks acting cooperatively. A model that is used to explain the differences in the rate of adjustment assumes that any given circadian rhythm is jointly controlled by two biological pacemakers.

Studies by Timothy Monk and colleagues at the Western Psychiatric Institute and Clinic of the University of Pittsburgh School of Medicine have led to the understanding that temperature rhythm alone does not control subjective alertness and the capacity to perform various cognitive tasks, although it is indeed an important determinant. Rather a cooperative relationship exists between inputs from at least two pacemakers, one that regulates body temperature and another the cycle of sleep and wakefulness.

## Suprachiasmatic Nucleus—The Master Clock

In mammals, the response to the light/dark cycle has an important biological function in sleep, activity, twenty-four-hour body temperature rhythm, and reproductive and perhaps social behaviors. Research studies have found that light exerts a dual influence on sleep and activity and other basic biological rhythms. The twenty-four-hour light/dark cycle acts as a synchronizer for the circadian rest/activity and sleep/wake, temperature, and melatonin rhythms, determining their period and relationship.

Although many sleep abnormalities occur in mood disorders, the most consistent and specific appears to be an abnormal distribution of REM during sleep. The first REM period occurs relatively soon after sleep onset, has a long duration, and often is of a high density. At least two biological clocks govern the regular transitions from waking to sleep and, within sleep, between the stages of active REM and deep non-REM sleep.

The suprachiasmatic nucleus sets the rhythm of so-called sleep propensity—the periods within the twenty-four-hour day when we are most likely to be able to fall into dream sleep. In humans, this is usually after lunch at midday and at around 11:00 to 11:30 P.M. These periods also occur at the same time that the twenty-four-hour body temperature rhythm begins to dip. At night, when body temperature reaches its lowest point of the day, the firing of norepinephrine-containing cells in the locus coeruleus all but ceases and the fast-activity desynchronized brain waves of REM sleep turn on. At the same time, complete muscular paralysis occurs and the body's primary heat loss and heat retention mechanisms almost completely lose their capacity to respond to changes in environmental temperature. All these functions are influenced by a third rhythmic clock in the midbrain, also synchronized to the REM/non-REM cycle, that uses acetylcholine as its chemical messenger.

REM/non-REM cycles alternate throughout the night, their duration strongly controlled by the difference in firing rates between the norepinephrine-producing midbrain locus coeruleus and the acetylcholine-producing giant tegmental cell nucleus (GTN). As with the autonomic nervous system—which receives, transmits, and integrates sensory information—the central nervous system uses a similar dual pattern of cooperation and opposition between norepinephrine and acetylcholine. The locus coeruleus is engaged in a nightly dance with the GTN, a competitive back-and-forth seesaw for dominance that produces the periodic alternations between REM and non-REM sleep states. During the sleep cycle the activity patterns of the norepinephrine and acetylcholine pacemakers are of similar frequency and amplitude, yet together they must be able to synchronize—one starting when the other leaves off—coupling and uncoupling multiple times throughout the night. Whether the transitions of consciousness that take place between REM and non-REM sleep are smooth or choppy depends on a well-oiled switch.

Non-REM sleep is thought to be controlled by the temperature-sensitive cells located in a biological clock in the preoptic/anterior nucleus of the hypothalamus that is near the suprachiasmatic nucleus, where circadian signals and homeostatic processes that regulate body temperature may be integrated. Dr. Pier Luigi Parmaggiani and his colleagues at the University of Bologna Medical School in Bologna, Italy, were the first to demonstrate that changes in the temperature sensitivity of these neurons was the basis for non-REM/REM transitions and could also be a primary component of the process for stabilization of arousal functions after transitions from wakefulness to non-REM sleep. The sleep arousals most commonly seen in childhood-onset bipolar disorder, including night terrors, sleep awakenings, bedwetting, sleepwalking, and abnormal movements (restless leg syndrome), are all examples of non-REM instability.

Does some timing disturbance affect the function of just one pacemaker, or could some disturbance in the rivalry for dominance between REM and non-REM sleep/wake cycles—what we might call a REM-dominant arousal state with non-REM instability—be due to a disturbance in timing regulation between two or more biological clocks? This same question must be asked about the finding of Drs. Pettigrew and Miller that binocular rivalry between left and right hemispheres is disturbed in patients with bipolar disorder. Is the slower alternation rates in interhemispheric switching they found in their study related to some common underlying biological disturbance that produces shortened REM latency and increases in REM sleep periods in patients with depression and perhaps even to the tendency to ultradian and seasonal cycling patterns?

## Seasonal Episodes of Depression and Mania

Since ancient times, remarkably regular seasonal recurrences of mania and depression have been an intriguing but unexplained phenomenon. Most contemporary studies have shown that spring and fall are peak times for depression. Hospital admissions for mania undergo seasonal variations as well. Several studies have reported that manic and depressive episodes increase with the difference between maximum and minimum daily temperatures. A high correlation also has been reported between monthly admission rates for mania in Great Britain and seasonal changes in mean monthly day length, daily hours of sunshine, and daily temperature that correspond to the vernal and autumnal equinox.

In one of the largest contemporary studies to examine this seasonal periodicity of episodes, Dr. Gianni Faedda and colleagues recruited a group of 175 patients in Caligari, Italy. In these patients, periods of depression followed one of two patterns: They suffered either fall-winter depression with or without spring-summer mania or hypomania, or spring-summer depression with or without fall-winter mania or hypomania. The two patterns occurred with almost equal frequency.

The idea that depression and mania can result from abnormalities of photoperiodic regulation draws further support from the known therapeutic effects of bright light treatment in seasonally cycling bipolar patients as well as from the studies of Dr. Alfred Lewy of the University of Oregon, in Portland. Lewy found that, compared to nonbipolar subjects, bipolar patients exhibited an abnormality in their capacity to suppress melatonin when exposed to bright light.

In a study of bipolar patients with seasonal episodes, Dr. P. A. Arbisi and colleagues at the Department of Psychology at the University of Minnesota in Minneapolis found that while depressed during the winter months, subjects had significantly impaired capacity to dissipate body heat after exercise.

Two primary environmental signals, the light/dark and temperature cycles, have daily and annual variations whose magnitude depends on the northern and southern latitudes. An annual sunshine record displayed in Figure 7.6 shows the periods of the year that correspond to the highest frequency of depression, hypomania, and mania. Strikingly, they occur at the times of the vernal and autumnal equinoxes—the times of the highest rates of change in dark to light or light to dark transitions. Recent studies have similarly found that these time intervals also correspond to the peaks of suicide and homicide in various parts of the world.

The suprachiasmatic nucleus and pineal gland form the biological timing device that measures the daily duration of darkness and light. By transmitting on-off signals at dawn and dusk, the suprachiasmatic nucleus and pineal gland mutually cooperate and oppose each other, much the same way the REM/non-REM pacemakers do, but at a slower pace, on a daily rather than an eighty- to one-hundred-minute time schedule.

The suprachiasmatic nucleus interacts with the environment via a direct connection to the retina and translates changing light intensity into information while regulating the circadian rhythms of body temperature, REM sleep propensity, and cortisol. The pineal hormone melatonin elicits two effects when applied directly to the suprachiasmatic nucleus: It causes immediate inhibition of pacemaker firing rates and, depending on the time of day, can advance or delay circadian rhythms. A timing glitch in this system might be more likely to be unmasked during periods of seasonal change when dramatic light/dark and temperature variations occur.

While it probably will be a number of years before the underlying biological basis of bipolar disorder is fully understood, the brain pathways contributing to many of the symptoms and behaviors are becoming more

**Figure 7.6 The Annual Light/Dark Cycle**
The variation in the intensity and amount of light in the Northern Hemisphere recorded each day and divided into twelve monthly intervals. The periods of time inclusive of the vernal and autumnal equinoxes and demarcated between late March through mid-April and mid-September to mid-October represent the peak periods of episodes of mania and depression during the year.

clearly delineated. Major contributions from molecular genetics and neuroimaging studies are adding daily to our fund of knowledge and should, in the near future, help us unlock the mystery of this illness. It is encouraging to think that much of the information presented in this chapter was unknown even ten years ago. From this perspective, there is every reason to hope that the next decade will bring an exponential increase in our understanding of the illness—and perhaps similar advances in its treatment.

# PART III

# Living and Coping with Bipolar Disorder

# The Impact
# on the Family

Just the simple word "family" conjures up more associations than probably any other word in the human language. On one level it represents an idealized state—a place where you are loved and supported, the *Father Knows Best* place where every daughter is "Kitten," where brother Bud works hard raking the leaves and shoveling the snow, and where mother Margaret somehow makes the mashed potatoes come out fluffy every time. And while there may be minor mishaps, everything gets worked out and seems warm and funny and complete.

The 1998 movie *Pleasantville* examined just such a world and found out that it all looked great as long as no emotions were expressed, no sexual thoughts ever passed through anyone's mind, and there were no bathrooms *anywhere*. (Nor was anyone ever seen looking for one.) There was no world outside of Pleasantville, and no one owned an umbrella because it never rained in Pleasantville.

And you can bet *no one* had bipolar disorder in Pleasantville.

Today's parents were brought up in this kind of fantasy idea of family life—no matter what their family life was actually like (and it may have been a frightening and dire world touched by the long reach of manic-depressive illness and alcoholism from generations before). But the all-powerful media image is what we carry around with us, despite any reality to the contrary.

So, in the TV series *Father Knows Best,* Bud never called his father a "fucking asshole" and threatened to kill him while he slept. He also never punched holes in the drywall. "Kitten" was never told to run to her room and lock the door because she might be hurt by Bud during a rage that could go on for three hours because his parents said he couldn't watch television. When Margaret was ready to serve those mashed potatoes, she had no trouble getting Bud to join the family. She also answered the phone with the most charming and upbeat voice, never afraid it might be the school calling to say that Bud was out of control again or that it might be a parent calling to complain that Bud had hit or frightened his child.

Family life in a household dealing with a bipolar child is about as un-Pleasantville as it comes. It is a virtual stew of guilt, powerlessness, denial, anger, anxiety, fear, uncertainty, confusion, blame, and shame. These are all very ugly words that make us flinch, arousing feelings that most of us would do anything to avoid, but all are feelings that a family with a bipolar child has to endure for months and years at a time.

The fact that most people don't see what goes on inside the home and have no idea what the family is dealing with makes it all the more terrible. All these awful emotions consume a family—chew it up—and no one understands or empathizes. The struggles for survival from one day to the next are invisible to almost everyone but another family dealing with a bipolar child.

This chapter is about reducing that invisibility, taking a good look at what is happening to a family, and talking about some ways of coping and steering the family onto higher ground—someplace not perfect but livable; where energy can be conserved and spent more wisely; where solutions can be found that allow all people within the family to grow and develop their potential; and a place where other emotions are allowed besides guilt and fear. Umbrellas still will be needed, but the weather report does not have to post hurricane warnings every day. The storms can be downgraded and life can go on.

But before any stage of mastery and acceptance is achieved, a host of overwhelming feelings are going to be part of the family's experience.

## DEALING WITH DAY-TO-DAY EMOTIONS

### Denial and Fear

Long before a diagnosis is made, parents have a nagging sense that something is not right with their child. He doesn't sleep like the books say a baby should; his reactions seem too extreme; he seems always on the go with a purposeful look on his face, but a shambles is left in his wake as he goes off to do yet something else. Parents in other families seem to enjoy their children more.

Some parents attempt to understand these temperaments and behaviors by telling themselves: "He's extremely bright"; "She's so sensitive and artistic"; "These traits are going to make him a very successful adult someday if we can only survive his childhood"; "It's just a phase—he'll grow out of it."

There are stages of recognition, adjustment, and adaptation to an illness, and each family travels through the stages in its own time and its own fashion. When the symptoms are mild and interspersed with periods of good functioning, it is not difficult to attribute them to events such as a death in the family, a divorce, or a temperament that is more sensitive and more easily upset or agitated.

Sooner or later, though, as the symptoms become more severe and disruptive, and as the external world begins bearing down on the parents for having no control over the child, the parents are going to begin looking for professional advice (or they are going to be directed toward professional advice by the preschool teacher or school psychologist).

While most parents who answered our survey said that it was a relief to finally find a name for what was happening inside their child, many reported absolute shock as well as the stranglehold of fear about their child's future. Questions such as: Will she live a normal life? Will she get married and be able to take care of children? Will she be able to live separate from us and be a contributing member of society? loom large and can paralyze a family.

Parents must try not to sap the little energy they have by imagining a future that probably will never be as dire as their fantasies. If parents can concentrate on finding solutions and build from feelings of competency today, tomorrow will sort itself out more easily.

As Helen Featherstone writes in *A Difference in the Family*:

Fears ease as experience discredits fantasy, as mothers and fathers learn that the actual problems of raising their child differ from the ones they imagined. Similarly, small victories over private demons reassure parents about their own ability to raise their child.

As time passes, both parents gain a measure of control, even though important parts of their child's future remain beyond their reach. They know a good deal more about their child's disabilities than they did at first; they no longer wait, bound and gagged, for the ax to fall. If they worry about school placement, they can talk to the teacher. In a medical crisis they know which doctor to call. They have learned to navigate in the sea of experts and services.

## SHAME

Learning how to steer through the enormously choppy waters of early-onset bipolar disorder is no easy task. Parents are expected to deal with an illness that doctors not only know little about but also are wary of diagnosing in the first place. Parents are set adrift inside a house that has become a war zone, dealing with feelings that alternate from extreme anger at the child to the most unbelievable yearning to help that child, from rage at the outside world for failing to understand what is happening to them to exhaustion in trying to deal with the child. And tucked into that welter of truly terrible feelings is shame—shame that one is unable to control his or her own child, and shame at what one begins to put up with and how abnormal one's life has become. One mother explained what her daily life was like:

> Connor would fly into a rage and start hitting and punching me. He had this wild look in his eyes and I couldn't reach him. I was literally straddling him, holding him down. He would then scream: "Help! Help! She's killing me, she's killing me" at the top of his voice. Then he said: "I can't breathe. It's over, Mom, it's over." And I let go and suddenly the head turns, I see the switch in his eyes, and boom!—the arm is there punching me. And this can go on for two to three hours.

Then she lowered her voice and you could feel her embarrassment even over the phone line:

> I'm ashamed to say that the last forty-five minutes I turned my back on him and let him beat on me as I stood at the kitchen sink, crying and feeling so alone in the world.
>
> At the end of the major rages, the tears come from Connor. He puts his arms around me and says: "Mommy, Mommy, you said the medication would work. I might as well be dead."

It takes many parents years to be able to tell a story like that. Often they can't tell anyone in the outside world until the child has long been stabilized and the violent rages cease. Like battered wives, they present a brighter face to the world and refuse to have outsiders picture their child or them this way.

## STRESS OF UNPREDICTABILITY

No childhood disability is easy for parents to deal with, but when one's child is bipolar, one never knows when a violent rage will ignite. Parents describe themselves as always walking on eggshells. One mother said she never knows whether she's going to be awakened with a kiss or a fist in her eye.

Another mother described it this way:

It keeps everyone on edge, on alert. He is so unpredictable that you can never slip into complacency for fear of ambush. We can't go out to dinner without wondering what disaster might be afoot at home. Once he locked a baby-sitter into the third-floor stairwell.

Things can be moving along at a nice pace, when something comes up and the child revs from zero to eighty in a split second. Not only is being on the scene a nightmare, but one father told us he couldn't even escape the stress from a distance:

I began to long for business trips. Any chance to be away and have *some* idea of how a day would unfold seemed like an oasis of sanity for me. I'm ashamed to say this, but I would dread making the call home at night to check on everyone. First I would have a few drinks, and then I would place the call with knots in my stomach as I waited for my wife to pick up the phone and give me the report. I felt awful that my wife was left with all of this (and we didn't even know what "this" was then), and then I felt more guilt and shame.

## EVERYONE'S A JUDGE AND A JURY

Life inside the home is bad enough, but a trip to the grocery store could unravel the most stable human being, because, sooner or later, the child is going to get tired or ask for a piece of candy, and if the answer forthcoming is "no," a meltdown is likely to occur on the checkout line. And this opens up the opportunity for strangers to offer their parenting advice and comment on the parent's and the child's lack of control.

American society is not tolerant of children in general. Children are not welcome at most restaurants; they're not supposed to make a ruckus. A visit to Italy or Israel would provide a contrast: Children are a part of every event, and the community expects to see them as well as hear them. But in this country, a parent is likely to hear: "Are you going to let her talk to you like that? If one of my kids ever said that to me, she'd rue the day," or (and this is the most popular) "Give him to me, for a week and he'll be an entirely different child." (We venture to guess that this man would be an entirely different man.)

Parents have some choices: They can ignore the comments, or they can choose to give a simple explanation, such as: "He has a neurological brain disorder that causes him to have something like a behavioral seizure. It's called early-onset bipolar disorder." Either way, the parent is going to feel criticized, humiliated, infantilized, incompetent, and extremely angry and stressed. One mother girds herself and takes control of such situations without even speaking. She hands the advice-giver a card while her son is on the floor kicking and screaming. On it is printed:

> Thank you for your advice and concern. My son is suffering with early-onset bipolar disorder, a neurological brain disorder which causes him to feel very irritable and anxious and culminates in tantrums and rages such as you are now witnessing. Screaming and threatening inflame the situation and are damaging to this child.
>
> Because it is obvious that you are concerned about this kind of behavior, may I suggest that you contact the Juvenile Bipolar Research Foundation at 973-275-0400 to learn more about this devastating illness of childhood and—if you can—please make a donation to support research so that no child should *ever* have to contend with this level of emotions in a little body and a developing brain. Thank you.

This mother tells us that she doesn't always feel the need to hand the card out, but just having it handy creates a sort of armor and empowerment when her anger at someone's intrusiveness and judgmental attitude threatens to derail her or makes her feel helpless and ashamed. She also said that when she does hand it out, she is doing something to raise awareness and to protect the next parent that the "helpful" person in the street may upset.

If trips to the grocery store and nights out to movies or special events or restaurants present multiple opportunities for a meltdown, the family is going to begin to withdraw so as not to stress the child or expose themselves to public attention and possible ridicule. Family forays outside the home will become few and far between. So many parents wrote and told us how guilty they feel that they can't provide a "normal" family life for their other children. One father wrote: "Everything depends on how Anna is feeling that day. We go or don't go depending on her mood. And if we do go, we are on tenterhooks until we get behind closed doors once again. It rips us apart to be viewed as incompetent and incapable in the public eye. I feel so sorry for my other children who are being cheated by Anna's illness."

Thus the family becomes an island unto itself. Even relatives can add to the stress by being very critical. While we were writing this chapter, we spoke with a woman who described her Thanksgiving day. Her daughter had been put on an antidepressant without the protection of a mood stabilizer, and she was irritable and becoming hypomanic. Before dinner, and while playing with another child, she lost control and hit him in the head with a toy car, in front of a shocked extended family assembled for the holiday. Everyone seemed to blame the mother, who spent the day after Thanksgiving in bed, depressed and terribly demoralized. She suspects that invitations will not be forthcoming and, even if they are, that she and her husband will stop accepting.

Even when people don't offer up criticism and advice, parents of a child with a problem of this magnitude find themselves pulling away from even well-meaning people who may be trying hard to understand. In the normal exchange of conversation, most parents find it agonizing to hear about their friends' healthy children and want desperately to shut themselves off from the envy and anger that they feel. Their friends are going to soccer games; *they* are going to psychiatrists. Their friends are visiting Ivy League schools; *they* are visiting children in inpatient units. Rather than feel this degree of pain, the families with a bipolar child avoid the social situations. Sadly, they become all the more withdrawn from social networks.

## THE GRIEVING PROCESS

It's impossible for parents not to train their eyes on the prize—bringing a baby home and daydreaming about family outings and holidays, baseball games, visiting college campuses. And sexist as it may sound, there are few mothers who don't anticipate the day when they can finger the lace on wedding dresses as they and their daughters plan that trip down the aisle. Farther into the future is the dream of grandchildren.

Bipolar disorder uproots all these hopes and expectations, as suddenly and violently as an earthquake. It shakes a family to its core; now parents suffer the anguish of watching their child in pain and fear for the quality of his or her future. Hopes and expectations may have to be modified and mourned. One mother whose daughter has the illness and who works with other families in crisis had this to say:

> There was a long time when I couldn't and wouldn't alter my expectations. I kept trying to make her more "normal"; I kept pushing her to be just the way I thought every little girl should be. I would not give up.
>
> Eventually I learned that I was the one who had to change. She wasn't able to just then, and it would take a much longer time for her to reach the goals that I was so desperate for her to achieve.
>
> I finally became more realistic and my priorities changed. The more I learned, the more I came to accept *this* child, the more I loved *this* child. I didn't give up hope, but I wasn't in a dream world either. But there's definitely a grieving process where you have to deal with the sense of loss. It's not that it can't be revitalized every time a friend's child graduates, it's just that we're at a different stage now and can feel the pain, rebalance, and go on.

## RECASTING THE PARENTING ROLE

Parents with a bipolar child have to give up on the idea of "typical" parenting skills. All the old bromides—consistency and authority, the parents must be in control so the child feels safe, and so on—don't carry the day inside this family (or at least they don't until the child is stabilized). Any assertion of authority is viewed by the child as the parent dominating him or her, a domination to be resisted at any cost. Something goes off in the child's brain, and a rage gathers. A simple "no" triggers a nuclear explosion. When the exasperated mother of a seven-year-old boy asked her son why he could *never* do anything she asked, he looked at her and said quite baldly: "Oh, I can't do that, that would mean you are in control of my life. I rule the world; what I say goes."

What would motivate this child to feel this way? This mother felt his statement came from a "great sense of grandiosity and perfectionism." Maybe it comes from a sense of defectiveness, and when an adult tries to subordinate the child to his or her will, it elicits feelings that are so bad or uncomfortable that they are not to be tolerated. Perhaps, as we suggested in Chapter 7, the anxiety level of these children is so high that they have to dig in their heels to feel a sense of control. No one really knows, but the Parenting 101 adage that discipline comes from the root "disciple" will seem almost funny after attempting to deal with a bipolar child. They are to be the parents' equals if not the parents' superiors.

So, the parent must step out of time and place and become the parent *this* child needs, not the parent that society (and the parent's ego) dictates. It requires an almost superhuman love, where the parent's expectations are set aside and the needs of the child are met first. A father wouldn't insist that a blind child play basketball because all the other sixth-grade kids are doing it; nor would he sign up his wheelchair-bound child for the football tryouts just because the other ninth-graders are doing it. Parents have to modify their ideas of parenting skills and be very, very brave.

Unfortunately, no one is going to give the mother or the father "Parent of the Year" award. Instead, parents will meet with criticism, dire warnings that they're spoiling the child, or even that they're "frightening the child" by not bending him or her to their will.

It all sounds good. It just doesn't work with a child who's struggling with bipolar disorder. In the next section, we'll talk about some techniques that may work and help to calm some of the disruptions to family life.

## DEALING WITH DAY-TO-DAY BEHAVIORS

### Raging

For a very long time parenting strategies revolved around adages such as "Spare the rod, spoil the child" and "Children are meant to be seen and not heard." While in some ways we are a more child-centered society, and parents tend not to be as autocratic as they were a few generations ago, most parents feel that to be a parent is to "be the boss," to have control, and to provide exact rules for the safety of the children and the smooth running of a household. After all, they are the adults, they understand consequences, and they know that they have to civilize children and prepare them to coexist in society. Easier said than done with a child who is oppositional and prone to violent outbursts where the parent can be injured both emotionally and physically—no matter how big and strong the parent is.

In order for a parent to begin to come to terms with oppositional and out-of-control behavior, he or she has to have an inkling of what is happening within the child and realize that what may work with a well child will rarely work with a bipolar child.

Why? Well, to begin with, these children don't start the day planning on screaming obscene phrases at parents or threatening them with forks and knives. They don't think to themselves: Today I'm going to trash my room, kick in a few walls, and break all of Mom's porcelain figures that seem to mean so much to her. Instead, they get caught up in a world that seems to demand things from them that they are not equipped to deal with: shifts from their own agendas to their parents' and teachers' demands and the quick changes that take place during the school day. Often these children are unable to make these shifts or comply with these requests. And to make matters worse, often these children are very smart and sensitive to the fact that other people can "go with the flow," so they feel doubly bad about themselves.

Sooner or later it all comes to a head with the phenomenon known, and feared, by parents as raging. Raging that can go on for hours at a time. It is rarely seen by the teachers and professionals but is reserved for the safe domain of home and family—most especially for the mother.

What causes these almost seizurelike rages, which seem to be most often triggered by the word "no"? The evidence points to neurochemical factors: With the right mood stabilizer or the right combination of mood stabilizers and perhaps atypical antipsychotic medications, these outbursts are often eliminated or become less frequent and intense.

But until the stabilization does happen, parents are going to have to deal with wild tantrums and tough times. And as most parents have found out, behavior management techniques do not work with these children: No amount of star-or-sticker charts or time-outs, and no threats of grounding or unplugged TVs and Nintendo sets, is going to make a whit of difference. These children are not moved by threats, explanations, or even bribes for very long.

As psychologist Ross Greene explains in his book *The Explosive Child*:

> Consequences can be effective if a child *is in a state of mind to appreciate their meaning* [emphasis added], but they don't work nearly as well if a child is not able to maintain such a state of mind. . . .
>
> What I've learned over the years is that some children become so overwhelmed so quickly by their frustration that their capacity to maintain coherence in the midst of frustration is severely compromised. I've seen that these children are also compromised in their ability to gain access to information they've stored from previous experiences and think things through so as to formulate a well-organized, reasoned response to frustrating situations.

One mother came to recognize the magnitude of the problem and began to think of her child as having a spasm in the emotional part of his brain. He seemed to be in an altered state of consciousness, and she began to realize that her anger and desire to assert her will over his was like pouring fuel on a fire. She wrote about her new awareness of what was happening and how she could best help her son through the rage:

> It is difficult to talk to him and get responses when he is out of control. He gets panicky when I try to restrain him. I am learning, though. At first I would get furious. I don't do that anymore since it is counterproductive and unkind, considering he seems to have little if any control of himself at those times. I've learned to listen to him very closely . . . and he often says "I'm scared." I now try to help him through these incidents. He is conscious, but just barely. I try to stay calm, I try to speak softly and in simple sentences. I avoid too much eye contact. I try to avoid patronizing or authoritarian statements. I don't threaten or shout. I try to help him feel control again. I remain very flexible though alert for my own safety.

Another woman said, "Humor is best. I can sometimes defuse very volatile situations by making jokes. Reasoning with the child is useless. So is force. I make every attempt to stay very calm."

## Personal Safety for the Family

Some children in a rage break only their own toys and possessions. Others, however, can do great damage to a house and cause personal injury to their parents or siblings. It serves no one to allow this to go on, but very often it is beyond the control of a parent. We know of fathers who are six feet tall who have had to stay home to protect their petite wives from the violence of thirteen-year-olds. Sometimes a raging child throws objects so forcefully as to cause a mild concussion to a family member unlucky enough to be targeted. To put it bluntly, many parents are being abused in their own homes. Many have had to protect themselves by working out emergency strategies to cope with assaultive behavior.

One mother from Michigan told us that she has an automatic dial to her parents' home, and her mother and father come running when her seven-year-old goes into a rage. They quickly roll him in a blanket and restrain him. They even had to construct a "quiet room" where he could cool down so as not to destroy the house or hurt his younger sister.

This woman was lucky because she had supportive parents close at hand who would do anything to help her, and her son was finally stabilized on medications and able to better control his emotions. But many mothers live far from family and are alone with children who suddenly explode. Most parents are loath to call the police to report the assaults of a six-year-old and alert the neighbors to a situation that will appear extremely shocking; many try to tough it out by themselves. Parents from all over the country have told us that they hide all knives and sharp objects and even baseball bats.

While some children get even more panicky if restrained, a therapeutic hold or restraint can help other children gain control and calm down. The parent should get behind the child, take him or her on a bed or floor with the parent's back against the headboard or wall. The parent should then put his or her legs over the child's, wrap the child's hands around the child's middle, and then hold his or her arms over the child's hands. All the time the parent should be saying in a calm, soft voice: "I'm going to hold you until the tantrum is over. I will not let you hurt yourself, or me, or destroy things. I will hold you until this is over and you are safe."

If the child is too big and strong to do this, and a spouse, friend, or emergency team cannot be summoned to the house in three minutes or so, a parent will have to consider bringing the police into the situation—

especially if the out-of-control son or daughter is older and much stronger and much more capable of doing horrific damage.

One woman who has had to call the police described her very wise plan:

> It is difficult to explain your child's situation and what you want done in the heat of a crisis. If violent acts are a possibility, it would make good sense to be proactive and make a plan when all is calm. Call it a "Family Crisis Emergency Plan" and include the child/adolescent, psychiatrist, or therapist in making the plan.
>
> I suggest an advance visit to the police station and talk with the social worker, who could then brief the local officers on how to handle a raging child or adolescent if they are called to assist. List on the plan how restraints will be used if necessary and where the adolescent will be taken (not to jail). The plan should list the phone numbers of the doctor, private therapist, family members, and anyone else who should be notified.

Given the severe consequences of these rages, it's a good idea to isolate what situations or comments trigger the bipolar child and attempt to deescalate the child before things reach the point of no return. In *The Explosive Child,* Dr. Greene suggests that a parent think in terms of three prioritized baskets: Basket A contains only things a parent should insist on—safety issues, for instance. Basket B holds items that are negotiable; and Basket C holds all the items that are not worth fighting about, given that they could detonate an explosion. Examples of Basket C items might be insisting the child sit at the dinner table and eat with the family, and eat the wholesome dinner the parent has prepared, *not* the pizza the child is screaming for. Give her the pizza, says Dr. Greene.

While the entire family sitting around the dinner table is a pleasant image, a child who has tantrums for three hours and throws food all over the kitchen as a result of a parent's strong "request" isn't. Such fantasies have to be let go of for a while.

Many parents have tried these strategies and fashioned others of their own, and have told us that they work. One mother said:

> I used to spend hours trying to get our older daughter to sit in her seat. Then I got more realistic. So when my husband and younger

daughter and I sit down to dinner, I wish she could join us, but if she can't, we three don't have to end up inside a tornado in the kitchen. And as she grows older and gets more stable, we've enjoyed more of a family life.

Another mother observed that whenever her son flew into a rage, he would run out the door. She understood that he needed a quiet place where he could be alone and calm down, and she designated three places on the property where he might go. She told him that she would give him twenty minutes and then come looking for him, and if he wasn't in one of those three places, she would call the police. Thus she understood and respected his way of dealing with his anger, but she placed safety limits around him.

It's obvious that dealing with a bipolar child requires superhuman strength and stamina and intelligently worked-out solutions. Parents will have to find the strategies that work best with the fit of their temperament and style and the child's temperament and needs. It's safe to bet, however, that the child won't be the one to change first. The parents, who are infinitely more flexible, will have to exercise that flexibility for quite a while. But there is every reason to believe that reasonableness will come back into the relationship once the child is medically treated and becomes stable.

## Mission Mode

Parents write to us often and mention that they are assailed all day long by their children's intense need to buy something or to do something. The children seem to wake up, decide they *have* to go to the pet store and purchase a hamster or a puppy, or they just *have* to have the expensive sneakers that their friend is wearing, and no amount of reasoning or discussion can deter them from what parents describe as "mission mode." Their sheer persistence is all-encompassing, and they become very adept at blocking out any agenda but their own (which they are feeling very intently and very urgently).

A mother from Oregon described her eleven-year-old daughter this way:

Lauren tends to get stuck in this mode over things like wanting to go to the mall and go shopping. Right then, right there. Period.

Doesn't matter that it's 9:00 at night or some other impossible, in-appropriate time. Trying to reason with her *never* helps. She often then feels picked on and "unloved" (her words) because I don't give in to her demands.

Sometimes mission mode can be a sign of impending mania, but not always; sometimes there is more of an obsessional, anxious component to it. Some of the answers may lie in the fact that many of the children have deficits in the frontal lobe regions (see Chapter 10). They are inflexible—they perseverate and can't move off a topic, they can't anticipate that this kind of behavior will bring negative reactions from others, and they have impulse control problems and cannot wait for something. (They may also be anxious that they will forget what it is they want; or they may be us-ing this sudden gusto about a project or new idea to focus their thinking.)

We spoke with Dr. Paul Schottland, a cognitive psychologist in Florham Park, New Jersey, about the bipolar child's often-relentless pur-suit of his or her own needs, and he said: "They don't realize their think-ing is rigid. They have to be taught to activate the flexibility of their thinking. They can't think: 'What would it be like for Mom to have to drive to the mall at this hour of the evening?' They lack the concept of compromise."

"It is not about the hamster, or the sneakers," says Dr. Schottland. "It's about the inability to cope with his not getting what he thinks he needs at that moment. This unreasonableness is a handicap, and it is the hand-icap that must be addressed."

## Installing the Software
We liked Dr. Schottland's computer analogy, where he instructs the par-ent to "install the software that isn't there on the hard drive." It doesn't come up on their screens naturally the way it does with other children, and it must be trained in by the parents.

"Let's go back to the sneakers," said Dr. Schottland. "They cost $125, and there is no way the parent can grant the request. Things escalate and the parent becomes more exasperated, and then the child blows. A rage ensues that shakes both the parent and the child." Dr. Schottland advises a parent to wait until the emotions settle. Then approach the child and talk about the situation. Say something like: "This is not a good situa-tion. We have to figure out a way to make it better next time because I love you and I don't want us to be this way."

And then the parent can ask: "What can you say in your own mind that could help you deal with something I can't do at that time?"

## Cognitive Mediators

Dr. Schottland gives children something called a "cognitive mediator"— a thought that can replace the uncomfortable thought they are thinking. This new thought can get them unstuck from the rigid place in their thinking. Dr. Schottland actually writes the cognitive mediator out on a card for the child.

Here's an example of a cognitive mediator:

In reality, you're lucky if you get what you want 50 percent of the time. You should ask for something, and then ask one more time, but if your parent says "no," can you picture yourself putting it on the shelf? Imagine saying to yourself: "She said no. I'll put it on the shelf and come back to it later." (This shifts the obsessive thought away from the child, and he or she spends time imagining it on the shelf. Chances are that the cognitive shift will help get the child "unstuck.")

Another cognitive mediator: "I won't get it this time but maybe I'll have a good shot at the next thing I ask for." (You're helping the child adapt to reality.)

"This is such a job for a kid," says Dr. Schottland. "Show him how you appreciate how hard he's working and every once in a while reward him." Dr. Schottland also warned that this requires a long training process. He tells the parents, only half-jokingly: "Get back to me after a thousand trials." He closed our conversation by adding: "You have to understand that you could do this all one hundred percent right . . . and you still might not get what you want. Don't judge yourself by how the child responds, but by how you respond. Are you responding neutrally, empathically, are you giving the child the tools? . . . If so, you've done your job."

## Boredom and Provocative Behavior

We all experience bouts of boredom in life, but children and adolescents with bipolar disorder seem particularly prone to them. It often seems difficult for these children to become engaged with projects, or to set goals, and though a parent can offer any number of choices of activities, the children can't seem to invest in any of them. They whine and complain constantly of being bored.

Often the children's response to this internal state of boredom is to provoke a stimulus from the environment—from a parent, usually, or from a sibling. They create chaos, despite the fact that it so often results in family members becoming angry at the provocateur in their midst. One mother wrote and described her thirteen-year-old daughter this way:

> She complains and whines constantly about being bored. When she realizes she has to stay at home, she starts "playing" with her little brother and sister. However, this playing is more in the form of torture. She tickles Maddy to the point of crying. She jumps into Jared's Nintendo game and makes him lose. She chases them, annoys them, pretends she is playing with them and lures them into a false sense of security, and then starts bothering them in any way possible. They cry and she seems happy not to be bored anymore.

Why are these children so often bored? Why do they "go on the prowl" and provoke someone close to them and create such chaos and bad feeling? The answers are multidetermined and no doubt a combination of psychological and biological factors.

## Some Possible Reasons for This State of Boredom

In children, a slowed-down depressed state may present as boredom. Children with bipolar disorder are both easily excited and easily disengaged and bored.

For many children, the provocative behavior that seems to follow a period of restlessness and boredom may be a way of connecting and even showing affection.

Sometimes the boredom is a result of the deficits that many of these children have in the realm of executive functions (see Chapter 10). If children have difficulty paying attention and planning, imagine how difficult it would be for them to sink their teeth into something and move themselves along toward a feeling of mastery, reward, and accomplishment.

These executive function deficits and the slow-down of depression may cause these children to lapse into periods where they cannot connect and they get no charge from the environment. They may feel they have no choice but to force the issue and make the environment respond to *them*. They pull others into their bored orbit in order to "fix" the problem.

*But How Can These States Be Handled in Real Life?*
Until we understand the biology of these states (and even then), isolating, labeling, and understanding the problem would be extremely helpful for the child and the family. We spoke with Dr. Schottland about this issue as well. He first talked about the sense of power the child gets from teasing and how that puts him or her in a better mood state. This power and sense of control can be almost narcotic-like to the child. But typically the person at the other end of the teasing becomes incensed, and the child realizes that things have gone badly once again.

Cognitive therapy can be extremely important and helpful. Dr. Schottland talks to his young patients and says:

> There is a very healthy part of you that can control or modify this behavior. You're a nice, sweet kid, but sometimes you go into this teasing, provocative mode that can be very upsetting to the people around you. When does this get activated? When you have nothing to do or when you are upset and feeling down—bored inside, and it feels so bad to you.

He continues, explaining to the children that everyone has a little bully inside of them, and everyone likes to tease, but when this gets activated in the child, it becomes hard to stop. "We need to construct a laundry list of items and ideas that may eliminate the bored state," he tells them.

He and the children enlist the help of the parents because these items must be in the house and available for such moments. When you're on your way to the store, it's too late to stop the mode from kicking in.

He also warns that the car is the "hell-on-earth mobile" for parents with bipolar kids. This is where they get extremely bored and begin to nudge their siblings. (They also may be hypersensitive to the closeness of bodies and loudness of sounds in the backseat of a car). The car is a prime breeding ground for blowups.

Dr. Schottland cautions parents never to get into a car with the kids—no matter how short the ride—without the bag of "distractors": handheld video games, CD players with headsets, a movie if the car is outfitted with a DVD or tape machine. "Parents should understand that these are therapeutic tools that result in better management of the problem and stop feeling guilt about appropriate video games and movies to keep things running smoothly."

However, a parent must be prepared that all their camp-counselor scheduling may be met with: "I hate that; I don't want to do that," and a string of negative and surly responses to each enthusiastic idea and suggestion.

It's good to remember that these are transient states and will resolve. (However, we understand that this is little consolation as you watch your child begin to go on "the prowl" and light on you or a sibling for this much-needed spark of life.)

## The Morning Battleground: Why Bipolar Kids Can't Get Up and Get Going

Every morning, in America and abroad, many parents of bipolar children wake up and experience dread as they prepare to get their children up for school. Contrary to cheery television commercials where families gather around quaffing fresh-squeezed orange juice, these parents often have to mount a siege simply to get their children out of bed.

A couple described a typical morning scenario:

Yesterday it took an hour and a half attempting to get him up. We kept shaking him, beseeching, threatening, beseeching anxiously. . . . We even called his cell phone thinking he might pick it up for a friend's call. He simply growled, muttered something we would have preferred not to hear, and turned over and went back to sleep.

We finally did see him rise from the bed and we ran the shower thinking that might wake him up. Ten minutes later we found him on the floor of the shower, curled up and sound asleep. It was as though he were anesthetized.

Although it may seem as if the child or adolescent is behaving in an oppositional manner, a great many of these youngsters actually suffer from something called *sleep inertia.*

### What Is Sleep Inertia?
Sleep inertia is a transitional state of lowered arousal occurring immediately after awakening from sleep and producing a temporary decrease in any subsequent performance. Studies show that sleep inertia can last from a few minutes to four hours. Youngsters with bipolar disorder are far

closer to the latter than the former. Several factors are involved in sleep inertia. A child may be depressed and chronically tired, or the thought of facing the school day may produce waves of anxiety or panic, forcing the child to choose sleep or somatic complaints over the trial of going to school. In many cases, the medications may be causing an early-morning sleepiness.

We do know that children with bipolar disorder have disturbances in the architecture of their sleep—they have sleep/wake reversals and are activated at night and slowed down in the morning (see pages 126–130). They also may have disturbances in their thermoregulatory systems— difficulty dissipating heat from the body. This can disturb sleep patterns, as can an irregular release of the peptide melatonin—often seen in adult sleep studies.

## What Can Be Done About Sleep Inertia?

A good plan of attack would be to discuss the timing of medications with the treating physician. If one or more of the medications is contributing to morning grogginess, then it might help to administer the drug at an earlier time the day before. If anxiety is causing school refusal, the doctor or therapist may ease the child's fears by helping him or her deal with the anxiety. Cognitive therapy may be particularly helpful.

Phototherapy, or light treatment (see Chapter 4), may entrain the rhythms and phase shift the dysregulation many of these children have. Some parents have reported that a dawn simulator is helpful in getting their children out of bed.

If the prescribing doctor thinks a trial of melatonin is a good idea, he or she will discuss the timing and dosage. Melatonin given approximately twenty minutes before bedtime may induce the earlier onset of sleep and produce a more restorative sleep. Melatonin is known to lower core body temperature, which may explain one of its effects on the regulation of the sleep/wake cycle.

Until the sleep/wake cycle is regulated (and a child may always be more of an owl than a lark), an accommodation in the school day may have to be made. It might help if the student is allowed a later start, and it would be wise to schedule all academics later in the morning and in the afternoon, when he or she would be more cognitively available for learning.

## Hypersexuality

It has long been accepted that adults who become manic or hypomanic and are experiencing an upswing in mood and energy also experience increased sociability and an increased sexual drive—hypersexuality. In children, the symptoms may manifest as a fascination with private parts and an increase in self-stimulatory behaviors, a precocious interest in things of a sexual nature, and language laced with highly sexual words or phrases.

Parents become paralyzed with shame and fear that people on the outside will assume that an overaroused child is an abused child. Fortunately there are data to back up the claim that children who are on the manic side of mood swings are often hypersexual.

Dr. Barbara Geller and her colleagues at Washington University in St. Louis looked at a group of ninety-three children and adolescents diagnosed with bipolar disorder as a part of an ongoing phenomenology study sponsored by the National Institute of Mental Health and found that 43 percent of this group who were manic were also hypersexual. The researchers looked carefully at the possibilities of abuse, and found that less than 1 percent of these hypersexual bipolar children had evidence of overstimulation or sexual abuse in the home environment. According to the conclusion of one journal article published about this ongoing study, "the 43.0% rate of hypersexuality in the prepubertal and early adolescent subjects strongly suggests hypersexuality as a symptom of mania."

Most of the parents we interviewed were very confused by their children's precocious knowledge. Knowing how sensitive and prone to night terrors these children are, the parents screened all television, movies, and popular media that might present anything scary, overstimulating, or sexual. It may be that these children are so exquisitely attuned to things they hear—snatches of lyrics in a parking lot as they walk to a store with a parent, or a television commercial at a friend's house, or something overheard at school—and it simply makes a bigger impression on them than on other children. Normal sensuality and desire for contact that is such a part of an adolescent's focus seems to occur years ahead of schedule.

### How Can Parents Deal Effectively with Hypersexuality?
Almost all the parents we interviewed said the hypersexual symptoms disappeared with proper mood stabilization, but until that day arrives, a

parent whose child is hypersexual is going to have to contend with conversations and behaviors and, embarrassed or not, model appropriate social behavior for the child—without making the child feel shame. (For a complete list of scenarios and a script of "fallback lines" that will help a parent respond to some of these behaviors and language, see the June 2002 issue of *The Bipolar Child Newsletter* at www.bipolarchild.com.)

## Hypersexuality in the Dreaded Teen Years

All systems rev up as children grow into adolescence. In a world where teens run out of the house with belly buttons exposed and multiple piercings flashing, it's hard to even know what is "normal" teen behavior and what is serious hypersexuality. Parents report their daughter caught making out in the school library and both males and females making serial 1-900 calls on their parents' credit cards. We have heard of girls who post explicit photos of themselves on the Internet.

This age group in American society is almost impossible to rein in, and the threat of impulsive sexual acts resulting in pregnancy or sexually transmitted diseases is enough to terrify any parent.

Most worrisome is the fact that many girls are at risk for rape; their skimpy clothing and "come-hither" sexual expressions give off signals that they might be game for anything.

Such girls should be kept home, off the computer, and should have their blood levels tested immediately to determine whether this hypersexuality is a sign of the need for a medication change.

Some parents have resorted to sending their daughters to residential treatment centers where they can be protected from themselves until they begin to put a higher premium on who they are and avoid the risk of rape and other horrible sequelae of being "out there."

## What Should a Parent Do to Protect the Child and the Family?

Many parents are worried sick that the child's flaunting of his or her body and suggestive talk could open the door to a perverse outsider taking advantage of the situation. They realize that they need to educate the child from a young age about possible consequences of such talk and behavior. One mother whose very young son became hypersexual told him: "If anyone ever tries to touch your body in any way, you tell Mommy and Daddy right away. No matter what you say, no one should ever be touching you anywhere near your private parts."

Siblings may be pulled into games of "Doctor." A few parents reported that, understanding there might be periods of hypersexuality, they watch their children like hawks. Most understood that the siblings should not bathe, shower, or sleep together, and that the child should be separated if signs of hypomania and hypersexuality were seen.

It would be wise to have the treating psychiatrist document the hypersexual behaviors or language in the child's medical records and to keep a copy of these in a binder at home. This way if Child Protective Services ever knocks on the door, a medical document exists detailing exactly what's been happening: that the child, when manic, may exhibit sexual behaviors or language.

## If Child Protective Services Visits

It's one thing to withstand the remarks of family members and the stares of people in the grocery stores, it's another to fear the knock at the door of Child Protective Services (CPS). Anytime a child screams at the top of his or her lungs for long periods of time, the thought of abuse will cross a neighbor's mind long before he or she thinks: I wonder if that child is bipolar.

Chances are that a parent of a bipolar child will entertain a visit or two before the child becomes stable. One mother wrote about her first visit with a sense of humor purchased only with the passage of time:

> When they showed up at my house, the air-conditioning was broken and my basement had flooded the day before. My house looked like a war zone, and all three of the kids were running around in their underwear (I was relieved they weren't nekkid).
>
> After talking with my husband and me, and the kids, and looking into my medicine box (so we could present all the medications), they were satisfied that I was doing the best job I could—and actually a very good job considering the circumstances. They closed the case altogether about six weeks later.

She went on to advise other parents: "Keep your chin up . . . and try to keep the house straightened" (usually they make a follow-up visit).

We spoke with this mother over the telephone and asked her if she didn't feel angry at and humiliated by CPS and the neighbor who had called them. She replied, "In my opinion, they all cared enough about the welfare of my child to investigate it. It was kind of a relief because once

I knew them and they knew me, I wasn't stressed about it anymore. I explained things to my neighbor in detail, and now she is a part of the team and is a great help and support to me. I respect her caring. What kind of neighbor could hear this and do nothing?"

Another mother we spoke to said that she keeps a binder of all the medications and charting she does and IEP materials for school, so it's easy to educate CPS if they come to investigate. The binder shows her to be an attentive mother dealing with an impossible situation, and she feels a sense of control.

Still, this wasn't quite what anyone pictured as she opened the gifts at the baby shower, and it takes time to get over your parenting being questioned by the state. Taking the time to get to know your neighbors and educating them about the illness and the child's behaviors may preempt this kind of upsetting visit and may net a supportive friend as well.

## Dealing with Suicidal Behavior

The emotional roller coaster that parents and siblings must ride is bad enough. But by far the most harrowing emotion is the fear that the child may kill him- or herself. Parents have said to us over and over: "Do you have any idea what it's like to hear our seven-year-old say, 'I'm a stupid dummy, everyone hates me and I may as well be dead'?"

Clinical reports show that children as young as five and six years old have made suicide attempts. Psychiatrist Cynthia Pfeffer of Cornell University Medical College has reported that her studies of children reveal that approximately 75 percent of children who are psychiatrically hospitalized are suicidal, while about 33 percent of those treated outside the hospital are suicidal.

The burgeoning statistics on adolescent suicides are deeply disturbing. It is estimated that five thousand teenagers kill themselves in this country every year. Suicide is the third leading cause of death in adolescence. In *His Bright Light,* author Danielle Steel wrote about her bipolar son's first suicide attempt:

I considered what had happened an aberration, because he had been off lithium at the time. I knew that once back on, it was unlikely to happen again. But what I uderestimated entirely, or had never been told, was how lethal his disease was. In my view, it was something that could make him unhappy all his life, but not something that could kill him. I missed that message completely.

This is not an easy message for a mother or father to absorb. It is almost impossible to second-guess what's going on inside a teenager's mind. Suicidal intentions are often expressed in subtle and ambiguous ways, and most families are not prepared to judge the seriousness of a threat.

If relatives even suspect that the child is thinking about suicide, they should call the treating psychiatrist immediately and alert him or her to that fact. Depending on a variety of factors, hospitalization may be required. Suicide is often an impulsive act: A child can have a glass of milk in the kitchen one minute and leap from a bedroom window the next. It happens that fast; it happens that unexpectedly. The notion that people who threaten suicide never actually go through with it is a dangerous myth.

## Warning Signs

Recently reported findings on factors associated with suicidal threats in children diagnosed with bipolar disorder suggest that the presence of aggression and impulsivity are importantly related to suicidal threats, independently of the risk of depressive symptoms. The study, published by Drs. Demitri Papolos, John Hennen, and Melissa Cockerham, M.A., in the *Journal of Affective Disorders,* found that 2,479 parents identified a group of specific symptoms and behaviors on the Bipolar Child Questionnaire (see page 433) as commonly co-occurring with frequent and severe suicidal threats.

Among the eight most prominent symptoms and behaviors were hallucinations, cursing and foul language, low energy and withdrawal, violent and gory imagery, destruction of property, low self-esteem, excessive risk taking, and excessive anxiety and worry. Girls who expressed suicidal threats were as likely as boys to experience and exhibit these symptoms and behaviors.

It is striking that this profile is, to a much greater degree, indicative of aggression, impulsivity, and psychosis than to parent-reported depressive symptoms.

However, in addition to the greater vulnerability when the aggressive, impulsive, and psychotic symptoms are present, other common warning signs of suicidal intention are:

- Depressed mood
- History of a previous attempt
- Decline in school performance
- Increased social withdrawal
- Loss of interest and pleasure in easily enjoyable activities
- Changes in appearance—for instance, no longer caring about one's hair or clothing
- Preoccupation with themes of death—the youngster may begin to read books with themes of death and dying
- Increased irritability and behavior problems
- Giving away important possessions
- Use of drugs and alcohol
- Changes in sleep and/or appetite patterns
- History of abuse and neglect
- History of a sense of failure
- Verbal expression about self-destruction—for instance, a youngster who actually says "I wish I were dead."
- No concern about making plans for the future

## Triggers

A bipolar adolescent or child may show a number of these signs at many times during the year, but one who is potentially suicidal may make an attempt after a variety of events. These may include the breakup of a romantic relationship, disciplinary problems with parents, difficulty with schoolwork, or an injury to self-esteem, such as a failure to win an important award or position.

The most dangerous situation where suicidal impulses may be acted on, however, is if the child is in a mixed state—he or she is experiencing a combination of the terrible feelings of depression with the frenzied agitation and energy of mania. While mixed states can occur naturally, very often they are induced by the use of antidepressant therapy in a bipolar individual. Antidepressant medications can increase the frequency of cycling and therefore produce protracted periods of mixed states.

When a child switches from one state to the other, he or she is experiencing symptoms from both poles of the condition. For example, the child may be very active and energized, and yet her mood may drop precipitously into a state of depression, accompanied by feelings of hope-lessness, helplessness, and rage. If, during this time, suicidal thoughts surface, as they frequently do, the energy to act on those suicidal thoughts is available.

Since it is well known that suicides in bipolar patients occur most fre-quently during mixed states, parents can help prevent this state from oc-curring by ensuring that the child is not placed on antidepressants without mood stabilizers. They should watch closely for any of the signs of mania or hypomania occurring simultaneously or depressive and manic symptoms alternating very rapidly back and forth. One young woman de-scribed this unbearable state as her mind being flooded with unstoppable frenetic energy and yet feeling physically immobilized.

A father whose daughter started to express suicidal thinking at the age of ten advised other parents on the BPParents listserv how he and his wife dealt with the problem:

> I think the basic rule of thumb is to take every sign seriously. First we let the psychiatrist and therapist know. We also immediately danger-proofed the house: We got rid of plastic cleaner bags; we put scissors, knives, and razors as far out of reach as possible. We locked up every bottle of aspirin and all pills in a tackle box with a combi-nation lock. Our daughter commented to us, even while having these suicidal thoughts: "Now I feel safer."
>
> We also learned how important it was for us to stay calm and look calm. She must be scared to death to have these feelings, and it's re-assuring to her that we're calm, in control, and will protect her.

Another mother wrote:

> I didn't leave her alone and we spent a lot of time together doing quiet things like reading stories. I let her talk about her feelings, but kept her as distracted (doing calm things) as possible.

We cannot emphasize how important it is that all guns be removed from the property and that the child not be allowed to spend any time over at a relative's or friend's house where there might be access to guns or other weapons. This is a time where only complete disclosure may pro-tect the safety of a child who may be dealing with suicidal impulses.

One mother told us that the doctor had talked with her suicidal nine-year-old son and told him some very helpful and reassuring things. She reported what the doctor said and how her son responded:

> He said that suicidal thoughts were a symptom of depression just like coughing and sneezing are symptoms of a cold. When the depression begins to subside, so will the suicidal thoughts, just like a cough goes away when you get over a cold. My son really latched on to this, it made him not feel so guilty and responsible for the terrible thoughts, and he made a pact not to try to hurt himself anymore.

Very often parents and teachers avoid introducing the subject of suicide because they are afraid it might "plant ideas." This is not so. Asking a young person about self-destructive wishes can help make him or her feel more understood and less trapped.

## Brothers and Sisters

In the middle of all this often stands a brother or sister—little people who have no way to fathom what is going on and no way to cope with the chaos in the household. The order of life and the hierarchy of a household seem suddenly out of whack. The other children see their mother and father—the authorities in their lives—tense and acting unauthoritatively in front of their sibling. The dog is being wagged by the terrible tail of a sickness they can't see, and the well siblings suffer significant losses. The first loss is that of their brother or sister.

While the sibling bond was long considered secondary—an adjunct to the parent-child relationship—recent research suggests that siblings can have as great an influence on each other as their parents, and sometimes an even greater one. As author Victoria Secunda writes in *When Madness Comes Home*:

> Siblings are each other's first and most enduring partners iin life. For one thing, they are of the same generation. They are partners in *time,* with an infinite future of mutual influence ahead of them. For another, they are partners in *development,* closer to one another in evolutionary steps than to the senior generation.
> Siblings are also partners in *distribution,* vying for the same parental "goods"—who has the bigger allowance, later curfew, larger

piece of the pie. And they are partners in *intimacy,* for the relationship is a dress rehearsal for friendships and romantic ties later on. Siblings often share their rooms, their toys, and their innermost secrets, the ones they wouldn't think of telling a grown-up.

But, she says, it's *because* of this identification that an illness of a sibling can be so damaging to a brother or sister. The partnership just spoken of is turned on its head when bipolar disorder affects one of the children. A host of traumatizing experiences can overwhelm the well siblings. Their privacy may be invaded, their toys and possessions destroyed or commandeered; they may suffer physical injury or even sexual molestation.

Many younger siblings become the target of the anger of an older ill brother or sister if they annoy or irritate him or her (an easy thing to do when someone is in a chronically irritable mood state). Mothers have confided to us that they watch their children like hawks because well siblings have been choked, had their ribs cracked, been hit in the head with rocks, and have been told that they would have their ears sliced off. When the ill child is raging, siblings have been told to lock themselves in their rooms or in the family car.

The well sibling will look desperately to the mother and father to provide protection against a brother or sister who may be threatening or abusive. What the well sibling probably will see are two exhausted, grief-stricken, and confused people, busy running to doctors' appointments, beginning to pull away from social networks as they become bankrupted of energy and joy by an illness they don't understand.

Not only do well siblings often feel unsafe, but they become consumed with resentment and jealousy because so much of the parents' attention and energy goes toward worrying over and solving the problems of the ill child and not to taking the well children's traumatization and fears seriously. They will feel angry that the ill child has so disrupted family life and quashed all the good times that families should share. Well siblings also can become socially isolated. The turmoil and uncertainty that overtake the household often prevent children from inviting friends home. They are embarrassed by their sibling and begin to worry that others will think that they have a "touch of it" also.

It is common for the well siblings to feel emotionally disenfranchised—that they are not allowed to express natural feelings of anger and fear. As Victoria Secunda writes:

They learn to suppress their own intense feelings, particularly of anger, which might be construed by the parents as a sign that these children, too, are going to pieces. Siblings often learn that *any* outbursts will be met with parental disapproval. To protect their parents, and to reassure themselves that they are not next to become ill, they may feel they have to act "weller than well." They can no longer be themselves.

Even in the best of situations, where the siblings love and appreciate one another, the well siblings will be bitter about the limit-setting that their parents enforce on *them*—and the seemingly disparate anything-goes attitude the parents adopt in response to the outrageous things their ill sibling does and says. Parents will hear loud refrains such as: "How come he gets away with everything?"; "Why doesn't she have to abide by the rules of the household?"; "Why do you let him use that foul language and tell me that I can't?"

Indeed, it's quite a feat for parents to be two-tiered disciplinarians, and parents may hold themselves to some impossible standard and suffer even more guilt. But parents have to remember that no parent—*anywhere*—gives attention that is microscopically equal to each of his or her children.

Parents should sit down with the well siblings and explain frankly some of what the ill child is experiencing. They can validate the well children's right to be angry and confused, the well children may have a different interpretation of what is going on around them. Parents can say something like:

You know that Ryan has unique problems, and for some reason, he experiences any limit-setting in a catastrophic way. If we tell you "no" you are able to hear us. But, unfortunately, Ryan cannot, and we feel that it is better for the family to eat dinner, do homework, watch a movie, or play a board game without a three-hour rage going on in the background. When that happens, nothing good can happen in this house.

The doctors are not even sure what is going on in Ryan's brain, and we are trying very hard to come up with some solutions that will keep everyone safe, while we and the doctors try to find out some answers and get Ryan more stable. But it's perfectly understandable that you feel angry and shortchanged, and we feel very bad about that.

However, you didn't cause this, you are not responsible for fixing it, and we will not let him hurt you. We will protect you.

The parents should encourage the siblings to ask questions and to register their fears and complaints. Sometimes it helps simply to be *heard.* It should not be assumed, however, that a lack of questions or curiosity implies that the children are not in turmoil. In fact, silence may be a clue as to how upset a child really is, and the parents may have to provide some prompting to get the conversation going.

We spoke with Dana, a thirteen-year-old girl whose older sister, Monica, had early-onset bipolar disorder and who had been in grave shape throughout Dana's early childhood. Dana remembers visiting Monica in the hospital, and to this day speaks with pain about seeing the "ugly, horrible little room with bars on the window that they put Monica in." She said she wanted to see Monica, but when we told her about Dr. Victor Fornari's advice in Chapter 12 of this book that siblings should see each other in a visiting room, not on the unit, she agreed that that would have been a much less traumatic memory for her. She also said: "I liked that my parents told me everything that was going on, but I wish I didn't know so many of the details because they were very disturbing to me. I couldn't bear hearing about Monica in restraints or having shock treatments. I would tell other parents to discuss things with their kids, but give a slightly softer and reassuring picture of things. Too much reality was hard for me to take." Dana concluded by telling us: "I think the best thing my parents did was try to give me extra attention; they tried to do special things with me, and they put me in therapy where I could really confide all my feelings in someone who could understand and not have her heart break as she listened to me. I will always be grateful to my parents for recognizing my need to be in therapy. It meant everything to me."

## WHEN MORE THAN ONE FAMILY MEMBER HAS BIPOLAR DISORDER

Studies have shown that the earlier the onset of bipolar illness, the more likely first-degree relatives (parents, grandparents, and siblings) are to have the illness. In many cases, the diagnosis of a child will reveal a formerly undiagnosed condition in one of the parents. Also, it is common that when a parent understands the presentation of symptoms in one child, he or she is quicker to recognize the early symptoms in a younger child (if they are present) or to reframe some of the behaviors in an older child that have been explained away by "a particularly rough adolescence."

Before we talk about the complexities of a family with more than one ill child, we'd like to focus on the family where both a parent and child have the disorder. We interviewed a mother who was formally diagnosed several years before her first child (a son) began to show the symptoms and behaviors of early-onset bipolar disorder. She spoke of the myriad feelings they both had about sharing the same diagnosis.

Certainly, as a bp parent, I have a tremendous compassion and understanding and patience for "acting out." While my husband has educated himself about the illness, he can't possibly truly understand the sometimes subtle differences between chosen behavior and when rage and heartbreak take over Greg's body and soul. I *know* that horrible feeling. I know what a relief it feels like to destroy, hurt, and self-mutilate in order to purge yourself of the monster within.

But maybe I identify too much with him—projecting my fears onto him. Maybe if I weren't bp, I could be firmer, establish boundaries . . . maybe being so forgiving hasn't been in his best recovery interest.

However, being a bp parent has, in a way, forced me to take real responsibility for illness management. No longer can I act out. I must model successfully life and coping strategies. But then, sometimes, my husband holds me up as a standard. For example, he'll say, "You're managing, why can't he?"

Greg is now fourteen years old and finally becoming stable after years of a distressingly jagged course. She speaks with such sadness about his early adolescence:

As Greg pushed further into adolescent behaviors and his bp behaviors became worse, layered with bitterness and hurt, even I have noticed that I have to distance myself from him. Before he stabilized he would spend all day raging, cursing, whining, complaining, picking fights, talking nonstop, basically exhausting everybody.

Then, just when I close my sweetly medicated eyes and float off to sleep, I'll hear him sobbing in bed. I'll go to him and talk softly to him, but part of me yearns for the simpler times of rage and outbursts of his younger years—cycles that could play out and end in cuddles and hugs. As he gets older and naturally separates himself from me, he is bound to me by his illness. He hurts me but also needs me.

Later on, as we continued this e-mail discussion, she wrote back in a lighter tone:

Just had a few thoughts about being "bp squared":

1. Humor. Because we are both bipolar, we can share "inside" jokes. For example, this morning there was an ad in the paper for the HBO show *Six Feet Under,* and I said: "Greg, isn't one of the people on the show bipolar?" "Yeah," he said. And I said, "You know, we are so hot in Hollywood right now. There's Sally Field on *ER,* that guy on *Once and Again,* Karen on *Will and Grace,* Robert Downy, Jr., . . . Tony Soprano's on lithium . . . it's just 'the thing' right now."
2. Medicating in company as a lifestyle.
3. He knows he holds a very special and unique spot in my heart because we are so alike.
4. "Normal" in our household is a very open and inclusive arrangement.
5. Greg gets the opportunity to nurture and give from his own life experience and therefore has moments of showing me the bright side too. He is not the only "patient" in the house and knows there is someone he can talk to about things only a therapist might understand. He knows I'm not going to judge him or say: "That's crazy."
6. We can learn from each other.

If this family is "bp squared," let us introduce you to a mother in Oregon who has what she refers to as a "bp-saturated family." Not only has her husband been diagnosed as having bipolar disorder, but her eleven-year-old daughter and her six-year-old son also have the illness. Her third child, a five-year-old, seems unaffected. She said:

My biggest frustration has always been trying to balance keeping a bipolar adult stable and giving my bipolar children the environment that they need in order to be stable. They often seem to have such opposite needs, and it is a juggling act trying to give one what he or she needs without triggering the others' issues. I very often point out to my husband that the "have-nots" are outnumbered by the "haves."

She goes on to explain what happens when one family member loses control. She has dubbed it "the bipolar bounce":

My son will run around all hyper and become annoying, which triggers a tantrum in my daughter. She then blasts her stereo so she doesn't have to listen to him. This triggers my husband, who begins to get annoyed and raises his voice so that everyone will stop. His upset unsettles me and makes the kids more anxious. . . .

My strategy when dealing with the bipolar bounce is to do all in my power to keep everyone separated. My eleven-year-old, Lauren, has a TV in her room with a VCR, and I offer a trip to Blockbuster to motivate her to stay in her room without feeling she is being punished. I couldn't let them all in the car with me as the car is one of the worst places when both kids are acting up. So I even bribe her to stay home with her dad with an extra rental of her choice. . . .

Two down. I then took my bipolar son and my youngest to Blockbuster. Blockbuster was tricky, but managed okay with just Sam and Cally. Had to pay the eighteen-dollar fine at Bbuster from our late returns of our last rentals (typical around here). However, still the best investment I know how to keep my bp kids separate when both cycling. This only works since we added a second VCR to the house. . . .

Sam was a handful all day, but managed to hold things together till about 6:00 P.M. I count down the hours of the day till 7:00 P.M. and I can give him his evening clonidine. Six P.M., dinner—ended up feeding everybody in a different part of the house. Not fun for me, but more fun than the alternative of sitting around the table feeling like Captain Bligh waiting for the mutiny. While having to be overinvolved with Sam, Cally colored all over the walls of her room with a black crayon. . . .

Just as I finally get Sam and Lauren and Cally asleep, my husband decides he wants to start working again. He has ended up spending the day isolated, feeling alone, wishing he and I could have time together and time to do some of the projects we need to get done. These are hard feelings for any adult, but harder for a bp adult who either internalizes it into a depression or externalizes it into a manic need to get the heck out of here and do something FUN!! . . .

I sleep from 11:00 P.M. until 3:00 A.M., when Cally gets up for a drink. Go back to bed with her till 5:30, when Sam wakes up, hyper and ready for a new day. I stay in his room with him in these early hours, trying to get him to quietly play Legos, Lincoln Logs, something—so he doesn't wake up the others. He wakes in an okay mood, but suddenly starts using the Lincoln Logs as swords and shouting and making fighting sounds. As I put them away and leave his room for a minute to check on the status of the others, he takes out a pair of children's scissors from his desk and cuts up all his pajamas from his drawer. . . .

So begins another day. . . .

This mother then told us:

The most important piece to put in place when raising two bp kids, or a bp child and spouse, or bp children and spouse—whatever you might want to call a multiple-affected bp household—is to build a support system for your family.

Building a support system:

1. It doesn't just happen. You have to create it.
2. Identify those people around your family that are in a position to be helpful to you or your kids. This might be family, teachers, administrators, neighbors, coaches, members of your church or synagogue, friends, doctors, other professionals such as a lawyer, dentist—whomever.
3. Once identified, educate. Be proactive. Let these people know about childhood-onset bipolar disorder (COBPD). Give them some basic information pertaining to your child and familial situation. If you stick your head in the sand and think people won't notice something is "different" with your child or "wrong" with your family, you are inviting trouble, and you are missing an opportunity to help your child and strengthen your family. Of

course it is important to use discretion and always protect the privacy of the bp kids/adult. Be certain you have identified those people who are in a position to help your family. I am not suggesting you broadcast to everyone that your children have a psychiatric illness. Be selective about the people who are in a position to be helpful and that you think are trustworthy.

4. Don't shelter these identified people. Let them see some of the rages. On several occasions when my child was raging in the car, I secretly dialed my parents' phone number from my cell phone and let them hear what I was dealing with. Once I even dialed our psychiatrist's office number after hours and the shouting, raging, screaming, "wanting to be dead" outburst she was having was left as a message on his answering machine. (This particular rage was over being told she couldn't have a hot dog as we left the skating rink because we were on our way home to eat dinner—and she was ten years old at the time!) If you try to shelter your child's behavior from everyone, they will not believe you when you describe the fits of rage.

5. Use the cybercommunity as a support. Learn from others' experiences, medicine trials, mistakes, victories. Use the Internet to stay as informed about COBPD as possible. This is important as you advocate for your child and continue to educate those around your child about his/her behavior.

Having a good support system is the only way I have survived, and the only way my children, both bp and not, have survived each other thus far. I know that in a crisis, there are at least four or five people I could call to come and help. This crisis might require separating my non-bp child from her siblings. It might require separating my two bp children from each other. It might require separating all the kids from their bp dad. Whatever the cause of the stressful situation, there will always be times when the best way to prevent one bp member from triggering another bp member is to separate them. Usually it is my wonderful parents who come to the rescue.

Both families who shared their stories spoke of the transformation that occurred when medical stability became the norm, and of the value of therapy—both individual and family. Each family does seem to work things out in its own way, its own time, and its own style. We are in awe, however, of the battles these families must wage and manage with minute-to-minute timing, and how they have developed intelligently worked-out coping strategies. This may not be *Father Knows Best*; it's simply love of the highest order.

## MARITAL RELATIONSHIP

The empathic reader may feel for the parents of children with early-onset bipolar disorder or recognize aspects in his or her own family life. These parents carry a terrible burden. They trained at no special school, they have no experience to guide them, yet they are forced to deal with an illness that they *and* the professionals know little about. If the emotions of the situation don't paralyze them, then dealing with the schools, hospitalizations, and cost of psychiatric treatments may. No matter what the parents do or don't do, say or don't say, it is likely they will feel they're doing it wrong, saying it wrong, and that the greater world and the rest of their family are holding them accountable.

Marriages are placed under heavy strain. The sheer exhaustion of trying to deal with all this leaves a husband and wife with little energy for evenings out. They may begin to realize that every conversation centers around the problems of their ill child and that they don't have the energy or wherewithal to demand and reserve time for themselves and to develop a plan for their own needs and pleasures in life. Yet if they don't, they'll have less energy. One woman wrote, "Your marriage can just disappear, as you become 'roommates' surviving a crisis together."

Indeed, without strong support, these marriages are at extremely high risk. Any chronic illness in a child places a terrible stress on a couple, but a couple with one (or more) bipolar children usually means that the mother or father has the illness him- or herself or grew up with the often-devastating consequences of it in the family of origin and may feel unable to deal with it again.

Denial abounds, especially, it seems, on the part of the fathers, who may feel the need to minimize the severity of the problem. This places most of the burden on the mother, who may resent the hand she's been dealt and feel an enormous amount of anger as her partner stays above the fray. He's at work; she's in the trenches.

Many mothers have told us that they give up career dreams and satisfactions so they can keep their child safe and that they spend most of their time running to doctors' appointments and dealing with schools. They feel that they are on the front lines alone all day, only to have their husbands walk in at night and offhandedly remark that the house is a mess. (One woman who had been dealing with a hypomanic child, trying to appease her so that raging wouldn't begin and the medications could kick in, responded to her husband: "Yes, I ate bon-bons all day and watched *Oprah* and then I took a nap. It was a totally relaxing day.")

Often the parents don't see eye to eye on the desperate need for treatment. If a mother knows in her heart that something is definitely wrong and her spouse's response is "You baby him, that's half the problem," then she will feel all the more isolated, alone, and accused.

A mother or father can be in denial and say things like: "All she needs is love" or "There's nothing wrong with her, she's just got strong feelings." While appearing to be at odds with each other, however, the spouse who makes the filled-with-denial but positive and hopeful statements actually may be acting out the silent wishes of the others to allay the terrible fears that haunt them both.

We also know women who try to protect their spouse from seeing the full extent of the problem. One doctor told the mother of a young girl whose father thought she was just dramatic and spoiled to step back and stop intervening to spare her husband the brunt of the girl's behavior, and to let him witness one of the meltdowns. She wrote:

So I did. One day she exploded in a rage when he needed to take a shower first to make the train to work (and her school didn't start for another hour). She went flying into her bedroom screaming "Then I'm going to turn on the cold water full blast in here and burn him!" The screaming and crying went on and on and she trashed her room. That night he said to me, "I think you're right." It took a month but I'm glad we waited until he was in agreement on the need for treatment.

Not all couples will be so logical. The stresses are so great that people without a mood disorder can crack and say or do abusive things. When one (or both) of the parents manifests the illness or carries genes for alcoholism or bipolar disorder, the situation becomes even more dicey. Grief and anger and confusion and grudges can build up to incendiary levels, and few people act maturely or kindly under this constant barrage of the ill child, the constant demands of the other children, and the demands from each other. If these marriages do not get support, they can be doomed as the couple are driven further and further apart, filled with disappointment, bitterness, and resentment. The marriage can become a kind of hell itself.

It is imperative that couples seek help from outside supports. Couples therapy is a safe place where both can air their feelings and attempt to come up with better coping skills. Plans for buffering them both can be made in this arena. A couple can begin to let go of some of the rancor and begin to pull together.

In order to pace themselves so that they can be a couple and be more effective parents, parents need respite—short-term specialized child care, the gift of time. They can't go this alone.

Where would they find a break from all the tension that they endure nonstop—twenty-four hours a day—and the debilitating stress that can affect their own mental and physical health? A call to the local department of mental health (children's services) may provide funds and a list of trained providers. Sometimes a local university with a psychology department can recommend an interested and energetic student who could do some respite care on weekends or afternoons.

The following organization offers programs and services for children with disabilities and their families:

ARCH National Respite Network
www.respitelocator.org
This network provides fact sheets and general resource sheets (including state contact sheets) about respite care. ARCH also operates the National Respite Locator Service, whose mission is to help parents locate respite care services in their area.

A husband and a wife need to learn to take care of themselves and each other, or they will never be able to deal effectively with their children and the unbelievably difficult and complex situations this illness will foist on them. Before it takes a village to raise a child, it takes a couple pulling in the same direction, seeing the illness for what it is (not what one wishes it to be), mourning what has happened to the family together, and working toward better solutions for everyone.

One mother said it well when she wrote: "Each time we fly anywhere, I listen as the flight attendant tells us to put on our oxygen masks first and then place them on our children. This was a hard life lesson for me to learn, but I've finally got it now. Putting on your 'oxygen mask' first enables you to properly adjust your children's."

# School: A Child's World Beyond Home

Children spend half their waking hours in school, a place that demands concentration and alertness, proper behavior, group and individual effort, and an ability to consolidate information quickly, to build on this information, and to reproduce it on pop quizzes, exams, and term projects. It is a fast-paced day with many transitions, much stimulation, and a host of complicated social interactions with peers.

Now take a child with bipolar disorder, who may have difficulty making transitions, or who may have comorbid syndromes that make him or her distractible, inattentive, anxious, or so perfectionist that he or she must complete everything to such an exacting standard that very little progress can be made. This child may be sleepy from medications or may have cognitive difficulties as a result of them. This child may be trying desperately to interpret social cues, may be feeling very bad about him- or herself, and possibly may be building up a head of explosive frustration. Additionally, as we will discuss in Chapter 10, these children commonly have associated learning disabilities, written expression difficulties, and executive function deficits that further complicate their acquisition of knowledge and adjustment to academic demands.

Add to this a child whose illness is waxing and waning, whose energy levels are often reduced or significantly increased, and whose thought and behavior and "availability for education" are variable, depending on the season and the severity of the cycling pattern, and it's not hard to see that many children with bipolar disorder need to be cut some slack in school—they need special accommodations.

## THE LAW

The Fourteenth Amendment of the Constitution of the United States provides that no state shall "deny to any person within its jurisdiction the equal protection of the laws." If a state provides free public education (and they all do), then that free public education must be available to all of America's children.

When we think of the case *Brown v. Board of Education,* we think of Kansas, Thurgood Marshall, and integration in schools. But this landmark case is cited not only for its racial finding but also for the proposition that the right to an equal education is a fundamental human right—no matter what a person's color, no matter what a person's disability.

And from this root source came the Rehabilitation Act of 1973, which made discrimination against individuals with disabilities unlawful in three areas: employment by the executive branch of the federal government, employment by most federal government contractors, and *activities which are funded by federal subsidies and grants.* Section 504 mandates that *individuals with impairments that substantially limit a major life activity, such as learning, are entitled to academic adjustments and auxiliary aids and services, so that courses, examinations, and services will be accessible to them.*

Two years later, in 1975, Congress enacted a statute titled the Education for All Handicapped Children Act, which is now referred to as the Individuals with Disabilities Education Act (IDEA). Reauthorized in 1997, IDEA provides funds to elementary and secondary schools for public education. Under IDEA, schools are responsible for identifying and evaluating students with disabilities who require special education and services and following through and providing them with a blueprint called an Individualized Education Program—the IEP we will talk so much about throughout this chapter.

But IDEA also stipulates that these services are to be provided in the least restrictive environment (LRE) appropriate to the child's needs and that the child should be integrated with other children, with and without disabilities, and still receive special services. Parents will hear this referred to as "inclusion."

# IDEA 2004

In December 2004 President George W. Bush signed into law the reauthorized Individuals with Disabilities Improvement Act. Called IDEIA by some and IDEA 2004 by most, the final bill was a compromise between bills proposed by the House and Senate. Much of IDEA 2004 is cued to the No Child Left Behind Act of 2002. IDEA 2004 took effect in July of 2005.

Once the law is established and states its intent, the U.S. Department of Education is authorized to write the regulations—the policies, procedures, and rules. As of this writing, these proposed regulations were being debated. So, for some time, state laws and regulations that currently exceed the IDEA 2004 minimum will remain in effect until they are repealed or revised to fall in line with the new to-be-established regulations. Parents should also keep in mind that no test cases have established any precedents, and much interpretation of the law remains to be parsed.

As with all things in life, the new law is a mixed bag, with some changes a probable plus for children and adolescents with bipolar disorder and any associated learning disabilities and others raising some possible red flags. We mention the relevant changes in IDEA throughout this chapter.

## A Closer Look at IDEA

Because IDEA provides money to schools to educate children with disabilities, the term "disability" must be defined. The statute reads like this (note that we have italicized the disabilities that are used most often to describe bipolar children):

(3) CHILD WITH DISABILITY—
(A) IN GENERAL—The term "child with a disability" means a child—
(i) with mental retardation, hearing impairments (including hard of hearing and deafness), speech or language impairments, visual impairments, deaf-blind, *serious emotional disturbance* (hereinafter referred to as "emotional disturbance"), orthopedic impairments, autism, traumatic brain injury, *other health impairments,* specific learning disabilities; and multiple handicaps and (ii) who, by reason thereof, needs special education and related services.

If a child's impairment is moderate, he or she may not qualify under IDEA, only under a Section 504 plan. This plan does not require formal evaluation of the disability, and it covers accommodations that can be implemented at the school building level and does not typically call in resources. A child who is undergoing the evaluation and IEP process probably should receive services under the Section 504 until the IEP is designed and implemented.

## The Question of Classification

Thirteen classifications entitle a child to full services and accommodations throughout the school day, but as we pointed out, the ones most likely to be applied to a bipolar child are "other health impaired" (OHI), "specific learning disability," or "serious emotionally disturbed" (SED), more often referred to as "emotionally disturbed" (ED).

Most parents should shoot for a classification of OHI, because it specifies that a child should have special education when he or she has

> limited strength, vitality, or alertness, including a heightened alertness to environmental stimuli, that results in limited alertness with respect to the educational environment, that—
> (a) is due to chronic or acute health problems such as asthma, attention deficit disorder or attention deficit hyperactivity disorder, diabetes, epilepsy, a heart condition, hemophilia, lead poisoning, leukemia, nephritis, rheumatic fever, and sickle cell anemia;
> (b) adversely affects a child's educational performance.

Pediatric bipolar disorder, like attention-deficit disorder, is a neurobiological illness: a medical condition. Certainly it is an illness that manifests with the decreasing energy of depressive episodes and the increasing energy, irritability, and even psychosis of a manic episode, that can result in hospitalization(s), and that "adversely affects a child's educational performance." Since over 90 percent of children with bipolar disorder have co-occurring attention ADHD, the OHI classification seems to fit best— for these and a host of other reasons.

In contrast, emotionally disturbed is *partially* defined as "an inability to learn that cannot be explained by intellectual, sensory, or health factors."

Many parents are told that an ED classification is the only way to ensure a therapeutic day or boarding school placement if it should be needed down the line or to protect a child should he or she act out and become a disciplinary problem. However, one "classification" does not offer any more protections than any other. The protections in the law are there for all students. If there are any issues relative to "discipline," it is incumbent on the school to be responsive by convening teams to determine if the behaviors are a manifestation of the disability (not the classification); if there needs to be an adjustment in the services, program, or anything else; and if more testing needs to be done and if that necessitates changes in the IEP.

The classification of OHI versus ED "frames" how the school views and will understand and work with your child from that day forward. An ED classification may help the school place the child in a classroom with students with more delinquent behaviors or may promote fear in a teacher or administrator when he or she considers that child. "Emotionally Disturbed" can also imply poor parenting instead of a medical illness beyond the child's control and adds to the already low self-esteem of a child or teen struggling with this disorder. An OHI classification, however, can promote more compassion from the school personnel and increase their desire to learn about this disorder.

Unfortunately, there are still some states that will not consider a more therapeutic placement for a child without the ED classification. Every state has slightly different ways to classify students, so it may be best to talk to an educational consultant or advocate before you set out on this journey (see below).

## EDUCATIONAL ADVOCATES

Because the entire IEP process is complicated—especially for parents dealing with it for the first time—it is often a good idea to find an educational advocate who can assist from the ground up. The advocate you choose should help draft all necessary correspondence, starting with the request for the evaluation, and then help draft the IEP and attend IEP meetings. To do so, the advocate must have a complete understanding of bipolar disorder and its impact on learning. A good advocate should also coach the parent and teach him or her the proper wording to use in person, on the phone, and in correspondence in order to achieve the necessary services the child needs. (The advocate also should coach the parent as to which phrases *not* to use and should outline how much information should be disclosed, and when.) Down the line the advocate can help measure the implementation and progress of the IEP and help make changes in course or, if necessary, make recommendations for an academic situation better suited to the child's needs.

When choosing an advocate, the Council of Parent Attorneys and Advocates (COPAA) advises a parent to select an advocate who is familiar with the local service providers, evaluators, local school districts, and special education administrators and the options they typically offer, and local customs. Ask a potential advocate about his or her background (that could range from being a paralegal, someone with a special education background and experience with the special educational needs of bipolar children and adolescents, to someone who is highly recommended by parents in your community). It is vitally important that any advocate you choose is extremely knowledgeable about IDEA 2004 and stays current with any regulation refinements in your state.

Currently, advocates are not certified, but COPAA is piloting a program that will train and certify advocates. COPAA offers an advocate locator on its website, www.copaa.org, and your state's Protection and Advocacy Agency can help you locate an experienced advocate. (Look in the yellow pages of your telephone book.)

Advocates may charge nothing for their time and expertise, but typically the fees range from $25 to $100 an hour. It is beneficial to both parent and advocate to spell out on paper exactly what the advocate's role and responsibilities will be, when the fees are to be paid, and how best to communicate with each other (phone, e-mail, office visits, and so on). In order for the advocate to prepare properly for any task that is required of him or her, the parent must alert the advocate in a timely manner of upcoming IEP meetings and any potential problems.

## INDIVIDUALIZED EDUCATION PROGRAM (IEP)

### How Does a Parent Initiate an IEP?

A child has to be deemed eligible to receive services, and that requires a complete evaluation of the child's weaknesses and strengths across all domains—academic skills, emotional functioning, and social skills. A parent should request the evaluation in writing but should first talk to the special education director and guidance counselor and ask how their system initiates the process. Most school districts ask parents to sign consent forms that make their child a "focus of concern." Once the process begins, the child is observed in the classroom, and a number of standardized tests that pinpoint IQ, specific academic strengths or weaknesses, and language and communication abilities are administered. Psychological assessment tests are administered as well.

The following sample "Request for Testing Letter" should help a parent get things moving. It should be sent by certified mail. (Keep in mind that not all parents will have independent testing, nor do they need independent testing, before such a request is made.)

### SAMPLE REQUEST FOR TESTING LETTER

Date


Dear _____ (Director of Special Education):

Our daughter, Maya, is starting the sixth grade at Hyde Park Middle School, and she has been diagnosed with juvenile-onset bipolar disorder. This is a medical illness that is characterized by rapid shifts in mood, energy, thoughts, and behavior.

Maya is relatively stable on medication and very compliant with treatment, but school can be difficult for her due to some seasonal fluctuations in moods and co-occurring attentional problems (some 94 percent of children with bipolar disorder have a co-occurring ADHD). She also has difficulties with organization and planning— she has executive function deficits. Maya's mood disorder and her attentional and organizational difficulties significantly impair her availability for education.

Therefore, we are formally requesting a complete evaluation of the impact of these problems, including academic, emotional, and social functioning, to determine Maya's eligibility for special education classification, accommodations, and services.

I would be happy to send you copies of all the independent testing we have for Maya and to supply you with any information that you need from her psychiatrist, therapist, and neuropsychologist.

Our address is 79 S. Green Acres Lane, Madison, CT 06990. Our phone number is 203-555-2345; fax: 203-555-5432; e-mail: Winnjk@gmail.com.

Please let us know what you need us to sign in order to make Maya a focus of concern and to initiate the process of evaluation as quickly as possible.

Thank you very much,
Jane and Kenneth Winnick

All the testing can be done by the school system and costs parents nothing, but parents should bring their own independent assessments to bear on the procedure. (Parents should remember that if a doctor feels these tests are "medically necessary," the insurance company may pick up a large percentage of the costs. Check with the insurance company first.)

We asked educational attorney Elizabeth Jester in Washington, D.C., whether a parent should make the effort and spend the money to have an independent assessment done. She said:

I strongly recommend it. Schools should certainly do more than a screening, but sometimes the testing is not in-depth, and if you go the independent route you can choose a very experienced tester who hopefully understands the panoply of symptoms and difficulties a child with bipolar disorder can suffer, and who will write a *very* specific report. Since the IEP is the critical document from which all services and progress benchmarks flow, the quality and comprehensiveness of the baseline assessments cannot be underestimated. If parents do get an independent assessment for their child, the school district should be notified at least two weeks before the IEP meeting, and the team should have a chance to go over the testing results and recommendations before the IEP meeting. Conversely, parents should be given all testing that the school has done.

## Who Attends the IEP Meeting?

The maximum amount of time allowed to pass between the parents' request and/or agreement to conduct the evaluation to the IEP development differs from state to state, but most regulations cite a time line somewhere between fifty and 120 days. A parent should begin this process as early as possible so that the school year does not slip by without modifications in the child's program.

Once the evaluation is completed, parents are contacted and a mutually acceptable time and place are set for the IEP meeting.

The following people are usually a part of the IEP development team:

- Parents
- Child's teacher or teachers
- District representative who is able to provide or supervise the provision of special education
- Special education teacher
- Guidance counselor
- School psychologist who conducted the testing
- Service providers

One or two parents will sit at a table with four, five, or six school professionals, which may be extremely intimidating. Therefore, parents should feel free to bring an advocate—the independent tester, the child's therapist, psychiatrist, educational consultant, and so on—if they feel it would present a more complete picture of the child, bipolar disorder, and its effects on learning and classroom behavior.

## HOW SHOULD A PARENT PREPARE FOR THE IEP?

### Recommendation 1: Be Prepared to Educate

If parents decide to disclose the bipolar diagnosis (and the general consensus is that parents should be open and aboveboard about it), they need to understand that few people realize that bipolar disorder can exist in childhood and that it can look identical to or be comorbid with attention-deficit disorder with hyperactivity and/or extreme anxiety, obsessive-compulsive disorder, and Tourette's syndrome. *It's up to the parent or the parent's professionals to educate the staff and ensure that everyone understands the condition and its effects on the child and the learning process, and what the child needs to be successful in school.*

One woman wrote of her efforts to do this education in preparation of her list of modifications in her son's program. She said:

I spent all weekend preparing a list of recommendations for his IEP. They were all-encompassing, covering every angle. I typed a brief description of bipolar disorder with mixed states so that the teachers who didn't know what it was could read it. I attached a few documents detailing different information about bipolar disorder, including Dr. Charles Popper's list of the differences between ADHD and bipolar disorder [see pages 39–41]. I wrote up a contingency plan for the occurrence of another manic episode. I also wrote a list of coping strategies for the teachers to deal with him in class. At the beginning of the packet, I took the time to list my concerns for my son and the reason why I called the meeting. I did a lot of work. I felt so empowered (and proud).

I walked in there with these big packets, and I passed them out and we went through them. My list of modifications was major, and they agreed to adopt all of my suggestions and modifications pretty much without question, and they are willing to test him further to help him.

People tend to be more helpful when they understand what they're dealing with, so preparing and educating the school personnel (graciously and sincerely) can move the process along because everyone is approaching it with the same fund of knowledge. (Elizabeth Jester, the educational attorney, suggests that a parent send the information about bipolar disorder to the planning team a week or so before the meeting, so the educators can read the materials, think about them, and view the child and the IEP modification requests through very different—and, it is hoped, more sympathetic—eyes.)

### Recommendation 2: Prepare a Binder
Another idea that proves a parent's credibility and braces his or her advocacy abilities is to *prepare a three-ring binder for the IEP.* It should have a large pocket on the outside into which a picture of the child can be slipped, along with his or her name. The picture helps humanize your child and reminds all involved that they are talking about a little human being and not just a problem. Also, if the child's artwork or writing are particularly wonderful, it is nice to show some of the child's strengths before launching into the catalog of weaknesses.

The spine of the binder should carry the name of the child and the year and grade the child is in. Use dividers and organize the following sections:

1. Important contacts and telephone numbers with any pertinent notes
2. All correspondence with the district and school system in chronological order

3. School (and any independent) assessments
4. Medical records
5. The child's report cards, progress notes, and discipline records
6. Examples of the child's work (to show which areas need remediation)
7. Any former Section 504 plans or IEPs
8. List of questions that need answering during the IEP
9. List of modifications and parent's expectations of this IEP
10. Long-term goals and short-term objectives
11. Information on parent's legal rights and due process
12. Any relevant articles or information

Thus organized, a parent can locate any relevant piece of information quickly and efficiently (and impressively).

A parent's clothing style, and even the briefcase he or she carries the binder and assorted materials in, adds or detracts from his or her credibility. A professional, polished, businesslike appearance not only adds to the appearance of competency and seriousness but makes the parent feel more competent and powerful in what is often an uncomfortable situation.

### Recommendation 3: Rehearse the Meeting

It is also an excellent idea to practice how the meeting will be started and how you will get across the points you want to make, even if there are objections. If both parents are attending, they should rehearse who will bring up what points and when in the presentation, and who will address possible objections. Parents should also decide which one is going to take meticulous notes of the meeting or operate the tape recorder.

## Starting the Meeting

Parents should do their best not to appear defensive. They can begin the meeting by introducing the advocates or professionals attending. A phrase such as: "We've brought _____, Sarah's _____, who has been helping us prepare for this IEP and would like to explain a bit about bipolar disorder and its impact on Sarah's performance in school."

Then the school professionals will discuss the results of the testing, where they've pinpointed weaknesses, and make suggestions for modifications in the academic program and daily schedule.

## Educating the Team About Accommodations That Will Benefit Your Child

Because a parent usually understands the illness and the side effects of the medications better than anyone, he or she should be ready to spell out a list of symptoms and medication side effects and proposed modifications in the academic schedule to accommodate the child's difficulties and to make the school day more productive and comfortable for the student.

By the time the team sits down to write the IEP, the parents and educators have a complete neuropsychological assessment that can pinpoint any specific learning disabilities, learning styles, and possible weaknesses in the domains of executive functions. (This neuropsychologist's report should make recommendations for the academic arena, and these recommendations should be addressed in the IEP.) See Chapter 10 for a complete discussion of neuropsychological testing.

We thought it would be helpful to divide the modifications into categories where parents and educators could see at a glance which symptoms the student has and which accommodations will have to be incorporated into the IEP. Four categories the IEP team should consider when developing an appropriate IEP for a student with a mood disorder are:

1. Symptoms caused by the mood disorder
2. Side effects of the medications used to treat the condition
3. Attention and organizational difficulties
4. Specific learning disabilities

## Possible Accommodations, Modifications, and Special Services

*Symptoms of the Illness*

SYMPTOM
The student has daily and seasonal fluctuations in mood and energy and is therefore more attentive to classwork at certain times and less attentive at others.

ACCOMMODATIONS
- Create formal contingency plans when the student is unstable and is experiencing periods of withdrawal or fatigue (a symptom of the illness and often a side effect of the medications).

SYMPTOM
The student can experience great irritability, building to a rage if not recognized and dealt with in an appropriate and timely manner.

ACCOMMODATIONS
- Assign a staff/school person whom the student can go see when he or she feels unable to cope. This can be a counselor, school therapist, teacher, or any other person (campus monitor, school nurse, etc.) with whom the student feels safe and whom the student trusts and chooses. Give the student a permanent pass and a private signal that only he or she and the teacher understand, so that the student can make a private exit in front of the rest of the class.
- Offer the student a private place to go to calm down when feelings are overwhelming.
- Schedule regular meetings with the school psychologist to teach the student self-calming and anger management techniques.
- Assign an aide in the classroom to prevent situations that may cause the student to lose control.
- Administer a Functional Behavior Assessment to identify triggers that cause the student to lose control. Then write a Behavior Intervention Plan to be added to the IEP, which provides appropriate interventions for problematic behaviors. This can be as simple as identifying stressors that cause untoward behaviors.

SYMPTOM
The student has periods of excessive anxiety and sadness.

ACCOMMODATIONS
- Assign a safe place where the student can regroup and calm down and a person with whom the student can talk easily.
- Have the student keep a journal in which he or she can address anxiety-producing thoughts and school experiences, which can be

shared with the school psychologist and the student's personal therapist.

- If the treating psychiatrist recommends the use of a light box, provide this daily during a study period in the resource room.

## SYMPTOM

The student has difficulty with peers. The student may have poor social skills, be bossy, misperceive the behaviors and intentions of others, and be socially inappropriate at times.

## ACCOMMODATIONS

- Arrange for the student to learn social skills and group behavior by meeting with the school social worker, school psychologist, or guidance counselor.
- Develop a social skills class and have the student participate in it.
- Place an aide in the classroom who can monitor social interactions and report incidents of social conflict. The aide can interpret and explain to the student how things occurred that may be outside the student's perception. This aide can advocate for the child, act as a friend, make the child feel safe, and alert the school if there are any incidents of bullying going on.

## SYMPTOM

Children with bipolar disorder often have a reversal in their sleep/wake cycle. It is extremely difficult for them to get to sleep at night and to wake up early in the morning. They may seem half comatose or extremely grumpy and sleep through first and possibly second period, often missing important class material and doing poorly on tests in the first two periods.

## ACCOMMODATIONS

- Schedule academic classes later in the day, when the student is more alert and emotionally available for learning.
- Allow the student to take important tests later in the day, when he or she may be able to focus better.
- Allow the student to begin the school day a little later.

SYMPTOM

The student is perfectionistic and has difficulty making transitions.

ACCOMMODATIONS

- Reduce writing by allowing the student to use a computer so the page looks neat to him or her.
- Allow student to finish tasks before moving on.
- Have all teachers cue the student as to transitions and the time they will occur.
- Provide an aide who will give support during nonsupervised periods of the school day (lunch, recess, escort to and from the bus waiting area, etc.).
- Allow the student to transition ahead of the rest of the class (going to lunch room, library, etc.).

SYMPTOM

The student becomes overheated and overstimulated in gym classes and begins to suffer discomfort or to cut class.

ACCOMMODATIONS

- If the student participates, he or she must always have access to water and rest.
- The student should have the option of less competitive physical activity, such as yoga, tae kwon do, weight training, aerobics, and the like.
- The student should be graded based on attendance rather than participation.
- If necessary for the student's emotional well-being, have an Adaptive P.E. written into the IEP until such time as the student is ready for mainstream physical education.
- If inclusion is an issue or a desire on the student's part, the student could be appointed scorekeeper or equipment manager.

## Side Effects of the Medications

SYMPTOM

The student is experiencing excessive thirst, a frequent need to urinate, or bouts of diarrhea as a result of some of the medications used to treat the illness (especially in the early stages of treatment).

ACCOMMODATIONS
- Allow the student to keep a water bottle at his or her side or to have unlimited access to (noncaffeinated) fluids.
- Allow unlimited access to the bathroom (with a signal to each teacher as to where the student is going—without announcing it publicly)
- Educate the staff (especially the school nurse) about medication side effects, which may include drowsiness, diarrhea, stomachaches, and cognitive dulling, and the need to accommodate for these.

SYMPTOM
The student is sleeping in class because his or her body is not yet accustomed to a new medication.

ACCOMMODATION
- Provide a place for the student to take a brief nap so that he or she can continue with the school day. (Sleepiness usually subsides as the body adjusts to the medication.)

SYMPTOM
The student is experiencing cognitive dulling and a lack of endurance as a result of the medication(s).

ACCOMMODATIONS
- Schedule frequent breaks.
- Provide extra time for work completion.
- Decrease workload and homework.

*Attentional and Organizational Difficulties*

SYMPTOM
The student has difficulty staying on task and paying attention for any length of time. The student is very fidgety in the classroom.

ACCOMMODATIONS
- Seat the student close to the teacher where the teacher can get the student's attention.
- Schedule frequent breaks.

- Offer choices, such as going to a study carrel in the library or to a quiet area outside the classroom.
- Assign a study buddy (use the phrase "study partner" for an older student). The students can focus each other and acquire strategies for learning from each other.

## SYMPTOM

The student is disorganized and often misplaces needed books and materials. The student often forgets to bring home assignments and/or fails to turn in work.

## ACCOMMODATIONS

- Use a "travel folder." This is a pocket portfolio that has necessary papers to complete on the left-hand side (mark this "To Do"). All completed homework is transferred to the right-hand side (mark this "Completed").
- Give the student a planner book and have the teacher check that daily assignments are recorded properly.
- E-mail or fax parents a list of assignments and news of upcoming projects or tests.
- Have the teacher or aide give the student a prompt before leaving school: "What do I need to do tonight and what materials would I need to accomplish it?" "I need: my coat, my recorder, my math book, my study sheet for French, my planner, my lunchbox, my travel folder (French sheet is there . . .)." The teacher or aide could photocopy lists of materials and clothing and have the student check items off as they are put in the bag. The student must be taught to pack a backpack to return to school the same way: with a prompt such as "What do I need for school today?" (A parent has to help out here.)
- Provide a second set of textbooks for the homework area.
- Teach the student to number assignments in the order in which they should be done before beginning a homework session. (Thus he or she will focus and begin to follow a set strategy.) Have the student start with an assignment that is short and easy, but avoid saving the hardest or longest assignment for last. Have the student estimate how much time it will take to complete each assignment and measure the estimates against the actual time. (These students have difficulty with time management.) Have the stu-

dent use a stopwatch to assign chunks of time to each step of a
study plan, which will help move him or her on to the next step.

- Teach the student to preview questions at the end of each chapter
  to focus on important concepts. The student should also preview
  photos, captions, and headings throughout the chapter before
  reading and when reviewing for a test.

- Color-code subject folders and notebooks to match textbooks. For
  instance, if the math text is orange, place an orange strip of tape
  on the math folder and notebook so that the student can quickly
  locate and assemble all materials needed for math. If the school
  requires the books to be covered, color-coordinate the books and
  folders.

- If the student uses a locker, teach him or her to place all morning
  textbooks, notebooks, and folders on the top shelf of the locker
  and all afternoon materials on a lower or the bottom shelf. This
  will help organize the student and ensure that he or she goes to
  class with the correct materials. Have the student (with the help
  of an assistant if necessary) clean out the locker at least once a
  week. Schedule that cleanup on Fridays to ensure that P.E. clothes
  and needed materials arrive home for weekend use.

## Specific Learning Disabilities

ACCOMMODATIONS FOR READING DISABILITIES OR DYSLEXIA
Children with reading disabilities, or dyslexia, have problems decoding
the phonetic structure of language, which negatively impacts comprehension. Once a difficulty in this area is discovered, IDEA spells out that an
"evidence-based" system of remediation be instituted. (A compilation of
evidence-based reading programs can be viewed at the Florida Center for
Reading Research at www.fcrr.org/FCRRReports/table.asp.) In addition,
the student may need some or all of the following accommodations.

- Provide the student with larger-print materials
- Arrange for the student to receive books on tape through the
  Recordings for the Blind and Dyslexic in Princeton, New Jersey.
  Contact them at www.rfbd.org.
- Provide books that have information highlighted.
- Have the student use a tape recorder in the classroom.
- Provide readers for tests.

- Allow extra time for tests.
- Provide materials that use lots of visuals.
- Provide information in bullet format.
- Teach the student to take notes and to study using visual techniques instead of words.
- Provide hard copies of notes to the student.
- Teach mapping techniques.
- Allow extra time for assignments.
- Do not penalize the student for spelling errors.
- Provide computer-based reading software, such as Kurzweil 3000 or Wordsmith, which scans textbooks or other reading material into a computer and audibly reads the scanned text back to the student. (In Wordsmith, the student has a choice of a male or female voice or a British or American accent.) Go to www.dyslexic .com to learn more about these products.

## ACCOMMODATIONS FOR WRITING DISABILITIES OR DYSGRAPHIA

Children with writing disabilities, or dysgraphia, generally have problems with handwriting (the actual formation of the letters), as well as deficits in written expression. When writing, these children may omit words or reverse them, and syntax and grammar are often incorrect. These students may also have difficulty deciding on a topic for an essay or organizing it so that the ideas flow in a logical manner. These problems may not show up in expressive language assessments and may be exhibited only in the written language assessments. Students with writing disabilities or dysgraphia will need some or all of the following accommodations.

- Teach and encourage the student to use a keyboard in class and to complete all assignments.
- Assign a scribe to write longer or timed writing assignments.
- Allow the student to tape record classes. Do not penalize the quality of note-taking or assume the student is not taking it all in aurally.
- Provide paper copies of notes to the student.
- Allow extra time for assignments.
- Assign a scribe for important tests, or allow the student to give answers orally.

- Do not penalize the student for handwriting or spelling errors.
- Have the parents investigate voice recognition software, such as Dragon Naturally Speaking (also available on www.dyslexic.com).

The remediation process will depend on the areas of difficulty that are impacting the child's written expression.

If the problem is dysgraphia, and the child is having trouble recalling the shape of letters (encoding) and sequencing them onto paper in a legible fashion, then a multisensory approach that is rehearsed and repetitive will help a great deal. An occupational therapist or a special education teacher may use a special pencil to encourage proper pencil grip, help a child align his or her arms and body in order to write, and use graph paper or a paper with raised lines to help the child recognize where to place and how to space letters. There are also slant boards that help the child work at a vertical surface, as this promotes the development of proper hand and wrist position and keeps the paper from sliding.

Special paper and slant boards are usually available in teacher supply stores, but teachers and parents should be aware of an impressive curriculum called Handwriting Without Tears. The method breaks down letters into kinesthetic lines, circles, and semicircles and helps a child organize and orient his or her writing with various paper options. Visit their website at www.hwtears.com. Therapro sells slant boards, pencil grips, and interesting products to promote better writing for youngsters. Visit their website at www.therapro.com.

Difficulties with spelling and the mechanics of writing, such as capitalization and punctuation, will also require a systematic, structured, and constantly rehearsed routine. The occupational services that help remediate dysgraphia and poor mechanics of writing should take place two to three times a week and should be written into an IEP.

Along with special services, an IEP should list a number of accommodations or modifications to the scholastic demands placed on a child with written expression difficulties. Certainly the amount of written work should be reduced, assistive technology should be employed, and extra time should be allowed for the student with disorders of written expression. An extensive discussion of disorders of written expression can be found in the next chapter.

## Constructing the IEP

The Individualized Education Plan, constructed by the school team, is a written statemnt of the goals, objectives, and services that will be delivered to assist a child with special educational needs. A well-written IEP will proceed from a listing of a general goal to very specific measurable objectives accompanied by a timetable in which those objectives will be met. Federal law dictates that it include six required parts:

1. A statement of the child's present level of performance
2. A statement of the goals and objectives
3. A statement of special education services to be provided
4. A statement of the extent to which the child will participate in regular education
5. The date the special educational services are to begin and the expected ending date
6. The criteria for determining if the objectives are being met

The IEP goals should be written in the order of priority—the most important goal is first, the second most important is next, and so on. The language should never be vague.

The following questions should be answered:

- What service is to be provided?
- Who will provide the service, the specialist, the teacher, the aide?
- What teaching methods will be used?
- Where will the services be provided, the regular classroom, the resource room, in a special education class? With a small group? Will it be one-on-one?
- How often will the services be provided? How many days per week?
- Will the sessions be thirty, forty-five, or sixty minutes in length?
- Are the services to be delivered to the child alone or to a small group? What is the cap on that group? (You want to see no more than four or five.) When will the services start? Immediately? Or within thirty days to allow time for the hiring of a qualified specialist?

## A Model IEP for a Child with Bipolar Disorder

Unfortunately, bipolar disorder is an illness with wide variations in energy, mood, and motivation, and it tends to be seasonal. This means that academic progress with modifications can work wonderfully for a while, but a child may experience breakthrough episodes at different times of the year, despite proper medication. There may be times when depression predominates and the child can barely get to school or produce close to his or her ability; other times the child may become activated and hypomanic and more difficult to handle in the classroom. Some children will experience a rocky road when new medication trials are initiated; some children may even require hospitalization during the school year and miss weeks and weeks of learning.

Therefore, we asked special education advocate Anne Marie Smith, M. Ed., in Agawam, Massachusetts, to construct a model IEP that might provide guidelines for educating a student with bipolar disorder. She explained that an IEP starts with a collection of assessments, typically done by the school but often augmented by the independent neuropsychological testing that the parent provides.

The baseline assessment serves as the foundation of the IEP. It describes the child's strengths and difficulties so that the IEP team can develop the specific annual goals that will ensure that the student receives an appropriate education. Please note: IDEA 2004 has authorized a three-year IEP for students in a limited number of states, but few think that this will ever serve the student or the school's and parents' ability to measure progress appropriately.

Moreover, IDEA 2004 dispensed with the mandatory short-term objectives or benchmarks heretofore required on IEPs. The lawmakers' reasoning is that children do not learn in a linear fashion, and lobbyists for school districts were attempting to reduce paperwork. However, short-term objectives or benchmarks are the incremental steps taken to accomplish an annual goal. Without these steps, parents and educators will have no way to assess whether the child is on the way to developing that skill or meeting that annual goal.

Since IDEA 2004 retains short-term objectives for students with serious and significant cognitive disabilities, parents of children with bipolar disorder should request that short-term objectives be retained in their children's IEPs. (Many school systems are doing this anyway.)

Every student is unique and will require the development of individual goals, accommodations, and services (that is why it is called an *Individualized* Education Plan). This hypothetical IEP was constructed to give parents and educators an idea of some of the possibilities. There may be several annual goals under each present level of performance category. Again, refer to page 295 to see a more comprehensive list of symptoms and potential accommodations.

## HYPOTHETICAL BASELINE INFORMATION AND DRAFT IEP FOR A STUDENT WITH BIPOLAR DISORDER IN MIDDLE SCHOOL

Joseph is a likable boy who was diagnosed with bipolar disorder three years ago. Early-onset bipolar disorder is a medical illness—a brain disorder that renders Joseph's academic and emotional availability variable and often unpredictable. His moods may veer from feeling hopeless and negative and depressed (typically in the fall), to times in which he will appear energized, grandiose, and superior to some of his classmates (typically in the spring).

Joseph sees a psychiatrist for medication and has had extensive independent neuropsychological testing that has pinpointed strengths as well as weaknesses. Both the psychiatrist and neuropsychologist have made recommendations for program modifications and remediation. The school has conducted its own assessments and has amassed much information about his functioning in all domains: academic, social, and psychological.

Joseph has been quite stable on medications, but side effects such as fatigue and cognitive dulling can impact his availability and ability to learn. He has trouble getting up in the morning (due to his medication regimen, if he is depressed, and sleep inertia) and tends to do well if his more difficult academic subjects are scheduled later in the day, when he is more alert.

Although Joseph is a bright student and wants to do well, at times he can appear bored, irritable, and oppositional in the classroom. He is somewhat inflexible and experiences extreme anxiety if he is unprepared for changes in his schedule. Transitions are difficult for him.

Joseph has executive function deficits that impair his ability to concentrate for long periods of time compared to his peers, and he is disorganized and cannot complete homework in a timely manner. He often turns it in late or forgets to turn in assignments that have been completed. Often he forgets to take needed materials home in order to finish assignments and projects.

Joseph can be impulsive and has poor judgment and decision-making skills. He lacks interpersonal skills and has difficulty making and maintaining friendships. He needs instruction to improve social interactions and a social skills class and counseling to support success in these areas.

Joseph has very poor self-esteem, and he needs calm, reassuring, and understanding teachers if he is to do his best.

## PRESENT LEVEL OF PERFORMANCE

Joseph can attend to independent structured learning tasks for a maximum of fifteen minutes and then requires a short physical break before he can complete any given assignment.

### ANNUAL GOAL

After being provided a cue by a staff member to take a break, Joseph will return to task and remain independently on task for structured independent learning for thirty minutes.

*Objectives*

- Joseph will remain on task for structured independent learning twenty minutes for the first marking period 80 percent of the time.
- Joseph will remain on task for structured independent learning twenty-five minutes for the second marking period 80 percent of the time.
- Joseph will remain on task for structured independent learning thirty minutes for the third marking period.
- Joseph will maintain the thirty-minute time frame for staying on task for structured independent learning for the fourth marking period.

## PRESENT LEVEL OF PERFORMANCE

Joseph has anxiety that expresses itself in school whereby he becomes oppositional and irritable, disruptive, and unable to stay in the classroom. This is not Joseph's regular demeanor; these traits become observable when he is extremely anxious.

ANNUAL GOAL
- Given a visual cue by staff, Joseph will utilize the permanent pass in his possession and seek out either the school guidance counselor or the school psychologist to utilize relaxation tools and strategies to reduce his anxiety and to reduce the chances of his becoming irritable, oppositional, or disruptive. He will do this without protesting or complaining 80 percent of the time.

*Objectives:*
- Given a visual cue by staff, Joseph will utilize the permanent pass in his possession and seek out either the school guidance counselor or the school psychologist 20 percent of the time for the first marking period.
- Given a visual cue by staff, Joseph will utilize the permanent pass in his possession and seek out either the school guidance counselor or the school psychologist 40 percent of the time for the second marking period.
- Given a visual cue by staff, Joseph will utilize the permanent pass in his possession and seek out either the school guidance counselor or the school psychologist 60 percent of the time for the third marking period.
- Given a visual cue by staff, Joseph will utilize the permanent pass in his possession and seek out either the school guidance counselor or the school psychologist 80 percent of the time for the fourth marking period.

**PRESENT LEVEL OF PERFORMANCE**
Reports from Joseph's psychiatrist and parents show Joseph to have very low self-esteem. He often makes negative comments about himself or his work, and parents and staff are concerned about the impact of this low self-esteem on his academic and social engagement.

ANNUAL GOAL
When Joseph makes a negative or self-deprecating comment, he will be redirected with a verbal cue to reframe his comments in a more positive light 50 percent of the time.

*Objectives*
- Joseph will convert his negative talk to positive commentary 25 percent of the time for the first quarter.
- Joseph will maintain the elimination of the negative commentary, replacing it with positive statements 25 percent of the time for the second quarter.
- Joseph will convert his negative talk to positive commentary 50 percent of the time for the third quarter.
- Joseph will maintain this 50 percent measurement for the fourth quarter.

## PRESENT LEVEL OF PERFORMANCE

When presented with a change in routine or a novel situation, Joseph can become overwhelmed, confused, and anxious. Because he has difficulty with transitions and anxiety, he resists engaging in any new event for which he is not prepared. He made progress this year when an appointed staff member reviewed his daily agenda before his first class, midday, and toward the end of the day, whereupon they discussed the upcoming school day. He feels more organized and in control, and certainly less anxious. This routine is to be kept in place.

### ANNUAL GOAL

Prior to any known change in schedule, routine, or curriculum, Joseph will be alerted and the assigned staff member will ensure that he marks the change in his daily agenda and is cued to the change prior to its happening. This should reduce his anxiety, and Joseph will be able to transition through a change in schedule and participate in the event(s) 90 percent of the time.

*Objectives*
- Given a change in schedule, Joseph will participate in the new event(s) 30 percent of the time in the first marking period.
- Given a change in schedule, Joseph will participate in the new event(s) 60 percent of the time in the second marking period.
- Given a change in schedule, Joseph will participate in the new event(s) 90 percent of the time in the third marking period.
- Joseph will maintain this 90 percent or better participation in the fourth marking period.

## PRESENT LEVEL OF PERFORMANCE

Joseph has no real friends at school. His mother brings him to school each day instead of his riding the bus because some of the kids tease him and he ends up fighting with them. He is viewed by some of his peers as bossy and authoritative. He does not seem to know how to access a social group and has trouble with the give-and-take of relationships. Joseph has told his counselor that he very much would like to be a friend and that he would like to have friends like the other children in his class.

### ANNUAL GOAL

Joseph will accomplish four out of seven of the following social skills on 80 percent of trials. The counselor is to take data and observe on a weekly basis.

*Objectives*

- Joseph will meet one new friend whom he does not know currently.
- Joseph will be able to demonstrate two characteristics of friendship learned in his social skills group in the school setting.
- Joseph will be able to demonstrate two characteristics of sharing learned in his social skills group in the school setting.
- Joseph will utilize one or two methods of anger management learned in his counseling session as an alternative to engaging in an argument with peers.
- During lunchtime Joseph will make three genuinely pleasant remarks to his peers over the course of a week.
- Joseph will choose to do one thing for someone else each week, inside or outside of school, without being asked and will record this act in his counseling journal.

## PRESENT LEVEL OF PERFORMANCE

Joseph does not complete all of his schoolwork on a daily basis. He is having trouble completing it because he cannot organize and plan and work efficiently due to executive function deficits. Joseph also has trouble remembering to bring needed materials home and returning homework to school.

ANNUAL GOAL

Given teacher assistance, Joseph will be able to utilize a homework journal to record and keep track of all assignments and necessary tools to complete the assignments 70 percent of the time.

*Objectives*
- With teacher assistance, Joseph will utilize his homework journal
  50 percent of the time for the first marking period.
- With teacher assistance, Joseph will utilize his homework journal
  60 percent of the time for the second marking period.
- With teacher assistance, Joseph will utilize his homework journal
  70 percent of the time for the third marking period.
- With teacher assistance, Joseph will maintain his utilization of the
  homework journal 70 percent or better for the fourth marking
  period.

## Functional Behavioral Assessments and Behavior Intervention Plans

While many children with bipolar disorder don't act out in school (but save
their pent-up frustration and upset for home and mother), some do. The
school may try to discipline, suspend, or expel the student due to unruly
or oppositional behaviors without understanding that many of the behaviors are a result of the student's condition. If you or the child psychiatrist
believe that these behaviors are sequelae of bipolar symptoms, you should
request that the school conduct a Functional Behavioral Assessment
(FBA). Based on the findings of the FBA, the school must write a Behavior Intervention Plan (BIP) into the IEP. This is now mandated by law.

### THE FBA/BIP PROCESS

The FBA is a formal assessment that can identify problem behaviors students are exhibiting, where they are having them, when they are having
them, and with whom they are having them. The data are analyzed and a
BIP is developed that provides goals to replace problem behaviors with positive behaviors.

Only trained professionals, such as psychologists or special education
teachers with specialized training, are qualified to conduct an FBA. It
cannot be stressed strongly enough that parents need to investigate the
level of experience of the people assigned to conduct the FBA. If it becomes obvious that experienced professionals are not available, then the

parents must insist that the school district bring in such professionals from the outside. Otherwise school districts will continue developing BIPs that are inherently flawed and subject to failure.

The data from the FBA are used by the BIP team (school psychologist, teachers, support teachers, and any other professionals who work with the child) to develop an appropriate intervention plan that will:

- Describe the behavior
- Determine the functions of behavior
- Develop interventions that will replace untoward behaviors with new behaviors
- Develop a time line for reviewing the plan

The school will implement the plan and, over time, evaluate the outcomes as outlined in the plan.

It is important when observing a child with bipolar disorder to differentiate between behaviors that can be modified and symptoms of the illness. For example, a child may be refusing to work because he or she is overwhelmed by the stimulation in the room, does not understand the assignment, and/or feels lethargic from the medications and/or the illness (or a combination of these factors). Therefore, the child simply is not able to perform to the teacher's expectations at that time, as opposed to being defiant to earn the respect of peers or some other outcome (known as a function) of the behavior.

It is necessary for the team to receive some training in childhood bipolar disorder before it can create an effective and appropriate BIP—one intended to identify the antecedents of the problem behaviors and modify them with positive behaviors.

The Behavior Intervention Plan should:

- Identify the antecedents to the problem behavior
- Focus on positive supports
- Teach replacement behaviors
- Manipulate antecedents
- Manipulate consequences
- Change curriculum or instruction
- Monitor and evaluate effectiveness and modify if necessary

Some examples of these interventions are:

| Behavior | Symptom (Antecedent) | Intervention |
|---|---|---|
| Child refuses to do classwork | •Lethargic from meds <br> •Cognitive dulling <br> •Overwhelmed by the assignment | •Allow student to work on a creative or interesting assignment <br> •Have an aide work one-on-one with the child. <br> •Reduce the length of the assignment. <br> •Allow the child to work in a study carrel. |
| Child interacts inappropriately | Inability to read social cues | Social FI skills training taught by the school psychologist or school social worker is offered. |
| Child pushes other children | Sensory integration issues | Student stands at the back of the line an arm's length away from other children. |

The Behavior Intervention Plan should be reviewed frequently to assess whether it is effective and whether the child might need a different placement.

Naturally, for a bipolar child, everything starts with proper mood stabilization and, in many cases, addressing the attendant learning disabilities that may be causing frustration, hopelessness, and perhaps anger when approaching work that uncovers these learning deficits.

The Center for Effective Collaboration and Practice is a national organization that helps students with emotional and behavioral problems succeed at school. The organization has a comprehensive website that discusses the philosophies of a Functional Behavioral Assessment and demonstrates how a team collects the data and writes the Behavior Intervention Plans. You can find them on the Internet at www.cecp.air.org/fba/problembehavior/main.htm.

## Other Sections on the IEP Form

After the baseline level and the goal and objectives are notated in the IEP, the IEP team notates how progress is to be measured. Some students will be tested periodically, or the teachers and counselor will fill out a standardized checklist, or progress will be charted every few days or on a weekly basis. (These measurement instruments are placed in the "Criteria" section on the IEP form.) Finally, a percentage goal is assigned that attempts to determine what percentage of mastery is realistic: 75 percent? 80 percent? 100 percent?

The goals are looked at every nine weeks or so. If progress is not being made, an IEP can be reconvened at any time to make adjustments or to put other modifications in place. It is important to remember that an IEP is an organic document that can be modified at any time. Parents who wish to reconvene the IEP planning team should put the request in writing.

Parents should keep in mind that the IEP must be constructed in just such a specific manner. If the time ever comes when they must prove that a small therapeutic school is better for their child, they're going to have to produce evidence that the child's needs cannot be met in the large public school environment, and everything will start with the IEP.

## Self-Contained Classroom Versus Scheduled Time in a Resource Room

The least restrictive environment is a regular classroom, with time scheduled in the resource room or school psychologist's office for remediation or therapy. But some schools have self-contained classrooms that have smaller numbers of students and less hustle and bustle, and that may be a more appropriate learning environment for a child having trouble with distractibility and overstimulation. Everything will depend on the grouping of students in that self-contained classroom and what each student's challenges may be. If a child with bipolar disorder is gifted in certain areas, the student should be placed in the high math or high science classes with the rest of the gifted students in the school, if possible, or have one-on-one tutoring.

## What Are the Possible Derailments on the Way to a Proper IEP?

It is hoped that everyone at the meeting is working in tandem and a proper IEP is under construction for the student; but comments or objections may arise that could derail the process and obstruct the parents' goals for the IEP. If a parent hears any phrases like: "We don't have this kind of money"; "We don't have this kind of specialist or staffing"; or "We have many students here. Your child is not our only concern"; the parent can respond calmly, "The law states that our child is entitled to a Free and Appropriate Public Education [FAPE], and a placement must be offered that allows our child's educational needs to be met and that can make our child 'available for education.' "

To put it another way: Legally, no school system can say any of those statements and be in compliance with the law. If they have to pull in private staffing to meet the child's needs, then that is what they'll have to do.

Teachers should recognize that these laws also can empower them and that they have every right to request additional in-service training, help within the classroom to manage that special ed child (an aide, a teacher who comes in part of the day to help, volunteer adults, a college intern, a psychology or social worker intern, or even a high school student assigned to help the student). No teacher should be asked to deal with all these modifications without complete training and adequate support services.

## The Meeting's End

At the end of the meeting, the parents may be asked to sign the IEP. No IEP should ever be signed on the spot but should be taken home and mulled over when the parents are a bit less spent and exhausted. If a day later there are some questions that need clarifying, the parent should call the special education director and discuss any changes. Only after clarification or correction should an IEP be signed saying that the parents accept the IEP plan.

If the plan has been well constructed and the school personnel have worked hard to promote success for the child, a phone call to the special education director and a note of thanks to each participant would be a very appreciated finale to the IEP process. Parents who have a positive response should bear in mind how much effort everyone is putting into this child and his or her problems. Much of the information about bipolar disorder is certain to be new to the school personnel, and they will be unsure as to what modifications will work (or will be less successful), and uncertainty can exist for them as well as the parents.

## Communication in Middle and High School

In elementary school, once the IEP is agreed on and signed, the special education team communicates the individual needs of each special education student with the primary classroom teacher and the specialists who work with the child once or twice a week, for art, music, gym, and so on.

In grades 6 to 12, however, the special education staff has a more complicated task in that the children are no longer in the same classroom with one or two teachers, but moving from class to class all day long. Somehow the special ed team must make each course teacher understand a number of children's difficulties and the specific accommodations and modifications from each IEP. We have watched special education teams work hard to communicate all the information to the numerous teachers who interact with the child throughout the week.

The following letter, sent personally to each teacher—with a picture of her son—was one mother's way of reaching out and introducing her child in an informal way. She wanted to connect with the teachers, give them some background, and ask for their help in making the school environment more comfortable for her son. She also wanted to facilitate the dialogue between the course teachers and the special education team.

The mother who composed this letter wanted us to pass this sample on to our readers. She would like parents to feel free to adjust the letter any way that would be appropriate to their son or daughter and his or her grade level.

*A Brief Introduction to Timothy Esterbrook*

Dear Mrs. Warner,

My son, Timothy, is very excited about starting school at the Southville Middle School next week. Although I know Mr. Dennis Rizzo and the special education team will be in close contact with you, I wanted to introduce myself and give you a brief background about Tim so that you may have a broader picture of who he is and the best way to help him learn and participate.

Tim was diagnosed with juvenile-onset bipolar disorder when he was six years old. He takes a combination of medications, including lithium, which help reduce the frequency and duration of "hyper" or "manic" moments. These medications also help him not to feel depressed. Basically, the best analogy I've used since Tim was young to help him understand his illness is to ask him to imagine that he is on the equator of the planet. I don't want him to go to the North Pole or to the South Pole. To the extent that he can moderate his moods and "stay somewhere near the equator," he will be fine.

Tim sees a wonderful psychopharmacologist every three or four weeks for medical management. As his teachers, however, your feedback and input are critical to Tim's success. Please contact me if you see anything troubling him or interfering with his ability to learn and communicate with his peers and teachers.

In addition to the burden of this biochemical brain disorder, Tim also struggles with several learning disabilities (they often travel hand-in-hand). Tim has problems with fine and gross motor skills, and he may need to type rather than write assignments. I am in the process of having him evaluated for assistive/adaptive techniques. In addition, Tim has just completed two days of extensive neuropsychological testing, and I will send you the results in a few weeks.

Tim has executive function deficits. As you get to know him, you will see that he struggles with organization and has difficulty planning, breaking things down, getting started, and estimating time. What comes natural to us is so very difficult for him. We are working on all of this at home, but your understanding and help will make him feel less anxious when he doesn't "get it."

Tim is also very sensitive to criticism. He wants so much to please and he gets frustrated when he does not succeed. He responds well if you assure him that you like him. There will be times that he will need to move around outside the classroom, as it's hard for him to sit still and concentrate for long periods of time. The special education team and I are determining appropriate places for him to walk off the energy (at times it will be the school psychologist's room), but if you need any chores done, Tim would be proud to help, and your giving him the responsibility would accomplish all this and more.

One last thing: Tim has difficulty estimating time and is sometimes unsure as to where he goes after your class, with which books and materials. If you could kindly let him know in a subtle way the answers to these unspoken questions, it will reduce his anxiety immeasurably.

Mrs. Warner, it would be my wish that you will find your work with Tim extremely satisfying, and that you will see the great difference a teacher can make in a child's life.

This is such a pivotal year for Tim, and I would welcome your suggestions and help and thoughts.

Please don't hesitate to call me at home at 973-555-5432 or on my cell at 908-555-4321; or to e-mail me at jestabrook@optonline.net.

I know we'll talk soon. Thanks you so much, Mrs. Warner.

Sincerely,
Jennifer Estabrook

## What If the IEP Is Unacceptable?

In the cold glare of morning, with no warmth shared around a table, parents may find themselves looking at an IEP that is not specific, that may be indifferent to some of their concerns and asked-for modifications, and that simply may not be right. It's so tempting to let it pass, hope for the best, and look like a "reasonable and nondemanding" parent.

Let that thought pass on by. The parent is the only one who can ensure that a child is more comfortable in school and thus gets a better education.

In most cases, the school will make the requested changes. Just calling the director of special education and announcing an intention to reject the IEP may result in the services requested. Sometimes, however, the school digs in its heels and thinks parents will go away. In such cases parents have three choices: They can call another meeting and go over their objections; they can go to mediation and hope to resolve the differences; or they can pursue their right to due process—they go to court. If parents decide to go to mediation or due process, they should hire an educational attorney to represent them.

It may be that the IEP is a beautifully written document, but a parent begins to notice that the promised services are not happening or that they happen in a very scattershot manner. This is a violation of a contract. The more documentation a parent has, the better the case for holding a due process hearing.

For instance, everything that is supposed to be happening according to the IEP and does not should be noted in a personal log and a letter should be sent to the director of special education about the omission. If a phone conversation was held between a parent and someone at school, a letter should be written that says: "This is to follow up in writing what we discussed on the telephone today. . . ."

A parent cannot assume the IEP is being followed (often the special ed department has the best of intentions, but the academic and other teachers outside that department are too busy to even look at the document and comply with its dictates). A personal log with all correspondence will graphically point out any lack of services or aids that will prove that the school is out of compliance with the IEP.

Before things escalate, parents should investigate calling their state's Protection and Advocacy group. This is a nationwide network that, among other things, devotes considerable resources to ensuring full access to inclusive educational programs. A phone call or letter from the Protection and Advocacy group requesting accommodations (or that accommodations be complied with) or the presence of one of their personnel at an IEP meeting almost always results in a parent getting what is needed for his or her child.

To find the P & A in your state, call the National Association of Protection and Advocacy Inc. at 202-408-9514; or look on the Web at www .protectionandadvocacy.com and click on "P & A's/CAPS."

## A Summary of Steps to Take When Things Go Wrong

Although the IEP is a legal document outlining the school's commitment of special education and related services and accommodations to a child, you may find that gaps in services are continuing to occur or that promised accommodations still are not happening. Or it may be that the child's classification, evaluation, program, or placement need adjusting, and the school system begins to dig in its heels.

Should that ever be the case, there are several steps parents can take. We'll outline them here so you get an idea of the sequence of legal actions available to you. Naturally, it would be best to resolve all the issues and sticking points at the IEP table, but sometimes parents will have to exercise other rights guaranteed under the law. For orientation purposes, this is the sequence of events that might be required in order to ensure your child an appropriate education.

1. *Go back to the IEP table.* You can reconvene an IEP at any time and voice your (carefully documented) complaints to the IEP team. Often this is enough to get things back on track or amend anything that needs amending.

2. *Request mediation.* If matters are not resolved, parents have a right to go to mediation. This is an informal and confidential procedure that brings the parents and the school personnel together with a trained impartial party—the mediator—in order to reach a solution to the problem. The mediator's role is to facilitate communication, keep some order in the room, and, it is hoped, persuade the two parties to come to a mutually satisfying agreement about the child's educational program. If a written agreement is developed in mediation, it is enforceable in any state court of competent jurisdiction or in any district court of the United States.

   Before entering mediation, parents should have the assistance of an experienced advocate and/or an educational lawyer.

3. *File for a due process hearing.* If you decide to file for due process, you should send in a request to the authority stated in your parents' rights manual. This request explains the background of the dispute and requests a "due process hearing under IDEA."

IDEA 2004 has changed some of the sequences moving forward from here, hoping to reopen lines of communication and to avoid a costly and typically ugly situation from developing.

*The Due Process Time Line*
A hearing is supposed to commence thirty days after the filing for a due process hearing (provided there are no objections). This thirty-day timeline can be interrupted by returning to mediation or by something called a "resolution meeting."

Within fifteen days of receiving notification that the parents have filed a due process complaint, the school must convene a meeting with them and the relevant members of the IEP team and a representative of the school who has decision-making authority. The purpose of this meeting is for the parents to voice their due process complaint so that the school has another opportunity to resolve the dispute. The school system cannot bring an attorney to the meeting unless the parents are accompanied by their attorney.

If a resolution is reached, the parents and school district execute a legally binding agreement that is enforceable in any state court of competent jurisdiction or in a district court of the United States. (Either party may void the agreement within three business days of execution of the agreement.)

If all concerns are not resolved in a written agreement, the due process hearing proceeds, but the clock is set back and the thirty days that the school district had to prepare for due process starts again at day one. A parent should have an educational attorney file the request and conduct the due process hearing hereafter.

Please note: Some situations need to be heard on an emergency and expedited basis. An educational lawyer will be familiar with the state regulations as to which matters qualify for an expedited hearing.

## EDUCATIONAL ATTORNEYS

The best way to find an educational attorney is to network with other parents who've worked with one and been pleased with the relationship and the outcome of his or her work on behalf of their child. Another way to get a recommendation is to talk to a trusted neuropsychologist. He or she may have testified in a case and be familiar with an outstanding attorney. The attorney must be very knowledgeable about bipolar disorder also or be willing to talk with the treating psychiatrist and find out how the illness is impacting the child's "availability for education."

Some lawyers require a retainer and, if the case drags on, the fees may become quite high. If the court finds for the parents, the attorney's fees are paid by the school system. (Parents who have paid the lawyer up front will be reimbursed.) If the school system prevails, however, the responsibility for the legal fees rests on the parents.

Sometimes the cost of representation is out of the reach of parents, but there are free legal services and law clinics throughout the country. The American Bar Association provides a listing of Legal Services and Pro Bono Programs in each state. Call the ABA at 312-988-5000, or sign on to its Web page at www.abanet.org to see a list for each state.

Another idea is to check the local phone book under "Community Services" and/or "Legal Services," or call a local agency that deals with children and family issues. Attorneys' fees are discussed next.

## Attorneys' Fees and the Due Process Hearing

Parents also need to know that—in many cases—they will have to pay the attorney and expert witness fees *up front* until the case is decided. In other words, they must advance the money and will be repaid if they win the case in court.

In some states there are caps on the fees charged, or there are educational attorneys who can do a certain amount of pro bono work and take fees only from the Board of Education if they win the case.

But parents need the best educational attorney they can find, and sometimes that means putting aside the money to pay for the case to proceed. Most educational attorneys do not work on contingency (check www.edlaw.net/service/attylist.html for a list of educational attorneys in your state).

Just what are those fees incurred by the parents throughout the due process hearing? We'll use the tristate area of New York City as an example on the high end, but your educational attorney will explain his or her fees so that you and your spouse can decide how far you want—and can afford—to take this.

The average due process hearing runs about ten days. Each day, before the hearing, you will be expected to show up with a check for $2,500 for your attorney's daily fee. One or two expert witnesses will be called, and their fees can range from $2,000 to $4,000 for a day of testimony (also paid by the parents up front). After both sides present their case, the hearing officer orders both the parents' and Board of Education's counsels to prepare and file briefs as well as reply briefs based on the testimony contained in the transcripts. This may take two and a half to three days of a lawyer's time. At $250 an hour, this may cost the parents over $5,000. Thus, a parent is looking at fees that run from $25,000 to $50,000. (Remember, this is the high end, but you have to know the realities of your situation.)

A new law states that a judge must order reimbursement if the parents win the case, and only then will most of the costs be returned to the parents. It's a lot to consider (especially if one or both parents are professionals who charge hourly fees themselves and must factor in the unrecoverable loss of income for all the time spent preparing for the hearing and being present at the multiple days of the hearing).

IDEA 2004 has inserted a new clause that states that if a complaint or course of action is instigated by a parent or the parent's attorney and is deemed "frivolous, unreasonable, or without foundation," the court can declare that the school district's attorney's fees are to be paid by the parents or their attorney. In addition, if the case brought by the parents is "presented for any improper purposes such as to harass, to cause unnecessary delay, or to needlessly increase the cost of litigation," the school district's legal fees will also be charged to the parents or the parents' attorney.

These clauses of IDEA 2004 have worried some children's educational advocates, who think they may deter parents from exercising their rights and seeking due process. However, few attorneys will argue a case that has no merits and will allow a client to get so out of control. The prohibitive costs and the emotional strain of going through due process will cause parents to think carefully before filing a complaint.

However, if your child needs several years of expensive schooling, and the merits of the case are good, you have to measure advancing $25,000 or $50,000 against the $175,000 or more such schooling would cost.

The other thing parents should understand is that the school system risks the possibility of losing and having to pay not only your attorney but also the attorney representing them, their expert witnesses, and the school placement you've requested. Your winning the case could also set a precedent for other parents in the state, so make no mistake about it, the case the Board of Education presents will be hard fought. In other words, the needs of the child will pale next to the money the school district stands to lose. Therefore, expect that it will be inferred that you and your parenting abilities are a significant source of your child's issues. Your "shortcomings" and virtually every excuse other than the school district's ability to appropriately address the educational needs of the child will be used as an explanation for the child's difficulties in school.

One mother we know was widowed in her thirties and had to work to support her daughter, who had a severe case of dyslexia. After exhausting all the opportunities for remediation in her school district, the mother brought a due process hearing to obtain a placement for her daughter in a special school for dyslexic children. During the hearing, her status as a single parent and her travel for work were brought up as a source of her daughter's learning problems.

If a parent does decide to push ahead, he or she should write a letter to the school district's special education director explaining the background of the dispute and requesting a "due process hearing under IDEA." This letter should be sent by certified mail.

A hearing must be scheduled within thirty days of receipt of this letter, and an "impartial hearing officer" will preside over it. If either the parent or the school feels the officer is not impartial, IDEA allows for an objection, and another person will be decided on or appointed by the state education department.

However, in November 2005 the U.S. Supreme Court ruled that parents filing a due process complaint must prove that the school district's special-education plans for their children are inadequate. In other words, the parents, not the school district, bear the burden of proof.

The justices who voted in the majority felt that the burden of proof in all suits is borne by the party who brings the claim to court, and that it should be no different in these educational cases. Advocates for children across the country greeted the news with concern; they fear that this ruling will intimidate parents who certainly don't have the resources that school districts have.

The truth is, some states shift the burden of proof to the school district and others shift it to the parents, and many of the states tend to follow their precedents. Connecticut law states that the burden of proof is on the school district. Connecticut's attorney general, Richard Blumenthal, was quoted in the *New York Times* as saying: "We believe that our regulation embodies a valid state policy that articulates our belief that school boards are in a better position to muster the facts and expertise in any contest with ordinary parents."

Parents will need to be more educated than ever. As Donna Gilcher, Ph.D., founder of the STARFISH Advocacy Association, writes:

> For the parents who are well prepared, have excellent documentation, completely understand their child's disability, what the impact of the disability is on the child's learning, as well as the learning style of the child and what learning supports and techniques the child needs to have in place to be successful in an educational placement, there is no change and they will continue to find success when the schools fail to serve or are under-serving the child.

The parents and their lawyer will present "evidence," such as independent testing and evaluations, the child's school records, and testimony from advocates, teachers, and the child's psychiatrist and other therapists.

The entire proceeding will be extremely clinical and businesslike; there will be nothing warm and fuzzy about it. Therefore, it can be a very trying situation for parents. But this is the nature of such a hearing.

## Disciplinary Issues

IDEA 2004 made some major changes in how a school district deals with violations of its code of conduct. Previously, if Jeremy had no classification or disability and Nicky did, Jeremy could be suspended from school for three days, but Nicky would have had a modification in his IEP exempting him from adherence to the code of conduct due to the behavior being a manifestation of his highly documented disability.

To put it in more practical terms: If both Jeremy and Nicky wore an inappropriate T-shirt to school and were told to change and did not obey the order, Jeremy would be suspended for three days, but Nicky would be granted some leeway due to his documented bipolar disorder and his oppositional behavior.

This is no longer the case, and both boys would be suspended from school.

However, if a Behavior Intervention Plan (discussed on page 312) has not been written into the IEP, it must be included as quickly as the assessment can be made. If such a plan already exists, the IEP team must examine it and amend it so that behaviors that result in suspension are dealt with in a timely manner.

### *Extremely Serious Discipline Issues*
No matter what a student's disability, and whether the behavior is a manifestation of that disability or not, a school district can now remove a student to another placement for forty-five days if:

1. The student carries a weapon onto school premises or to a school event.
2. The student knowingly possesses, uses, sells, or solicits illegal drugs, controlled substances, or alcohol on school premises or at school events.
3. The student inflicts serious bodily injury on another person in school or at a school event.

Before IDEA 2004, a student committing such serious infractions would have been hauled off to jail, and the law enforcement officers would not have had access to any records that might present mitigating circumstances surrounding the behavior. IDEA 2004 now says that, if the parents give permission to the school to transmit the records, the school may do so. (The parents, under the Family Educational Rights and Privacy Act—FERPA—must sign a release of the records for the law enforcement officers to read.)

The IEP team will decide an alternative placement for the student for not more than forty-five days. If the parents disagree with the placement, they should have their lawyer appeal to a hearing officer at the State Department of Education. This hearing officer can do one of two things:

- If there was a violation of the child's procedural rights, the hearing officer can return the child to school.
- If the hearing officer determines that the infraction was a manifestation of the child's disability, an expedited due process hearing may take place.

It is easy to see why parents should disclose the child's medical illness to the school (and on a yearly basis), but many parents who are lucky enough to have a child who functions well at school and in the sports program are loathe to do so.

Even if the parents choose *not* to disclose the illness, advocate Anne Marie Smith advises them to note the disability on the yearly medical record that is kept on file by the school nurse. Thanks to the Health Insurance Portability and Accountability Act (HIPAA), all medical records are confidential, but if a hearing were to take place, parents can give the nurse permission to release this heretofore confidential notation.

## TRANSITION BEYOND HIGH SCHOOL

Students classified with a disability will need careful preparation for life beyond high school. Congress, unequivocal about this need, placed great emphasis on the importance and necessity of "transition services" in the new IDEA 2004 statutes.

This means that no later than the age of sixteen, the IEP team shepherding the student through high school must conduct an assessment about the adolescent's life in the years beyond and develop a plan to help the student meet his or her goals—whether they are to attend college, learn a trade, or land a job. Some students will need assistance with life skills and finding their place in the community.

In other words, a results-oriented and coordinated plan and set of activities must be designed for the student based on his or her hopes and aspirations, and measurable goals for postsecondary transition services must be written into the IEP.

What does this mean? If a student's goal is to go to a university, then the school district has the responsibility to offer and provide opportunities to that student that will make that goal possible—for instance, ensuring that the student takes the required courses in order to be a qualified applicant. (Note: The school can only offer and provide, not ensure success.)

Then, in the second semester of the junior year and the first semester of the senior year, school and guidance counselors will help the student look at appropriate colleges and programs in the lead up to the college application deadlines. Once the college application process begins, the guidance counselor helps organize the essays and myriad requirements of the applications. (This is confusing even for an organized adult.)

If a student is not ready to go to college or decides that the work world seems a better fit, he or she should be given career-interest inventories, or the school should teach the student how to job search and interview well. (Sometimes the school will have to contract with an outside career vocational agency. The responsibility rests with the school district, however.)

## The Freshman at College or the New Member of the Workforce

Once a student protected under IDEA leaves high school and begins college or enters the work world, he or she is no longer classified under IDEA. Instead, any protections are supplied by the Americans with Disabilities Act.

However, IDEA 2004 states that students who were eligible under IDEA must leave high school with a summary of academic achievement and functional performance, which will include recommendations on how to assist them in meeting their postsecondary goals. This Summary of Performance (SOP) is to be developed within the IEP eighteen months before graduation—with the student's input—and is designed to provide useful information to colleges and agencies to which the exiting student goes next. The SOP is to be developed in lieu of an exit IEP.

The Association for Higher Education and Disabilities (AHEAD) has published a comprehensive Summary of Performance template that is extremely helpful for parents, educators, advocates, and lawyers. It is available at www.ahead.org/resources/ideaintro.html.

## WHEN IS IT TIME TO SEEK OUT A THERAPEUTIC DAY SCHOOL?

The time may come, even with a comprehensive IEP in place with full implementation, when it becomes clear that the public school situation is not the appropriate place for a child with bipolar disorder, and he or she might be far better off in a small, therapeutic program. This is a separate school (public or private), usually with a small number of children with a small class size (six to eight children), in a classroom with a trained special education teacher and a trained aide. The children receive academic subjects along with group therapy, individual therapy, and sometimes family therapy, and art and music therapy.

Now the job of the parents is to prove to the school system that an "appropriate" education for their child cannot take place in the larger public school environment: Rather, the appropriate program for the child is one designed to deal with children who have these types of learning impediments and a waxing and waning set of symptoms.

Most public schools start a child in a regular classroom, then add services, then possibly place the child in a self-contained classroom within the public school setting. If the child has been hospitalized or has made a suicide attempt, there will be documentation of a severe problem that probably can't be handled within the public school setting, but parents typically have to fight to secure placement in a therapeutic day school. Start pursuing a placement while the child is in the hospital, or step down to a day hospital (the child spends part of the day at a hospital program) temporarily until a placement can be found.

A meeting is held and everything is laid out on the table. The child will not qualify for a special school unless the IEP is written in such a way that it cannot be implemented in the regular classroom, since the law requires that a child must be educated in the "least restrictive environment" that meets his or her educational needs. The IEP must specify that the child is to have a small, structured, self-contained classroom taught by a special education teacher. In addition, mental health staff should be on hand to perform one-on-one services and monitoring.

Parents may want to consult an educational consultant for guidance on which schools are state-approved or most appropriate for their child. (Some school districts are not totally forthcoming about all the possibilities.) Networking with other parents can clue a parent in to good schools that have been paid for with district funds in the past. The State Education Department Special Education Division can also give a list to parents.

To locate reputable consultants in your area, go to the website of the Independent Educational Consultant Association (www.iecaonline.com) to obtain names and phone numbers. Make sure the consultant is familiar with special education schools.

Parents should visit each school, but they should understand that, before they can visit, a "formal referral" package consisting of all the child's records must be sent from the referring district. This process can take two weeks or longer if the public school performs this service. Educational attorney Elizabeth Jester told us that she gathers the entire packet (the medical records, the IEPs, hospital records, if any, the psychiatrist's recommendations, the school records, etc.) and sends them to potential schools immediately so that parents can begin looking at the programs.

Parents should note their impressions on paper to help remember what each school has to offer. These will be useful to support—or refute—a placement in that particular school. The following list can be typed up as a form, photocopied, and kept in a binder so that information on all the schools is in one place.

Name of school
Phone number, address, directions to school
Principal, headmaster, or director's name
Cost of annual program
Does program run nine months, ten months, twelve months?

## 1. Curriculum and Level of Challenge
Describe the type of students (and their families) who attend this school.
What are their educational labels—OHI (Other Health Impaired)? ED (Emotionally Disturbed)? What are their major difficulties?

What is the number of students in the school? What is the gender
   ratio?
What is the average IQ of students in this program?
Is there a minimum IQ cutoff for admission?
Are there enrichment programs for gifted students?
Is there access to computers?
What is the curriculum?
Are classrooms graded or ungraded?
Are classrooms structured by subject, grade, or ability?
How many students in each class? Ratio of teachers to students? Stu-
   dents' age range?
Is the academic program adjustable according to the student's vari-
   ation in energy level, mood, and motivation?
Does the child have free time during the day? How is it structured?

## 2. Teachers and Staff

How many teachers?
Certified to teach individual subjects?
Certified in special education?
Are there psychiatric nurses or aides?

## 3. Treatment, Discipline, and Social Development

### DISABILITIES/SPECIAL SERVICES

What proportion of the students are on medication?
How are medications administered? Is there a doctor or nurse on
   staff?
Is there a hospital affiliation?
What is the training and background of the therapeutic staff?
Psychiatrist on staff? Psychologist on staff?
Other mental health professionals?
Are there any rules about not permitting outside prescribing psychi-
   atrists for students who are enrolled in school? Will their psychi-
   atrists willingly consult with child's present doctor?
Is there therapy or counseling? How often and who provides it?
Are there groups? Social skills groups?
Is the family invited to school and involved in a family therapy? Is
   it mandatory? If yes, it should be noted in the IEP. Once on the

IEP, the parents are in a strong position to have the costs they incur in attending the therapy (transportation, lodging, etc.) paid for by the school system.

What is the psychological orientation of the school?

Strictly behavioral?

Psychodynamic?

Cognitive therapy?

Combination or other?

### DISCIPLINARY PROBLEMS, POLICIES, AND PROCEDURES

Do they call parents?

If school uses a point system, is it based on taking away points for bad behavior, or earning points and privileges for good behavior?

If the school uses a level system, what are the new privileges and responsibilities that come with each level?

### OVERALL PHILOSOPHY

Describe the philosophy of the school and what kind of success rate it's had with students. What colleges do their students go on to attend?

## Difficulties in Finding the Right Fit

Unfortunately, many geographical areas have few good placement options. If a school's reputation is good, there is a waiting list to fill limited seats. Some schools are for lower-functioning children (children with mild to severe retardation or other neurological problems), and some schools are mainly for children with behavioral disorders (BD). Parents of children with bipolar disorder need to stress how "vulnerable" their child is, and how impulsive, and that it would be potentially harmful to put the child in a school with mostly behavioral disordered children, who may teach them delinquent behaviors.

A parent should not come back and say to the school system: "This is not the best school for my child" because the law states that an "appropriate" education is required, not the "best" education. ("Appropriate" is usually interpreted as "minimally appropriate.") Be prepared to suggest alternatives and support the choices with expert recommendations from the psychiatrist and educational consultant or attorney.

## Homebound Instruction

Homebound instruction is considered a "general education" placement, but it is considered the most restrictive placement because it removes the student from the mainstream and peers. However, it is frequently used for a student who is too symptomatic or too emotionally fragile to attend school in the school building. It is considered a temporary placement until the student is able to return to school or until a more appropriate placement can be procured.

Parents need to know that a doctor's "order" must accompany the request for home instruction. An IEP meeting will determine how often the tutors for each subject will come to the house to provide instruction and lessons for the student. Some school districts require a doctor's therapy or treatment plan to accompany any application for homebound instruction.

## Home Schooling

If an appropriate learning situation is not available in your geographic region, and if the stresses of school—any kind of school—are making it difficult for the child to function or to recover from an episode or hospitalization, some parents may want to consider the option of home schooling.

Home schooling was viewed, not too long ago, as very counterculture, or something that people did solely because of religious beliefs. As outcomes of home schooling were measured, however, and the home-schooled children often tested two years ahead of their in-schooled peers, home schooling has become more generally accepted. All fifty states allow for it as long as the parent completes the necessary paperwork with the state's Department of Education.

Thanks to advances in technology, home schooling can be done richly and effectively on computers with CD-ROM curricula or even over the Internet. This mode of learning may be particularly beneficial for a bipolar child because it focuses learning and helps students with attentional problems. One such curriculum, OdysseyWare from Pathway Publishers, is an advanced multimedia-based learning environment that incorporates video clips, sound files, animations, computer games, drills, and tests. With earphones, a parent can home-school several children. Visit Pathway on the web at www.pathwaypublishers.com.

The student works at his or her own pace. If a hospitalization should interrupt learning, the student doesn't miss the work but just picks up where he or she left off.

Switched-On Schoolhouse pioneered this curriculum for grades 3 to 12, with Christian content woven sporadically throughout the text. Calvert Academy offers a correspondence course that one mother felt was excellent and added another authority to the experience of home-schooling. (She wasn't testing her own children constantly.) The Calvert Academy has been supplying home-schoolers with curricula for a hundred years, and it is worth investigating. Visit www.calvertacademy.org.

Another program parents should investigate is the Laurel Springs School, which offers distance learning and a learning-style model teaching method. After a child's learning-style profile is determined, a customized program that plays to the student's strengths and interests is created by a learning-success coach. The curricula may be web- or text- or project-based, or a combination of all three. Frequent conversations between the student, parent, and teacher are integral to the program.

Laurel Springs School may be especially interesting to parents of children with co-morbid learning disabilities such as dyslexia, written expression difficulties, or dyscalculia, as the learning coach can design remediation programs in all areas. Visit www.laurelsprings.com.

## Access to Public School Programs for the Home-Schooled Child

What happens if a home-schooled child wishes to participate in extracurricular activities at the public school such as sports teams, the band, or clubs; or enroll during the school day in classes such as advanced calculus or a foreign language? After all, the parents are paying taxes to the town or city.

Fourteen states already require the home-schooled child such access, and last year, bills were introduced in approximately fourteen state legislatures to open up these activities and honors classes to home-schooled children. Unfortunately, many school districts in many states list a host of reasons why a child who leaves the public school cannot participate in public school programs. However, we expect that to change as more tax-paying parents who home-school begin to push for access.

To further explore the prospect of home-schooling, take a look at the following websites:

**Homeschool World (www.home-school.com):** Official website of *Practical Homeschooling Magazine.* Has lists of home-schooling organizations in your area, the *Home Life* catalog, and discussion forums.

**Kaleidoscopes Refugees Homeschooling Forum (www.network54.com/Forum/180575):** Interesting discussion forums for parents who are home-schooling or are thinking about it.

## WHEN IS RESIDENTIAL TREATMENT THE RIGHT WAY TO GO?

Sometimes a school that meets the needs of a student just doesn't exist in the area close to home, or the time comes when a child cannot be managed effectively at home. It becomes obvious that a change in environment with a twenty-four-hour peer group and a number of nonparental authority figures may be in the child's best interest. This residential placement is one of the most difficult decisions to make. Parents will suffer guilt, feelings of having failed the child, and grief that they're sending their "baby" away.

Educational attorney Elizabeth Jester always tells the parents she works with: "Nothing is forever. You're not putting your child away, you're enabling the child to get an education and learn skills he or she may not be able to learn inside the family. I've worked with numerous students who, after twelve to eighteen months in a residential school, really get their act together. Away from the close atmosphere of the home environment, they can blossom and mature. And the entire family gets to put itself back together again as well."

Parents should bear in mind that residential schools are not institutions or jails; they more resemble boarding schools, but they have a staff and a program equipped to deal with and especially designed for students having specific problems.

Residential schools cost a whopping amount of money. We've heard fees that range from $56,000 to $125,000 per year. School districts may pay a part or most of the fee for such a placement, if they fail to offer an appropriate educational placement that meets the child's needs. However, a due process hearing would no doubt take place first.

Parents should definitely seek the help of a professional consultant with the search process. (The child psychiatrist should also be involved.)

Websites that are particularly helpful are Family Light (www.familylight .com) and Lon Woodbury's Struggling Teens (www.strugglingteens.com).

## EDUCATION OF THE PARENTS

It will seem obvious—from all of the above—that parents will have to immerse themselves in basic educational law, public education, the educational needs of a child with bipolar disorder, and various programs that may be effective for their child. Just as finding the right doctor, getting the right diagnosis, and getting the child properly medicated are the first steps, the educational piece of the child's life is also critical.

As we close this chapter, we'd like to point out some resources that will make the entire journey through the educational maze a far easier one. For information on state regulations, IDEA, and IEPs, contact the state Department of Education, or log on to the following websites:

Wrights Law (www.wrightslaw.com)
LD OnLine (www.ldonline.org)

For information about therapeutic schools or summer character-building programs, contact:

Family Light
www.familylight.com

The National Association of Private Special Education Centers (NAPSEC)
www.napsec.org

The National Association of Therapeutic Schools and Programs
www.natsap.org

Peterson's Private Secondary Schools
www.petersons.com/private/select/pssns.html

Woodbury Reports Online
www.woodbury.com

# The Neuropsychological Testing of a Bipolar Child

On the front lines of a war, medical personnel learn to triage and deal with the most dire cases first. Parents of a bipolar child also triage naturally and spend all of their energy trying to cope with the child's out-of-control behavior, the other siblings in the home, and the public at large. They run themselves ragged looking for a doctor who can give a name to the problem and who can begin treatment so that the rages cease, the mood is stabilized, and the child and the home life become more peaceful and predictable.

Until that time arrives, however, parents are going to start each day filled with anxiety as they attempt to get the child up and out to school, and try to divine the child's mood and whether he or she can sustain the school day without incident. The behaviors of everyday life, the simple things that other families take for granted, are such all-consuming tasks that rarely on the front burner is the question: I wonder what my child's academic strengths and weaknesses are and how I can get a comprehensive evaluation of them.

But evidence is emerging that learning disabilities, attentional problems, and deficits in the area known as executive functions are a significant associated feature of early-onset bipolar disorder. One hundred sixteen parents answered the question "Does your child have a learning disability?" in our original study for this book. Sixty of them (52 percent) indicated that their child had an identifiable learning disability. (Few of these children had had comprehensive neuropsychological evaluations that examine the area of executive functions that we will talk so much about in the pages that follow.)

Any deficits that impede the acquisition of knowledge and impact a child's performance in school compound the effects of a mood disorder and erode an already compromised sense of self-esteem. These learning difficulties tax, frustrate, and irritate the child, and it becomes difficult to know which behaviors are a result of irritability caused by shifting moods and which behaviors are a response and rally to the narcissistic injury caused by the child's feelings of inadequacy as he or she is steadily challenged by greater academic expectations with each advancing school year.

In other words, an underlying neuropsychological deficit or an unrecognized learning disability could independently produce low self-esteem, irritability, and angry outbursts relating not so much to the mood disorder but to the child's inability to perform academic tasks. In fact, these learning disabilities can continue to exert significant influence long after the mood has been stabilized. That is why we so strongly recommend a complete neuropsychological battery for every child diagnosed with bipolar disorder.

## WHAT EXACTLY ARE LEARNING DISABILITIES?

A learning disability is assumed to be present when a child with a normal or high IQ is two years or more behind his or her classmates. Another definition of learning disabilities can be gleaned in public law books. U.S. Public Law 94–142 of the Federal Register, Section 121A, Volume 5 of 1977, states that learning-disabled individuals are:

> Those who have a disorder in one or more of the basic psychological processes involved in understanding or in using language, spoken or written, which disorder may manifest itself in imperfect ability to listen, think, speak, read, write, spell, or do mathematical calculations.

These are broad and rather noninclusive definitions of learning disabilities that address mostly verbal disabilities and fail to take into account the nonlanguage domains and areas of executive functions. A specific learning disability is a breakdown in one particular task area, whereas executive function deficits cut across many domains and impact all arenas of life—both academic and nonacademic.

Therefore, children with bipolar disorder should be tested with a comprehensive battery of intelligence, academic, neuropsychological, and psychological tests. These tests identify areas of strengths and weaknesses. Not only do the tests do much to explain the problems to the parents and the teachers—and to the child—but their findings direct remediation efforts. Parents and the school system need this critical evaluation when developing an Individual Education Plan—the IEP, which we discussed in Chapter 9.

Treatment can then focus on a three-pronged approach: stabilizing the mood with medications; addressing the cognitive, organizational, and sensory problems through tutoring, remediation, or occupational therapy; and instituting psychotherapy to help the child realistically assess his or her talents and areas of vulnerability, and to help the child come to terms with the distressing and disturbing feelings that both the illness and a learning disability may engender.

A neuropsychological evaluation also gives parents and the professionals a baseline so that they can retest periodically and see if medication, remediation, and therapy are having the desired effects.

## Who Should Test and How Do You Find This Person?

Children should be tested by a child neuropsychologist. This is a professional who has specific training and supervised experience in the assessment and treatment of patients with brain disorders and disorders of the central nervous system. Typically, a neuropsychologist has a doctorate in psychology and two years of postdoctoral training within a neurological or neurosurgical setting (one year in a general setting; one in a children's unit). A neuropsychologist is licensed by the state.

The child's psychiatrist should be familiar with good neuropsychologists; the pediatrician can often be of help, or a pediatric neurologist will undoubtably know the best neuropsychologists in the area.

## How Much Does Testing Cost?

A comprehensive battery of tests can easily require eight hours of direct consultation, as well as additional hours for reviewing records, data analysis, and the preparation of a written report, and will cost in the range of

$2,400 to $3,000. Some insurance companies may reimburse a certain amount of testing fees, but many do not. It's a good idea to call your insurer and see if they do cover it, and whether a precertification is required.

## The Battery of Tests

We spoke with Dr. Steven Mattis, clinical professor of neurology at Weil-Cornell University Medical Center in New York City, who has been focusing much of his research attention on the neuropsychological profiles of children with bipolar disorder and is one of the nation's authorities in this area. We asked him to give us a list of a standard battery of tests that might be given to every child with bipolar disorder. While there are over a thousand instruments of assessment utilized, and each neuropsychologist will use those based on his or her training and clinical experience, Dr. Mattis listed the ones he frequently relies on as the screening battery. (Naturally, as problems are uncovered, other instruments will be recruited to examine the hypothesized deficit more closely.)

We list the complete battery as a total and then describe certain measures in detail. A full discussion of each test and each learning disability would require a book of its own, but we focus on several tests, as they seem to reveal something significant about the cognitive and motor difficulties often seen in children with bipolar disorder.

### TESTS OF INTELLIGENCE

"First you need a good test of general intellectual ability," says Dr. Mattis. "The Wechsler Intelligence Scales for Children (WISC-IV) is the most commonly used and it is the jumping-off point of neuropsychology."

The intelligence test *samples* many of the cognitive skills that are needed to learn in school; thus it is considered a predictor of academic capabilities.

### The WISC-IV

Until 2003, the WISC-III was the most widely used test of intelligence, but it has been replaced by a newer version—the WISC-IV. The WISC-III was made up of thirteen subtests: six had a higher verbal loading and were scored as the Verbal IQ; seven were less dependent on language and could be viewed as an indication of the child's nonverbal reasoning, spatial processing skills, attentiveness to details, and visual-motor integration. These seven subtests were scored as the Performance IQ. Thus, three scores were computed: the Verbal IQ, the Performance IQ, and the full-scale IQ.

In 2004, the WISC-IV replaced the WISC-III. The WISC-IV added several new subtests and eliminated a few others from the WISC-III. Now ten "core" and five supplemental subtests are grouped into four indices called "factor scores." These factors measure various dimensions of functioning. These factors are:

Verbal Comprehension Index (VCI)
Perceptual Reasoning Index (PRI)
Processing Speed Index (PSI)
Working Memory Index (WMI)

The WISC-IV deemphasizes crystallized knowledge (facts such as "What is the capital of Italy?") and increases the contribution of fluid reasoning, working memory, and processing speed. The new test and its scoring are influenced by current research and neurocognitive information-processing models.

## Why Is My Child's IQ Score Lower on the WISC-IV Than on the WISC-III?

Children and adolescents will test lower on the WISC-IV for a number of reasons. First, the norms for the newer test are somewhat harder due to something called the Flynn effect.

The Flynn effect is so called because, in the 1980s, a political scientist from New Zealand, James Flynn, observed that the results of intelligence tests in different countries showed that each generation scored higher on tests of intelligence than the generation before it. (For example, students in Belgium, Holland, and Israel scored over 20 points higher over a thirty-year period.)

This increase in intelligence may be explained partially by factors such as better nutrition, longer schooling, and more parental attention bestowed on fewer children born to a family. But without a doubt, a child today is exposed to technological and scientific advances that boost abstract reasoning and nonverbal abilities. Even young children can program a microwave or work a VCR, and mastering these appliances and then computers and video games tends to fine-tune abstract thinking and visual-motor abilities, as well as processing speed.

The constructors of the WISC-IV updated the test and established more rigorous norms. Children will typically score three to five IQ points lower on this test compared to their test scores on the WISC-III. In some cases, depending on the child's individual weaknesses, which may be tapped more effectively by the new test, the IQ score may be more than five points lower.

Moreover, gifted students may score lower on the WISC-IV as they tend to value accuracy over speed. (The WISC-IV emphasizes processing speed.) Also, the IQ subtests in which gifted children have traditionally done well, such as arithmetic and information, have been removed from the core subtests to supplemental subtests that usually do not enter into scoring unless a core subtest is spoiled or invalidated.

### Why Students with Bipolar Disorder May Score Lower on Tests of Intelligence Compared to Tests Administered in Their Younger Years

Beyond the more rigorous norms of the WISC-IV, it is not unusual for parents of bipolar children to see a drop in IQ on more recent testing. Parents want to know if brain damage is a possibility. Dr. Mattis said it is extremely rare for a child actually to lose brain cells, although a large decrement in scores must be taken seriously. There may be several reasons for this decrement in scores, and parents should not panic.

Scores may be lower simply because the child's ability to pay attention may differ with each testing period or the time of day in which he or she is tested, or there may be a difference in testers and their interpretation of the child's responses.

Then again, children dealing with a mood disorder, medication trials, attentional problems, and perhaps multiple learning disabilities may fail to keep pace with their age group and may begin to fall behind in their general fund of knowledge or their capacity to learn new information. They may test less well as their cohort goes on to attain information, unburdened by the above-mentioned factors.

However, Dr. Mattis shared an interesting insight into the bipolar children he has been testing. For every subtest, a child must fail several consecutive items before the subtest is terminated. The examiner then moves on to the next task.

In his entire career, Dr. Mattis has seen only one group of children intentionally give incorrect answers to move the tester along: the children who come to him diagnosed with bipolar disorder. Whether this is a form of control, oppositional behavior, inability to deal with failure so they control the failure, or something we can't yet identify is a question that remains to be answered. It's just a fascinating observation that bears further scrutiny. But this attitude and behavior would also contribute to what is seen as a decrement in the testing scores.

### An Explanation of the WISC-IV Subtests and Scoring

Most parents receive the WISC-IV scores and don't understand what domains of neurocognitive functioning they tap and how the scoring is calculated. In this section, we want to explain what each subtest is out to measure.

This diagram of the four composite scores that comprise the Full Scale IQ and the number of subtests that are administered for each of the indices may help organize the information to be presented.

### Diagram of Organization of Four Indices

1. Verbal Comprehension Index (VCI)
2. Perceptual Reasoning Index (PRI)
3. Working Memory Index (WMI)
4. Processing Speed Index (PSI)

Source: Radford University Department of Psychology

### The Subtests and What They Measure

*Note:* An asterisk indicates the test is a supplemental and is generally not included in the index total score. A supplemental test is a backup test if a core subtest is spoiled (e.g., if a fire drill interrupts a test that is being timed, or the child has to go to the bathroom). A few of the supplemental tests may help demonstrate giftedness. Also, if the tester knows that a child has fine motor coordination difficulties, he or she can choose a supplementary subtest that does not have a significant fine motor component.

### Verbal Comprehension Index

This test is an index of a child's verbal knowledge as well as his or her ability to use verbal skills in new situations.

1. *Vocabulary.* Measures verbal expression and knowledge of spoken words

2. *Similarities.* Measures logical and abstract thinking ability necessary in recognizing essential relationships between objects and ideas.

3. *Comprehension.* Measures social judgment, practical knowledge, and common-sense reasoning.

*4. *Information.* Measures the child's fund of general knowledge and reflects on his or her alertness to the everyday world.

*5. *Word Reasoning.* Measures verbal reasoning ability in which a child is given successive cues and must identify an underlying concept.

### Perceptual Reasoning Index

This index reflects the child's ability to think about and organize visual material minus the use of words.

1. *Block Design.* Measures spatial visualization, perceptual organization, abstract conceptualization, and motor speed. (It is timed.) Red and white designs are shown on cards, and the child is asked to use blocks to reproduce the design.

2. *Picture Concepts.* Measures perceptual organization, nonverbal reasoning, and an ability to categorize objects. The child is asked to select objects that can be grouped together based on an underlying concept.

3. *Matrix Reasoning.* Measures nonverbal reasoning, as the child is showed an incomplete design or grid and is then asked to find the piece that completes the matrix.

*4. *Picture Completion.* Measures a child's ability to attend to visual details. The child is shown colorful pictures and is asked to identify missing details in each.

### Working Memory Index

This index explores a child's ability to hold information in short-term memory while manipulating it toward problem solving or sequencing it in a logical order.

1. *Digit Span.* Measures short-term auditory rote-sequential memory, concentration, as well as spontaneous organizational ability.

The child repeats numbers that the examiner reads, forward and backward.

2. *Letter-Number Sequencing.* Measures working memory. The child hears a string of random numbers and letters and then has to repeat the numbers in numerical order followed by the letters in alphabetical order.

*3. *Arithmetic.* Measures arithmetic reasoning and facility with numbers using mental math.

## Processing Speed Index

This index gauges the speed at which children can process visual information, such as designs or numbers, without making errors. The subtests have a motor component that follows a scanning task.

1. *Coding.* Measures a child's ability to learn something new and measures speed, accuracy of visual-motor coordination, attention, and short-term visual memory. The child is asked to copy symbols paired with other symbols.

2. *Symbol Search.* Measures visual alertness and motor speed under the pressure of a time limit.

*3. *Cancellation.* Measures processing speed as it asks a child to cross out certain objects on the page.

The Full Scale IQ is calculated by combining the scores of the core subtests.

The IQ test results of a twelve-and-half-year-old girl with bipolar disorder looked like this:

## VERBAL COMPREHENSION INDEX SUBTESTS

| SUBTEST | SCALED SCORE | PERCENTILE | RANGE |
|---|---|---|---|
| Similarities | 12 | 75 | High Average |
| Vocabulary | 15 | 95 | Superior |
| Information | 15 | 95 | Superior |

## PERCEPTUAL REASONING INDEX SUBTESTS

| SUBTEST | SCALED SCORE | PERCENTILE | RANGE |
| --- | --- | --- | --- |
| Block Design | 10 | 50 | Average |
| Matrix Reasoning | 11 | 63 | Average |
| Picture Completion | 8 | 25 | Average |

## WORKING MEMORY INDEX SUBTESTS

| SUBTEST | SCALED SCORE | PERCENTILE | RANGE |
| --- | --- | --- | --- |
| Digit Span | 9 | 37 | Average |
| Letter-Number Seq. | 11 | 63 | Average |

## PROCESSING SPEED INDEX SUBTESTS

| SUBTEST | SCALED SCORE | PERCENTILE | RANGE |
| --- | --- | --- | --- |
| Coding | 3 | 1 | Extremely Low |
| Symbol Search | 6 | 9 | Low Average |

## COMPOSITE SCORES SUMMARY

| SCALE | COMPOSITE SCORE | PERCENTILE | RANGE |
| --- | --- | --- | --- |
| Verbal Comprehension (VCI) | 124 | 95 | Superior |
| Perceptual Reasoning (PRI) | 98 | 45 | Average |
| Working Memory (WMI) | 99 | 47 | Average |

## COMPOSITE SCORES SUMMARY

| SCALE | COMPOSITE SCORE | PERCENTILE | RANGE |
|-------|-----------------|------------|-------|
| Processing Speed (PSI) | 70 | 2 | Borderline |
| Full Scale IQ (FSIQ) | 100 | 50 | Average |

The WISC-IV indicates that this girl's general intellectual abilities were highly variable. She demonstrated a specific strength in verbal reasoning (Superior range), a specific weakness in processing speed (Borderline range), and adequate performance on tasks involving perceptual reasoning and working memory (Average range). Most striking was her variability on tasks involving aspects of processing speed and the extraordinary superiority of her verbal-reasoning skills.

In other words, there should be some consistency or similarity. If, as is so often seen with children with bipolar disorder, ADHD, and other disorders, there is significant intertest variability, the tester has to begin asking why and continue testing various domains.

## What Does the IQ Really Mean?

Intelligence test scores are plotted against a normal bell curve. The WISC-IV has a mean IQ score of 100 and a standard deviation of 15, so, statistically, 68 percent of people will obtain scores that fall between 85 and 115.

Below are the scores and general population statistics:

| 130+ | Very Superior | About 2 percent of the population |
| 120–129 | Superior | About 7 percent of the population |
| 110–119 | High Average | About 16 percent of the population |
| 90–109 | Average | About 50 percent of the population |
| 80–89 | Low Average | About 16 percent of the population |
| 70–79 | Borderline | About 7 percent of the population |
| Below 69 | Extremely Low | About 2 percent of the population |

Other tests of general intellectual ability may be administered, depending on the age of the child and the tester's preference: the Stanford-Binet, Raven Progressive Matrices, and so on. Children older than sixteen are often given the Wechsler Adult Intelligence Scale (WAIS-IV). Children between the ages of four and a half and six are often given the Wechsler Preschool and Primary Scale of Intelligence (WPPSI-R).

## A SUGGESTED BATTERY OF TESTS

After the testing of intellectual ability, Dr. Mattis recommends a test of sustained attention. Sustained attention is different from the ability to mobilize attentional processes for brief episodic periods. The Connors Continuous Performance Test and the Tests of Variable Attention (the TOVA) examine attention over a much longer period—fourteen to twenty-two and a half minutes—and one or the other is frequently administered.

Both of these measures of sustained attention are computerized tests that are able to measure discrete aspects of attentional functioning.

Below are other tests that should be included in the battery:

### Tests of Academic Achievement
The Woodcock-Johnson Psychoeducational Battery—Revised is a norm-referenced test for ages three to eighty. This battery provides extensive testing of reading, decoding, comprehension, and mathematical calculation and the ability to understand math concepts and apply them. It yields samples of dictation and writing. It measures the child's understanding of content in science, social studies, and the humanities.

The Wide Range Achievement Test-3 (WRAT-3) is a norm-referenced test for use with children five and up. It tests decoding, spelling, and arithmetic.

Two other tests that may be utilized are the Gates-MacGinnite Reading Test and the Gray Oral.

### Tests of Language
An evaluation of expressive and receptive language function should also be conducted. Dr. Mattis often includes the Spreen-Benton Token Test as a measure of receptive language; and the Boston Naming and the Picture Vocabulary (Peabody) as tests of naming ability and sentence repetition ability. He assesses Buccal-Lingual Praxis when he has a child repeat different phonemes or multisyllabic words.

*Tests of Executive Function*
In the evaluation of bipolar children, Dr. Mattis places a heavy emphasis on tests of executive and motor function. Many of these tests are described in detail later in this chapter.

*Motor Tests of Sequenced Movement*
  Fine Motor Coordination
  Hallstead-Reitan Finger Tapping Test
  Luria Test of Praxis
  Purdue Pegboard or the Grooved Pegboard

*Projectives*
  Rorschach Inkblot Test
  Thematic Aperception Tests (TAT)
  Three Wishes

## What Are Executive Functions and Why Is Everyone Talking About Them?

As we delve into this huge and complicated subject, let's recall that the frontal lobes of the brain (including the prefrontal cortex, which is a layer of tissue that lies just behind the forehead) are the most forward part of the brain, in front of the motor areas.

The frontal lobes coordinate speech, reasoning, problem solving, strategizing, working memory, attention, self-control, motor sequencing, and other processes central to higher functioning. As Dr. Elkhanon Goldberg writes in his elegant book *The Executive Brain: Frontal Lobes and the Civilized Mind*:

> The frontal lobes perform the most advanced and complex functions in all the brain, the so-called executive functions. They are linked to intentionality, purposefulness, and complex decision making. . . . The frontal lobes are to the brain what a conductor is to an orchestra, a general to an army, the chief executive officer to a corporation. They coordinate and lead other neural structures. Frontal lobes are critical for every successful learning process, for motivation, and attention. . . . True to its "executive" functions, the prefrontal cortex is probably the best-connected part of the brain. The prefrontal cortex is directly interconnected with every distinct functional unit of

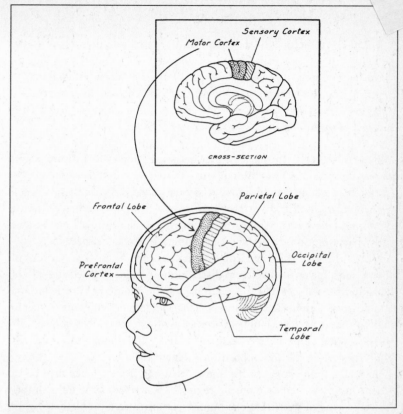

Figure 10.1 The Left Hemisphere, Showing the Cortical Lobes, Sensory Cortex, and Motor Cortex

the brain. It is connected with the posterior association cortex, the highest station of perceptual integration, and also with the premotor cortex, basal ganglia, and the cerebellum, all involved with various aspects of motor control and movements. . . . [It is connected to] the hippocampus and related structures, known to be critical for memory; and with the cingulate cortex, presumed to be critical for emotion and dealing with uncertainty. In addition, this command post connects with the amygdala . . . and the hypothalamus. Last but far from least, it is connected with the brain stem nuclei in charge of activation and arousal.

He concludes with this powerful statement:

Of all the structures in the brain, only the prefrontal cortex is embedded in such a richly networked pattern of neural pathways. This
unique connectivity makes the frontal lobes singularly suited for co-
ordinating and integrating the work of all the other brain structures—the conductor of the orchestra. . . . *This extreme connectivity
also puts the frontal lobes at particular risk for disease* (italics ours).

Research has shown that children with attention-deficit disorder with
hyperactivity, as well as children with Tourette's syndrome, have deficits
in the areas of the frontal lobes. It is now suspected that most children
with bipolar disorder have problems in the frontal systems. When the
prefrontal lobes don't work correctly, there is a major impact on the ability to pay attention, to devise plans, and to alter them if needed.

The child with this impairment is more prone to reckless and impulsive actions. He or she will seem distractible and disorganized and will often skip from subject to subject, fail to develop a fount of knowledge, and
often display a motoric restlessness. This problem or problems in the domain of executive functioning, governed by the frontal lobes, may be why
there is such comorbidity between ADHD and bipolar disorder, and
Tourette's syndrome and oppositional defiant disorder.

Actually, brain imaging has shown that the frontal lobes may be divided into seventeen or more subregions, each responsible for a slightly
different kind of work that the human performs, so a problem anywhere
in this area will impact the way a child approaches and performs any task.

Let's delve a little deeper. Whenever a human being approaches a problem or a project, he or she must recruit the following executive functions:

Analyze the problem.
Plan and implement the strategy.
Anticipate problems.
Organize the way the strategy will be accomplished (break it down
    into its components and effectively assign a time segment for each
    substrategy to be accomplished).
Monitor the progress and assess whether the plan is working.
Remain flexible and reformulate the plan of attack if the monitoring
    and assessment process shows it not to be working.

Reassess the new strategy that has been implemented.
Follow the adjusted plan through to the finish.

Executive processes have been described as a group of diverse integrative, organizational, and supervisory functions that primarily involve the control and regulation of attention, cognition, and behavior according to the demands of a certain situation and a person's needs, plans, and goals. As one can see, strategizing, organizing, marshaling intention into movement, flexibility (changing set when it is recognized that the original strategy isn't working), and constant monitoring are crucial to the completion of any task. The "executive" must relinquish a strategy that is not working and employ cognitive and motor skills to move onto something else.

Children with bipolar disorder often can't organize and break down the problem and assign time factors to each subunit; they are inflexible when they need to move off track and try something new. They will continue to attempt the same strategy when it is apparent to others that it is not working (they will "perserverate"), they might not be able to put a plan into action or sequence it (exhibiting problems with intentionality or motor sequencing difficulties), and they won't be able to attend and follow through.

## Working Memory

Also guided by the frontal lobes, and a significant part of the executive functioning of the prefrontal cortex, is working memory. We are constantly selecting bits of information stored in memory and bringing them to bear on any task we choose to perform and carry out. Short-term memory is remembering a phone number for a few seconds; working memory involves the ability to hold data in short-term memory while manipulating it toward problem solving or sequencing it in a logical order.

Studies conducted using functional magnetic resonance (fMRI) have examined working memory and found that if subjects were shown faces or consonants, they would process them in visual processing areas in a rear part of the brain initially, but as pauses were built into the test and the memory load grew heavier, activity increased in the front area of the brain. A key part of the prefrontal cortex and certain other brain areas stayed active, impressing researchers that these areas were involved in the active maintenance of information in working memory. Bipolar children also seem to have problems with working memory.

## An Explanation of Some of the Tests of Executive Function

Some of the major tests of executive function include:

The Wisconsin Card Sort
Tower of London
Tower of Hanoi
Trails A and B
Stroop Color and Word Test

The Wisconsin Card Sort is a measure of abstract conceptual skills, cognitive flexibility, and the ability to test hypotheses and utilize error feedback. It also measures the ability to relinquish a hypothesis when it is no longer applicable. This test can be done manually with cards or on a computer.

The child is given a set of stimulus cards that differ according to several different principles. Four of the cards are laid down as target cards, and the child must generate a plan to sort or match each card to one of the targets. The examiner will inform the child if his or her response was right or wrong. The child then continues sorting according to the "correct" criterion.

At some point, the criterion shifts and the child must adjust to the new principle and change strategies. This continues over a number of trials.

Patients with lesions of the lateral portion of the prefrontal lobes often perseverate on the first sorting criteria, tend to finish significantly fewer categories, and make more total errors than controls or individuals with other types of brain lesions. Bipolar children tend to get stuck in the use of the previously correct principle as well—they perseverate. They find it hard to "change set" and smoothly assume the new strategy and then change set again as they respond to the feedback that was deemed correct previously but is currently not working. The Wisconsin Card Sort often reveals these difficulties and the inflexibility of bipolar children.

The Tower of London requires children to move colored beads onto pegs with the least number of moves so that they achieve an arrangement (a model) that is in their view.

The Tower of Hanoi uses three pegs also. The goal is to move all the discs from the left to the right one, moving only one disc at a time and never allowing a larger ring to rest on a smaller one. The number of moves and the time it takes is scored by the tester.

Trails A and B are timed paper-and-pencil tests. They have a motor component and examine sequencing and set-changing abilities. Again, children with deficits in the frontal lobes—such as bipolar children and children with ADHD—may perform poorly on these tests.

Stroop Color and Word Test has various formats, but it is basically a sensitive measure of perceptual interference. Names of colors are written on a sheet in inks that don't match the verbal spelling "blue" or "green," and so on. The child is asked to override the visual signal and interpret the literal symbol (the word). In other words, one has to inhibit the response to name the color in order to read the word.

The Stroop tests the ease with which the child can shift his or her perceptual set and conform to changing demands. Children who are impulsive have trouble doing this, as do children who have executive function difficulties.

This test is given to older children whose reading skills are fluent and intact (a dyslexic child will happily ignore the words and focus on color only, thus negating the gauge of the test).

## EXECUTIVE MOTOR SKILLS

Almost all tasks—by definition—involve not only analysis, planning, monitoring, and adjustment of strategy, but the translation of images and ideas into sequenced motor acts. This activity most likely involves the prefrontal cortex and the motor cortex—the strip that begins the frontal lobes. *Praxis* is a Greek word meaning "doing, action, practice." It is the ability to interact successfully with the physical environment and to plan, organize, and carry out a sequence of unfamiliar actions. When a child persists in a motor activity or has an inflexibility or difficulty in initiating an activity, he or she is said to have a dyspraxia.

The Luria Test of Praxis asks a child to imitate a one-handed task requiring three sequenced hand positions while saying the verbal commands aloud. An inability to perform a sequenced motor act while stating the commands reflects a disassociation within the individual between his or her own thoughts and actions that is distinctly characteristic of a marked defect in executive processes. Dr. Mattis has observed that most bipolar children will have difficulty performing the Luria Test of Praxis smoothly and without perseveration.

## PROJECTIVE TESTS

Almost everyone is familiar with the Rorschach Inkblot Tests. Children look at the images and describe what they see. In some ways the inkblots are mirrors of the mind.

Other projective tests, such as the Thematic Aperception Test—the TAT—show children a scenario and ask them to make up a story around the picture. What the children produce is often an expression of their private world of thoughts, fears, and wishes.

Dr. Mattis also noted differences in the bipolar children's answers or thoughts in the projective tests. "I tend to hear more about blood and guts and people being ripped apart and death; or the children are so affected by unsettling imagery that they report that they see 'nothing,' " he said. (This gory imagery would fit with the night terrors these children suffer and sometimes remember; see our discussion in Chapter 6.)

## HELPING THE CHILD WITH SPECIFIC LEARNING DISABILITIES

Children with specific learning disabilities, such as dyslexia or written expression problems, need remediation provided by a teacher or tutor trained in special education techniques. The school may have someone on staff who is highly competent, but this may be the only learning specialist covering four hundred children. If the remediation is handled by the school, we strongly suggest that an independent tester monitor the progress each year. The school will do a triennial review if the child is classified and has an IEP, but three years is too long to wait to find out that the child is not making appropriate progress. Some parents will want to deal with private tutors after school. Again, we suggest independent testing on an annual basis (not an entire neuropsychological evaluation, just tests that probe the disability the child has).

## MORE ABOUT DISORDERS OF WRITTEN EXPRESSION

There are no statistics, but some psychiatrists and neuropsychologists who treat and test children with bipolar disorder estimate that at least half of these children have disorders of written expression. The numbers may even be higher. Children with this learning difficulty will resist writing very vehemently, and with increasing frustration and anger.

The problem for some children is language-based (and may coexist with dyslexia); for others it may be a motor outflow difficulty.

During the physical act of writing, we control certain muscle groups to keep the writing tool flowing in a direction—moving vertically, horizontally, and in a circular fashion (rotary movement). Fine-motor coordination is key as we stimulate certain muscle groups; inhibit others; and balance, flex, and contract movements. If letters are poorly formed, and there is a difficulty with the spatial organization of the letters and words on a page and heavy line pressure, the child is having difficulty in the graphomotor domain. This area of disability is called *dysgraphia*—a glitch between motor memory and its connection to the fingers.

Writers perform motor and cognitive sequences as they must summon from memory the shapes and sequence of letters to form words (spelling) and must integrate the mechanics of writing, such as periods, commas, and capitals.

In addition to performing the mechanics mentioned above, students have to develop ideas, organize and sequence thoughts, have the flexibility to relinquish those original ideas and reformulate them (draft, redraft, and polish), and marshal energy and attention to complete the assignment. They must also draw heavily on working memory. Children with problems in this domain will forget the topic of the essay as they fret over a comma or a semicolon.

If a piece of writing is to be rich and persuasive, layers of thought and creativity, organization and logical sequencing, elaboration and sustained attention must be brought to bear upon the assignment. Weaknesses in executive functioning and graphomotor glitches will make any demand to complete written work untenable. If students with a written expression difficulty do write, they "dumb down" the output and produce as little as possible on the written page.

Pity the parent who has to motivate the child to write essays or book reports. Parents find themselves increasingly anxious, frustrated, and angry at the child who puts off any writing assignment until the last minute. When attempting to motivate the child doesn't do the trick, negative feelings quickly arise as evenings and weekends go sour or escalate to very ugly scenes. This is exhausting and demoralizing for the child as well as the parent.

## What Tests Would Reveal These Areas of Weakness in Written Expression?

Many tests can be administered to determine which areas of the writing process are problematic for a child. Again, each educational psychologist or neuropsychologist will use those based on his or her training and clinical experience. However, most evaluators on a child study team in a school system will rely on the following battery of tests.

The Woodcock-Johnson Psychoeducational Battery, Revised, is a norm-referenced test for ages three to eighty. Among other skills, it yields samples of dictation and writing.

The Wechsler Individual Achievement Test (WIAT-II) is a measurement tool used to gauge achievement skills and to help diagnose learning disabilities for preschool children through adults.

The Test of Written Language (TOWL-3) is a written language assessment tool used with individuals ages seven and a half to seventeen. It measures expressive skills in written language, including use of established rules for punctuation, capitalization, and spelling; the use of serviceable syntactic and semantic structures; and the ability to write logical, coherent, and sequenced written products.

Tests that measure sustained attention are recommended, as well as the battery of tests mentioned earlier that assess the domains of executive functioning and executive motor skills. Chapter 9 gives a complete list of accommodations that should be written into the IEP of a child with written expression difficulties as well as the services that may be required for remediation.

## HELPING THE CHILD WITH EXECUTIVE FUNCTION DEFICITS

While methods of remediating dyslexia are well established, helping the child with deficits in the areas of executive functioning is not so prescribed. "This is the child who may need help in many areas of daily living," says New York City neuropsychologist Dr. Dana Luck. Children with executive function difficulties are highly dependent on adults to help them structure and organize their environment.

Dr. Luck told us that most often it is the parents who have to provide a highly structured home environment to help the child accomplish certain routines successfully. Each routine—each "package of behavior"—

must be broken down and rehearsed independently before a complete set of responsibilities can be fulfilled.

For instance, to complete the morning routine, certain grooming, dressing, and organizational tasks must be addressed. All clothing should be simply organized, all books, music, and sports equipment should be in one place and always in that place. If the child dallies in the bathroom with too many choices of toothpaste and mouthwash, there should be nothing there but the toothbrush and one tube of toothpaste. In other words, streamline all possible distractions.

The child should be given prompts: "In order to go out to the school bus I need . . . my book bag, my coat, my recorder . . ." The prompt before the child leaves school is: "What do I need to do tonight and what do I need in my book bag in order to do it?" At school, a teacher or aide should help the child follow a set of steps to accomplish the prompt. In effect, the parents and teachers become the frontal lobes of the child.

## How Does the Child with Executive Function Difficulties Fare at School?

Not well. These children might always seem disorganized. Homework, notes, workbooks, and planners might make it home some nights and not others; homework that is completed may never make it back to the teacher.

If this student has a major project assigned for three weeks hence, he or she may have trouble remembering to bring everything home in order to plan the project and may have difficulty getting organized in one place. Then he or she can find it difficult to settle on a topic.

These are the children who sometimes can't "see the forest for the trees." If they do choose a topic, they might not be able to break it down, outline the way it will be explored in the paper, and discuss the subunits in an organized, sequenced fashion. (For children with written expression difficulties or graphomotor problems, the task becomes all the more daunting.)

These children also have difficulty with timing and pacing. They underestimate how long each section will take to accomplish, they have trouble "getting going," and they tend to procrastinate and leave everything until the last minute. Parents and teachers may grow exasperated and view the children as lazy, "not trying hard enough," or stubborn and oppositional.

Actually, because of the problems with executive functioning (and any other learning disabilities they may have), they can't seem to find their way into what often seems a gigantic and undoable task. This has a serious impact on the children's feelings of self-worth. Their self-confidence and self-esteem plummets, and most academic tasks become so unpleasant and engender so much anxiety that they begin to refuse to even try or give up quickly if they can be coaxed to give it a try. Naturally, this anxiety impacts their level of attention, exacerbates any learning disabilities, and seriously impacts the children's mood (the very thing the doctors and parents are working so assiduously to keep stable and in the positive range).

When children find things so effortful, it takes a toll on them. They may become irritable, fatigued, hyperactive, and begin to avoid situations that require extended effort or feign disinterest in them. The children may simply "quit the playing field." As Dr. Luck says: "Even for a child who doesn't have a specific learning disability, problems in executive function can significantly impact his or her academic performance and progress and achievement, particularly as the task demands require greater independent functioning."

Dr. Luck also told us:

In lower grades, the academic work is often organized and separated for the child—for instance, a work sheet will be all addition or all subtraction. Later on, when academic work is more integrated, the child must be monitoring, asking "Which problem is this and what am I supposed to do?" When the child gets to higher level reading where paraphrasing is required and inferential and deductive thinking come into play, children with executive function difficulties are going to experience more problems. Here these children have difficulty sorting out details or they may get stuck in a detail, and since they often can't prioritize the level of importance of details, they begin underlining everything in a textbook or fail to get started doing anything. . . . Homework is almost always a hot spot. The child should have a place to work that has pencils and other supplies always available. Then the child must learn that it's normal to spend ten minutes setting everything up to begin the homework. It may help if the parent sets an external timer so that the child becomes aware of pacing and moving along. The tone of the time spent working should be kept "cool." Anger and frustration should be minimized both by the child and the parent.

Dr. Luck suggested some highly useful techniques to help these children. She said that because these children can't separate out main themes from supporting detail, they should be taught to utilize the cues in a textbook, such as pictures, captions, and headings.

It is perfectly acceptable to look at the questions at the end of the chapter first so that children are primed as to what is considered important and can read looking intently for that information and give less weight to some of the other information. They shouldn't underline until they've looked at those discussion questions and all the pictures, captions, and headings. These children need to think macro rather than micro.

If all the work can't be finished (and most nights it won't be), this should be added into the IEP (see Chapter 9). There should be constant communication with the school. The parent should understand how difficult this is for the child, and the child should be encouraged and rewarded.

Dr. Luck said that the children need to learn to advocate for themselves. They need to understand how to ask for help and to accept some responsibility. They should learn how to go to the resource room for help. If they do something with a partner, they shouldn't work with a best friend, but with someone who needs their strengths and has strengths they don't have. If a child recognizes that he or she is lively and dynamic and presents well, he or she should pick a partner who organizes and researches well. Choosing people who complement your strengths and compensate your weaknesses is smart choosing and is something children should continue to do throughout life in work and social situations.

"Always the children should compartmentalize their difficulties," concludes Dr. Luck. "Just because they have difficulty in one area doesn't mean they're not truly strong in another."

In fact, these children often have gifts and see things in novel ways that result in very creative thinking and performance. They are often referred to as out-of-the-box thinkers. Children with learning disabilities often are keen observers and notice things others don't. Children with high energy and a motoric restlessness may grow up and be able to work long hours with an intense focus. Many children with dyslexia have strong visual abilities, and many have an enhanced sense of vertical balance and may excel at sports such as riding, skiing, or diving. Parents and teachers need to see the unique talents these children have and build on them.

If parents can get their children evaluated well before they reach the higher grades in school, and help relieve the potentially snowballing pressures as a result of these sometimes hidden disabilities and deficits, then they won't be blindsided as adolescence enters the picture. They won't think that every problem has a root cause in hormonal cascades or the condition of adolescence itself. Nor will everything be laid at the door of the mood disorder. The parents will have explored and dealt with one of the problems certain to impact profoundly on the child's sense of mastery and self-esteem. It is hoped that the child then reaches this critical passageway in life with the academic playing field a bit more level—paved by understanding and remediation.

The tasks of adolescence—complicated by a mood disorder—are challenge enough for any teenager.

# Navigating the Shoals of Adolescence

Parents look forward to the teenage years with all the enthusiasm they reserve for an extended stay in Dracula's castle with the crucifixes confiscated from their suitcases. In fact (and just to continue the horror-story metaphor), most parents seem to equate an emerging adolescent with the Frankenstein monster—docile one day, then suddenly zapped with a bolt of electricity (the hormones) and rising quickly to pillage the countryside.

But for parents of bipolar children, such nightmarish forebodings are even worse. Hormonal surges can trigger cycling (or more severe cycling). These adolescents can be impulsive, hypersexual, and indulge in extremely risky behaviors. Grave dangers abound: unwanted pregnancy, sexually transmitted and life-threatening disease, recklessness behind the wheel of a car, and substance abuse. Their outrageous, provocative, and oppositional stunts can land them in the juvenile justice system, and their poor judgment can cause dire consequences out in the world.

Every parent we spoke to voiced terrible fears about such possibilities. All asked: "What will happen to our children in adolescence and the aftermath?" All assume that because the illness began so early and appears so pernicious, the course will go from bad to worse.

But according to investigators who have followed bipolar teenagers over a period of years, these forebodings do not necessarily become fact. To the contrary, there is reason for parents to feel hope.

Dr. Thomas McGlashan followed thirty-five adolescent-onset bipolar patients for fifteen years. He found that although the adolescent-onset patients displayed more delusions and hallucinations and were more explosive and disorganized than the adult-onset patients, the adolescent patients went on to have an equal or superior outcome to those with the adult-onset form of the disorder.

Dr. McGlashan's study, published in the *American Journal of Psychiatry* in 1988, examined the lives of a group of people in their mid-forties who became symptomatic in the teenage years and compared their outcomes to a group of people in their fifties who became symptomatic as adults. He failed to find significant differences in their marital status, parental status, living situations, length and number of hospitalizations, and amount and severity of symptoms. But where differences did exist—for example, in the frequency of social contacts and amount of work time in the previous year—the adolescent-onset patients were "consistently superior."

Dr. McGlashan himself was surprised by the findings and offered two hypotheses:

First, adolescent-onset mania may be a milder variant that, however, looks more severe because it emerges during a developmentally vulnerable period when defenses are in flux and coping strategies are poorly developed. With the passing of adolescence, however, the disorder becomes less penetrating in its virulence. Second, adolescent-onset mania may not be a milder variant but may emerge at a time when personality structure is flexible enough that the individual can develop ways of coping more effectively with the illness.

Dr. McGlashan speculated that adults who develop the illness may be more set and rigid, temperamentally less flexible and able to adapt to the vagaries of the illness.

More recently, Dr. Michael Strober, director of the Adolescent Mood Disorders Clinic at the University of California, Los Angeles, and a leading researcher who has followed bipolar teenagers from the age of thirteen into their late twenties and early thirties, had even more promising data to offer parents. During a phone interview, he said: "There is no basis for assuming automatically that just because the illness is more familial and presents earlier these young people are going to have a chronic relapsing course. In fact, our data suggest a less malignant course than what is reported in the adult literature."

We asked Dr. Strober what he has seen happen to his study group as the youngsters move through adolescence. He replied, "The course is quite variable and difficult to predict. Some kids emerge into a more sort of classically identifiable cycling affective illness. Others continue to have a persistence of extreme, irritable, explosive, and emotionally labile behavior. On the other hand, I have seen kids who have actually quieted down."

Dr. Strober recommends, as we do, that psychopharmacological treatment administered *with* psychotherapy is imperative to treat the illness. He talked of how mood states have influenced the development of personality and interpersonal relationships and also how the mood states affect intrapsychic development. Not only does a supportive therapeutic therapy address all these issues that are intertwined with the illness, but having a close, trusting relationship with a doctor can help a teenager make better choices for him- or herself.

We then asked Dr. Strober what factors seem to predict a better course of illness and about the results of the ten-year study that he and his group were about to publish. He said:

> In our studies, the kids who do best are the kids who have the classic manic-depressive cycles, the kids with pure mania bounded with well periods. The kids with pure manias have the lowest likelihood of relapse. Granted, you're less likely to see these well-defined patterns in kids. Mixed states by and large do not do as well, but that's not to say that a number of these kids don't do just fine. We've seen kids with mixed episodes who've done very well.
>
> In our experience, many teenagers go into very long and stable periods of remission. These kids can look horrible, be dysfunctional, need hospitalization, but then they can go into remission. Yes, it's a lifelong illness, but people can have periods of time where they don't cycle. You can't really predict.

So, with this hope about the teenager's future firmly in mind, let us discuss some of the truly dark moments that a parent and a bipolar adolescent are bound to experience during the teenage years. There will probably be disagreements over medication compliance, acting out at home, and situations where the teen's judgment is simply bad or nonexistent. Such issues as the choice of friends, behavior in school and in the community, sexual promiscuity, and alcohol and drug abuse may pit parents and children against each other.

The task of adolescents is to separate from their parents and step out into the world as people with ideas and goals that need to be accomplished. Adolescents are typically in a state of expectation, excitement, and vulnerability. They are searching for their place in the world and are extraordinarily concerned with the opposite sex and what their peer group thinks of them.

They become desperate to fit in. Because adolescents know that social acceptance depends on how good they look and how cool they are, no flaws can be tolerated.

It's a wonder how anyone survives adolescence unscathed (and maybe nobody does). But now take a teenager who has bipolar disorder. He or she may enter adolescence with a reputation in shambles, a deteriorated relationship with exhausted and wary family members, a scholastic record hobbled by bad grades and time lost from school, and few champions among the school's administration or faculty. A teenager who takes medication may enter adolescence with even more acne than his or her nonbipolar peers and almost always with more weight than is acceptable in the perfect, perfect world most teenagers long to belong to. (For an individual with a penchant for perfectionism, as is the case with many bipolar kids, adolescence throws up a mirror that reflects every painful flaw imaginable.)

If a typical teen has to deal with a life now infused with sexual feelings and longings, a bipolar teen may have to deal with a much more intense hypersexuality. If a typical teen has to deal with the task of separation, the bipolar teen has to deal with severe separation anxiety, which makes it extremely difficult to negotiate the primary developmental task posed by adolescence. If the nonbipolar adolescent can experiment with alcohol and marijuana, the bipolar adolescent is more prone to addiction, and he or she may see the course of the illness worsen as the moods fluctuate with the use of alcohol and drugs.

Bipolar teenagers arrive at young adulthood with so much baggage, with such low self-esteem, that they can feel very isolated and defective.

Meanwhile, this is all unfolding as parents are entering middle age and worrying about their own increasingly elderly and infirm parents. At the same time, the parents may be going through their own identity and marital crisis. How are their own careers going? How is their marriage? Is their retirement income going to be sufficient? In addition, their child's college or post–high school years are fast approaching, and the future has to be reckoned with. Where will their child go to college—especially if his or her grades are not good or the child has learning disabilities or a history of suspension and poor attendance? How will this young person who has always been so dependent move away from home and into the hustle and bustle of college life or vocational school? Many difficult decisions await this already stressed family.

In the pages that follow we discuss these issues and some ways of smoothing the transition into these years.

If the teenager had early-onset bipolar disorder or had early symptoms but the full force of the disorder is only beginning to manifest itself, then nothing good can happen until there is stability. Medication compliance is going to be one of the major negotiating tasks of the teenage years.

## MEDICATION COMPLIANCE

Teenagers are extraordinarily concerned with their body image. They are going through a period when everything is changing, and they are growing at a rate not experienced since the first year of life.

As a young person's hormonal levels shift, teenage acne sprouts on the face and body, and an adolescent can become obsessed with every pimple and blackhead. After a lot of hyperfocusing on the face and its deficiencies, this intense and very unforgiving gaze moves down to the body. Every curve is examined, breasts are found to be too small or too large; dieting becomes a major activity. Boys have their own concerns: Their chests are too concave, their voices are not low enough or crack embarrassingly.

Now imagine asking a teen to take a medication that causes acne and weight gain. Medication compliance is going to be a major problem.

The support and sympathy of a confiding relationship with a therapist is invaluable in trying to help teenagers cope with the upsets of an illness like this and the side effects that arise from its treatment.

Medications also can become a power struggle between the parents and the adolescent. The parents who've lived through instability and episodes can become desperate for the teenager to stay compliant with the medication regimen, and a clash of wills may ensue as the adults pressure, hover, question, and cajole.

Adolescence is such a vulnerable time: A young person is struggling to move out of the orbit of parental supervision and to achieve independence. The idea of taking any medicine, and especially a psychotropic drug, can activate highly charged psychological issues. The medicine becomes a reminder that something within is not working as it should. This deficit makes the teenager more vulnerable in relationship to his or her peers and has the potential for decreasing the teenager's sense of self-worth. There may be a strong motivation to deny the illness and stop taking the medications entirely.

Parents will have to learn to play a different part around the medication treatment once a child becomes an adolescent. Where once they were the sole dispensers, now their involvement can become a problem for the teenager and a source of conflict. Teens may find the taking of medications an ideal subject to fight about and exhibit their own sense of control over the illness and the parents' wishes.

If parents can recognize the changes taking place in the teen and back off a bit, and let him or her discuss all of this with the therapist, the young person probably will make the right decision. In most cases the terrible feelings the adolescent had before the medications worked are usually not worth reexperiencing for the sake of some weight loss. Many teenagers reach this conclusion if it doesn't become the issue to fight over.

Parents should encourage their teenager to fill the prescriptions at the pharmacy and to set up a schedule for remembering to take the medicines. Also, the teen should be encouraged to keep a diary of side effects and how well he or she thinks the medications are working, and discuss everything with the psychiatrist. These children need to learn to own their illnesses. A support group of teenagers with bipolar disorder would be ideal, and parents could talk to the guidance counselor at school or a psychiatrist in the area to help organize one.

The leader of a National Alliance on Mental Illness Child and Adolescent group told us that one of the most often asked questions by parents at the monthly meetings she chairs is how to get an adolescent to be compliant with the medications. Her answer? "The dangle of car keys. Teenagers will do anything for the privilege of the car. Sometimes that's your only ace in the hole." Parents who live in a city will have to find an equally regarded privilege.

## ALCOHOL AND DRUGS

Parents who believe that drugs and alcohol are not easily accessible to any teenager are burying their heads in the sand. Thirteen-year-olds from "nice" suburban families are smoking pot and getting drunk—and on a regular basis. A leftover hippie from the 1960s has a harder time finding drugs than a teenager in America today.

Bipolar teenagers have an inordinately high risk of becoming addicted. It was commonly thought that people with mood disorders who abuse substances were self-medicating—they were either prolonging the highs of hypomania with stimulants or calming the anxiety and the irritability of depression with alcohol.

But recently researchers have begun examining the pairing of substance abuse and bipolar disorder more closely. They are asking the following questions about this "comorbidity": Is the association actually due to attempts at self-medication? Is the tendency to crave drugs and alcohol something heritable that travels in the company of the gene or genes that predispose one to mania or depression? Or do abused substances induce cycling? Or, as we mentioned in Chapter 5, is alcoholism a different manifestation of bipolar disorder?

Whatever the answers, the comorbidity of substance abuse and mood disorders has been vastly underestimated. In a random sample of five hundred members of the National Depressive and Manic-Depressive Association, almost half of the members reported that they abused alcohol and drugs prior to the correct diagnosis and treatment of the mood disorder, compared to 13 percent among patients properly diagnosed and treated.

The Epidemiologic Catchment Area data compiled early in the 1990s pinpointed an even higher statistic. It revealed that 61 percent of bipolar patients had a history of substance abuse. Of that number, 15 percent used drugs alone, 20 percent used alcohol alone, and 26 percent used both substances.

Dr. Kathleen T. Brady, the clinical director of the Center for Drug and Alcohol Programs at the Medical University of South Carolina, and Dr. Susan C. Sonne found that patients with substance abuse disorder and bipolar disorder have a much earlier age of onset—some seven years earlier. Other studies have found that substance-abusing bipolar patients are more likely to have irritable and paranoid episodes of mania rather than the elated kind. They are also more likely to relapse and have 50 percent more hospitalizations.

All this means that it is vital for parents to talk with their children and warn them that they will more likely become addicted to alcohol or drugs and suffer a worse course of illness. For the bipolar teen, drugs and alcohol are not "recreational" and something "everyone experiments with." They are mood-altering substances that impact powerfully on a very easily disturbed central nervous system. In this case, it's important for the teenager to view him- or herself as different, likely to have a far more serious reaction to the drugs than a hangover, and to remove him- or herself from the scene. Too much is at stake here, and the teenager needs to know that the consequences are not worth the short-term activity.

## When All Your Efforts Fail

Despite all the family discussions, parents may come to learn that their son or daughter is abusing drugs or alcohol and spending time with a crowd of like-minded teenagers. It is natural to think that "all kids experiment, hopefully this is just a passing phase." But if it becomes apparent that the adolescent is spiraling downward and the teenager is becoming more unstable and his or her future is becoming closed off (or there is trouble with the law), parents will have to have a plan and be ready to enact it.

Some teenagers recognize they need help and know deep inside that they need to be separated from their peer group. If the family has economic means, a therapeutic boarding school that has a dual-diagnosis program may be what's truly needed. However, the child may not be allowed to come home for months or even a year, and the costs are prohibitive (ranging from $4,500 to $9,000 a month, and the adolescent typically attends such a school for a year or eighteen months).

Twelve-step programs that are in or nearby almost every community in this country may be helpful, but a person experienced with teenagers and recovery must be guiding the adolescent and family members. (Parents should understand that the twelve-step program was originally designed for adult men and that the needs of an adolescent are different.)

These programs seem to work best when the family attends Alanon meetings while the teenager attends his or her meeting. The family must work as a unit on recovery. People who have had experience with these programs advise attending a particular meeting at least three or four times before trying another group in the area.

When the best answer is to remove the adolescent from the negative peer environment, parents can investigate one of the so-called wilderness programs. These are typically eight-week programs that take place in states out west, such as Utah, Colorado, and Montana, although there are also programs in the Carolinas.

In a wilderness program, teenagers learn not just to "talk the talk" but also to "walk the walk." They are outside learning to love and respect the environment, themselves, and each other. This program involves the family initially, and one day is spent where the adolescent can only listen to the family members' point of view and say nothing; the next day the family has to listen to the teenager and say nothing. After three days the family leaves and the teen lives in a small group, learns to make fire, cook (think *Survivor*), takes night hikes, and learns to trust him- or herself and others. This program incorporates a drug rehab program with the wilderness program.

Getting the adolescent to such a program may be so difficult that a parent has to resort to an escort service. This is a situation where two people come to the house and escort the teenager to the airport, onto the plane, and then into the program. This is harrowing for parents, but, expertly handled, it often goes more smoothly than expected. Most kids, once they find themselves in a no-exit situation, make the best of it and eventually see that the parents were trying to save their lives.

A book called *Shouting at the Sky* by Gary Ferguson profiles the Aspen Achievement Academy and gives an accurate picture of the essence of these kinds of programs, why they work, and how the teens, the staff, and the parents feel during the experience.

An eight-week experience like this costs in the neighborhood of $20,000 and may be the beginning of the road back. "I have found the wilderness programs to be the most effective way to get teenagers to internalize the need for profound change," says Thomas J. Croke, educational consultant and president of Thomas Croke and Associates in Latrobe, Pennsylvania. "For recovery to last, however, it must become as much a part of the teenager's lifestyle as drug-related activity has been." In other words, the adolescent may still need a more structured environment than home can reasonably provide following that wilderness experience.

If a family can afford it, a therapeutic boarding school may offer the teenager the best chance to consolidate recovery and self-esteem. David L. Marcus recently published a book entitled *What It Takes to Pull Me Through: Why Teenagers Get into Trouble and How Four of Them Got Out*. The author follows the students, staff, and parents at the Academy at Swift River in western Massachusetts. The book is worthwhile reading for any parent considering a therapeutic boarding school. If it is decided that the teenager should stay closer to home, many communities have intensive outpatient facilities—typically associated with a psychiatric hospital— that offer special programming for adolescents (often they attend after school). If you look in the yellow pages of the phone book under "Drug Abuse and Addiction Information and Treatment," you will find programs offered in your community.

To investigate wilderness programs or therapeutic boarding schools, log on to www.familylight.com and check the listings. Educational consultants throughout the country can help match your teenager or young adult to special schools or programs that deal with bipolar disorder and substance abuse problems. To locate someone who serves your area, contact the Independent Educational Consultant Association at www.iecaonline.com or by calling 703-591-4860. Members have to have experience, credentials, and ethics, and must have visited over one hundred programs prior to membership so that they can truly match a teenager to a program.

## SEXUALITY

It is estimated that well over half of American high school students are having sex. The question becomes not should they have sex but how should a parent prepare a teenager about sex in the likelihood that he or she starts "dating" someone and the opportunities keep presenting themselves? Teens must be counseled to protect themselves both from pregnancy and a life-threatening disease.

If parents of typical teenagers are in a quandary about the entire subject of sex, consider the even more complicated situation parents of a bipolar teen may be dealing with. Their teenager—if not medicated properly—can have periods of hypersexuality where the drive is *imperative.*

So many parents have described watching with horror as their daughters get "dressed" in the skimpiest of outfits and attempt to go out flaunting their bodies to cadres of boys in the neighborhood and school. One girl we know was so hypersexual that she and her boyfriend were practicing heavy petting in the school library for all to see.

The first thing the parents of such a teenager should do is call the treating psychiatrist and get the teen's blood levels checked. The hypersexuality may be a sign that the levels have dropped or the teen is being noncompliant. (In an adolescent with no history of the disorder, hypersexuality may be a symptom of the impending illness, not an indication that the teen is amoral.)

Perhaps the adolescent should be kept home from school for a few days while the meds are adjusted and to keep her or him out of trouble. If there is a party that Saturday night, common sense dictates that this adolescent should not be allowed to attend. Sending a hypersexual teen to a party is an incendiary situation—one that can bring grave consequences to a teenager and the family.

The provocative dress and behavior may not be a sign only of hypersexuality; it may be very tied to the psychology of the teen. Having a mood disorder can leave an adolescent feeling so defective and with such low self-esteem that the arena of sex may be a place where a girl finally feels attractive, valued, and in control. The girl may need to be so desired and loved that the cravings may be just as psychological as physical.

Parents will be desperate to avoid a pregnancy and the trauma of abortion or adoption. They will be so afraid of their daughter's impulsiveness and lack of forethought that the idea of a shot of Depo-Provera—a hormone that suppresses ovulation for about ninety days—seems to cover a lot of bases. But Depo-Provera contains medroxyprogesterone acetate, and progesterone is known to cause depression or exacerbate a mood disorder. And if it does so, it is present in the bloodstream for at least ninety days. Therefore, it's not a good option for a girl with bipolar disorder.

The minipill—oral progesterone—may be a better option because it can be stopped if it becomes apparent that the progesterone in it is adversely affecting the mood disorder. But parents and teenagers should be aware that the mood stabilizers carbamazepine (Tegretol), oxcarbazepine (Trileptal) and lamotrigine (Lamictal) can interfere with the contraceptive ability of birth control pills. They accelerate their normal breakdown and make them less reliable. (Depakote and lithium do not cause this.) Tegretol also diminishes the accuracy of pregnancy tests.

In the best of all possible worlds, a sexually active teenager would use a combination of a condom and a diaphragm with the spermicide and HIV-killing nonoxynol-9 gel with every sexual act. But teenage sex doesn't often afford such privacy and planning, and, paradoxically, many teenagers feel that if it just "happens," they won't be embarrassed by seeming aggressive and calculating.

Probably the only thing parents can do is ensure that their children are well informed and understand the risks of pregnancy and sexually transmitted disease so that their fear overcomes any embarrassment and they take care of themselves. They need to know the benefits of monogamy and of knowing who their partner is. There are no easy answers here.

## LYING

In our survey, some 50 percent of the parents responding checked the phrase "Frequently lies" about their children. In many in-person and over-the-telephone interviews as well, parents discussed their children's lies. These parents were confused and upset because, even when confronted with evidence of the lie, the children and teenagers continued to deny their guilt. Audacious as it may sound, the teenagers—knowing full well they were lying—got angry at the parents for even *suggesting* they were not telling the truth.

But is lying a symptom of bipolar illness? Studies show that almost all teenagers lie. They do so to avoid getting into trouble, to maintain a certain zone of privacy, and to avoid confrontation. They often do it to manipulate a situation or to get what they want. They may lie at home and not so much in the outside world. As author Anthony E. Wolf writes in *Get Out of My Life, but First Could You Drive Me and Cheryl to the Mall?*:

> Lying as a teenager is not an especially reliable indicator of whether or not that teenager is, or will become, an honest person. A good part of teenage lying is a function of the strange amorality of the at-home self. We should always confront them with their deceit when they are caught, and we must communicate our outrage. But a disaster, a tragedy, such deceit is not. Their sliminess may be deplorable, it is also normal, as it was when we were adolescents.

Dr. Wolf's wise discussion helps take the fear and steam out of the issue and place everything in perspective. But we need to explore this issue a bit further in the case of bipolar children.

There may be additional reasons why these kids lie. Some lies help establish the child's power. The child knows he or she is lying, and the parent knows it as well but is helpless to prove it. By lying, the child can test and challenge authority, and this may be an especially attractive form of power to a bipolar child who cannot accept parental authority without feeling a loss of self. In Chapter 1 we described a young boy who in response to his mother's exasperated question: "Why can you never listen to me and do as I say?" responded: "Oh, I couldn't. That would mean you had power over me. I am the master of my universe."

Lying would certainly be a provocative and teasing way to keep that power challenge going in the right direction for that child. There may be some other specific reasons for lying also. A twenty-one-year-old girl filled out our questionnaire and frankly checked off "Lies frequently" on the symptom checklist all through her childhood and adolescence. Since she was being so forthright about it, we homed in on this and asked: "How often do you lie, and why do you think you do it?"

She described what she felt was the underlying basis for her lying:

> I lie all the time. It's a compulsion. It's easier to lie than to tell the truth. It's more comforting. It removes me from the constant feeling that I am incompetent and always failing.
>
> For instance, this morning I was a half an hour late for work because I was sitting and daydreaming and time just passed. I don't know what happened to it, it just passed, and I couldn't pull everything together. So I told my boss that there was a three-car accident on the road and a slew of helicopters and all the news media blocking the way and I couldn't get through. The drama appealed to me. I don't know why I do this. I know they know it's not true. I don't know what they must think of me.

## School Avoidance

According to Dr. Russell Barkley, the director of the Child and Adult Attention-Deficit Disorder Clinics at the University of Massachusetts and a leading authority on attention-deficit hyperactivity disorder, approximately 21 percent of teenagers with ADHD skip school. They are also at risk for dropping out (35 percent) or of being suspended (45 percent). Adolescents with ADHD and mood disorders may find school such a place of failure because they are so distractible and can't concentrate, and feel themselves slipping farther and farther behind.

While no statistics exist for bipolar teenagers, those just quoted don't bode well for this population.

Many teenagers with bipolar disorder experience school phobia and tell their parents they have stomachaches, headaches, and impending flus in order not to have to attend. When parents detect signs of school refusal, they have to act quickly and locate the source of the problem.

If the adolescent has never been tested for learning disabilities, or never had special accommodations put in place to compensate for symptoms of bipolar illness, this avenue should be explored immediately (see Chapters 9 and 10). It could be that the teenager is falling behind and feeling a lot of stress at school and trying to avoid that stress. While parents get to the bottom of things academically, they must make it very clear that unless the teenager has a fever, he or she is going to school. Parents should not cover for their child.

Certain medications can be very sedating and can make it difficult for someone taking them to get up in the morning. This possibility should be assessed by the treating physician, who can perhaps advise that the medications be taken earlier in the evening or who can make some changes in the medication regimen.

At the same time, parents should be noting what time the teenager is getting to sleep at night. If he or she is having difficulty getting to sleep, it may be a sign that the condition is beginning to influence the sleep cycle—hypomania may be beginning to develop. Again, the doctor should be consulted, and he or she can assess the situation.

## CURFEWS

Most teenagers, in their effort to establish independent relationships and a social identity apart from their parents and family, need to be with their peers constantly. They tend to congregate or "hang" into the late hours of the night.

Unfortunately, for a person with bipolar disorder, a disturbance in the sleep/wake cycle can become a window through which hypomania or mania can occur. A regular bedtime is essential to the teenager's health.

Parents should explain that they understand how important their teenager's social life is but that an irregular sleep/wake cycle can trigger episodes of illness. This needs to be addressed with the treating psychiatrist, and a reasonable curfew should be imposed, perhaps with some latitude on one weekend evening. If the teen is going to sleep at a friend's house, it must be made clear to the parents of that friend that "all-nighters" are dangerous for their son or daughter; their help must be enlisted to make sure the teens get to sleep at a decent time.

## SPECIAL ISSUES FOR TEENAGERS

Unlike their classmates and others in their age group, teenagers with bipolar disorder have far more complicated concerns and burdens.

Stigma is not a thing of the past, and these adolescents are always faced with the questions: Whom do I tell? Whom do I trust? How do I define myself minus the illness? Rather than risk rejection, these adolescents can become socially withdrawn, remain very isolated, and feel that they are "odd" and totally unacceptable.

We talked recently with Laurie Austin, M.S.W., a therapist in Westport, Connecticut, who treats a number of adolescents and helps them come to terms with their illness. She told us:

> The middle school kids I treat can have a very hard time. If they have finally been diagnosed and stabilized, they see with 20/20 hindsight that they have been so buffeted by mood cycles they've failed to develop social skills and often have very few friends. They get very demoralized as a result of that dawning realization. These feelings amplify periods of depression and contribute to lowering self-esteem.
>
> If their parents and therapists see the depression as merely a manifestation of the mood disorder and lose sight of the social and self-esteem consequences wrought by having this disorder, the young adolescent loses a chance to examine these important issues apart from the mood disorder. They may become enraged at the adults for attributing all of their feelings of despair to a biological condition that simply awaits the right drug at the right dose.

No one should be cavalier when advising an adolescent or young adult about full disclosure. One girl found that her friends all turned away; another heard her friend say brightly: "Everyone I know is bipolar!"

Some kids want very much to be in the mainstream and decide to keep their problems close to the chest, while others may defensively embrace an "out there" or "Goth" style as if to announce to the world: "Yes, I'm different. I march to a different drummer, and you're going to see it big time."

Individual therapy with a professional who understands the illness and all the fallout it causes is vital to adolescents working through the loneliness, the anger at being stuck with a genetic illness, and the conflicted feelings they harbor about the parent or grandparent who passed the disorder on to them. Family therapy can do much to work out many of the tangled feelings and behavioral patterns that have arisen as a result of the bipolar disorder.

While teenagers wrestle with issues of disclosure, parents are making the same dicey decisions. "Mothers and fathers tend to fall into one of two categories," says therapist Laurie Austin: "Those who don't want to broadcast their child's diagnosis and those who decide to fight stigma and who want to lay everything out on the table."

Whichever choice the parents make (and the decision must, by nature, be an individual one), mothers and fathers should realize that either course of action is bound to have a strong impact on the teenager and any siblings in the family. A parent's fear of stigma may bother and shame an adolescent greatly; and a parent's open disclosure and involvement in the bipolar community may be viewed by the teenager as a co-opting of the teen's illness.

Today there are so many in-person and online support groups that it is easy for a parent's social life to begin to revolve around the illness. (Involvement with the bipolar community is one of the best ways to ensure proper treatment for the child and to give and gain support to and from others who have walked the same path.) However, no youngster appreciates a parent tethered to a computer or a phone line, and it is easy to see that attention given to *other* people dealing with bipolar disorder can provoke adolescents. (Even though they can act as if you're dirt beneath their feet, they also really want your attention more than they can admit.)

Therefore, it is important for a parent to attempt to limit involvement with the outside bipolar world when the adolescent is around and certainly to make the subject of bipolar disorder off limits at dinnertime. Phone calls with support group members or any volunteer work should be conducted when the adolescent is not at home, if possible.

Looking at the paragraphs above, we see highly emotive words such as "fury," "enraged," "anger," and "provoked" flying off the page. While not all adolescents react with these feelings, many do—those with or without bipolar disorder—and parents need to find some balance and to try not to overreact to everything the teen says or seems to feel.

## The Big Question: When Do I Tell Someone I Date and Like?

In late adolescence or early adulthood, a young woman or young man will have to decide when and how to disclose the illness to a potentially serious boyfriend or girlfriend. New and serious and urgent questions arise once more: Will I be rejected by someone who matters so much to me? Can the relationship be stable? Will his or her parents accept a son-in-law or daughter-in-law with this illness? (The parents of the affected young adult will face their own worries about the reaction of potential in-laws.)

Again, there are no pat answers here. Sometimes the relationship will not survive the disclosure; sometimes the boyfriend or girlfriend will divulge his or her own psychiatric problems (which definitely compounds the risk of passing the illness on to children), and sometimes the love and commitment that a couple share override the problems—especially if the young adult has taken charge of his or her illness and is stable.

We spoke to the boyfriend of a young woman named Elyse and asked him to tell us his reactions when she told him about her bipolar disorder after they had dated for a few months:

> I wondered what Elyse had in store for me when she said she had something important to tell me. I think I reacted pretty well. I was fortunate to know what bipolar disorder was, as I had been a resident assistant in college and I received a lot of training in how to help a person with depression, contemplating suicide.
>
> At worst, I was probably a little disappointed. There is no cure for bipolar disorder, which meant that if I would spend the rest of my life with this girl, with whom I was already beginning to fall in love, bipolar disorder would always be there. Elyse was afraid I would want to end the relationship, but this was definitely not the case. Elyse was just too amazing of a person, and many things which I adore, including her personality and creativity, are largely due to her bipolar disorder.
>
> She is very stable most of the time, but sometimes I see her get depressed. Sometimes I see her obsessing and counting things, and that is very eerie for me.

He concluded:

We are not completely free and clear, and I know it will be very difficult when we have children as she will not be able to take medications and we both worry about passing the genes onto our children. Then I think that there are no guarantees in life. Settling down with someone and having children requires a huge leap of faith and many hopes that life will work out for the best. Some things are just not in your control.

## COLLEGE BOUND

Before a parent turns around, his or her world becomes filled with the subject of SATs and grade-point averages, and the coffee table overflows with brochure packets and videotapes from colleges and universities across the nation. Spring and summer vacations turn into car trips to campuses near and far. It's a heady and frightening time. This child is about to be launched.

Many, many questions and considerations are going to arise for bipolar adolescents. How far should they go away from home? Who will treat their disorder in a different community? Can they deal with the academic and social demands of campus life? What kind of school should they look for? At what point do you address the medical diagnosis and academic disabilities that may accompany the disorder?

Today, many colleges have developed learning centers where students who have a disability can get help, tutoring, and have programs designed for them that take their disability into consideration (after acceptance evaluations and other documents supporting disability are sent to the college's disability coordinator). An educational consultant would be a good person to turn to for advice on suitable programs.

Jayme Stewart, the director of College Guidance at the Yorke Preparatory School in New York City, advises a bipolar student to look for a small, nurturing school (with about 1,500 to 2,000 students), one with an active learning center. It is extremely important that the dean of freshman students be contacted and put on notice that the student needs special accommodations. The parents need to let the dean know that they are expecting him or her to keep an eye out for that student. She gives all the parents of her learning-disabled graduates the following letter for them to make that contact. This letter should be sent return receipt requested:

Dean of Freshman Students                                Date
College
Address

Dear Dean of Freshman Students:

Our (son/daughter) is about to enter (college name) as a freshman in the class of 20_____. We are writing to you now at the suggestion of (his/her) high school guidance counselor. We would like to have an understanding with (college) that (child's name) is a documented LD student (see enclosed reports). Should it become necessary, we request that (name) will be allowed to take untimed exams in college, have a note taker for certain courses, have a lighter-than-usual course load, and be able to use "books on tape" if available. (He/She) will, of course, fulfill the required work during summers or as part of a fifth year.

In addition, we will arrange with the Academic Support Center to set up a tutoring schedule in order to give (name) whatever help (he/she) needs outside of class. Please feel free to contact me if you need any further information.

We, and (name), are very happy about (his/her) enrollment at (college) and we look forward to (his/her) becoming a productive and successful member of your student body.

Sincerely,
Your Name

Enclosure

Ms. Stewart also advises parents to arrange—and pay for—the services of a mentor—a junior or senior with good grades who can tutor the new student and assist him or her socially. She said: "A student mentor is more natural than an adult tutor, and has the added advantage of taking the new student to parties and helping him or her assimilate into campus life. Knowing a mentor is in place means knowing that someone is checking in on the young adult and making sure everything is going smoothly."

Ms. Stewart definitely recommends that a bipolar student look into something called a "quiet dorm." This is something new on college campuses; these dormitories have rules that forbid loud music or parties so that students can study without distraction and get enough rest. However, she does not think a bipolar student should ever have a single room.

"This student could disappear from the scene and no one would know it. A roommate is company and can get help for the student if a period of instability arises," she explained.

It will be important for parents to contact and stay in touch with the senior resident assistant (RA) of the dorm. Because the school must view its students as adults and not intrude on them, the senior RA may be the only person who can keep an eye out for the young person who may become noncompliant with medications or begin to founder.

Ms. Stewart had several other recommendations to help ease the way into an entirely new life. She said: "I think bipolar students should schedule classes later in the day, as I know getting up in the morning can be difficult. I also think there is nothing wrong with taking five years to complete a degree (this is becoming common even among non–learning-disabled students). If the pressures and stresses are kept to a minimum, the student has a better chance of experiencing success and really blossoming as a student and as a young adult."

If the adolescent is not stable and is still acting out, it may be a better idea for him or her to attend school locally with the full support of the home environment and the treating psychiatrist and therapist. There may be excellent schools within driving distance of the home, and as the young person matures and stabilizes, he or she probably can attend another college full time, but then with a more secure academic and social base.

## To Everything There Is a Season

It is interesting to note that adolescence in western society was something reserved only for the upper social classes until the early twentieth century. The poor never experienced adolescence because they were expected to proceed dutifully from an obedient childhood into an obedient adulthood without benefit of the period of transition from childhood to adulthood.

So, thanks to the emancipation of the working classes and the advent of the youth movements of the early 1900s, adolescence is something all parents get to "enjoy." As Dr. Louise J. Kaplan writes in her book *Adolescence,* "Now that adolescence is accessible to the multitude and not restricted to gentlemen and lords, many adults are taking alarm at what seems to be a barbaric horde of scruffy girls and boys out to dismantle the structures of society. It is hard to see any virtue at all. What the grown-ups see in its stead is considerable evidence of pride, covetousness, anger, gluttony, envy, sloth, and a great deal of lust."

We hope this chapter has provided some perspective for the dicey years the parents of a bipolar teen will have to endure. Adolescence is a difficult phase—for any family.

But that's what it is, a phase, and one that passes. In the majority of cases, a more reasonable, more centered adult rises from the ashes of adolescence. It's never easy, but parents should remember that much of what they say, teach, and advise eventually does get through, despite all evidence to the contrary.

Surprisingly, the parents of a bipolar adolescent may have a unique advantage over other parents: They have become particularly attuned to this child and his or her emotional state, and they may be in a better position to troubleshoot and stave off potential problems. They have had to confront uncomfortable truths early on. These parents have been tempered by the fires of a bipolar childhood and may be more flexible, more realistic, and better able to withstand the shock of adolescence without losing their footing. In fact, these parents—*and* their teenagers—may be surprised at their ability to handle adolescence and all its accompanying tumult.

# When a Child Is Hospitalized

Parents who've brought a newborn home from the hospital nursery usually have an indelible memory of the experience. It's impossible to pass through the hospital's corridors on that first journey home and not encounter people smiling broadly and voicing good wishes for the fledgling family. There is such excitement and hope about the special days and months ahead. And as the new young mother and father head out toward a brand-new future, all of their love, thoughts, efforts, and intentions are focused on helping this infant thrive and get off to the best possible start in life.

Never, *ever,* do parents dream that—not so many years later—they may be forced back into another kind of hospital because that child has a psychiatric condition that now makes him or her "a danger to self or others." Parents who make the agonizing decision to hospitalize a child will never forget either the events that led up to its necessity or those first disorienting days on a child psychiatric unit.

It is not uncommon for a child or adolescent to require hospitalization, and families should almost expect that a crisis might occur at some point in the child's life. Therefore, we want to outline the procedures and introduce the professionals that a child and his or her family encounter throughout the period of a hospitalization. We also want to include the wise advice and counsel of other parents who have had a child in crisis and

who, in hindsight, assessed the hospitalization as a positive experience—
for their child as well as for the family as a whole.

## WHEN SHOULD A CHILD BE HOSPITALIZED?
## WHAT CAN IT ACCOMPLISH?

It's time to think about a hospitalization when a child is so out of control
that he or she may be hurting him- or herself, threatening to harm a family member, unable to stop raging, experiencing delusions or hallucinations, or talking about or planning suicide.

*No two human beings, no matter how dedicated, have the stamina to see a child
through the intensity of such a crisis alone.* The right and appropriate course
of action is to have a professional staff take over at this time.

A psychiatric unit is a protected environment where a team of professionals can keep the child safe, observe the child's full range of behaviors
and reactions, meet with and talk to the family on a regular basis, participate in the diagnosis (or rediagnosis) of an illness, order and administer
medication trials, and note any untoward effects.

Years ago a psychiatric hospitalization often lasted a month or two. Today, with the cost-containing practices of managed care, a child is typically preauthorized for a number of days on a psychiatric unit, and all
future days must be reauthorized as the insurer's utilization review board
monitors the progress of the child's condition. Doctors often have to fight
to make a case for additional hospital days, but the average length of stay
ranges from six to fourteen days. A Band-Aid, yes, but a necessary one.

We asked one father to tell us about his twelve-year-old daughter's hospitalization in the adolescent psychiatric unit of a Chicago teaching hospital. While he talked about the trauma of making the decision, he said
that ultimately there was no choice. She became more and more agitated
and began acting in a threatening manner. He picked her up, put her in
a taxi, and headed toward the emergency room of the hospital. Looking
back, he felt that it was absolutely the right thing to have done, and he
ticked off the benefits:

- It offered respite and safety for her.
- It offered respite and safety for us.
- We got to "fast-track" a medication regimen.
- It supplied a concrete recognition of her illness and the crisis we
  were in.

- We got eight more confirmations of her diagnosis as the staff got to talk with her and observe her behavior. When people asked, "Did you get a second opinion?" we were able to answer: "Yes. We got eight of them."
- She got to meet other teenagers struggling with bipolar disorder, and she didn't feel so alone or alien. They liked her and helped prove to her that she was okay, despite her problems.
- The other kids told her never to go off her medications. (They had, and that is why they were repeating the hospital experience.) They also told her that she should "never mess with alcohol and drugs" because it would make everything worse. (No one but another teenager could have made that all-important message stick.)

Other parents we interviewed had experiences that, on the whole, paralleled this family's, where the hospitalization—although traumatic for everyone at first—made perfect sense in view of the crisis situation and ultimately proved beneficial in many other ways.

But make no mistake, psychiatric hospitalization always raises the issues of stigma. No matter how enlightened, most people feel a sense of shame and disgrace that the private life of their family is now no longer private. The absence of the child from home must be explained, the seriousness of his or her illness must be acknowledged, and all of this must be thought through at a time when the family is exhausted and grief-stricken.

One mother who felt protective of her son's reputation (Would other parents let their children play with him when he got home? Would people gossip? Would they blame her and her husband?) admitted: "I found myself saying 'he has a neurological illness.' I felt ashamed telling people that I had put him in a psychiatric unit. When I had a choice between two hospitals, and one was Children's Hospital and the other began with 'The Psychiatric Institute of . . .' I opted for the name that revealed the least, or didn't make my heart skip a beat every time I was forced to mouth it."

Sadly, stigma adds to the already overwhelming burden these families feel. However, this mother has since rallied and was very eager to tell other parents how to avoid falling into the trap that had made her situation all the more difficult.

She said:

Your tendency is to contract and isolate yourself. But it's so important that the parents push themselves to reach out and break down the barricades of their isolation. I advise them to go home, and get on the phone with a National Alliance for the Mentally Ill (NAMI) or Depressive and Bipolar Support Alliance (DBSA) chapter and ask someone at the chapter to put you in touch with another family who's had to hospitalize their child. I finally did this, and when a family member called me, it was such a lifeline. Here were people who were so empathic, who had been through the experience and who had survived it, and who could walk us through the days ahead and offer counsel and comfort.

This mother also had great praise for her son's psychiatrist during this crisis period:

She expressed such compassion. She acknowledged our struggle and offered us hope that this crisis would pass and we would have our little boy back. She also encouraged me to call her as often as I wanted and cry my heart out. Often I didn't need to speak to her, I just left messages on her machine. I needed to keep connected, keep her informed and vent a little.

## IF YOU HAVE A CHOICE, WHICH HOSPITAL SHOULD YOU CHOOSE?

Since over 85 percent of the people who are insured in this country are enrolled in some type of managed care insurance program, today parents have limited choices when it comes to a psychiatric hospitalization. As we discuss in Chapter 13, most managed care plans have contracted with a few hospitals in your area for behavioral health treatment, and you will have to hospitalize your child in one of these facilities.

Most hospitalizations must be preauthorized and planned forty-eight hours in advance. (If it's an emergency and you cannot get preauthorization from the insurer, you have no choice but to go to the emergency room of a hospital and wait for a bed there.)

If a hospitalization seems imminent, it's best to call your insurer and get it on record that matters are deteriorating and find out your choices (if any). The child's psychiatrist arranges the preauthorization, but one mother whose two children had been hospitalized advises parents to do a lot of checking and even to tour the units and get a gut feeling about the facilities. Hospitals vary, and she wrote:

My oldest son was just hospitalized two months ago. I took him to University Hospital in San Diego. They got him a bed right away. The staff was great, I feel that it did help him. He says he wasn't scared and that they were good to him. He liked the classes and I liked his new child psychiatrist. So, it was a positive experience for us.

However, my youngest son is ten years old and is bipolar also. We had to put him in the hospital when he was nine years old because he tried to kill himself. We took him to a different hospital required by our insurance company. It was awful. He was there for seven days. He was only allowed to call home once a day and cried, told me how scared he was, and that the people were mean. I could hear the staff shouting in the background at him to get off the phone. He was scared of the dark and I had told them that, but they continued to close his door at night. They would only allow me to visit him for one hour each night. My son begged me to take him home every day. After four days I tried to and they told me it was against the doctors' advice and that basically Special Services would take him away from me if I did. I felt completely guilty for taking him there. I was a nervous wreck and cried all the time. I felt like an awful parent.

When he came home he was scared to leave my sight. He followed me everywhere, including the bathroom. He slept with my husband and me for a few weeks. We had to constantly reassure him that he was safe and he would never go back to that hospital again. He still is scared to tell things to his therapist because he says the therapist will send him back to the hospital. So, his therapist wrote a promise note telling my son that he promised he would never send him back to *that* hospital. He is just now, one year later, feeling okay to talk to his therapist about everything.

The only positive thing about my younger son being in the hospital—and this is not insignificant—was that his doctor there did properly diagnose him.

I would tell other parents—and I do tell them at groups I attend—to check out the hospital yourself first.

We asked Dr. Victor Fornari, the associate chairman for education and training at Schneider Children's Hospital in New Hyde Park, New York, if it is typical for a parent to tour the hospital. "If you have some choice," he said, "by all means make an appointment and come in to see the facility, meet some of the staff and become familiar with the point of view of people who might be working with your child. You may not be taken up to the children's unit, but you'll get a feel for the facility and the people in charge of its program."

We then asked him: "If you had to hospitalize one of your children on a psychiatric unit, what would you look for and what would you tell other parents to assess?"

He advised a parent to:

- Learn about the leadership of the unit. Who runs it and what is his or her philosophical orientation? What is the staff-to-patient ratio?

- Make sure you see more registered nurses than psych technicians (often called milieu therapists) and aides. One registered nurse is not enough. Naturally, the units with small children should have a greater ratio of staff to children than an adolescent unit.

- Research the policies and procedures governing seclusion and restraints and involuntary administration of medication. While each state has regulations governing seclusion and restraint, there's a philosophy that guides how liberally either seclusion or restraints are used, and you want to know that it's for the safety of the child, used infrequently and as a last resort, and never applied punitively.

- If the child is very young and the separation from the parent is going to be a big problem, ask if the hospital will let you "shadow" the child—sleep in the parents' lounge and participate in some of the day activities. If the staff doesn't advise that, listen carefully to their reasons and determine for yourself if they seem reasonable.

- Take a look at the programs for parents. Is there an attempt to educate parents and help them work through the trauma? Is there a siblings group? And how much thought seems to go into discharge planning? There are alternate levels of aftercare that include more than discharge to home and therapist.

Parents should also keep in mind that private rooms and fancy facilities are not assurances of quality treatment. One family from Florida admitted their son to a psychiatric hospital with tennis courts and swimming pools, and for three weeks the staff did nothing to benefit the boy positively. When their insurance ran out, he was transferred to the county hospital. There he was looked after by a doctor who diagnosed him correctly and prescribed a combination of medications that worked. This child has been stable for a year. He had formerly suffered school phobia, and the school year was a nightmare for him and his family. His mother told us with such joy in her voice that he recently returned to school and he came home one week and announced: "You know, I'm really loving school and I think my teacher is great and I'm going to work hard this year and move ahead."

The diagnostic abilities and treatment philosophy of the psychiatrist running the unit are far more important than the interior design and the gym equipment.

## COSTS OF A HOSPITALIZATION

Parents are going to need to read all the fine print on their insurance policies and probably log a bit of time on the phone with their plan's administrators, so that they understand completely what they will be responsible for when the bill for a psychiatric hospitalization is finally tallied.

Some of the questions that need to be asked are:

- How many days in a psychiatric hospital are covered?
- Do you have a choice in the hospital, or must it be in one of the plan's participating hospitals?
- If a child is hospitalized through the emergency room of a hospital not in the plan, how much of the bill will be covered?
- Is there a ceiling to the dollar amount reimbursed?
- What is the deductible?
- Are partial hospitalizations (for instance, day hospital programs) and other alternatives to inpatient care covered? For how many days or weeks?
- If you have several policies, when does one pick up from the other?

We discuss all of this in Chapter 13. We understand how difficult it is to read fine print and legalese in the middle of a crisis, but the more information you have going in, the less likely you'll be to fantasize financial ruin over a hospitalization, and the more secure you'll feel when the issues of money and insurance are raised.

If your coverage is inadequate, the hospital's business office may be able to initiate a Medicaid application, help arrange a bank loan, or negotiate another payment method.

Families should also be aware that there is a form of hospital "Catastrophic Medicaid" that covers patients who are not currently receiving Medicaid and whose inpatient hospital care exceeds 25 percent of their annual income. This coverage is valid for only six months from the date of application and covers only inpatient care.

What would twelve days of a psychiatric hospitalization of a child or adolescent cost? The charges are variable, and a city, county, or state hospital will naturally cost less, but a child admitted to a private hospital would incur bills that would range from $10,000 to $17,000.

Every parent should examine his or her insurance situation with a magnifying glass. If a person does not have coverage and lacks financial resources, a hospital will take care of the treatment and initiate a Medicaid application.

## PREPARING FOR ADMISSION

### What to Take to the Admissions Office

A telephone call to the admissions office of the child psychiatry unit will fill you in on what's required for the admitting procedure. In all probability you need to take the following:

- Completed questionnaires and paperwork sent to you by the hospital prior to admission; similarly, any questionnaires completed by your child's teacher
- Your child's immunization record
- Any previous psychiatric, psychological, or medical reports
- A complete listing of all medication trials and the responses your child had to them
- Your child's insurance card

- The Social Security card or phone number of the person who will bear the responsibility for the bill
- Name, address, and phone number of the person to be notified in case of an emergency
- A checkbook or credit card (some hospitals require a deposit)

### What Clothing Should You Pack for Your Child?

While each unit is different and will advise you about clothing and personal articles, many units ask that you supply enough clothing for one week and recommend that you iron in name labels or identify all clothing. Typically, a child needs:

Underwear  7 sets
Socks  7 pairs
Pajamas  3 sets
Bathrobe  1
T-shirts  7
Tops  7
Sweater  1
Pants/jeans  4
Slippers  1 pair
Shoes  1 pair
Sneakers  1 pair
Shampoo (in a plastic container)
Comb/brush (plastic)
Toothbrush/toothpaste
Soap
Coins for phone calls
A favorite stuffed animal, but no other toys, cords, or strings, which may be dangerous for a child in crisis

For the safety of the child and others on the child unit, do *not* pack or take the following: scissors, glass objects, tobacco products, matches, clippers, cameras, medications, MP3 players, radios, hair dryers or other electrical items, glue, paste, or soda cans.

## AFTER ADMISSION

After the parents sign authorization-for-treatment papers, the family is escorted to the unit. In many hospitals, the nursing staff handles the orientation and intake procedure. Most hospitals hand you brochures with a Patient's Bill of Rights and a statement of the unit's philosophy of treatment as well as all kinds of information about life in this therapeutic community. The parents and the child will be told all about the therapy programs, the rules of the unit, visiting hours, the daily schedule, and so on.

Next the nurse takes a medical and psychiatric history from the parents. The nurse's intake not only helps orient the child and family to the new surroundings, but gives the people who are working most closely with the child a chance to get to know him or her and you.

Once the intake is complete, the psychiatrist responsible for the child begins a medical and psychiatric workup. In some cases, the private psychiatrist who admitted the child to the hospital will be his or her private attending physician and will thus be familiar with the child's history; in units that assign their own staff to each new patient, typically there will be an extensive workup of the child's developmental, medical, and psychiatric history. The family history should be explored and all medication trials and responses will be noted.

## Physical Examination

All children admitted to a unit are given a physical exam and routine screening tests, such as blood tests and a urinalysis. The results of these tests may point to a physical cause of the psychiatric problem or may unearth a coexisting medical problem. They also will guide the psychiatrist in the choice of psychotropic medication. For example, a child with a history of seizures would need psychotropic medications that would have less of a potential for lowering the seizure threshold. (Many neuroleptics lower it to some degree, as does the antidepressant Wellbutrin.) Depending on the clinical picture, the psychiatrist may call for a medical consultation with a neurologist, an endocrinologist, or a cardiologist.

After all of these exams are completed, the treatment team and plan are put into action. Under the psychiatrist's direction, a team of psychologists, social workers, the nursing staff, occupational and activities therapists, and an education specialist continuously review, discuss, and treat the child.

## Hospital Team

The child will be evaluated and treated by different staff professionals throughout the hospital stay, and it is important for parents to know who they are, how they can help, and what kind of training they have. The following brief descriptions should answer these questions.

- The *child psychiatrist* is a medical doctor who specializes in the diagnosis and comprehensive treatment of psychiatric disorders. After completing four years of medical school, he or she completes three years of an adult psychiatric residency and two additional years of a child psychiatry fellowship. The education encompasses medical treatment approaches as well as psychotherapeutic approaches. The child psychiatrist, as a medical doctor, is the only mental health professional (in most states) who can prescribe medications and perform electroconvulsive therapy. The child psychiatrist supervises and coordinates the entire treatment team and plan.

- The *clinical psychologist* is also called "doctor," but here the title refers to a Ph.D. degree or its equivalent in clinical psychology. The psychologist completes three years of course work as well as an internship in a psychiatric hospital or mental health clinic. In addition, most Ph.D. programs require a dissertation on a research topic. While a psychologist cannot prescribe medication, he or she is trained to do psychological testing, psychotherapy, and research.

- *Psychiatric nurses* are registered nurses who have been specifically trained to work with children who have psychiatric disorders. These are the professionals who spend the most time with the children on a psychiatric unit, and their manner can set the tone of the whole unit and do much to make a child and his or her family feel safe and at home. Not only do the nurses dispense the medications ordered by the child psychiatrist, but they closely monitor the side effects. The nurses' daily report gives the rest of the treatment team valuable information about the child's medical and mental status. Some nurses have master's degrees, and some are nurse practitioners trained to do psychotherapy and run groups, and even prescribe medications in some states.

- The *psychiatric social worker* can be invaluable to the family as well as to the child. After four years of college, the psychiatric social worker completes a two-year course with an internship in a psychiatric setting and is awarded the degree of master of social work (M.S.W.). If the initials

A.C.S.W. appear after the social worker's name, it means that he or she has met the requirements of and is certified by the Academy of Certified Social Workers. L.C.S.W. means that the social worker is a licensed clinical social worker. Not only can this professional conduct group and individual therapy sessions, but he or she assesses and coordinates the needs of the child and family members during and after the hospitalization. The social worker helps with the discharge treatment plan and may initiate Medicaid applications where they are appropriate.

• The *rehabilitation therapist* on some children's units coordinates each child's daily schedule, which includes school, therapeutic activities, group therapy, and other milieu groups. He or she plans and leads a variety of action-oriented groups that address the child's problems and assets and focuses on skill development.

• Many units also have *activities therapists* who specialize in art therapy, dance or music therapy, or recreational therapy. They are graduates of accredited bachelor's or master's programs that emphasize the therapeutic application of art or physical education. The activities programs are designed to encourage self-awareness and the exploration of feelings as well as to provide the children with an opportunity to engage in structured leisure activities that promote socialization and the improvement of interpersonal skills. (These activities could include sports, hobbies, woodworking, crafts, cooking, and the like.) The activities therapist understands the treatment goals for each child and attempts to reinforce them through the projects undertaken.

• Most child and adolescent units have a *teacher* who conducts a school program for two to three hours a day. He or she keeps in close contact with each child's home teacher and receives the assignments and curriculum so they may be completed during school hours on the unit. This way the child can keep from falling far behind classmates during the hospitalization.

In addition to the professionals just mentioned, the child comes into close contact with other hospital personnel: the physician's assistant, who may do physical exams, psych technicians, and nursing aides. In a good hospital, these people not only do their jobs but offer children reassurance and encouragement.

## Daily and Weekly Schedule on a Children's Unit

Treatment for children suffering with psychiatric disorders begins with an integrated plan to diagnose, ameliorate the symptoms of the illness, help the child reestablish a sense of self-esteem, educate the child and the family as to the nature of the illness, and develop a practical outpatient treatment that will serve to prevent rehospitalization. The many meetings, medical rounds, and social and therapeutic interactions throughout the hospital stay are aimed at accomplishing these agendas.

Typically each morning the staff assembles for "rounds." This is the nurses' report on the medical and behavioral status of each child on the unit. If there are psychiatric residents and child fellows on the unit (as there would be in a teaching hospital), the residents may report at this time also. Any questions about changes in the treatment plans, or concerns about a response to a medication or a family visit, are brought up at this time.

Many psychiatric units divide the patient responsibilities into two teams. Detailed discussions of each child are conducted in team meetings several times a week. If a child is experiencing any neurological or medical problems, consultants are called in and supplemental medical rounds are conducted.

Individual, group, and family meetings are scheduled throughout the week. Naturally, there are hours set aside for school, meals, showers, quiet times, and visiting hours.

## Behavioral Programs on an Inpatient Unit

Every unit runs differently, but most have a system or set of rules designed to encourage behavior that will help a child reach his or her therapeutic goals as well as limit behaviors that result in distress or that are dangerous or disruptive. Some units run on a point system with a token economy. The more often the child maintains control and achieves certain goals set for him or her, the greater the number of points he or she receives, and these points can be converted to "behavior dollars" at the unit's store or result in special treats or privileges (such as time at the Nintendo game).

Behavioral programs should be explained thoroughly to the parents and the child during the intake process.

## Safety Measures and Discipline

Some children are so aggressive, suicidal, or out of control that it is decided they need more contact with the nursing staff. Part of the treatment plan, then, is a period of time where the child has "one-on-one," or constant observation. This means that a nurse or milieu therapist is assigned to stay close to that child at all times and make frequent or verbal contact with the child.

If a child cannot control his or her behavior, there are a number of disciplinary procedures designed to keep the child safe, help him or her regain control, and also keep the other children as well as the staff on the unit safe.

One of these procedures (familiar to all parents) is a "time-out." When there is a problem behavior, the child is asked to sit in a chair, away from social stimulation. If a parent visits during a time-out, the parent is usually asked to wait for the completion of the time-out before the visit can begin.

At the conclusion of the time-out, the staff discusses with the child what happened and how he or she might have dealt with the situation more appropriately.

Ideally, the child goes to a "time-out chair" cooperatively; if, however, he or she does not respond to the request to take a time-out, the child is typically helped to the chair by a staff member who holds the child's hand or arm. The child is given three chances to sit down. If he or she does not or cannot, the child is informed that he or she has the alternative of the quiet room.

If no cooperation is forthcoming, the child is gently escorted to the quiet room. The door is locked only if it is necessary to provide safety, and a doctor must order this and assign a staff person for constant observation for the time the child is in seclusion. Children should never be alone.

## The Quiet Room, Seclusion, and Physical Restraints

Strict state regulations govern any use of a quiet room or seclusion. The following discussion may sound awful to people who've never dealt with a raging, aggressive, and abusive child, or a child who is hallucinating and feeling panicked or paranoid, but parents who've tried to deal with such a child by themselves have told us that they *wished* they had a seclusion room at home to protect their child, their other children, themselves, and all of their possessions when their child is totally out of control and kicking in the walls of their home. (At least four parents wrote and said they *had* jerry-rigged their own versions of a seclusion room at home. They felt it was necessary to keep the entire family safe.)

In a hospital setting, a seclusion room is a room stripped of any sharp or heavy objects that could be used by a patient to hurt him- or herself or the staff. Often the walls are covered with padding, and there is a mattress on the floor for the patient to rest and sleep on. (A bed frame has too many sharp angles.)

The seclusion room is a measure of last resort. It can be used only to prevent a child from hurting himself or others, and only when other treatments are ineffective. The psychiatrist must write the orders for seclusion, the child's behavior must be observed and documented frequently (there is a window in every seclusion room), vital signs (blood pressure, pulse, respiration rate, and temperature) must be taken periodically, and if the child is not sleeping, he or she must be released and taken to the bathroom every two hours.

There may be times—for instance, if the child is banging his or her head against the wall or trying to do damage to him- or herself in some way—that physical restraints are deemed appropriate. Again, each state has laws determining what kind of restraints can be used. (A rubber blanket that limits kicking and punching may be placed over a very agitated child, or a restraining sheet with special padding may be used.) Again, this may look medieval to someone who has never dealt with this kind of extreme rage or aggression, but many parents have spent hours in their own homes holding a raging child down or wrapping a child in blankets. The authorized hospital restraints limit the potential damage to self or others that a child may cause. They may lessen the stimulation and feelings of overarousal a child is experiencing; they also may frighten a child terribly. Parents need to make sure that the policy of the unit is to have an empathic adult with that child at all times and to inform the family when restraints or seclusion are being used.

Having strangers make a decision to seclude or restrain your child is bound to bring up a lot of feelings of uneasiness and guilt for family members. But one young woman who was secluded in a quiet room for a time recalled how she felt about it on the "inside":

I had been running around trying to do a thousand things and my mind was going a million miles a minute. I was exhausted, and the room seemed a quiet and simple place for me. The pressure was off. I didn't have to accomplish anything. I could just slow down and rest. I'm sure a seclusion room must enrage or frighten some people—it's all so individual—but for me, the time in a seclusion room was a retreat. It seemed an appropriate place for me to be at that time.

## Whom Can You Call to Check on Your Child and Whom Do You Turn to If You Have a Complaint?

It's always a good idea to ask who will have the most contact with your child and whom you can call to check in and see how he or she is doing. Typically, one nurse on each shift is assigned to each child, and that professional is in the best position to answer your questions. When you have the nurse's name, ask him or her when would be the best time to call.

If there is anything that concerns you about the treatment of your child, do not hesitate to talk to the unit chief or the head nurse. If you are still not satisfied, make an appointment to speak to the doctor in charge of your child or to the director of clinical services. He or she should be able to resolve any problem, but if not, consult the admissions brochure you were given at the start of your child's hospitalization and look for the name of the patient representative. This person is a direct link to the hospital's administration and should be able to help find a solution.

## Should Siblings Visit?

Parents have a tendency to try to shield their children from situations that seem unpleasant, but when we asked Dr. Victor Fornari whether siblings should visit, he said:

> By all means. Everyone is affected by the hospitalization, and siblings need to understand what is happening and see their brother or sister. In addition, the hospitalized child needs to be kept involved in their family's life. I do think, however, that the visit should take place not on the unit, but in a waiting room or some other room off the unit.
>
> At Schneider Children's Hospital, we have a sibling group that meets once a week where the brothers and sisters can talk about their

many feelings about the patient and his or her hospitalization and the problems that led up to it. They begin to see that they are not alone with all their feelings.

Parents should not underestimate their other children's extreme sensitivity and capacity to imagine things far more terrible than reality. Watching their sibling removed from the home may have filled them with fear or triumph or any of a number of complicated feelings. There has been a supreme rupture in family life. Seeing their brother or sister at the hospital would do much to help these children replace uncomfortable fantasies with firm and guilt-free facts. Also, during a visit they get to witness the parents' deep involvement and concern for their ill child; this will allay any anxiety that the parent sent the ill child away because he or she was "bad" or "too much trouble." They may fear that this will also happen to them if they misbehave.

## WHILE YOUR CHILD IS IN THE HOSPITAL

Parents need to remember to take very good care of themselves during this time of crisis. They are grieving. Experiencing your child grabbing on to you crying and begging "Don't leave me, Mommy, please don't leave me here alone" is not something easily forgotten. The guilt parents feel and the uncertainty about the drastic measures they've been forced to take are very unbalancing at first. A mother from Texas whose young son had several hospitalizations devised a way to deal with some of the sadness for everyone in the family:

When Billy is in the hospital, we do "Billy" projects—something that sort of "commemorates" him. During one hospitalization I made a quilt. Every stitch I took in was filled with my thoughts and love for him. It was very therapeutic for me because it was a way of keeping him close. It gave me a way to deal with the fact that someone else was taking care of him. It also gave me something to tell him about on visits and phone calls. He would get all excited and want to know how far I'd gotten each time. He sleeps with that quilt now, and it's his prized possession.

We also do projects to give the same "therapy" to his sister, Jamie. For example, we each have scrapbooks for Billy that we work on during hospitalizations. We incorporate photos, drawings, thoughts, and all kinds of things. She gets very sad when we see something or go somewhere and Billy's not there. So I encourage her to take pictures for the scrapbook—anything that she wants to share with him. He loves feeling like she's his "eyes" on the outside. He gets a sense that he's with us always and that we've not forgotten about him.

Parents are often confused as to what to tell neighbors, friends, and schoolmates. Several parents mentioned how kind neighbors were and how meals appeared at their doorsteps nightly. But one mother said, "No one can help you if you keep it all secret. You just feel more isolated."

Not all parents will want the child's classmates to know what has happened, but classmates can't send cards and stuffed animals unless they know your child is in the hospital. It's very sad that stigma keeps such natural inclinations at bay, so a parent has to think long and hard how his or her child is going to take a lack of contact and warm wishes from friends while in the hospital, as well as the possible future teasing that could result from some children frightened about the thought of a psychiatric hospitalization. Much depends on you, your child, the teacher, and the community you live in. A mother whose daughter was hospitalized told us that her daughter's classmates sent a big poster on which all of them had signed their names and written little notes. "She put it up on the wall in her room and she was so proud," said the mother. "The nurses told me that this was the first time a child on the unit had received anything from his or her classmates."

## COMING HOME

A three-week hospitalization gives a medical staff time to titrate medications and stabilize a child. Unfortunately, today's insurance companies want a child out of a hospital as soon as the child is nonpsychotic and seems less "a danger to self or others." Thus a family may have a child who is not stable coming home in six or twelve days.

Before the child comes home, however, the staff meets to determine a discharge plan. It is hoped that the staff has given this a lot of thought, and each child is not discharged simply to "home and therapist." Alternate levels of care should be explored with the parents: Would a partial hospitalization, a day school, intensive outpatient care, a residential placement, or a private school be more appropriate aftercare? Much will be determined by the parents' insurance or ability to fight for funding, but all alternatives should be explored and some kind of plan be detailed.

When the child does return home, it's best if the parents don't expect too much, or press their other children to turn the homecoming into a joyous celebration unless the sisters and brothers want to mark the return of their sibling that way. The family needs some time to get used to each other again and to let the harshness of the preceding crisis fade a bit.

## PARTIAL HOSPITALIZATION

After a hospital stay, a partial hospitalization or day program is often the best step-down level of care for a child who has been in crisis. Also, if a child is not dangerous to "self or others," is not psychotic, does not need twenty-four-hour medication monitoring, and has a stable living environment, then a partial hospitalization is not an unreasonable option to pursue in lieu of a complete hospitalization.

Partial hospitalization is usually a day program where a child spends from four to six hours a day, three to five times a week, and receives some of the support and therapeutic benefits of a full hospitalization without being separated from his or her family.

Typically a child attends a partial hospitalization program for several weeks, or again, as long as the insurer authorizes the treatment option. Sometimes school districts pay for a day program if they do not have an appropriate placement available (see Chapter 9).

Each morning the child is seen for a medical evaluation; there also are group meetings, therapy, school, classes in coping skills, and recreational activities. The parents are usually involved in a weekly meeting with the child and the psychiatrist, and there is a communications log where the therapists report to the parents each afternoon and the parents write back about the events of the evening.

A mother of a young boy wrote about day hospitalization:

I had to put Robby in this kind of program when he was twelve. It was a "kinder, gentler" place. He was there Monday through Friday from 7:45 to 3:15. In addition to therapy, he had regular seventh-grade classes so the psychiatrist, the social worker, and the special ed teacher could all observe him in a real environment. I really had to fight my insurance company over this, but now they are believers.

Another level of care is an *intensive outpatient program* (IOP), sometimes referred to as a "partial-partial." This is a program that lasts two to three hours a day and often takes place after school. The child attends his or her own school most of the day and then goes to the hospital to receive clinical services.

Parents should also investigate a new type of program known as a *subacute program.* This is overnight care that may provide respite for the child and the family and a very structured environment at a time when the child may still be fragile.

It has to be said: The insurers are going to want to see a reduction in services as quickly as possible, and the psychiatrist involved in the child's care will have to be very smart and persistent to make sure the child's interests are best served. A solid alliance between the parents and the psychiatrist is invaluable at all times, but especially during and after a crisis situation.

## COMMITMENT LAWS FOR OLDER ADOLESCENTS OR "EMANCIPATED MINORS"

A parent of a young child or adolescent can simply sign commitment papers requesting psychiatric hospitalization. But at a certain age, and in certain circumstances, a young person is no longer considered a minor, and the commitment process becomes much more complicated. In most states, once a "child" reaches the age of eighteen or twenty-one, he or she is viewed by the law as having reached adult status; or if an adolescent has been living away from home for a certain period of time, he or she is regarded as an "emancipated minor." A fifteen-year-old girl who has given birth may be by definition a mother *and* an emancipated minor. And if that young adult or emancipated minor does not see the need for a psychiatric hospitalization, and the parents do, then the only recourse the parents have is to pursue an involuntary commitment.

And now we enter the very complicated world of commitment law and all its attendant guilt and furor.

The purpose of commitment law is to enable persons who are mentally ill to be hospitalized for treatment before they harm themselves or others, even if they do not believe they need treatment. Each state enacts its own legislation governing commitment, and the laws of each state are constantly changing.

Commitment laws actually rest on two legal foundations: (1) *parens pa-*

*triae,* the right of the state to act as a parent and protect the well-being of a citizen who cannot care for him- or herself (this concept evolved from English common law, which held that the king was "father" of all his subjects); and (2) the right of the state to protect its citizens from a person who is dangerous. This means that if a person is so disabled that he or she cannot recognize the need for treatment, cannot provide for his or her own basic needs, or may otherwise be dangerous to him- or herself or to others, that person may be committed to a psychiatric treatment hospital for a specified period of time.

In the 1960s, however, civil libertarians focused on issues of freedom for individuals and pushed for tighter and tighter restrictions governing involuntary commitment. In 1975, a U.S. Supreme Court ruling dictated that a state cannot confine a patient who refuses voluntary hospitalization and who can manage outside a hospital alone, or with the help of family or friends. Thus states began to demand proof that a person is mentally disturbed and a danger to self or others.

Some states are a little more flexible and do not rely strictly on "dangerousness" criteria. (The *parens patriae* rationale still plays a part.) For example, the state of South Carolina says that a person can be committed if "he is mentally ill, and needs treatment because he (1) lacks sufficient insight or capacity to make responsible decisions with respect to his treatment, or (2) there is a likelihood of serious harm to himself or others." The chances of getting a commitment in a state such as this are greater than in New Hampshire, whose law has no such latitude and states that a "person must exhibit dangerousness to self or others."

But what proof demonstrates that a person is dangerous to self or to other people? The least stringent level of proof is "clear and convincing evidence," while the "beyond a reasonable doubt" level of proof demanded by states such as California, Kentucky, Massachusetts, New Hampshire, and Oregon makes commitment more difficult.

State law also dictates the procedure for initiating commitment. The following paragraphs describe the process in the state of New York, but the reader can check the procedure in his or her state by calling the admissions office or emergency room of the nearest hospital, by calling the police, or by contacting the county mental health association or the state's local NAMI chapter (see Resources on page 437).

In the state of New York, if a family member or responsible adult sees that a person is exhibiting conduct that is dangerous to self or others, he or she can try to get the person into a hospital either by calling the police or by going to the State Supreme Court and filing a petition for commitment. (The patient must have made a suicide attempt or have acted in a menacing fashion, such as punching people or harboring a weapon such as a knife; or the patient must be dazed or confused and seem unable to take care of him- or herself.) If the responsible adult calls the police and they fail to check out the situation (they more often do respond—and quickly), the responsible adult must go to the Supreme Court and file a petition (an affidavit) setting forth the reasons why this person needs to be hospitalized and why the person is a danger to self or others.

If the judge who hears the argument is convinced of its validity, a warrant is issued, and the police can then find the person and take him or her to the emergency room of a hospital for an evaluation. In order for the patient to be admitted, the evaluating psychiatrist must decide that the person is a danger to self or others. Within seventy-two hours, a second doctor must confirm that opinion or the patient is released. However, if the second doctor does confirm the need for hospitalization, the patient can be held under an emergency commitment status for a period not to exceed fifteen days. The patient is released at the end of this time unless the director of the hospital or the family petitions the court for a longer period of commitment.

If the person is still delusional or dangerous at the end of the fifteen days, his or her status can be converted to a longer-lasting commitment only when two psychiatrists sign a certificate and a family member or responsible adult living with the patient signs a petition requesting a longer commitment and outlines the reasons for doing so.

At any time, the patient has the right to go to court and contest the commitment. A mental health information lawyer represents him or her at a hearing held before a judge. (Usually a judge's chambers are located in the hospital.) The patient, family members, and examining psychiatrist testify at the hearing, and normal judicial rules of evidence and due process apply.

Today the national trend is toward making it easier to commit involuntary patients with psychiatric illnesses. Addressing the issue, the American Psychiatric Association has devised a model commitment law that would allow commitments not only when patients are dangerous to self and others but also when they are suffering and would likely deteriorate without treatment; in the presence of a major psychiatric illness that could be treated, provided the treatment is available; and when patients are incapable of deciding for themselves.

In the past few years Arizona, Delaware, Hawaii, Iowa, Oklahoma, New York, and South Carolina have amended their laws and made it easier to commit a psychiatrically ill patient to a hospital.

It takes an enormous amount of stamina and courage to press for an involuntary commitment, but the relative who decides to do so needs to understand that he or she is probably the only person who stands between the patient and the dangers that exist during an acute phase of the illness. We have had patients write to us and tell us that once they became stable, they were grateful to the relative who took such a stand. One person who had been in a delusional state said: "If a family member won't take care of me when I'm in this condition, who will?"

We wish we could say that, with excellent treatment, a child will never need hospitalization. But the very nature of being a child—a growing person whose height and body weight and metabolic processes change daily—makes treatment a tricky proposition. In puberty, the cascade of estrogens, progesterone, luteinizing hormone, and gonadotropins can induce or inhibit genes that affect neurotransmission and neuropeptide systems and potentially make the adolescent more vulnerable to breakthrough episodes (episodes that occur despite treatment) or relapse. And most adolescents decide to stop taking their meds at least once, either because they are uncomfortable with the idea of being different or uncomfortable with the side effects, or they feel well and are convinced that they don't have a problem anymore. Hospitalizations may be needed to fine-tune the medications, to calm extreme agitation, or to prevent self-injurious behavior.

This is why we so strongly suggest that parents check their insurance policies and visit the hospitals in the networks of managed care companies. Then, if anything happens, the family is more comfortable with their decision. Naturally, the ideal would be complete stabilization at home, but hospitalization is not a sign of failure. Remember, the goal is not to avoid hospitalization so much as it is to keep the child alive and well.

# The Insurance Maze

We doubt that there's a person on the planet who, when asked the proverbial question "What do you want to be when you grow up?," answers enthusiastically: "I want to accumulate an absolutely enormous amount of knowledge about neurological brain disorders; I want to know as much about Section 504 of the law as any educational attorney; and I want the vocabulary of managed care to come so trippingly off my tongue as to astonish all those around me."

And yet the parents of a child with bipolar disorder must assimilate and master all this and much, much more.

These parents have an enormous burden: Life inside the home can be a virtual war zone; life outside the home seems fair game to the intrusion of strangers. September is a nightmare because the stresses of the school year begin; June is a nightmare because just as the stresses of the school year end, the unstructured, endless days of summer begin. . . . Nothing is simple; nothing can be taken for granted, and parents are always scrambling for new strategies and better solutions.

So to add financial strain, serious debt, and, in some cases, near-financial ruin in order to pay for diagnostic consultations, weekly visits to psychopharmacologists and psychologists, neuropsychological testing, multiple medication trials of long-term and often costly prescriptions, and individual, couples, and family therapies seems downright unfair.

While there is much we can't change, we hope that this chapter serves to allay some of the anxiety and clear up the confusion about paying for this enormously expensive illness. After we discuss the sea change in the delivery of mental health care that arrived with managed care, we'll move into the world of public insurance. These discussions should help children get the services they need—even when it looks as if all avenues are closed. Built into the system are options and appeals and "unadvertised" financial support programs. In the following pages, we explore some of them as well as the economic realities of the mental health marketplace.

## PRIVATE INSURANCE FOR MENTAL HEALTH CARE

Private medical insurance and all the plans that, for a premium, seek to cover doctor's fees and hospitalization fees are called *fee-for-service* plans. The insurance company underwrites some of the patient's health care, but it is the patient's responsibility to locate the doctor to supply it and then file the claims for reimbursement. The doctor determines the medical treatment, and the insurance company asks few questions. Once a person meets a *deductible,* the service is reimbursed; typically the insurance company covers 80 percent of the incurred medical fees; the patient, the remaining 20 percent.

But the provisions for mental illness in such plans have always been more restrictive than for "medical" illness. Insurance companies typically limit their risk by capping the dollar amounts of annual and lifetime mental health benefits; requiring preadmission certification for hospitalization; limiting services covered, often with incentives for outpatient care; charging higher copayment and deductible amounts; and excluding coverage for certain disorders. These practices are discriminatory, and people with serious psychiatric illnesses are often denied sufficient coverage and have few choices but to try to obtain treatment from public mental health services or even to go without treatment entirely.

Group policies that cover employees through their place of business, union, or professional organization are much less expensive and usually more generous than individual policies, but not always when it comes to psychiatric coverage. Often an employer can choose just how broad or limiting the psychiatric coverage might be, but the standard policy typically pays for thirty to sixty days per year of inpatient care and for perhaps twenty office visits for therapy per year. Employees are used to paying most of their own therapy bills themselves. (Due to stigma, many people never avail themselves of the little coverage offered because they refuse to process claims for mental health services through the company.)

And then there are preexisting illness clauses written into most policies. Questions such as "Have you or any named dependent within the past five years had any mental or physical disorder?" may eliminate benefits for a certain period of time or deny them completely.

So, it's good to keep in mind that psychiatric coverage never really had a "Golden Age." In almost all cases it was inadequate, but especially for someone with a chronic psychiatric disorder.

## MANAGED CARE: A RADICAL CHANGE IN THE DELIVERY OF HEALTH CARE

Today some 85 percent of America's employees are enrolled in some kind of managed care program. It is a system of organizing, financing, delivering, and evaluating services that deliberately seeks to control costs while promising to deliver high-quality health care.

The original idea behind the health maintenance organization (HMO) concept was to have health insurance and health services integrated by the same organization, under the same roof. This system provides a follow-through on patient care and an emphasis on preventive care. HMO members pay a fixed monthly or quarterly premium and receive health care from a team of physicians, nurses, technicians, and other health professionals. This model for the delivery of health care eliminates deductibles, reimbursement forms, charges minimal copayments, and provides plenty of patients for doctors.

Today's managed care organizations are simply networks of independent physicians who are called *providers* and who sign on to panels and agree to direct a patient's treatment according to guidelines set by the managed care companies. The doctors are reimbursed according to a fee structure also set by the managed care company.

Why on earth would doctors agree to this system? Well, as employers thrilled to the idea that there might be a brake on skyrocketing costs of health care and signed contracts with managed care companies to provide health care for their employees, physicians not associated with these managed care networks lost the possibility of treating many of these patients. Most doctors simply decided to ride the horse in the direction it was going.

Moreover, managed care companies instituted a system known as *capitation*. They give doctors a fixed amount of money every month and guarantee them a certain income if the doctors agree to provide a range of services to a specified group of patients. If the patient never shows up, or if the doctor can provide the services for less than the capitation received, the doctor can keep the difference. If, however, the doctor provides more extensive services than the capitation covered, the doctor underwrites the difference.

But built into this system is an incentive to limit the range of services or watch profit margins slip to razor-thin proportions.

The balance of power has shifted from the physician to insurers. Insurers decide which tests financially (not medically) can be conducted, what kind of treatments may be offered, and how often those treatments can occur by limiting what they will pay for. And because many of today's managed care companies are "for-profit" organizations, insurers are looking to the bottom line and are answering to shareholders, not necessarily to the patient's needs or the doctor's medical opinion of these needs.

Some organizations forced doctors to sign (the now-infamous) "gag rules": Doctors were told not to inform patients of alternative treatment strategies or medication options if they were viewed as more expensive. Fortunately these restrictive practices are being regulated out of existence.

Not only are doctors chafing under this new system of care, but patients are extremely anxious about physician choice. If their doctor is not on the panel of the company that provides their benefits, then they must leave their physician in order to receive maximum reimbursement. Most managed care plans do have a *dual-option plan* that allows a patient to seek care outside the network, but the patient must pay deductibles and co-payments and claims are reimbursed at a far lower rate. And the specialist must be referred to by the *primary care physician* (the PCP) whom the patient accepts when he or she signs on for the insurance.

A PCP is typically a family practitioner or an internist who acts as a "gatekeeper" to a network of specialists. Managed care philosophy is that a patient should first see a generalist who can explore whether a patient really needs the attention of a more expensive specialist or further testing.

For example, under the old fee-for-service plans, a patient who was troubled by headaches could make an appointment with a neurologist of his or her choice. The neurologist, in turn, would probably order a brain scan and other expensive tests, and the patient would then submit the bills to the insurer for reimbursement.

The managed care company argues that the patient should see a generalist first—a doctor who knows and understands the patient—and who may determine that the headaches are caused by stress, by allergies, by the wrong eyeglass prescription, or by masked depression, and attempt to solve the problem with commonsense, low-tech, and certainly less costly solutions. If none of these possible causes is at the root of the problem, then the patient may be referred to a specialist.

This sounds good and reasonable until you learn that managed care companies are not fond of doctors who make too many referrals to specialists and spoil their profit picture. Since the doctor's referral rate is keenly watched by the managed care company, there is a subtle pressure to be very conservative with referrals to specialists. Access to care is a grave concern.

Another thorn in the health care professional's side is that he or she must answer to an employee of the managed care company—the *case manager*—who has nowhere near the physician's level of training and expertise and who questions the physician about his or her treatment plans based on formulas and company policies driven by economic considerations. Add to these intrusions the lack of confidentiality between doctor and patient that this system insists on, endless paperwork, and often slow-paying methods of the managed care companies, as well as the fact that the reimbursement fees are far below doctors' customary fees (moreover, an established authority in his or her specialty is reimbursed with the same fee as a doctor straight out of a residency-training program), and you have a group of disgruntled, demoralized people providing you with health care.

Oddly, the managed care companies have taken a combative stance with the very people who are the bedrock of their existence: doctors and patients. Many doctors are disenrolling from panels; some are leaving medicine entirely.

Patients are beginning to fear that although preventive care is handled nicely by managed care, a truly serious illness would find them fighting for their lives as well as their pocketbooks. A poll taken by *Time* magazine and CNN in July 1998 found that fewer than half of the people questioned were confident that their current managed care health plan would pay for treatment if things turned serious and expensive.

Something else is being lost in this bottom-line mentality. America's academic training and research center hospitals are in great jeopardy. Because these institutions are traditionally more expensive than nonacademic ones—due to their taking on the most severely ill patients and the costs of education—managed care companies tend to contract with the nonacademic hospitals for the sake of cost efficiency. Thus important centers of research and postgraduate training, which typically develop and offer more innovative treatments, are suffering financially, and parents with bipolar children often don't have the option of having their child hospitalized in such centers.

These days no one can afford to blink when observing the managed care revolution. As quickly as employers embraced the HMO models, this form of restricted care is being superseded in recent enrollments by the *preferred provider organization* (PPO) model. Members can go to doctors and hospitals outside of the network, but it costs them more. At least they don't have to be funneled through gatekeepers to specialists who may not be of their choosing.

There may be some good news in the mental health arena of managed care, referred to as "behavioral health care." Some of its benefits and philosophies (at least on paper) may be more advantageous than those offered in the fee-for-service policies.

For example, one policy we looked at offered a choice of three hospitals in the area, and there was no lifetime cap on psychiatric inpatient days. Many families with fee-for-service policies have lifetime caps of $25,000 for mental health. Since children develop bipolar disorder early in life and may undergo several hospitalizations, the lifetime cap can be reached after one or two hospitalizations.

The lifetime cap on psychiatric benefits is something every family with a child with bipolar disorder needs to investigate. Thanks to the passing of the 1996 Mental Health Parity Act, all group health plans with fifty or more workers must equalize the annual and lifetime limits imposed on mental and physical health care. This means that if there is a $1 million lifetime cap on medical illness, then the theoretical lifetime cap on psychiatric hospitalization must be the same. But we hear stories of health plans limiting access in subtle ways. (This also means that companies with under fifty employees are exempt from this law, and companies that have opted to choose policies that have medical caps can legally have caps on mental health benefits also.)

Although many policies offer about twenty outpatient office visits to a psychiatrist a year, a senior staff psychiatrist at Kaiser Permanente told us that medication visits (office visits where prescriptions are reviewed, renewed, or written) are unlimited. This is a vital benefit for families of children with early-onset bipolar disorder who will need medication and monitoring for such a long time.

Parents should ask their insurers about a *conversion of benefits* provision. A policyholder can choose to convert inpatient days for outpatient psychotherapy visits as well as aggregate visits for family therapy. For example, if a family decides that family therapy is the most appropriate use of outpatient visits, they can utilize twenty visits of one family member, and then the twenty visits of the next, and so forth. Medical directors are aware that the people closest to the patient—the family—can suffer from stress-related medical illnesses, and they view family therapy as a preventive type of medicine.

This all sounds good, and the prescription coverage of most policies is a boon that cannot be underestimated, but the doctor who understands how to treat bipolar disorder in children is the cornerstone on which any quality of life for the child and the family rests. If possible, it is best to check which child psychiatrists are on the panel before signing on. Not only is it terribly difficult to find a child psychiatrist who understands this illness, but it's not clear how many of those who participate in a panel that reimburses them far below their customary fee do have such knowledge and skill.

## How Does Your Policy Read?

Look carefully at the wording of any policy before or even after enrolling. (Even if you have no choice, it's important to imagine a future in which there might be a crisis or a need for extensive psychiatric care.) If a benefits package uses phrasing such as "adequate mental health care" or "care where medically necessary," find out what this means in the insurer's lexicon. Find out the answers to the following questions:

• Which child psychiatrists, pediatric neurologists, and psychologists are on the panel of this insurer? In other words, which doctors are "in-network"? What if none of these physicians has experience treating early-onset bipolar disorder? How will I be reimbursed if my child continues to see his or her out-of-network psychiatrist?

• Will the psychologist's bills be covered if there is no psychiatrist practicing in the same office?

• How many outpatient visits are allowed each year? If the visits are for medication monitoring, are they unlimited? At what point does the psychiatrist have to ask approval for additional sessions?

• For hospital care, what is the maximum amount of days and the dollar cap per year allowed by the policy? What is the lifetime cap, assuming that the company has less than fifty employees and is exempt from the Mental Health Parity Act?

• Should my child need psychiatric hospitalization, which hospitals in my area are in-network? If I go to the emergency room of an out-of-network hospital, will it be covered? How much of it will be covered? What if the hospitals are unsatisfactory to me?

• What is the prescription plan? Is there a limit on the number or total costs of medications each year? What is the charge if I choose brand-name medications over generic ones? (See discussion of the differences in Chapter 4.) Are expensive, nongeneric medications such as Risperdal, Abilify, and Lamictal on the list of approved prescription medicines (the formulary) that the health plan agrees to pay for? Is the child psychiatrist allowed to prescribe these expensive brand-name drugs, or must he or she get authorization from the managed care company beforehand? Will this approval be difficult to get and be frowned on, adding to the doctor's discomfort and reluctance to prescribe?

• Does the plan offer alternative service options such as day treatment (partial hospitalization), residential care, or intensive outpatient care in time of crisis? How many days are usually covered?

• How do I appeal decisions and file a grievance if I am not satisfied with the decisions being made about the psychiatric care of my child or my child's access to care?

If you feel you're being denied access to care, each managed care company has a phone number to call and a procedure for initiating an appeal process. Consumers and physicians sit on the grievance committee. (And new legislation may provide the right to appeal a managed care decision by going to an outsider.) It's not unlikely that an appropriate request will be granted in the appeals process. Managed care companies are very concerned about consumer satisfaction because if valued employees are not happy, then the employer paying for the coverage is going to consider switching managed care companies when the contract comes up for review.

One mother (who said she was willing to go to any lengths to avoid confrontation) described her mother lioness behavior when it became important to face off with the managed care company in order to ensure the proper treatment for her twelve-year-old son. She said:

> We are in an HMO insurance plan and we live out of the network area. For our mental health benefits we were referred to a gatekeeper. The gatekeeper psychiatrist met with us for fifteen minutes and then referred us to a psychiatrist in their network. She was good with Daniel but was clueless as to what his problems were. She diagnosed him ADD and maybe depressed and put him on Ritalin and Adderall. BIG MISTAKE! He was soon out of control big time, and she said that she had done all she could and he needed a "higher level of care."
>
> At this point the insurance company wanted to send him to a psychiatric hospital in our area, but one that cared mostly for kids with drug problems.
>
> I threw the biggest fit and told them I was not putting a twelve-year-old on a unit with drug addicts. I refused to back down and kept going up their higher chain of command. I literally had to browbeat the insurance company into placing him in a child and adolescent psych center that I approved of. It wasn't an easy or pleasant thing to go through, but now the insurance company listens to me. Anytime Daniel needs something they won't provide, I start going up their chain of command again and they back off.
>
> I would advise people not to let an insurance company make them use a psychiatrist they are not comfortable with. (After all, it was the psychiatrist's incorrect diagnosis and prescription of Ritalin and Adderall that precipitated the mania and resulted in the need for hospitalization.) Never back off—it's our right and we are the ones paying for the insurance.

## Public Insurance

People who work full time for a company that employs more than fifty people on its payroll usually receive health benefits through that company. But employees whose place of work has fewer than fifty people may have to purchase medical coverage for their families by themselves, at huge costs.

Self-employed workers also have to purchase their own policies. If they belong to a professional organization that offers a group health plan, most likely they can purchase coverage through that association, but the premiums to cover a family typically cost more than $650 a month. (Buying a single-family policy without benefit of a group is prohibitive for most families, in the range of $1,200 a month.)

What happens to people who don't work full time or who are out of work? How do these parents obtain medical insurance for their families? What if they had a child suffering with bipolar illness—how would they cover the phenomenal medical expenses?

Fortunately, the federal government—acting through state programs—provides money for public health insurance and disability insurance to those who can't afford private medical coverage and who qualify for these programs.

"Qualify" is the operative word here. There are strict guidelines governing the granting of the entitlement programs. First we'll discuss Medicaid and Medicaid waiver programs mandated by certain states that offer financial aid to children who have special needs. Then we'll explore the new children's insurance program that was passed by Congress in 1998. It is called the State Children's Insurance Program (SCHIP), and it expands health insurance to a great many uninsured children. Finally we'll discuss Supplemental Security Income (SSI), which is available for some children who are disabled by a psychiatric problem.

## Medicaid

Medicaid is a federally mandated national program of medical assistance for people and families who have limited incomes. The program is financed by federal, state, and local taxes and administered by local public assistance programs. (Look in the telephone book under City Government Departments and scan down the sublistings until you find Social Services; or sometimes it's listed under Government and Community Services under the heading "Medicaid.")

The Medicaid program provides children with mental illnesses with a comprehensive benefits package. It covers diagnostic screening and assessment, psychological testing, psychotherapy, prescription drugs, lab tests, and hospitalizations (inpatient and partial as well as day treatment), and the family is not responsible for deductibles or copayments. The disadvantage of Medicaid is that it reimburses professionals and hospitals with very low fees. Consequently, many doctors and hospitals do not accept Medicaid patients, and most often a child will be hospitalized in a city, county, or state facility. (But as we mentioned in Chapter 12, that is not necessarily a bad thing.)

How does a family qualify for Medicaid? It's complicated. Children under the age of six whose family income is up to 133 percent of the national poverty level—and children born after September 30, 1983, whose family income is up to 100 percent of the poverty level—now qualify for Medicaid in every state.

If the national poverty level for a family of four in most states is $19,350, multiply that figure by 100 or 133 percent and you will arrive at the allowable family income that qualifies a family for Medicaid.

Certain income, assets, and possessions are excluded when determining the family's income: The home the family lives in and the land it's built on are not counted; the family car usually does not count either.

Once the family meets the poverty guidelines, the child has to be suffering with a disability that is on the Supplemental Security Income (SSI) medical listing.

Generally, the definition of "disability" for children requires that:

- A child have a physical or mental condition or conditions that can be medically proven and results in marked and severe functional limitations
- The medically proven physical or mental condition or conditions must last or be expected to last at least twelve months
- The child cannot be working at a job that is considered substantial work

So a child with a documented history of bipolar disorder should be able to obtain a Medicaid card if the family income and the clinical history meet the disability criteria requirements.

Every three years a child has a disability review, and, at the age of eighteen, the child's eligibility is redetermined.

## Medicaid's Home and Community Waivers and the Katie Beckett Story

Medicaid's limitations on income levels are quite rigid, but in some states there are exceptions to the rules. These exceptions are referred to as *waivers,* and they come into existence when a state applies for (and is granted) exemptions from the standard Medicaid regulations. In other words, waivers allow the state to provide services that are not available under the state Medicaid Plan. These waivers are often referred to as Katie Beckett Waivers or Home and Community Waivers.

You can call your local Medicaid office and ask if you qualify for such a waiver. These waivers are not advertised. Just ask: "What waivers do you have, and what populations do they serve?" You're looking for one that serves children with severe psychiatric disorders.

All families should know about a wonderful grassroots organization called Family Voices in Albuquerque, New Mexico. Family Voices is a network of families and friends speaking on behalf of children with special health care needs. The people at this organization can give you all the information about each state's waiver programs. They will tell you if you qualify, refer you to your state coordinator, and match you with a family that has applied for the Katie Beckett or Home and Community Waiver and who can guide you through the process. Contact Family Voices at 1-888-835-5669 or at www.familyvoices.org.

## State Children's Insurance Program (SCHIP)

On August 5, 1997, Congress signed the Balanced Budget Law, which, among other things, created a new children's health program that purchases health insurance for uninsured children. The legislation became effective on October 1, 1997.

Each state has the opportunity to create its own children's health program or to expand its current Medicaid program. If the state does choose to create a new children's health program, it has enormous flexibility in defining the benefits covered, selecting health plans, using managed care, and setting payment rates, but each state's proposed plan must meet the requirements outlined in the law and be approved by the secretary of Health and Human Services.

SCHIP is a program designed for the working poor—for people whose incomes are somewhere between 150 and 300 percent of the poverty level. Again, if the national poverty level for a family of four is $19,350, then a family in the state of South Carolina (a 150 percent state) must make less than $29,025 to qualify; a family in the state of Missouri (a 300 percent state) must make less than $58,056 to qualify. (We have heard repeatedly that some people with children suffering with bipolar disorder look carefully at a state's SCHIP before taking a job in that state. For a family without private insurance, and with one or two children with bipolar disorder, this decision is not something to treat lightly.)

To check on your state's plan and get eligible children enrolled in SCHIP, call toll-free at 1-877-KIDSNOW (543-7669), or go online at www.insurekidsnow.gov/.

## Supplemental Security Income (SSI)

Supplemental Security Income (SSI) is a federal program that provides financial and medical assistance to children under the age of eighteen who are blind or who have a severe disability or chronic illness and who are financially needy. In 2002 children who were eligible received close to $545 a month (and more in the states that supplement this federal benefit; for instance, the state of Massachusetts will contribute an additional $100 per month). A child qualifies solely because of need, and naturally the more money the family makes, the smaller the check will be. But once a child receives even one dollar a month from SSI, he or she always receives free health care through Medicaid. And it's the Medicaid benefits that are so important to the parents of a bipolar child.

Once a child has been diagnosed as having bipolar disorder, it is not hard to document that the child is disabled and "has marked and severe functional limitations" from a mental condition, and that the condition is expected to last at least twelve months. Social Security has a "Listing of Impairments" that are laid out in its book *Disability Evaluation Under Social Security.* It lists the criteria for mood disorders in children with a requirement that a number of symptoms be present to meet the impairment. A child with bipolar disorder would meet every one of the criteria listed, so the impairments of early-onset bipolar disorder will not be in dispute (especially if all records of hospitalization, time lost from school, and documentation from doctors are included with the application), but it's the financial piece of the picture that is very complicated and takes a bit of explaining.

*Financial Eligibility*

If a child with bipolar disorder lives with parents or stepparents who do not receive SSI themselves, Social Security counts the parents' income and resources, then subtracts certain types of resources and income. The resources that are not counted are:

- The family home and the land it sits on
- Personal belongings, furniture, and other household goods worth up to $2,000
- A car
- Life insurance policies that, combined, have a cash surrender value of less than $1,500; a pension fund or Individual Retirement Account; and property needed for work, such as farmland and equipment

Not counted as income are:

- Benefits received by other family members, such as welfare payments, SSI, and veteran's pensions
- Food stamps and housing or home energy assistance
- Foster care payments
- One-third of child support payments received
- Grants or loans for education

So what does count as income? Any wages, salary, or tips paid to family members through employment by others or for themselves (earned income) and any monies that don't come from employment. This includes a portion of child support, veteran's benefits, interest, unemployment, or workers' compensation, and most public benefits.

The chart that follows should give an idea of the maximum amount of monthly earned and unearned income parents can have to be eligible for SSI benefits for their child. Two parents with two children—one with bipolar disorder and one without—can earn about $39,600 a year before their child would become ineligible, and more than that amount in states that provide supplements.

*Income Eligibility*

Parents' maximum monthly income for a child with a disability to be eligible for at least $1 of SSI. (The dollars are for 2005. They change each year to reflect inflation.) *The maximum levels are higher in states that supplement SSI.*

### COUNTABLE *EARNED* MONTHLY INCOME

| Number of Other Children with No Disability in the Household | When Eligibility Ceases | |
| --- | --- | --- |
| | One-Parent Household | Two-Parent Household |
| 0 | $2,411 | $3,015 |
| 1 | $2,728 | $3,302 |
| 2 | $2,945 | $3,589 |
| 3 | $3,302 | $3,876 |

### COUNTABLE *UNEARNED* MONTHLY INCOME

| Number of Other Children with No Disability in the Household | When Eligibility Ceases | |
| --- | --- | --- |
| | One-Parent Household | Two-Parent Household |
| 0 | $1,198 | $1,485 |
| 1 | $1,485 | $1,772 |
| 2 | $1,772 | $2,059 |
| 3 | $2,059 | $2,346 |

Note: The monthly limit for either type of income increases by $272 for each additional child with no disability in the household.

### *What Kind of Documentation Does Social Security Require?*

If it looks as if the child will qualify for SSI, the parent should go to the local Social Security office or call Social Security at 1-800-772-1213 between 7:00 A.M. and 7:00 P.M. on weekdays. Try to avoid Mondays and the first week of every month, because they are very busy.

A parent needs to bring the following items and documentation when filling out the forms and talking with the Social Security worker:

- Child's Social Security number.
- Child's birth certificate or proof of age.
- Information about the family's income and resources: payroll slips,

income tax return of the year before, bank books, insurance policies, and car registration.

- Medical records and documents from doctors' offices and hospitals
that detail the child's condition and limitations.
- Reports from any provider who has worked with the child in the
past year: psychiatrists, psychologists, therapists, social workers,
teachers, and so on. (Ask providers to submit short written reports
with their formal records. In these reports they should list specific
examples of the child's medical, mental, and functional limitations.)
- Any charting of the illness the parent has recorded.

Social Security now offers a "Child Starter Kit" online for children
eighteen and under. The kit provides general information about the disability programs and the decision-making process that can help take
some of the mystery out of applying for disability benefits.

The Child Starter Kit includes a list of frequently asked questions, a
checklist, and a worksheet to help a parent gather and organize the information and documents needed for the disability interview. The Starter
Kits are available in Spanish and English at www.ssa.gov/disability/
disability_starter_kits.htm. (Note: Any parent who is more comfortable
in a language other than English will be provided with an interpreter by
Social Security.)

All of this information will be sent to an examiner at the state Disability Determination Service. This examiner may call or write for more information, and it should be supplied as quickly as possible. It is not
unusual for a psychological exam to be scheduled also.

Typically it takes three to five months for a determination of disability
to be made. If the child qualifies, a letter will come in the mail and the
SSI payments will be paid retroactively back to the first day of the month
after the parent filed the application.

## Appeals

If the child is not considered eligible, a parent has sixty days to appeal to
the next level of decision making. The form that requests reconsideration
should be filed immediately. Any new reports about the child's condition
should be submitted with the reconsideration request.

If the answer is still no, the parent should not give up. The next step
is a hearing before a Social Security Administrative Law Judge (ALJ).

This is the only chance to meet with the person who will reconsider the decision made about the disability. Parents should know that ALJs reverse more than half of all denials. It is advisable to bring a trained advocate or lawyer to this informal hearing. The local legal aid or bar association or the state Protection and Advocacy agency can usually supply a lawyer. (Call 202-408-9514 to find the state P&A agency; or check the National Association of Protection and Advocacy Systems, Inc., at www.napas.org.) Witnesses such as doctors, teachers, social workers, therapists, and friends can testify and discuss the child's functional limitations at this hearing.

If the child is found not eligible at this level of appeal, a parent has sixty days to request a review by the Social Security Appeals Council, and from there the matter can go to a federal court.

Once a child is found eligible, his or her case is reviewed and reevaluated every three years.

As we were writing this chapter, we often needed to call government agencies (or to find out which government agencies we should call). We spent whole days listening to recorded messages prompting us to select any of a number of options, only to feel that we'd simply gone around in circles. When we did link up finally with a helpful person, all the "Title-this" and "Title-that" programs and the unfamiliar phrasing of the laws and regulations were hard to grasp. And no sooner had we nailed down one piece of information than we were told that each state had its own regulations or that legislation was pending that would amend that rule or limit that program or, in the case of SCHIP, expand that program. One young woman in charge of a Connecticut entitlement program finally said: "You want 'one-stop shopping' and it just doesn't exist in the world of insurance."

But it does, sort of, we came to find. There *are* grassroots organizations that are willing and able to guide the consumer through the maze of insurance and to help parents get their children the medical care they need. The day we stumbled across Family Voices on the Internet (www .familyvoices.org) and called their number in New Mexico, we felt as if we'd come in from the cold. Finally we'd found an organization that knew every state Medicaid waiver and was set up to help a family apply for those as well as for SSI benefits if they qualified. And it's comforting to think that an organization like NAMI can also offer guidance and direction.

You are really not alone, but you will need patience and a lot of persistence. New and dense and difficult subjects take getting used to. After some exposure a few things make sense, and in a while more things make sense, and one day soon you'll be speaking the lingo so well you'll be able to explain it knowledgeably to someone else. Best of all, armed with a newfound understanding of the system and your rights, you'll be able to advocate for your children and get them the treatment they need and are entitled to have.

# PART IV
# Life Goes On

# Agenda
# for the Future

The year we spent on the BPParents listserv not only gave us a rare view of the day-to-day lives of hundreds of families with bipolar children but allowed us to watch the arc of emotional growth that these parents were experiencing. When these mothers and fathers first introduced themselves to the group, you could sense how tentative they were—how hard it was for them to step out and tell their stories. Many wrote how relieved they felt to find out that they weren't the only parents whose children were having these problems. (For years they'd thought they were all alone.) They felt blamed by others for their child's illness, intimidated by mental health professionals, and totally confused about the medications and their side effects. Most were angry at managed care companies and all the "ifs, ands, or buts" of the policies surrounding psychiatric care. All were mystified by the laws that governed accommodations in schools.

Months later, however, these parents were reaching out to welcome other newcomers to the listserv, eager to share the information they'd gained from sitting down every day and reading 175 posts; purchasing and reading the recommended books; and searching for—and absorbing—article after article in the professional literature. We were watching these parents turn into fledgling advocates.

What impressed us time and time again was that these people were on the front lines of a war inside their own homes, getting little support from the outside world, yet wanting to turn a nightmare into something shining and good by helping others in the same situation.

These parents want to channel their anger and energy in a direction that will create a better future for their children and others like them. Currently their "voices" exist only on screens in cyberspace (and now in the pages of this book), but they are beginning to be heard in their own communities. Soon they will make inroads beyond. As one woman put it, "I am now so knowledgeable about early-onset bipolar disorder that I've gone from shaking my head to nodding my head; and now I'm going to find a place to direct all this anger and knowledge and sorrow."

When Tomie Burke invited us to become members of the listserv, we opted not to post directly to the group because we did not want to intrude on this special community. As we read through the seasons of their year, however, we were able to hear time and time again what these parents need and want and are beginning to advocate for. A national agenda could be discerned among the blizzard of pages we downloaded from their daily postings over a twelve-month period, an agenda that requires the talents and energies of physicians, mental health professionals, policy makers, educators, and all family members to highlight areas of neglect and develop models of treatment, research, services, information, and advocacy. Such a national agenda would help ensure a better future for all children suffering with bipolar disorder.

### Parents Want a Quicker Diagnosis and Less of a "Wait-and-See" Attitude

Parents want mental health professionals to leave the *DSM-IV* on the bookshelf and make the diagnosis based on current understanding of how early this illness can onset and how different it appears from the adult form of the disorder. They want doctors to take a long, hard look at the family history and at the subtle signs of a developing mood disorder—to recognize that this illness has myriad symptoms that can look like other childhood psychiatric disorders—and to intervene quickly and knowledgeably with medications that *will not worsen the course of the illness.* They want the residency training programs and the continuing medical education programs to begin to teach what is already published in the psychiatric literature and is becoming increasingly obvious in the psychiatric research community. In short, they want doctors to practice medicine based on today's findings, not yesterday's myths.

### Parents Want the DSM-IV *Updated to Reflect the Realities of Early-Onset Bipolar Disorder*

Until the editors of *DSM-IV* form some kind of emergency committee and amend the criteria for mood disorders in children, diagnosis, research, and clinical treatment is going to founder on the shoals of outdated and skewed information.

### Parents Want the Mental Health Professionals to Regard Them as Collaborators on the Treatment Team for Their Children

They do not want to be blamed or told that they are "overinvolved." They want doctors to anticipate their questions and needs, and recognize that the parents are the on-site experts who are responsible for administering all the medications, watching carefully for side effects, and dealing with the child on a twenty-four-hour basis.

They do not want to hear: "I'll call you if there's a problem with the lithium level; you don't need to know it." *These parents need to know it.* They are charting their sons' and daughters' course of illness, and they will likely need to make corrections in the treatment plan with that doctor or another. Would a doctor tell a parent of a child with cancer "You don't need to understand the treatment?"? We think not.

### Parents Want All Doctors—Whether Psychiatrists, Neurologists, or Pediatricians—to Know About New Treatment Trials

Some children will not respond—or will respond only partially—to commonly prescribed medications. Their parents need to know what other options exist in the psychiatric research community. They need doctors to look for and learn about any new protocols that may help their children.

### Parents Want Managed Care Companies to Stop Placing Limitations on Access to Care

They want managed care companies to understand that when their children are at risk for suicide, they need immediate hospitalization. They do not want to be told: "She's only slightly suicidal, so we can't admit her." (One mother read that story on the listserv and shot back, "Oh, and if she kills herself, will she be only slightly dead?")

They want the parity laws spoken about in Chapter 13 to be adhered to so that families do not "max out" on their insurance benefits. They want the government to take a closer look at the subtle ways mental illness discrimination is being practiced all over the land and access to care is being denied.

Managed care companies, parents, and doctors who treat these children know that it takes weeks to stabilize a child, not six "preauthorized" days. Doctors are not being allowed to use their best judgment; often they are forced to plead for authorization for a few more days of hospitalization. That is an untenable situation for a physician to be in. More often than not, these children are sent home sick and unstable, only to return to the hospital several days or weeks later. In between, the parents are playing ER at home with a child in crisis, at a soul-crushing cost to the family.

## Parents Want More Research Focused on This Devastating Illness of Early Childhood

In 2004, the NIMH spent three times as much money on research in the field of schizophrenia versus that of bipolar disorder. How much of that is dedicated to the field of pediatric bipolar disorder is not known. Certainly not enough. Stepping into the breach are two foundations: the Stanley Medical Research Institute (SMRI) and the National Alliance for Research on Schizophrenia and Depression (NARSAD).

The Stanley Medical Research Institute (SMRI) is the largest private provider of research on schizophrenia and bipolar disorder in the U.S. Each year, SMRI spends approximately $40 million on research on the causes and treatment of both illnesses. This includes approximately two hundred treatment trials, which help develop better medications for children and adolescents with bipolar disorder.

Since 1987, NARSAD has awarded over $180 million to scientists on the faculty or staff of 330 universities and medical research institutions around the world. NARSAD is dedicated to the idea that all funds solicited go exclusively for research grants. In other words, a dollar donated is a dollar spent on scientific research. (See Resources for NARSAD's address and phone number.)

The Juvenile Bipolar Research Foundation (JBRF) is solely dedicated to funding research that will advance our knowledge about childhood-onset bipolar disorder. Current areas of study include diagnosis and phenomenology, neuroimaging, neuropsychology, molecular genetics studies, chronobiology, and neuroendocrine studies (see Resources for JBRF's address and website).

*Parents Want More Outreach to, and Education for, Families
Struggling with This Disorder*

Several national organizations are addressing these issues; all addresses
and phone numbers are in the Resources section.

In 1999, just as we were readying the manuscript of the first edition
for publication, a group of parents and one physician who met on Tomie
Burke's BPParents listserv founded the Child and Adolescent Bipolar
Foundation. True to its mission, the foundation offers a great deal of information, support, and advocacy for families with children suffering
with early-onset bipolar disorder.

In the winter of 2002, the National Alliance for the Mentally Ill created the Child and Adolescent Action Center to focus attention on systems of care reform and to help young families in need. The Center
intends to drive the debate on child and adolescent psychiatric illness system reform, ensure improved treatment outcomes for children and adolescents by advancing evidence-based practices, and provide outreach to
underserved populations, among other agendas. A free quarterly newsletter called *NAMI Beginnings* offers up-to-date information on legislation,
research, and treatments, as well as model programs that help families
cope.

The National Mental Health Association (NMHA) has 340 affiliates
around the country. The NMHA advocates on the state and federal level
with the juvenile justice system and for juvenile justice legislation, and is
responsible for several initiatives that focus on children's mental health.

The Depression and Bipolar Support Alliance (DBSA), which has over
one thousand affiliates in the United States, is an organization of individuals who have been diagnosed with depression or bipolar disorder and
their family members. Many of the affiliates are beginning to start groups
for the parents of bipolar children and adolescents. DBSA publishes a
newsletter, runs a national bookstore, and is a good source of information
and referral.

*Parents Want Schools to Educate Teachers and Other Staff About
This Disorder*

Because so many students are suffering from mood disorders, there should
be annual educational seminars for teachers, psychologists, guidance
counselors, and administrators to raise awareness about these disorders.
Model IEPs—taking into consideration periods of depression and activation—should be developed and implemented. Bipolar students should

have a place to go to pull themselves together and a person on staff who understands what they are going through. Social skills programs should be offered.

### Parents Desperately Need a Greater Choice of Smaller, Therapeutic Schools That Would Be Appropriate for Children with Bipolar Disorder

There are far too few specialized schools and programs, often long bus rides away, and far too many waiting lists. Bipolar children do not belong in classes with children whose IQs are far below theirs; nor do they belong in classes with juvenile delinquents. New programs are going to have to be instituted.

### Parents Want Drug Prevention Programs in Schools Tailored to Their Children

Students in middle school should be taught about the risks of addiction. Parents want the programs to incorporate the findings that people with bipolar disorder are vulnerable to becoming addicted to alcohol or drugs.

### Parents Do Not Want the Juvenile Justice System to Become the Hospitals of the Future

Because many states have slashed budgets for adolescent psychiatric hospitals and managed care makes it so difficult to hospitalize an adolescent, and because adolescents with bipolar disorder and conduct disorder act out so many of their problems, there's a good chance that the only place they can be "parked" is in jail. Adolescents do *not* belong in juvenile detention centers. Communities and policy makers must make major efforts to create more child and adolescent psychiatric units in general hospitals. Parents are going to have to survey their communities, identify the services lacking, and start fighting to get them in place. The Federation of Families is working to create wraparound services that bring together families, personnel from child welfare, juvenile justice, and the school system, who, as a team, help devise an integrated plan that fits the needs of the child and the family and keeps the child in the community. Federation of Families has a program that trains people to deliver these integrated systems of care.

The Child & Adolescent Bipolar Foundation is advocating for the establishment of juvenile mental health courts that will help divert adolescents with bipolar disorder away from the criminal justice system and into court-supervised treatment programs. It is a huge agenda, and one that has been jump-started by parents and family members. Organizations like NAMI, the National Mental Health Association, and the Depression and Bipolar Support Alliance have been advocating on behalf of the mentally ill for years, but only recently with a focus on children with psychiatric disorders. The ranks of such organizations as these and the Child and Adolescent Bipolar Foundation need to be swelled by these families so that legislators listen even more carefully to their concerns.

## CLOSING THOUGHTS

We wish our readers could see the hundreds of e-mails and letters that parents from all over the country sent helping us to better understand the problems that bipolar children and their families face. We have been inspired by their dedication to their children and their heroic efforts to find solutions. We are in awe of these children who get up every morning and struggle through each day, knowing—and never knowing—how a day will unfold. We have felt privileged to have been a part of this community.

A few months ago, the father of a young woman named Becca sent us a newspaper clipping profiling his daughter's early struggles with bipolar disorder. With Becca's permission, we reprint a section of the article here:

> Living with bipolar as a child, Becca suffered many symptoms of the disorder. She suffered with night terrors. She talked uncontrollably. Although she was extremely bright and gifted, she was often in trouble with teachers for distracting other students. She was unable to concentrate on her studies. She was misdiagnosed for years, first with ADD and ADHD, then with acute anxiety disorder, and finally with obsessive-compulsive disorder. Between ages 7 and 16, she saw seven doctors, none of whom was able to pinpoint the source of the problem. A move at age 14 triggered her most difficult period. Although she and her parents believed she was suffering from bipolar disorder, she was misdiagnosed with major depression, and prescribed an antidepressant in error. At 15, she attempted to end her life.
>
> Looking back, she is grateful that her parents admitted her to a psychiatric hospital, where she began her journey to health. She finally found the right psychiatrist: someone who truly listened,

helped put the pieces of the puzzle together, and prescribed a medication that worked.

Today, with three years of stability under her belt, two years of college behind her, and a very strong support system of friends and family around her, she beams with self-confidence and hope.

Becca talks freely about living with bipolar disorder and how it has affected her life, both positively and negatively. "I think it has made me more self-aware than most people my age," she says. "And I really had to learn how to take care of myself . . . using exercise, nutrition, my support system, all these healthy ways of dealing with stressful times."

Becca is emphatic about her goals. "I want to educate people so they understand what it is like to live with a psychiatric illness. I want them to open up and realize that there is no reason to stereotype, no reason to discriminate. That's really my life goal." She plans on getting her Ph.D. in psychology, specializing in bipolar disorder in children.

We hope the day comes soon when these children can run and play and swing on swings that have *nothing* to do with shifts in moods. When parents can rejoice in the great creativity this illness can confer but can watch a child grow with stability, reaching toward a future that is bright, filled more with sunlight than threatening clouds.

This will happen only if we *all*—researchers, doctors, parents, educators, drug companies, journalists, and policy makers—get involved and make these children's future a national public health priority. We need to reach, so they can reach. We need to reach, so they can soar.

# The Bipolar Child Questionnaire

This questionnaire was displayed on the website Parents of Bipolar Children, and copies were distributed by the leaders of NAMI Child and Adolescent Support Groups and through mental health professionals in our network.

Age
Date of birth
Current grade level
Are you the child's mother, father, or other?
Child's current psychiatric diagnosis
State of residence
Age and sex of siblings

1. How old was your child when you first noticed any behavioral symptoms (e.g., temper tantrums, night terrors, excessive clinginess, separation anxiety, hyperactivity, rapid speech, periods of sadness, periods of irritability or elation, obsessive thoughts)? Please describe what you observed.
2. What did you think these symptoms represented? What did your family, friends, or even strangers tell you they represented?
3. Did any school professionals suggest that your child receive a psy-

chological or psychiatric evaluation? Which school professional made the recommendation? What did he or she think the diagnosis might be? How old was your child at the time?

4. At what age did your child first see a mental health professional? Did you see a social worker, psychologist, psychiatrist, pediatric neurologist, or other? What were the conclusions reached at that evaluation? Were medications prescribed? If yes, which ones? Did the mental health professional inquire about a possible family history of psychiatric illness or alcohol and/or substance abuse?

5. Is there a history of alcohol or substance abuse in the family? If yes, who has the problem?

6. Do you or your spouse suffer with any of the following psychiatric disorders?
Mother: depression, manic-depression (bipolar disorder), phobias, obsessive-compulsive disorder, panic disorder
Father: depression, manic-depression (bipolar disorder), phobias, OCD, panic disorder

7. Do you or your spouse take psychotropic medications? If so, who is taking them, and which ones have been effective?

8. Have you or your spouse ever been hospitalized for depression, mania, or a mixed state?

9. Does anyone on either side of the family have recurrent depression or manic-depression? If yes, who has the illness (e.g., maternal or paternal grandmother or a maternal or paternal uncle, sibling, etc.).

10. Have there been any suicides in the family? Please specify.

11. Were you aware that manic-depression (bipolar disorder) can be manifested in childhood?

12. Did you or your spouse experience symptoms of a mood disorder or any other psychiatric condition in childhood? Please specify.

13. Were you or your spouse ever afraid to have children because of a personal or family history of mood disorders? If yes, please explain.

14. Did you worry about and/or watch your children uneasily?

15. Before your child received any medications, how would you describe your child's behavior in the classroom? Did the child have attentional problems? Did the child fidget and not sit still? Did the child skip school or disregard authority? Did he or she at-

tempt to be the class clown? Was it hard for your child to make and sustain peer relationships?

16. Please describe what problems your child may have had with peer relationships.

17. Does your child have any learning disabilities? If yes, please specify.

18. Was your child ever put on Ritalin or another stimulant? Who prescribed the medication? How did your child respond to the medication?

| Attention: | Improved | No change | Became more distractible |
| Mood swings: | Improved | No change | Mood swings increased |
| Hyperactivity: | Decreased | No change | Increased |

If the behavior of the child worsened after treatment with Ritalin or another stimulant, please describe what you observed.

19. If your child was initially diagnosed as depressed, was antidepressant medication prescribed?

Which one(s)?

If yes, how did he or she respond?

| Mood improved | No change in mood | Mood swings increased |
| Became more aggressive | Had trouble sleeping | Other (please specify) |

If the behavior of the child worsened after treatment with an antidepressant, please describe what changes in behavior you observed.

20. If your child was diagnosed with bipolar disorder, was he or she placed on a mood stabilizer such as lithium or Depakote or some other medication(s) in combination or alone? If yes, please detail the type of medications, the maximum daily dose, the length of the trial, and the response.

21. Once your child was diagnosed with bipolar disorder, how did you and your spouse initially react to the diagnosis? Did you seek a second opinion? How did you feel about putting your child on medication?

22. What was the original episode of illness? Depression or hypomania or mania? What was the duration of the first episode? What is the episode frequency pattern now? Full episode within a 24- to 48-hour period? Full episode within a week? One episode per month? Four or more full episodes per year? One episode per year?

23. How would you describe your child's daily activity level (e.g., ample, difficult to arouse in the morning and increasingly active at night)? Is there a discernible pattern? If so, please describe.

24. Were the child's educators supportive? What did they say or do?

25. How did you explain the illness to your child? How did you explain the illness to his or her siblings?

26. How has the illness changed the relationship between the child and his or her siblings? How has the illness affected the family as a whole?

27. How did you and your family attempt to deal with your child's difficult behaviors? Were any measures particularly effective?

28. Were there any stressors (i.e., a job loss, a move to another community, marital difficulties, or a death in the family) that affected your family in the year prior to the emergence of symptoms in your child? If so, please describe.

29. Has any form of talking therapy been recommended for your child? If yes, what kind (individual, family, group, other)? How has it been helpful?

30. What in your opinion constitutes a good doctor? What would you advise someone to look for?

31. Would a support group for parents of children with bipolar disorder be helpful? Why? If you belong to a support group, how does it help?

32. Is there anything you would especially like to say to us, or any issues you hope will be covered in this book?

33. About early-onset bipolar disorder: What do you know now that you wish you had known when the illness first manifested itself in your child?

# Resources

**ORGANIZATIONS**
The Juvenile Bipolar Research Foundation (JBRF)
550 Ridgewood Road, Maplewood, NJ 07040
973-275-0400
e-mail: info@jbrf.org
www.jbrf.org

Child & Adolescent Bipolar Foundation (CABF)
1000 Skokie Boulevard, Suite 425, Wilmette, IL 60091
847-256-8525
www.bpkids.org

Depression and Bipolar Support Alliance (DBSA)
730 N. Franklin Street, Suite 501, Chicago, IL 60610
1-800-826-3632
www.dbsalliance.org

The National Alliance for the Mentally Ill (NAMI)
200 N. Glebe Street, Suite 1015, Arlington, VA 22203
703-524-7600
www.nami.org

S.T.E.P. Up 4 Kids, Inc.
P.O. Box 65, North Scituate, MA 02066
1-866-922-KIDS
www.stepup4bpkids.com

STARFISH Advocacy Association (SAA)
3341 Warrensville Center Road, Suite 203, Shaker Heights, OH 44122
216-283-2377
www.starfishadvocacy.org

The Stanley Medical Research Institute (SMRI)
5430 Grosvenor Lane, Suite 22, Bethesda, MD 20814
301-571-0760
www.stanleyresearch.org

NARSAD (National Alliance for Research on Schizophrenia and Depression)
60 Cutter Mill Road, Suite 404, Great Neck, NY 11021
1-800-829-8289
www.narsad.org

The National Mental Health Association
2001 N. Beauregard Street, Alexandria, VA 22311
1-800-969-NMHA
www.nmha.org

Federation of Families for Children's Mental Health
1101 King Street, Suite 420, Alexandria, VA 22314
703-684-7710
www.ffcmh.org

Family Voices
2340 Alamo SE, Suite 102, Albuquerque, NM 87107
1-888-835-5669
e-mail: kidshealth@familyvoices.org
www.familyvoices.org

Lithium Information Center
c/o Madison Institute of Medicine
P.O. Box 628365, Middleton, WI 53562-8365
608-827-2470/FAX: 608-827-2479

International Society for Bipolar Disorders
P.O. Box 7168, Pittsburgh, PA 15213
412-605-1412
www.isbd.org

## INTERNET RESOURCES
The Bipolar Child (website of Demitri Papolos, M.D., and Janice Papolos)
www.bipolarchild.com
In-depth information about the disorder, noteworthy e-mail newsletter, model IEP, book-
    store, advice on starting a support group, and authors' contact page and lecture schedule.

Juvenile Bipolar Research Foundation ( JBRF)
www.jbrf.org
Descriptions of foundation-sponsored research, the Child Bipolar Questionnaire translated
    into several languages, the Jeanne and Jeffrey Illustrated Interview for Children (a diag-
    nostic and research screening battery for children with or at risk for bipolar disorder), in-
    formation about juvenile bipolar disorder, professional listservs for physicians and
    therapists treating the children, educational forums for parents and teachers, *Educating and
    Nurturing the Bipolar Child* DVD.

Child and Adolescent Bipolar Foundation (CABF)
www.bpkids.org
Important interactive website offers online support groups, chat rooms, message boards,

learning center, database of professional members and local support groups, mood charts, resource page with information on Social Security, drug database, and international resources.

STARFISH Advocacy Association (SAA)
www.starfishadvocacy.org
Offers excellent online educational classes that help parents become advocates in their children's schools; parents' and teachers' message boards; chat rooms; newsletter; and parent-to-parent support programs.

S.T.E.P. Up 4 BP Kids
www.stepup4bpkids.com
Information about the disorder, promotes parent support groups, holds educational conferences for families and professionals, and advocates for public awareness.

BPSO (Bipolar Significant Others)
www.BPSO.org (click on Children and Adolescent icon)
Internet support group for people in relationships with someone who has a bipolar disorder (children, parents, siblings, spouses, etc.).

McMan's Depression and Bipolar Web
www.mcmanweb.com
Award-winning online weekly newsletter presents the latest research, new therapies, social and legal issues, and book and movie reviews. This site also contains nearly two hundred superb articles, including articles on early-onset bipolar disorder.

National Library of Medicine
www.nlm.nih.gov/medlineplus
Free access to Medline, where over four thousand biomedical journals are archived. Click on "Other Resources" and then on "MEDLINE" to conduct a search of articles dating back to the 1960s. Some full-text articles are available; others are abstracts. Refine your search by using Boolean operator "and." For instance, if you search "lithium" and "neuroprotection" and limit the search from 1996 to 2002, ten references appear.

BipolarNews.org
www.bipolarnews.org
Home of the *Bipolar Network News* newsletter and the latest on bipolar disorders research. This website is divided into three main areas: Life Charting (the Kiddie Chart); the newsletter, which is published three times a year; and daily abstracts from the scientific literature. A primary source for learning about the latest research and discoveries in bipolar disorder.

Teaching LD.Org
www.teachingLD.org
The website for the Division of Learning Disabilities for the Council of Teaching Exceptional Children, this should be a great resource for teachers who are working with children with bipolar disorder. Not only are there general discussion bulletin boards, but the site features information on research-based teaching strategies and approaches and interviews with experts in all aspects of learning disabilities. Particularly helpful to teachers with questions about the best way to work with bipolar children is the "Find a Colleague" section, in which a teacher can build a profile and search a database in order to find other teachers and mentors who are dealing with a child of the same age with the disorder and then share knowledge and strategies of what has been effective.

## Other Websites and Helpful Products

www.BPChildren.com

Offers mood charts, posters, a newsletter, and excellent books such as *Brandon and the Bipolar Bear* (also available in a DVD storytelling format), *Anger Mountain,* and *My Bipolar Roller Coaster Feelings Book and Workbook.*

Tourette Syndrome "Plus"

www.tourettesyndrome.net

Dr. Leslie E. Packer's website provides articles and ideas to help the child with executive function deficits organize homework, estimate time, and make transitions ("switch jobs"). Parents will find the glossaries, the organizers, and the advocacy tutorial extremely helpful. Winner of a Bright Spot on the Web Award.

The Mood Tree

www.moodtree.com

Helps parents and therapists chart the child's moods, feelings, and actions at a particular point in time. This tangible communication tool is rather like a board game with Colorform-like apples. The child can choose these apples and place them on the tree to illustrate what he or she is feeling. High-energy states as well as low ones and mixed states can be captured by the placement of the apples. The Mood Tree is available in a child or adolescent version for $39.95. Order online or call 850-386-3455.

Sensory Comfort Catalog

www.sensorycomfort.com

Provides a selection of products that help children with sensory integration difficulties and attentional problems, such as seamless socks, junior ear muffs that reduce noise levels, blankets that don't itch, soothing tapes that calm or aid attention, and an Easy Focus Center (portable study carrel) that reduces visual stimulation and aids in concentration. Order online or call 1-888-436-2622.

The Courage to Change Catalog

www.couragetochange.com

This catalog for life challenges is a resource for children and their parents, teachers, and therapists. Features products such as games and books that help children deal with anger and low self-esteem, as well as improve social and decision-making skills. Catalog also includes the popular *Magic Island* audiotapes: guided imagery that helps to quiet the mind, soothe the emotions, and expand the imagination. Call 1-800-440-4003.

SparkTop.org

www.SparkTop.org

This site, developed by Schwab Learning, offers children with learning disabilities and/or ADHD ages eight to twelve a number of games, mini-movies, creative opportunities, and a large community of other preteens struggling with the same difficulties. The mini-movies starring Tim and Moby (look under "Explore" and then "BrainPOP") are charming and informative. Cutting-edge technology allows a youngster to compose music, perform and record, write, and create art. They then can post their work to the World Wide Web through the SparkTop Gallery. SparkTop.org helps kids appreciate and understand their own unique brains and discover new ways to succeed in school and life.

# Appendix

## ORGANIZING AND PUBLICIZING A SUPPORT GROUP FOR PARENTS OF BIPOLAR CHILDREN

Years ago, we included a sample press release for publicizing a support group in the back of our book *Overcoming Depression*. Apparently scores of groups mushroomed across the country using that one-page press release and the instructions on how to reach the media. We would like to offer that same help to parents and professionals who would like to start groups in their local communities.

Although online support groups are invaluable for daily support, and you don't need to find a sitter and leave home, an in-person support group increases your chances of finding friends you can socialize with (and call when you're feeling blue) and provides access to resources in your own community. Plus, you may find you can arrange stress-free play dates for your child with other children who have the disorder (it is so important that the children don't grow up feeling they are the only ones who have bipolar disorder), and you can be absolutely sure the other parents in the support group won't be judging your child's behavior and wondering what's going on in your home.

### How to Form a Support Group

Initially you can print up a flyer that says nothing more than: "If you are interested in joining a support group for parents of bipolar children, e-mail me at ____ or call me at ____."

You can put this notice in therapists' and pediatricians' offices, or find out the name and address of social workers who work in a nearby children's psychiatric unit of a hospital and ask them to pass the flyer along to families who have children diagnosed with the disorder.

You also should list the announcement of the group start-up at the website of the Child and Adolescent Bipolar Foundation, as it has a state-by-state directory: www.bpkids.org/supportgroups.

As responses come in, get a feeling for where, when, and how often people are available to meet. Get contact information for each person. E-mail is an effective and easy way to contact many people at once. After you receive your first few responses, make decisions regarding meeting locations, dates, and times. Evening meetings work well for parents who work. Meetings should occur at least once a month to be effective.

### Find a Meeting Location

A good location for a support group meeting is a quiet place, with enough room for everyone to sit comfortably in a circle. Nongroup members should not be able to overhear what is being said in a meeting. Local libraries usually have rooms available for meetings such as these. Check with other group members who may belong to a club, a church, or a synagogue or other organization that will let you use their facility.

Once you have a core group of people and have decided where and when you'll hold the first formal meeting, advertise your fledgling group to the surrounding community. Local newspapers in the area and radio and cable television stations will write about or announce the new group, but you need to write a press release and gather the names and addresses of editors and producers.

### Writing a Press Release

An entire communications network that needs ideas and information exists in each community in this country. The editors—the people who receive the notices of community events—will view you as a reporter in the field, but there are contact formats and skills that you must understand in order to gain coverage. If you send a correctly constructed, properly worded press release, you increase the chances of obtaining publicity for your organization and spreading the message to the public.

The press release is the announcement of your new organization, its intentions, and information concerning its first meeting. Basically it should follow the format of the sample release that follows, but there is plenty of room for variation in the body of the copy. Tell the editor what is happening: when, where, and why. Then follow this information with some background or facts.

If your new group has letterhead stationery, type the release double-spaced on it; if not, plain bond paper will do. The release can be duplicated on a copy machine. Typically releases are mailed out six weeks before scheduled meetings, but it's always a good idea to check the deadline requirements for each publication.

To compile a list of the editors and announcers you should contact with the release, call the general numbers of the newspapers and radio and television stations. (Check your local yellow pages under "Newspapers," "Radio," and "Television—Cable.") Explain that you wish to publicize the start-up of a support group for parents of children with bipolar disorder and that you need to know who handles articles on health-related topics and who handles calendar listings for the community events. Send each of these people a copy of the release. (Don't forget to get e-mail addresses for e-mail press releases also.)

Don't stop there. Follow up within a few days with a telephone call to see whether the editor received the release and to find out if he or she needs any further information. You can be warmer and more immediate on the phone, and you might just stir up enough interest to persuade the editor to do an article about your group. This would be a great coup, as many people in the community who might really benefit from your efforts can read about the group in the local paper, give you a call, and get involved. Interested physicians and mental health professionals will also know how to get in touch with you and will refer parents, and perhaps offer their services to help launch the group.

Once the group is launched, send monthly e-mail announcements to the calendar-listing editor of each paper so that each meeting is noted by the community.

Contact: Maureen Kaylin
(203) 555-4321
mkaylin@aol.com
FOR IMMEDIATE RELEASE
June 26, 2006

## SUPPORT GROUP FOR PARENTS OF BIPOLAR CHILDREN TO HOLD ITS FIRST MEETING — JULY 10, 2006

A newly formed support group for parents of children who have been diagnosed with bipolar disorder will hold its first meeting in the undercroft of St. Stephen's Church, 230 Maple Avenue, Newtown, at 8:00 p.m., July 10, 2006. The public is welcome and encouraged to attend.

Bipolar disorder in children is thought to affect over one million children in this country alone, but it is often mistaken for ADHD or depression. The cardinal symptoms of early-onset bipolar disorder are rapid shifts in mood: The child can veer from irritable, easily annoyed, angry mood states to silly, goofy, giddy elation, and then just as easily descend into low-energy periods of intense boredom, depression, and social withdrawal, fraught with self-recrimination and suicidal thoughts. These abrupt shifts in mood can occur several times a day. Temper tantrums—rages—that go on for protracted periods and during which the child can become very aggressive are also common, as are grandiose thinking and behavior, racing thoughts, and a decreased need for sleep. These children are very often oppositional and defiant and may also suffer severe separation anxiety, night terrors, distractibility, and impulsivity.

Families dealing with such an ill child can quickly become exhausted, traumatized, and isolated. This new group intends to provide support, friendship information, and referrals to the parents and siblings, grandparents and friends. Monthly meetings will feature psychiatrists, researchers, and health professionals who will provide the most current information about the disorder.

For further information about the group and the meeting, please call (203) 555-4321.

# Bibliography

CHAPTER I
Duke, Patty, and Kenneth Turan. *Call Me Anna.* New York: Bantam Books, 1990.
Geller, Barbara, Marlene Williams, et al. "Prepubertal and Early Adolescent Bipolarity Differentiate from ADHD by Manic Symptoms; Grandiose Delusions; Ultrarapid or Ultradian Cycling." *Journal of Affective Disorders* 51 (1998): 81–91.
Gershon, Elliot, et al. "Birth-cohort Changes in Manic and Depressive Disorders in Relatives of Bipolar and Schizoaffective Patients." *Archives of General Psychiatry* 44 (1987): 314–319.
Hershman, D. Jablow, and Julien Lieb. *Manic Depression and Creativity.* Amherst, N.Y.: Prometheus Books, 1998.
Hunt, Swanee. "I Couldn't Help My Daughter." *Good Housekeeping* (November 1996).
Klerman, Gerald, L. Lavori, et al. "Birth Cohort Trends in Rates of Major Depressive Disorder Among Relatives of Patients with Affective Disorder." *Archives of General Psychiatry* 42 (1985): 689–693.
Kramlinger, K. G., and Robert Post. "Ultrarapid and Ultradian Cycling in Bipolar Affective Illness." *British Journal of Psychiatry* 168 (1996): 314–323.
Kranowitz, Carol Stock. *The Out-of-Sync Child.* New York: Penguin Putnam, 1998.
Lewinsohn, Peter M., Daniel N. Klein, and John R. Seeley. "Bipolar Disorders in a Community Sample of Older Adolescents: Prevalence, Phenomenology, Comorbidity, and Course." *Journal of the American Academy of Child and Adolescent Psychiatry* 34 (1995): 454–463.
McInnis, Melvin G., Francis J. McMahon, et al. "Anticipation in Bipolar Affective Disorder." *American Journal of Human Genetics* 53 (1993): 385–390.
Papolos, Demitri, and Janice Papolos. *Overcoming Depression,* 3rd ed. New York: HarperCollins, 1997.
Popper, Charles. "Looking at Anger." *American Academy of Child and Adolescent Psychiatry Newsletter* (Fall 1990).
Popper, Charles. "On Diagnostic Gore in Child's Nightmares." *American Academy of Child and Adolescent Psychiatry Newsletter* (Spring 1990).
Steel, Danielle. *His Bright Light.* New York: Delacorte Press, 1998.
Torrey, E. Fuller. *Surviving Schizophrenia,* 3rd ed. New York: HarperCollins, 1995.

## CHAPTER 2

Adams, F. *The Extant Words of Aretaeus, the Cappadocian.* London: The Sydenham Society, 1856, 301–302.

Akiskal, Hagop S. "The Prevalent Clinical Spectrum of Bipolar Disorders Beyond DSM-IV." *Journal of Clinical Psychopharmacology* 16, Supplement 1 (1996).

Akiskal, Hagop S. "Subaffective Disorders: Dysthymic, Cyclothymic, and Bipolar II Disorders in the 'Borderline' Realm." *Psychiatric Clinics of North America* (April 1981): 25–46.

Akiskal, Hagop S., Walker Parks, et al. "Bipolar Outcome in the Course of Depressive Illness: Phenomenologic, Familial, and Pharmacologic Predictors." *Journal of Affective Disorders* 5 (1983): 115–128.

American Psychiatric Association. *Diagnostic and Statistical Manual of Mental Disorders,* 3rd ed. Washington, D.C.: American Psychiatric Association, 1980.

American Psychiatric Association. *Diagnostic and Statistical Manual of Mental Disorders,* 4th ed. Washington, D.C.: American Psychiatric Association, 1994.

Anthony, E. James, and Peter Scott. "Manic-Depressive Psychosis in Childhood." *Journal of Child Psychology and Psychiatry* 1 (1960): 53–72.

Ballenger, James C., Victor I. Reus, and Robert M. Post. "The Atypical Clinical Picture of Adolescent Mania." *American Journal of Psychiatry* 139 (May 1982): 602–606.

Biederman, Joseph. "Is Childhood Oppositional Defiant Disorder a Precursor to Adolescent Conduct Disorder?: Findings from a Four-Year Follow-up Study of Children with ADHD." *Journal of the American Academy of Child and Adolescent Psychiatry* 35 (September 1996): 1193–1204.

Biederman, Joseph, Steven V. Faraone, et al. "Attention-Deficit Hyperactivity Disorder and Juvenile Mania: An Overlooked Comorbidity?" *Journal of the Academy of Child and Adolescent Psychiatry* 35 (August 1996): 997–1008.

Biederman, Joseph, Steven V. Faraone, et al. "Panic Disorder and Agoraphobia in Consecutively Referred Children and Adolescents." *Journal of the American Academy of Child and Adolescent Psychiatry* 36 (1997): 214–223.

Birmaher, Boris, et al. "Is Bipolar Disorder Specifically Associated with Panic Disorder in Youths?" *Journal of Clinical Psychiatry* 63 (2002): 414–419.

Bleuler, Eugen. *Dementia Praecox or the Group of Schizophrenias.* New York: International Universities Press, 1950.

Bolton, P. F., A. Pickles, et al. "Autism, Affective and Other Psychiatric Disorders: Patterns of Familial Aggregation." *Psychological Medicine* 28 (1998): 177–183.

Bowring, Margaret Ann, and Maria Kovacs. "Difficulties in Diagnosing Manic Disorders Among Children and Adolescents." *Journal of the American Academy of Child and Adolescent Psychiatry* 31 (July 1992): 611–614.

Carlson, Gabrielle A., Shmuel Fennig, and Evelyn J. Bromet. "The Confusion Between Bipolar Disorder and Schizophrenia in Youth: Where Does It Stand in the 1990s?" *Journal of the American Academy of Child and Adolescent Psychiatry* 33 (May 1994): 453–459.

Carlson, Gabrielle A., and Frederick K. Goodwin. "The Stages of Mania." *Archives of General Psychiatry* 28 (February 1973): 221–228.

Chen, Yian-Who, and Steven C. Dilsaver. "Comorbidity of Panic Disorder in Bipolar Illness: Evidence from the Epidemiologic Catchment Area Survey." *American Journal of Psychiatry* 152 (1995): 280–282.

Davis, Richard E. "Manic-Depressive Variant Syndrome of Childhood: A Preliminary Report." *American Journal of Psychiatry* 136 (May 1979): 702–705.

Delong, George Robert. "Children with Autistic Spectrum Disorder and a Family History of Affective Disorder." *Developmental Medicine and Child Neurology* 36 (1994): 659–660.

Delong, George Robert, and J. Dwyer. "Correlation of Family History with Specific Autistic Subgroups: Asperger Syndrome and Bipolar Affective Disease." *Journal of Autism and Developmental Disorders* 18 (1988): 593–600.

Duke, Patty, and Kenneth Turan. *Call Me Anna.* New York: Bantam Books, 1990.

Faedda, Gianni L., Ross J. Baldessarini, Trisha Suppes, et al. "Pediatric-Onset Bipolar Disorder: A Neglected Clinical and Public Health Problem." *Harvard Review of Psychiatry* 3 (1995): 171–195.

Faraone, Stephen V., Joseph Biederman, et al. "Bipolar and Antisocial Disorders Among Relatives of ADHD Children: Parsing Familial Subtypes of Illness." *American Journal of Medical Genetics (Neuropsychiatric Genetics)* 81 (1998): 108–116.

Faraone, Stephen V., Joseph Biederman, Janet Wozniak, et al. "Is Comorbidity with ADHD a Marker for Juvenile-Onset Mania?" *Journal of the American Academy of Child and Adolescent Psychiatry* 36 (August 1997): 1046–1055.

Feighner, John P., Eli Robbins, Samuel Guze, et al. "Diagnostic Criteria for Use in Psychiatric Research." *Archives of General Psychiatry* 26 (January 1972): 57–63.

Filipek, P. A., P. J. Accardo, G. T. Baranek, E. H. Cook, Jr., et al. "The Screening and Diagnosis of Autistic Spectrum Disorders." *Journal of Autism and Developmental Disorders* 29 (1999): 439–484.

Filipek, P. A., P. J. Accardo, S. Ashwal, G. T. Baranek, E. H. Cook, Jr., G. Dawson, et al. "Practice Parameter: Screening and Diagnosis of Autism: Report of the Quality Standards Subcommittee of the American Academy of Neurology and the Child Neurology Society." *Neurology* 55 (2000): 468–479.

Frazier, Jean A., Robert Doyle, et al. "Treating a Child with Asperger's Disorder and Comorbid Bipolar Disorder." *American Journal of Psychiatry* 159 (2002): 13–21.

Geller, Barbara, and Joan Luby. "Child and Adolescent Bipolar Disorder: A Review of the Past Ten Years." *Journal of the American Academy of Child and Adolescent Psychiatry* 36 (September 1997): 1168–1176.

Geller, Barbara, Louis W. Fox, and Karen Clark. "Rate and Predictors of Prepubertal Bipolarity During Follow-up of 6–12-Year-Old Depressed Children." *Journal of the American Academy of Child and Adolescent Psychiatry* 33 (May 1994): 461–468.

Geller, Barbara, Louis W. Fox, and Miriam Fletcher. "Effect of Tricyclic Antidepressants on Switching to Mania and on the Onset of Bipolarity in Depressed 6–12-Year-Olds." *Journal of the American Academy of Child and Adolescent Psychiatry* 32 (January 1993): 43–50.

Geller, Barbara, Kristine Bolhofner, et al. "Psychosocial Functioning in a Prepubertal and Early Adolescent Bipolar Disorder Phenotype." *Journal of the American Academy of Child and Adolescent Psychiatry* 39 (December 2000): 1543–1548.

Geller, Barbara, Kai Sun, et al. "Complex and Rapid-Cycling in Bipolar Children and Adolescents: A Preliminary Study." *Journal of Affective Disorders* 34 (1995): 259–268.

Geller, Barbara, Betsey Zimmerman, et al. "Bipolar Disorder at Prospective Follow-up of Adults Who Had Prepubertal Major Depressive Disorder." *American Journal of Psychiatry* 158 (January 2001): 125–127.

Geller, Daniel A., Joseph Biederman, et al. "Obsessive-Compulsive Disorder in Children and Adolescents: A Review." *Harvard Review of Psychiatry* 5 (1998): 260–273.

Goodwin, Frederick K., and Kay Redfield Jamison. *Manic-Depressive Illness.* New York: Oxford University Press, 1990.

Henry, Chantel, Donatienne Van den Bulke, and Frank Bellvier. "Anxiety Disorders in 318 Bipolar Patients: Prevalence and Impact on Illness Severity and Response to Mood Stabilizer." *Journal of Clinical Psychiatry* 64 (2003): 331–335.

Johnson, J. G., Cohen, P., and Brook, J. S. "Associations Between Bipolar Disorder and Other Psychiatric Disorders During Adolescence and Early Adulthood: A Community-based Longitudinal Investigation." *American Journal of Psychiatry* 157 (2000): 1679–1681.

Kestenbaum, Clarice J. "Children at Risk for Manic-Depressive Illness: Possible Predictors." *American Journal of Psychiatry* 136 (September 1979): 1206–1208.

Kovacs, Maria. "Presentation and Course of Major Depressive Disorder During Childhood and Later Years of the Life Span." *Journal of the American Academy of Child and Adolescent Psychiatry* 35 (June 1996): 705–715.

Kovacs, Maria, and Myrna Pollock. "Bipolar Disorder and Co-morbid Conduct Disorder in Childhood and Adolescence." *Journal of the American Academy of Child and Adolescent Psychiatry* 34 (June 1995): 715–723.

Kraeplin, Emil. *Manic-Depressive Insanity and Paranoia.* Edinburgh: E. & S. Livingstone, 1921.

Lewinsohn, Peter M., Daniel N. Klein, and John R. Seeley. "Bipolar Disorder in Community Sample of Older Adolescents: Prevalence, Phenomenology, Comorbidity and Course." *Journal of the American Academy of Child and Adolescent Psychiatry* 15 (1995): 219–226.

Lisch, Jennifer D., Susan Dime-Meenan, et al. "The National Depressive and Manic-Depressive Association (DMDA) Survey of Bipolar Members." *Journal of Affective Disorders* 31 (1994): 281–294.

Maj, Mario. "Evolution of the American Concept of Schizoaffective Psychosis." *Neuropsychobiology* 11 (1984): 7–13.

Masi, Gabriele, Christina Toni, Guillo Purugi, et al. "Anxiety Disorders in Children and Adolescents: A Neglected Comorbidity." *Canadian Journal of Psychiatry* 46 (2001): 797–802.

Mellior, C. S. "First-Rank Symptoms of Schizophrenia." *British Journal of Psychiatry* 117 (1970): 15–23.

Papalos, Demitri F. "Bipolar Disorder and Comorbid Disorders: The Case for a Dimensional Nosology." In *Bipolar Disorder in Childhood and Early Adolescence,* ed. Barbara Geller and Melissa P. Delbello. New York: Guilford Press, 2003.

Papalos, Demitri F., and Janice Papalos. *Overcoming Depression,* 3rd ed. New York: HarperCollins, 1997.

Papalos, Janice, and Demitri F. Papalos. "Anxiety Symptoms in Children and Adolescents with Bipolar Disorder." *The Bipolar Child Newsletter* (July 2003). At www.bipolarchild.com.

Piven, Joseph, Jeanne Gayle, et al. "A Family History Study of Neuropsychiatric Disorders in the Adult Siblings of Autistic Individuals." *Journal of the American Academy of Child and Adolescent Psychiatry* 29 (1990): 177–183.

Piven, Joseph, Gary A. Chase, et al. "Psychiatric Disorders in the Parents of Autistic Individuals." *Journal of the American Academy of Child and Adolescent Psychiatry* 30 (1991): 471–478.

Pope, Harrison G. "Distinguishing Bipolar Disorder from Schizophrenia in Clinical Practice: Guidelines and Case Reports." *Hospital and Community Psychiatry* 34 (April 1983): 322–328.

Pope, Harrison G., and Joseph F. Lipinski, Jr. "Diagnosis in Schizophrenia and Manic-Depressive Illness: A Reassessment of the Specificity of 'Schizophrenic' Symptoms in Light of Current Research." *Archives of General Psychiatry* 35 (1978): 811–822.

Pope, Harrison G., Joseph F. Lipinski, Jr., et al. "Schizoaffective Disorder: An Invalid Diagnosis? A Comparison of Schizoaffective Disorder, Schizophrenia, and Affective Disorder." *American Journal of Psychiatry* 137 (August 1980): 921–927.

Popper, Charles. "Diagnosing Bipolar vs. ADHD: A Pharmacological Point of View." *The Link* 13 (1996).

Puig-Antich, Joaquim, et al. *Schedule for Affective Disorders and Schizophrenia for School-age Children (Kiddie-SADS).* Pittsburgh: Western Psychiatric Institute and Clinic, 1986.

Schneck, Jerome M. *A History of Psychiatry.* Springfield, Ill.: Charles C Thomas, 1960.

Strober, Michael, Carolyn Lampert, et al. "The Course of Major Depressive Disorder in Adolescents: Recovery and Risk of Manic Switching in a Follow-up of Psychotic and Nonpsychotic Subtypes." *Journal of the American Academy of Child and Adolescent Psychiatry* 32 (January 1993): 34–42.

Taylor, Michael A., and Richard Abrams. "The Phenomenology of Mania." *Archives of General Psychiatry* 29 (October 1973): 520–522.

Torrey, E. Fuller. *Surviving Schizophrenia,* 3rd ed. New York: HarperCollins, 1995.

Weller, Elizabeth, Ronald Weller, and Mary Fristad. "Bipolar Disorders in Children: Misdiagnosis, Underdiagnosis, and Future Directions." *Journal of the American Academy of Child and Adolescent Psychiatry* 34 (June 1995): 709–714.

Weller, Ronald, Elizabeth Weller, and Mary Fristad. "Mania in Prepubertal Children: Has It Been Underdiagnosed?" *Journal of Affective Disorders* 11 (1986): 151–154.

Whybrow, Peter C., Hagop S. Akiskal, and William T. McKinney, Jr. *Mood Disorders: Toward a New Psychobiology.* New York: Plenum Press, 1984.

Wozniak, Janet, and Joseph Biederman. "A Pharmacological Approach to the Quagmire of Comorbidity in Juvenile Mania." *Journal of the American Academy of Child and Adolescent Psychiatry* 35 (June 1996): 826–828.

Wozniak, Janet, Joseph Biederman, et al. "Parsing the Comorbidity Between Bipolar Disorder and Anxiety Disorders: A Familial Risk Analysis." *Journal of Child and Adolescent Psychopharmacology* 12 (2002): 101–111.

Wozniak, Janet, Joseph Biederman, et al. "A Pilot Family Study of Childhood-Onset Mania." *Journal of the American Academy of Child and Adolescent Psychiatry* 34 (December 1995): 1577–1583.

CHAPTER 4

Allison, D. B., J. L. Mentore, M. Heo, L. P. Chandler, et al. "Antipsychotic-induced Weight Gain: A Comprehensive Research Synthesis." *American Journal of Psychiatry* 156 (1999): 1686–1696.

American Academy of Child and Adolescent Psychiatry. "Practice Parameters for the Assessment and Treatment of Children and Adolescents with Bipolar Disorder." 36, Supplement 176 (October 1997): 157.

American Psychiatric Association. "Tardive Dyskinesia: Summary of a Task Force Report of the American Psychiatric Association." *American Journal of Psychiatry* 137 (October 1980): 1163–1172.

Balaban, M. T. "Affective Influences on Startle in Five-month-old Infants: Reactions to Facial Expressions of Emotions." *Child Development* 66 (1995): 28–36.

Baldessarini, Ross J. *Chemotherapy in Psychiatry,* 2nd ed. Cambridge, Mass.: Harvard University Press, 1985.

Baldessarini, Ross J. "Fluoxetine and Side Effects." *Archives of General Psychiatry* 47 (1990): 191–192.

Baldessarini, Ross J. Personal written correspondence, September 12 and 25, 2000.

Baldessarini, Ross J., and Leonardo Tondo. "Antisuicidal Effect of Lithium Treatment in Major Mood Disorders." *Harvard Medical School Guide to Suicide Assessment and Intervention.* Douglas Jacobs, ed. San Francisco: Jossey-Bass Publishers, 1998.

Baldessarini, Ross J., and Leonardo Tondo. "Does Lithium Treatment Still Work?" *Archives of General Psychiatry* 57 (2000): 187–190.

Baldessarini, Ross J., and Martin H. Teicher. "Dosing of Antipsychotic Agents in Pediatric Populations." *Journal of Child and Adolescent Psychopharmacology* 59 (1995): 1–4.

Baldessarini, Ross J., Leonardo Tondo, Gianni Faedda, et al. "Effects of the Rate of Discontinuing Lithium Maintenance Treatment in Bipolar Disorders." *Journal of Clinical Psychiatry* 57 (October 1996): 441–448.

Bertogali, Mark W., and Carrie M. Borcharch. "A Review of ECT for Children and Adolescents." *Journal of the American Academy of Child and Adolescent Psychiatry* 29 (1990): 302–307.

Biederman, Joseph. Personal correspondence, September 21, 2000.

Biederman, Joseph. "Olanzapine in the Treatment of Bipolar Disorder in Juveniles." An abstract presented at the 2000 annual meeting of the American Psychiatric Association; Chicago, Illinois.

Botteron, Kelly N., and Barbara Geller. "Pharmacologic Treatment of Childhood and Adolescent Mania." *Child and Adolescent Psychiatric Clinics of North America* 4 (April 1995): 283–304.

Brunet, G., et al. "Open Trial of a Calcium Agonist, Nimodipine, in Acute Mania." *Clinical Neuropharmacology* 13 (1990): 224–228.

Burgess, John R., Laura Stevens, et al. "Long-chain Polyunsaturated Fatty Acids in Children with Attention-Deficit Hyperactivity Disorder." *American Journal of Clinical Nutrition* 71 (2000 supplement): 327–329.

Burris, K. D., T. F. Molski, et al. "Aripiprazole: A Novel Antipsychotic Is a High-affinity Partial Agonist at Human Dopamine D$_2$ Receptors." *Journal of Pharmacological Experimental Therapeutics* 302 (2002): 302–389.

Cade, John F. "Lithium Salts in the Treatment of Psychotic Excitement." *Medical Journal of Australia* 195 (September 1949): 349–352.

Calabrese, Joseph R., Charles L. Bowden, et al. "A Double-Blind Placebo-Controlled Study of Lamotrigine Monotherapy in Outpatients with Bipolar I Depression." *Journal of Clinical Psychiatry* 60 (1999): 79–88.

Calabrese, Joseph R., Tricia Suppes, et al. "A Double-blind, Placebo-controlled Prophylaxis Study of Lamotrigine in Rapid-cycling Bipolar Disorder." *Journal of Clinical Psychiatry* 61 (2000): 841–860.

Chen, Guang, Wei-Zhang Zeng, et al. "The Mood-Stabilizing Agents Lithium and Valproate Robustly Increase the Levels of the Neuroprotective Protein bcl-2 in the CNS." *Journal of Neurochemistry* 72 (1999): 879–882.

DelBello, Melissa, C. M. Adler, et al. "Quetiapine Efficacy in Bipolar Adolescents with Depressive Symptoms." A poster presented at the Sixth International Conference on Bipolar Disorders; Pittsburgh, Pennsylvania, 2005.

DelBello, Melissa P., et al. "Prior Stimulant Treatment in Adolescents with Bipolar Disorder: Association with Age at Onset." *Bipolar Disorders* 3 (2001): 53–57.

Delong, G. Robert. "Lithium Carbonate Treatment of Select Behavior Disorders in Children Suggesting Manic-Depressive Illness." *Journal of Pediatrics* 93 (1978): 689–694.

Denicoff, Kirk D., Earlian E. Smith-Jackson, et al. "Comparative Prophylactic Efficacy of Lithium, Carbamazepine, and the Combination in Bipolar Disorder." *Journal of Clinical Psychiatry* 58 (November 1997): 470–478.

Dose, M., et al. "Use of Calcium Agonists in Mania." *Psychoneuroendocrinology* 11 (1986): 241–243.

Dubovsky, Steven L., and Randall D. Buzan. "Novel Alternatives and Supplements to Lithium and Anticonvulsants for Bipolar Affective Disorder." *Journal of Clinical Psychiatry* 58 (May 1997): 224–242.

Dubovsky, Steven L., and Ronald D. Franks. "Intracellular Calcium Ions in Affective Disorders: A Review and Hypothesis." *Biological Psychiatry* 18 (1983): 781–797.

Dunn, Robert T., Mark S. Frye, et al. "The Efficacy and Use of Anticonvulsants in Mood Disorders." *Clinical Neuropharmacology* 21, no. 4 (1998): 215–235.

Earl, N., Ascher J., et al. "New Information Confirming the Importance of Dosing and Rash with Lamotrigine." Presented at the 41st annual meeting of the New Clinical Drug Evaluation Unit; Phoenix, Arizona, May 2001.

Emrich, H. M., M. Dose, and D. von Zerssen. "The Use of Sodium Valproate, Carbamazepine, and Oxcarbazepine in Patients with Affective Disorders." *Journal of Affective Disorders* 8 (1985): 243–250.

Emrich, H. M., T. Okuma, and A. A. Muller, eds. *Anticonvulsants in Affective Disorders.* Amsterdam: Elsevier Science Publishers, 1984.

Faedda, Gianni L., Ross J. Baldessarini, et al. "Pediatric-Onset Bipolar Disorder: A Neglected Clinical and Public Health Problem." *Harvard Review of Psychiatry* (1995): 171–195.

Faedda, Gianni, Leonardo Tondo, Tricia Suppes, Mauricio Tohen, and Ross J. Baldessarini. "Outcome After Rapid vs. Gradual Discontinuation of Lithium Treatment in Bipolar Disorders." Paper presented at the fifth meeting of Biological Psychiatry; Florence, Italy, June 1991.

Fatemi, S. H., D. J. Rapport, et al. "Lamotrigine in Rapid-cycling Bipolar Disorder." *Journal of Clinical Psychiatry* 58 (1997): 522–527.

Fine, Max. "ECT Update—1997." *Psychiatric Times* (April 1997).

Frazier, J. A., M. C. Meyer, et al. "Risperidone Treatment for Juvenile Bipolar Disorder: A Retrospective Chart Review." *Journal of the American Academy of Child and Adolescent Psychiatry* 38 (1999): 960–965.

Geller, Barbara, L. W. Fox, and M. Fletcher. "Effect of Tricyclic Antidepressants on Switching to Mania and on the Onset of Bipolarity in Depressed 6–12-Year-Olds." *Journal of the American Academy of Adolescent Psychiatry* 32 (January 1993): 43–50.

Gershon, Elliot, et al. "Birth-cohort Changes in Manic and Depressive Disorders in Relatives of Bipolar and Schizoaffective Patients." *Archives of General Psychiatry* 44 (1987): 314–319.

Goodnick, Paul J. "Treatment of Mania: Relationship Between Response to Verapamil and Changes in Plasma Calcium and Magnesium Levels." *Southern Medical Journal* 89 (February 1996): 225–226.

Goodnick, Paul J., and J. M. Jerry. "Aripiprazole: Profile on Efficacy and Safety." *Expert Opinion on Pharmacotherapy* 12 (2002): 1773–1781.

Gorman, Jack M. *The Essential Guide to Psychiatric Drugs,* 3rd ed. New York: St. Martin's Press, 1997.

Green, Wayne Hugo. *Child and Adolescent Clinical Psychopharmacology,* 2nd ed. Baltimore: Williams & Wilkins, 1995.

Hibbeln, Joseph. "Fish Consumption and Major Depression." *The Lancet* 351 (1998): 1213.

Horrobin, David. "Depression and Bipolar Disorder: Relationships to Impaired Fatty Acid and Phospholipid Metabolism and to Diabetes, Cardiovascular Disease, Immunological Abnormalities, Cancer, Aging and Osteoporosis: Possible Candidate Genes." *Prostaglandins, Leukotrienes and Essential Fatty Acids* 60 (1999): 217–234.

Horrobin, David. Personal correspondence, April 20, 2001.

Hughes, Jennifer, B. Barraclough, and W. Reeve. "Are Patients Shocked by ECT?" *Journal of the Royal College of Medicine* 74 (April 1981): 283–285.

Isovari, Jouko I. T., et al. "Polycystic Ovaries and Hyperandrogenism in Women Taking Valproate for Epilepsy." *New England Journal of Medicine* 329 (1993): 1383–1388.

Kafantaris, Vivian, Daniel J. Coletti, et al. "Adjunctive Antipsychotic Treatment of Adolescents with Bipolar Psychosis." *Journal of the American Academy of Child and Adolescent Psychiatry* 40 (2001): 1448–1456.

Kafantaris, Vivian, Magda Campbell, et al. "Carbamazepine in Hospitalized Aggressive Conduct Disorder Children: An Open Pilot Study." *Psychopharmacology Bulletin* 28 (1992): 193–199.

Kaplan, Arline. "FDA-Approved Office Lithium Test Expected to Enhance Clinical Care." *Psychiatric Times* (August 2005).

Katz, Abraham. "Magnetic Depression: Scientists May Zap the Blues Away." *New Haven Register,* September 4, 1997.

Klerman, Gerald L., et al. "Birth Cohort Trends in Rates of Major Depressive Disorder Among Relatives of Patients with Affective Disorder." *Archives of General Psychiatry* 42 (1985): 689–693.

Knoll, James, Kristine Stegman, and Trisha Suppes. "Clinical Experience Using Gabapentin Adjunctively in Patients with a History of Mania or Hypomania." *Journal of Affective Disorders* 49 (1998): 229–233.

Krauchi, K., C. Cajochen, and Anna Wirz-Justice. "Waking Up Properly: Is There a Role of Thermoregulation in Sleep Inertia?" *Journal of Sleep Research* 13 (2004): 121–127.

Krauchi, K., C. Cajochen, and Anna A. Wirz-Justice. "Warm Feet Promote the Rapid Onset of Sleep." *Nature* 401 (1999): 38–39.

Kusumaker, Vivek, and Lakshami N. Yatham. "An Open Study of Lamotrigine in Refractory Bipolar Depression." *Psychiatry Research* 72 (1997): 145–148.

Kutcher, Stan. *Child and Adolescent Psychopharmacology.* Philadelphia: W. B. Saunders Company, 1997.

Loppman, Steven. "A Comparison of Three Types of Lithium Release Preparations." *Hospital and Community Psychiatry* 34 (February 1983): 113–114.

McClellan, Jon, and John S. Werry. "Practice Parameters for the Assessment and Treatment of Children and Adolescents with Bipolar Disorder." *Journal of the American Academy of Child and Adolescent Psychiatry* 36, Supplement (October 1997): 157–176.

Meesters, Ybe. "Case Study: Dawn Simulation as Maintenance Treatment in a Nine-Year-Old Patient with Seasonal Affective Disorder." *Journal of the American Academy of Child and Adolescent Psychiatry* 37 (September 1998): 986–988.

Moise, Frantz N., and George Petrides. "Case Study: Electroconvulsive Therapy in Adolescents." *Journal of the American Academy of Child and Adolescent Psychiatry* 35 (March 1996): 312–318.

Morrow, David J. "Lusting After Prozac." *New York Times,* October 11, 1998.

Nugent, Clare, and Dorie Geraci. "Pill Swallowing Tips." website of the Child and Adolescent Bipolar Foundation. At www.bpkids.org.

Papolos, Demitri F., and Janice Papolos. *Overcoming Depression,* 3rd ed. New York: HarperCollins, 1997.

Papolos, Janice, and Demitri F. Papolos. "Aripiprazole (Abilify): A Novel Atypical Antipsychotic." *The Bipolar Child Newsletter* (February 2003). At www.bipolarchild.com.

Pazzaglia, Peggy J., Robert M. Post, et al. "Preliminary Controlled Trial of Nimodepine in Ultra-Rapid Cycling Affective Dysregulation." *Psychiatry Research* 49 (1993): 257–272.

Reinstein, Michael J., John G. Sonnenberg, et al. "Comparative Efficacy and Tolerability of Oxcarbazepine versus Divalproex Sodium in the Treatment of Mania." A poster presented at the 2001 American Psychiatric Association Conference; New Orleans, Louisiana.

Rosenthal, Norman E. *Winter Blues,* rev. ed. New York: Guilford Press, 1998.

Rosenthal, Norman E., Alytia A. Levendosky, et al. "Effects of Light Treatment on Core Body Temperature in Seasonal Affective Disorder." *Biological Psychiatry* 27 (1990): 39–50.

"Safeguards Needed for Carbamazepine." *FDA Drug Bulletin* 20 (1990).

Sandrolini, Mark. Telephone conversation with Janice Papolos, September 20, 2000.

Schou, Mogens. "Lithium Perspectives." *Neuropsychobiology* 10 (1983): 7–12.

Schou, Mogens. *Lithium Treatment of Manic-Depressive Illness,* 2nd ed. Basel: Karger, 1983.

Segal J., M. Berk, and S. Brook. "Risperidone Compared with Both Lithium and Haloperidol in Mania: A Double-blind Randomized, Controlled Trial." *Clinical Neuropharmacology* 21 (1998): 176–180.

Simoupoulos, Artemis P. *The Omega Diet.* New York: HarperCollins, 1999.

Spencer, Thomas, Timothy Wilens, and Joseph Biederman. "Psychotropic Medication for Children and Adolescents." *Pediatric Psychopharmacology* 4 (January 1995): 97–121.

Stevens, L. J., S. S. Zentall, et al. "Omega-3 Fatty Acids in Boys with Behavior, Learning, and Health Problems." *Physiological Behavior* (April–May 1996): 915–920.

Stoll, Andrew. *The Omega Connection.* New York: The Free Press, 2001.

Stoll, Andrew L., Emanuel Severus, Marlene P. Freeman, et al. "Omega-3 Fatty Acids in Bipolar Disorder: A Preliminary Double-Blind, Placebo-Controlled Trial." *Archives of General Psychiatry* 56 (1999): 407–412.

Suppes, T., S. L. McEroy, et al. "Use of Quetiapine in Bipolar Disorder." *Clinical Psychopharmacology* 19 (2004): 173–174.

Tassi, P., and A. Muzat. "Sleep Inertia." *Physiological Behavior* 68 (1999): 55–61.

Tohen, Maurizio. Telephone conversation with Janice Papolos, September 22, 2000.

Tohen, M., T. G. Jacobs, et al. "Efficacy of Olanzapine in Acute Bipolar Mania: A Double-blind, Placebo-controlled Study." *Archives of General Psychiatry* 57 (2000): 841–849.

Tohen, M., T. M. Sanger, et al. "Olanzapine vs. Placebo in the Treatment of Acute Mania." *American Journal of Psychiatry* 156 (1999): 702–709.

Tohen, M., Zarate C. A., Jr., "Antipsychotic Agents and Bipolar Disorder." *Journal of Clinical Psychiatry* 59, Supplement 1 (1998): 38–48.

Tondo, Leonardo, and Ross J. Baldessarini. "Reduced Suicide Risk During Lithium Maintenance Treatment." *Journal of Clinical Psychiatry* 61, Supplement 9 (2000): 97–104.

Tondo, Leonardo, Ross J. Baldessarini, et al. "Lithium Treatment and Risk of Suicidal Behavior in Bipolar Disorder Patients." *Journal of Clinical Psychiatry* 59 (1998): 405–414.

Valenstein, Elliot S. *Blaming the Brain: The Truth About Drugs and Mental Health.* New York: The Free Press, 1998.

Wehr, Thomas A., and Frederick K. Goodwin. "Can Antidepressants Cause Mania and Worsen the Course of Affective Illness?" *American Journal of Psychiatry* 144 (November 1987): 1403–1411.

Wehr, Thomas, Frederick Goodwin, Anna Wirz-Justice, et al. "48-Hour Sleep-Wake Cycles and Manic-Depressive Illness." *Archives of General Psychiatry* 39 (1982): 559–565.

Willins, Timothy E. *Straight Talk About Psychiatric Medications for Kids.* New York: The Guilford Press, 1999.

Wong, Ian, George E. Mawer, and Josemir W. Sander. "Factors Influencing the Incidence of Lamotrigine-Related Skin Rash." *Annals of Pharmacotherapy* 33 (1999): 1037–1042.

Zarate, C. A., Jr., J. A. Quiroz, et al. "An Open-label Trial of the Glutamate-Modulating Agent Riluzole in Combination with Lithium for the Treatment of Bipolar Depression." *Biological Psychiatry* 4 (2005): 430–432.

**CHAPTER 5**

Egeland, Janice A. "Amish Study, III: The Impact of Cultural Factors on Diagnosis of Bipolar Illness." *American Journal of Psychiatry* 140 (January 1983): 67–71.

Fibiger, H. C. "Neurobiology of Depression: Focus on Dopamine." *Neurobiology to Treatment.* New York: Raven Press, 1995.

Ginns, Edward I., Pamela St. Jean, et al. "A Genome-Wide Search for Chromosomal Loci Linked to Mental Health Wellness in Relatives at High Risk for Bipolar Affective Disorder Among the Old Order Amish." Proceedings of the National Academy of Science 95 (December 1998): 15531–15536.

Guttmacher, Alan, and Francis Collins. "Genomic Medicine—A Primer." *New England Journal of Medicine* 347 (2002): 1512–1520.

Hakkarainen R., C. Johansson, et al. "Seasonal Changes, Sleep Length and Circadian Preference Among Twins with Bipolar Disorder." *BMC Psychiatry:* Epub, June 9, 2003.

Hamilton, David. "Gentic-Variation Map Gains as Biotech Firm Donates Some Data." *Wall Street Journal,* February 15, 2005.

Iarovici, Doris. "New Hints About Genetic Factors in Psychological Traits." *Journal of NIH Research* 7 (November 1995).

Lachman, Herb. Personal correspondence, September 21, 23, 2005.

Lachman, Herb. Telephone interview, September 21, 2005.

Lachman, Herbert M., Bernice Morrow, et al. "Association of Codon 108/158 Catechol-O-methyltransferase Gene Polymorphism with the Psychiatric Manifestations of Velo-cardio-facial Syndrome." *American Journal of Medical Genetics* 67 (1996): 468–472.

Lachman, Herbert M., Demitri F. Papolos, et al. "Human Catechol-O-methyltransferase Pharmacogenetics: Description of a Functional Polymorphism and Its Potential Application to Neuropsychiatric Disorders." *Pharmacogenetics* 6 (1996): 243–250.

Lubs, H. A., et al. "Genetic Bases of Developmental Dyslexia: Molecular Studies." *Neuropsychological Foundations of Learning Disabilities.* San Diego: Academic Press, 1994.

Luscher, J. M., B. Mohler, et al. "The Corticotropin-releasing Hormone Gene and Behavioral Inhibition in Children at Risk for Panic Disorder." *Biological Psychiatry* 57 (June 2005): 1485–1492.

McGuffin, Peter, Michael J. Owen, et al. *Seminars in Psychiatric Genetics.* London: Gaskell Press, 1994.

McManamy, John. "A Genome Primer." Website of McManweb.com.

Matthews, C. A., and V. I. Reus. "Assortative Mating in the Affective Disorders: A Systematic Review and Meta-analysis." *Comprehensive Psychiatry* 42 (July–August 2001): 257–262.

Merikangas, Kathleen, and David G. Spiker. "Assortative Mating in Patients with Primary Affective Disorder." *Psychological Medicine* 12 (November 1982): 753–764.

Mishima, K., T. Tozawa, et al. "The 3111T/C Polymorphism of hClock Is Associated with Evening Preference and Delayed Sleep Timing in a Japanese Population Sample." *American Journal of Medical Genetics, Part B: Neuropsychiatric Genetics* 5 (February 2005): 101–104.

Papolos, Demitri F., and Herbert M. Lachman, eds. *Genetic Studies in Affective Disorders.* New York: John Wiley & Sons, Inc., 1994.

Papolos, Demitri, Sabine Veit, and Robert Shprintzen. "Chromosomal Abnormalities and Bipolar Affective Disorder: Velo-Cardio-Facial Syndrome." *Medscape Psychiatry Journal* 2 (August 1997): 1–13.

Papolos, Demitri F., Sabine Veit, Gianni Faedda, et al. "Ultra-ultra-rapid Cycling Bipolar Disorder Is Associated with the Low Activity Catecholamine-O-methyltransferase Allele." *Molecular Psychiatry* 3 (1998): 346–349.

Philipkoski, Kristen. "Chips Show DNA Differences. *Wired News,* May 8, 2001. At www .wired.com.

Plomin, Robert. "The Role of Inheritance in Behavior." *Science* 248 (April 1990): 183–188.

Schwartz, C. E., C. I. Wright, et al. "Inhibited and Uninhibited Infants" 'Grown Up': Adult Amygdalar Response to Novelty." *Science* 300 (June 20, 2003): 1952–1953.

Stipp, David. "Speed Reading Your Genes." *Fortune Magazine,* September 1, 2003.

Tiihonen, Jari, Tero Hallikainen, Herbert Lachman, et al. "Association Between the Functional Variant of the Catechol-O-methyltransferase (COMT) Gene and Type I Alcoholism." *Molecular Psychiatry* 4 (1999): 286–289.

Todd, Richard D. "The Link Between Parental Alcoholism and Childhood Mood Disorders: A Family/Genetic Perspective." *Medscape Mental Health* 2, no. 4 (1997).

## CHAPTER 6

Anch, A. M., and C. P. Browman, et al. *Sleep: A Scientific Perspective.* Englewood Cliffs, N.J.: Prentice-Hall, Inc., 1988.

Arkin, A. M., et al. *The Mind in Sleep: Psychology and Parapsychology.* Hillsdale, N.J.: Lawrence Earlbaum Associates, 1978.

Borbely, Alexander. *Secrets of Sleep.* New York: Basic Books, 1986.

Borzel, Nicolas L. "Nightmares and Night Terrors: The Horror Movies of the Mind." www .sawka.com/spiritwatch/borzel.htm.

Bowlby, John. *Separation.* New York: Basic Books, 1973.

Bowlby, John. *Attachment,* 2nd ed. New York: Basic Books, 1982.

Brazelton, T. Berry, and Bertrand G. Cramer. *The Earliest Relationship.* New York: Addison-Wesley, 1991.

Dubovsky, Steven L., and Ronald D. Franks. "Intracellular Calcium Ions in Affective Disorders: A Review and an Hypothesis." *Biological Psychiatry* 18 (1983): 781–797.

Hershman, D. Jablow, and Julian Lieb. *Manic Depression and Creativity.* New York: Prometheus Books, 1998.

Hofer, Myron. "Early Social Relationships: A Psychobiologist's View." *Child Development* 58 (1987): 633–647.

Joels, Marian, and E. Ronald De Kloet. "Effects of Glucocorticoids and Norepinephrine on the Excitability in the Hippocampus." *Science* 245 (September 1989): 1502–1505.

Kagan, Jerome, Richard B. Kearsley, and Philip R. Zelazo. *Infancy: Its Place in Human Development.* Cambridge, Mass.: Harvard University Press, 1980.

Kramer, Mark S., Neal Cutler, John Feighner, et al. "Distinct Mechanism for Antidepressant Activity by Blockade of Central Substance P Receptors." *Science* 11 (September 1998): 1640–1645.

Mahler, Margaret S. *The Selected Papers of Margaret S. Mahler: Volume 2.* New York: Jason Aronson, 1979.

Mahowald, Mark W., and Carlos H. Schenck. "Diagnosis and Management of Parasomnias." *Clinical Cornerstones (Sleep Disorders)* 2, no. 5.

Ohayon, M. M., P. L. Morselli, and C. Guilleminault, "Prevalence of Nightmares and Their Relationship to Psychopathology and Daytime Functioning in Insomnia Subjects." *Sleep* 20, no. 5 (1997): 340–348.

Ohayon, M. M., et al. "Night Terrors, Sleep Walking, and Confusional Arousals in the General Population: Their Frequency and Relationship to Other Sleep and Mental Disorders." *Journal of Clinical Psychiatry* 60 (April 1999): 268–276.

Papolos, Demitri F., and Janice Papolos. *Overcoming Depression,* 3rd ed. New York: Harper-Collins, 1997.

Papolos, Demitri, John Hennen, and Melissa Cockerham. "Obessive Fears About Harm to Self or Others and Overt Aggressive Behaviors in Youth Diagnosed with Juvenile-onset Bipolar Disorder." *Journal of Affective Disorders* (in press).

Pine, Fred. *Developmental Theory and Clinical Process.* New Haven, Conn.: Yale University Press, 1985.

Popper, Charles. "On Diagnostic Gore in Child's Nightmares." *American Academy of Adolescent Psychiatry Newsletter* (Spring 1990).

Reich, Annie. "Pathologic Forms of Self-esteem Regulation." *Psychoanalytic Study of the Child,* vol. 15. New York: International Universities Press, 1960.

Salzman, Leon. *Treatment of the Obsessive Personality.* New York: Jason Aronson, 1980.

Winnicott, D. W. *The Maturational Processes and the Facilitating Environment.* Madison, Conn.: International Universities Press, 1965.

Winson, Jonathan. *Brain and Psyche: The Biology of the Unconscious.* Garden City, N.Y.: Anchor Press, 1985.

## Chapter 7

Aston-Jones, G., and Floyd E. Bloom. "Activity of Norepinephrine-containing Locus Coeruleus Neurons in Behaving Rats Anticipates Fluctuations in the Sleep-waking Cycle." *Journal of Neuroscience* 8 (August 1981): 876–886.

Berger, Ralph J., and Nathan H. Phillips. "Regulation of Body Temperature During Sleep." *Comparative Physiology of Sleep, Thermoregulation, and Metabolism from the Perspective of Energy Conservation.* New York: Wiley-Liss, 1990.

Blakeslee, Sandra. "Biologists Close in on the 'Tick-Tock' Genes." *New York Times,* December 15, 1998.

Bradley, M. M., P. J. Lang, and B. N. Cuthbert. "Emotion, Novelty, and the Startle Reflex: Habituation in Humans." *Behavioral Neuroscience* 107 (December 1993): 970–980.

Cahill, L., et al. "Amygdala Activity at Encoding Correlated with Long-term, Free Recall of Emotional Information." *Proceedings of the National Academy of Sciences* 15 (July 1996): 8016–8021.

Changeux, Jean-Pierre. *Neuronal Man.* New York: Pantheon, 1985.

Charney, Dennis S., et al. "A Functional Neuroanatomy of Anxiety and Fear: Implications for the Pathophysiology and Treatment of Anxiety Disorders." *Critical Review of Neurobiology* 10 (1996): 419–446.

Chorpita, B. F., and D. H. Barlow. "The Development of Anxiety: The Role of Control in the Early Environment." *Psychology Bulletin* 124 (July 1998): 3–21.

Conlan, Roberta, ed. *States of Mind: New Discoveries about How Our Brains Make Us Who We Are.* New York: John Wiley & Sons, Inc., 1999.

Coscina, Donald V., et al. "Induction of Rage in Rats by Central Injection of 6-Hydroxy-dopamine." *Pharmacology Biochemistry and Behavior* 1 (1973): 1–6.

Ehlers, C. L., et al. "CRF/NPY Interactions: A Potential Role in Sleep Dysregulation in Depression and Anxiety." *Depression Anxiety* 6 (1997): 1–9.

Evans, B. "Cyclical Activity in Non-rapid Eye Movement Sleep: A Proposed Arousal Inhibitory Mechanism." *Electroencephalography and Clinical Neurophysiology* 86 (February 1993): 123–131.

Farrant, Mark, and Stuart Cull-Candy. "Gaba Receptors, Grabule Cells, and Genes." *Nature,* January 28, 1993, 302–303.

Fibiger, H. C. "Neurobiology of Depression: Focus on Dopamine." *Depression and Mania: From Neurobiology to Treatment.* New York: Raven Press, 1995.

Glavin, Gary B. "Stress and Brain Noradrenaline: A Review." *Neuroscience and Biobehavioral Reviews* 9 (1985): 233–243.

Goleman, Daniel. *Emotional Intelligence.* New York: Bantam Books, 1997.

Halaris, Angelos, ed. *Chronobiology and Psychiatric Disorders.* New York: Elsevier, 1987.

Inui, A., M. Okita, et al. "Anxiety-like Behavior in Transgenic Mice with Brain Expression of Neuropeptide Y." *Proceedings of the Association of American Physicians* 110 (May 1998): 171–182.

Jacobson, Lauren, and Robert Sapolsky. "The Role of the Hippocampus in Feedback Regulation of the Hypothalamic-Pituitary-Adrenocortical Axis." *Endocrine Reviews* 12 (1991): 118–134.

Joels, Marian, and Ronald De Kloet. "Effects of Glucocorticoids and Norepinephrine on the Excitability in the Hippocampus." *Science* 245 (September 1989): 1502–1505.

Kramer, Mark S., Neal Cutler, et al. "Distinct Mechanism for Antidepressant Activity by Blockade of Central Substance P Receptors." *Science* (September 1998): 1640–1645.

Kranowitz, Carol Stock. *The Out-of-Sync Child.* New York: Penguin Putnam, 1998.

Lachman, Herbert M., and Demitri F. Papolos. "Abnormal Signal Transduction: A Hypothetical Model for Bipolar Affective Disorder." *Life Sciences* 45 (1989): 1412–1426.

Landsberg, Lewis, and James B. Young. "Fasting, Feeding, and Regulation of the Sympathetic Nervous System." *Seminars in Medicine of the Beth Israel Hospital, Boston* 298 (June 1978): 1295–1300.

LeDoux, Joseph, and William Hirst. *Mind and Brain.* Cambridge: Cambridge University Press, 1986.

Lee, Gregory P., David W. Loring, Kimford J. Meader, and Betty B. Brooks. "Hemispheric Specialization for Emotional Expression: A Reexamination of Results from Intracarotid Administration of Sodium Amobarbital." *Brain and Cognition* 12 (1990): 267–280.

Leeman, Susan E., James E. Krause, and Fred Lembeck, eds. *Substance P and Related Peptides.* New York: New York Academy of Sciences, 1991.

Logothetis, Nikos K., David A. Leopold, and David L. Sheinberg. "What Is Rivalry During Binocular Rivalry?" *Nature,* April 18, 1996, 621–624.

Lombroso, Paul J., and Robert Sapolsky. "Development of the Cerebral Cortex: Stress and Brain Development." *Journal of the American Academy of Child and Adolescent Psychiatry* 37 (December 1998): 1337–1339.

Lumer, Erik D., Karl J. Friston, and Geraint Rees. "Neural Correlates of Perceptual Rivalry in the Human Brain." *Science* 280 (June 1998): 1930–1934.

Malkoff-Schwartz, Susan, Ellen Frank, et al. "Stressful Life Events and Social Rhythm Disruption in the Onset of Manic and Depressive Bipolar Episodes." *Archives of General Psychiatry* 55 (August 1998): 702–707.

Mandell, Arnold J., and Suzanne Knapp. "Asymmetry and Mood, Emergent Properties of Serotonin Regulation: A Proposed Mechanism of Action of Lithium." *Archives of General Psychiatry* 36 (July 1979): 909–916.

Manji, Husseini K., Gregory J. Moore, and Guang Chen. "Bipolar Disorder: Leads from the Molecular and Cellular Mechanisms of Action of Mood Stabilizers." *British Journal of Psychiatry* Supplement 41 (2001): s107–s119.

Manji, Husseini K., Gregory J. Moore, et al. "Neuroplasticity and Cellular Resilience in Mood Disorders." *Molecular Psychiatry* 5 (2000): 578–593.

Marder, Eve. "From Biophysics to Models of Network Function." *Annual Review of Neurosciences* 21 (1998): 25–45.

McGeer, Patrick L., John C. Eccles, and Edith G. McGeer. *Molecular Neurobiology of the Mammalian Brain.* New York: Plenum Press, 1978.

Migliorelli, Ricardo, Sergio E. Starkstein, et al. "SPECT Findings in Patients with Primary Mania." *Journal of Neuropsychiatry and Clinical Neurosciences* 5 (1993): 379–383.

Mirabile, Charles S., and Bernard C. Glueck. "Separation of Affective Disorder into Seasonal and Nonseasonal Types Using Motion Sickness Susceptibility as a Marker." *Journal of Neuropsychiatry* 5 (Summer 1993): 330–334.

Monk, Timothy H. "Research Methods of Chronobiology." Chapter 2 in *Biological Rhythms, Sleep, and Performance,* Wilse B. Webb, ed. New York: John Wiley & Sons, Inc., 1982.

Moore, Gregory J., Joseph M. Bebchuk, et al. "Lithium-induced Increase in Human Brain Grey Matter." *The Lancet* 356 (2000): 1241–1242.

Murphy D., B. Costall, and J. W. Smythe. "Regulation of Hippocampal Theta Activity by Corticosterone: Opposing Functions of Mineralocorticoid and Glucocorticoid Receptors." *Brain Research Bulletin* 45 (April 1998): 631–635.

Ostrow, David, Angelos Halaris, et al. "State Dependence of Noradrenergic Activity in a Rapidly Cycling Bipolar Patient." *Journal of Clinical Psychiatry* 45 (1984): 306–309.

Papez, James W. "A Proposed Mechanism of Emotion. 1937." *Journal of Neuropsychiatry and Clinical Neurosciences* (Winter 1995): 103–112.

Pettigrew, John D., and Steven M. Miller. "A 'Sticky' Interhemispheric Switch in Bipolar Disorder?" *Proceedings of the Royal Society of London* 265 (1998): 2141–2148.

Papolos, Demitri F., and Janice Papolos. *Overcoming Depression,* 3rd ed. New York: Harper-Collins, 1997.

Restack, Richard. *The Brain.* New York: Bantam Books, 1984.

Schulkin, Joseph, P. W. Gold, and Bruce S. McEwen. "Induction of Corticotropin-releasing Hormone Gene Expression by Glucocorticoids: Implication for Understanding the States of Fear and Anxiety and Allostatic Load." *Psychoneuroendocrinology* 23 (April 1998): 219–243.

Tache, Yvette, and Catherine Rivier, eds. *Corticotropin-Releasing Factor and Cytokines: Role in the Stress Response.* New York: New York Academy of Sciences, 1993.

Teicher, Martin H., Carol Glod, et al. "Circadian Rest-Activity Disturbances in Seasonal Affective Disorder." *Archives of General Psychiatry* 54 (February 1997): 124–130.

Tornatzky, Walter, and Klaus A. Miczek. "Long-term Impairment of Autonomic Circadian Rhythms After Brief Intermittent Social Stress." *Physiology and Behavior* 53 (1993): 983–993.

Trimble, Michael R., and E. Zarifian, eds. *Psychopharmacology of the Limbic System.* Oxford: Oxford University Press, 1985.

Warren, Wade S., Thomas H. Champney, and Vincent M. Cassone. "The Suprachiasmatic Nucleus Controls the Circadian Rhythm of Heart Rate Via the Sympathetic Nervous System." *Physiology and Behavior* 55 (1994): 1091–1099.

Webb, Wilse B., ed. *Biological Rhythms, Sleep, and Performance.* New York: John Wiley & Sons, Inc., 1982.

Wehr, Thomas A. "A Brain-Warming Function for REM Sleep." *Neuroscience Biobehavioral Review* 16 (Fall 1992): 379–397.

Whybrow, Peter C., Hagop S. Akiskal, and William T. McKinney, Jr. *Mood Disorders: Toward a New Psychobiology.* New York: Plenum Press, 1984.

Winson, Jonathan. *Brain and Psyche: The Biology of the Unconscious.* Garden City, N.Y.: Anchor Press, 1985.

## CHAPTER 8

Featherstone, Helen. *A Difference in the Family.* New York: Penguin Books, 1981.

Geller, Barbara, Kristine Bolhofner, et al. "Psychosocial Functioning in a Prepubertal and Early Adolescent Bipolar Disorder Phenotype." *Journal of the American Academy of Child and Adolescent Psychiatry* 39 (December 2000): 1543–1548.

Geller, Barbara, Betsey Zimmerman, et al. "Diagnostic Characteristics of 93 Cases of a Prepubertal and Early Adolescent Bipolar Disorder Phenotype by Gender, Puberty, and Comorbid Attention Deficit Hyperactivity Disorder." *Journal of Child and Adolescent Psychopharmacology* 10 (2000): 157–164.

Geller, Barbara, Betsey Zimmerman, et al. "DSM-IV Mania Symptoms in a Prepubertal and Early Adolescent Bipolar Disorder Phenotype Compared to Attention-Deficit Hyperactive and Normal Controls." *Journal of Child and Adolescent Psychopharmacology* 12 (2002): 11–25.

Greene, Ross J. *The Explosive Child.* New York: HarperCollins, 1998.

Krauchi, K., Cajochen, C., and Anna Wirz-Justice. "Waking Up Properly: Is There a Role of Thermoregulation in Sleep Inertia?" *Journal of Sleep Research* 13 (2004): 21–27.

Papolos, Demitri, and Janice Papolos. *Overcoming Depression,* 3rd ed. New York: Harper-Collins, 1997.

Papolos, Demitri, John Hennen, and Melissa Cockerham. "Factors Associated with Parent-Reported Suicide Threats by Children and Adolescents with Community-Diagnosed Bipoolar Disorder." *Journal of Affective Disorders* 86 (2005): 267–275.

Papolos, Janice, and Demitri F. Papolos. "Boredom and the Provocative Behavior of Children with Bipolar Disorder." *The Bipolar Child Newsletter* (February 2004). At www.bipolarchild.com.

Papolos, Janice, and Demitri F. Papolos. "The Irrepressible Agendas of Children with Bipolar Disorder." *The Bipolar Child Newsletter* (October 2002). At www.bipolarchild.com.

Papolos, Janice, and Demitri F. Papolos. "The Morning Battleground: Why Bipolar Kids Can't Get Up and Get Going." *The Bipolar Child Newsletter* (October 2004). At www.bipolarchild.com.

Popper, Charles W. "A Haven from Rage." *American Academy of Child and Adolescent Newsletter* (Spring 1991).

Popper, Charles W. "Looking at Anger." *American Academy of Child and Adolescent Newsletter* (Fall 1990).

Secunda, Victoria. *When Madness Comes Home.* New York: Hyperion, 1997.

Tassi, P., and A. Muzat. "Sleep Inertia." *Physiological Behavior* 68 (1999): 55–61.

Wehr, Thomas, Frederick Goodwin, Anna A. Wirz-Justice, et al. "48-Hour Sleep-Wake Cycles and Manic-Depressive Illness." *Archives of General Psychiatry* 39 (1982): 559–565.

CHAPTER 9

Anderson, Winifred, Stephen Chitwood, and Deidre Hayden. *Negotiating the Special Education Maze: A Guide for Parents and Teachers.* Bethesda, Md.: Woodbine House, 1997.

Congressional Research Service Report for Congress on IDEA 2004.

Council of Parent Attorneys and Advocates. *Full-Text Comparison of IDEA 2004 and IDEA '97.*

Cutler, Barbara Coyne. *You, Your Child, and "Special" Education: A Guide to Making the System Work,* 3rd ed. Baltimore: Paul H. Brookes Publishing Co., 1997.

Dao, James. "Schooled at Home, They Want to Play in School." *New York Times,* June 22, 2005.

Davidson, Howard. *Just Ask!: A Handbook for Instructors of Students Being Treated for Mental Disorders.* Calgary: Detselig Enterprises Ltd., 1993.

Dornbush, Marilyn P., and Sheryl K. Pruett. *Teaching the Tiger.* Duarte, Calif.: Hope Press, 1995.

Gilcher, Donna. Child and Adolescent Bipolar Foundation Review of IDEA 2004. At www.bpkids.org.

Gootman, Elissa. "Special Education Ruling's Effects Unclear." *New York Times,* November 17, 2005.

Haerle, Tracy. *Children with Tourette Syndrome: A Parents' Guide.* Bethesda, Md.: Woodbine House, 1992.

Latham, Peter, and Patricia H. Latham. *Attention Deficit Disorder and the Law.* Washington, D.C.: JKL Communications, 1997.

Lynn, George T. *Survival Strategies for Parenting Your ADD Child.* Grass Valley, Calif.: Underwood Books, 1996.

Quackenbush, Doug, Stan Kutcher, et al. "Premorbid and Postmorbid School Functioning in Bipolar Adolescents: Description and Suggested Academic Interventions." *Canadian Journal of Psychiatry* 41 (February 1996): 16–22.

Smith, Anne Marie. Personal correspondence with Janice Papolos, June 26, 27, August 4, 13, 16, 2005.

Wright, Pete, and Pam Wright. *IDEA-Wrightslaw.* At www.Wrightslaw.com.

CHAPTER 10

Bearden C. E., K. M. Hoffman, and T. D. Cannon. "The Neuropsychology and Neuroanatomy of Bipolar Affective Disorder: A Critical Review." *Bipolar Disorders* 3 (2001): 106–150.

Cohen, Jonathan D., et al. "Temporal Dynamics of Brain Activation During a Working Memory Task." *Nature* 386 (1997): 604–608.

Comings, David. *Tourette Syndrome and Human Behavior.* Duarte, Calif.: Hope Press, 1990.

Courtney, S. M., et al. "Transient and Sustained Activity in a Distributed Neural System for Human Working Memory." *Nature* 386 (1997): 608–611.

Dornbush, Marilyn P., and Sheryl Pruitt. *Teaching the Tiger.* Duarte, Calif.: Hope Press, 1995.

El-Badri, S. M., C. H. Ashton, et al. "Electrophysiological and Cognitive Function in Young Euthymic Patients with Bipolar Affective Disorder." *Bipolar Disorders* 2 (2001): 79–87.

Goldberg, Elkhonon. *The Executive Brain: Frontal Lobes and the Civilized Mind.* New York: Oxford University Press, 2001.

Harwell, Joan M. *Complete Learning Disabilities Handbook,* 2nd ed. Paramus, N.J.: The Center for Applied Research in Education, 2001.

Kay, Kiesa, ed. *Uniquely Gifted: Identifying and Meeting the Needs of the Twice-Exceptional Student.* Gilsum, N.H.: Avocus Publishing, Inc., 2000.

Levine, Mel. *A Mind at a Time.* New York: Simon & Schuster, 2002.

Luck, Dana, and Steven Mattis. Telephone interview with Janice Papolos, July 8, 2005.

Ratey, John J. *A User's Guide to the Brain.* New York: Pantheon Books, 2001.

Roberts, A. C., T. W. Robins, and L. Weiskrantz. *The Prefrontal Cortex.* New York: Oxford University Press, 1998.

Wechsler, David. *WISC-IV.* New York: The Psychological Corporation, 2003.

**CHAPTER 11**

Alexander-Roberts, Colleen. *ADHD and Teens: A Parent's Guide to Making It Through the Tough Years.* Dallas: Taylor Publishing Company, 1995.

Austin, Laurie. Interview with Janice Papolos, June 30, 2005.

Bauman, Lawrence, and Robert Riche. *Ten Most Troublesome Teen-age Problems: And How to Solve Them.* Secaucus, N.J.: Citadel Press, 1998.

Cassell, Carol. *Straight from the Heart: How to Talk to Your Teenagers About Love and Sex.* New York: Simon and Schuster, 1987.

Dendy, Chris, and A. Ziegler. *Teenagers with ADD: A Parents' Guide.* Bethesda, Md.: Woodbine House, 1995.

Ekman, Paul. *Why Kids Lie.* New York: Charles Scribner's Sons, 1989.

Kaplan, Louise J. *Adolescence: The Farewell to Childhood.* New York: Simon and Schuster, 1984.

Marcus, David L. *What It Takes to Pull Me Through.* New York: Houghton Mifflin, 2005.

McGlashan, Thomas. "Adolescent Versus Adult Onset of Mania." *American Journal of Psychiatry* 145 (1988): 221–223.

Park, Alice. "What Makes Teens Tick." *Time,* May 10, 2004.

Pogany, Susan Browning. *SexSmart: 501 Reasons to Hold Off on Sex.* Minneapolis: Fairview Press, 1998.

Wexler, David B. *The Adolescent Self.* New York: W. W. Norton & Company, 1991.

Wolf, Anthony E. *Get Out of My Life, But First Could You Drive Me and Cheryl to the Mall?* New York: Farrar, Straus, Giroux, 1991.

**CHAPTER 12**

Levy, Robert M., and Leonard S. Rubenstein. *The Rights of People with Mental Disabilities.* Carbondale, Ill.: ACLU Southern Illinois University Press, 1996.

Papolos, Demitri F., and Janice Papolos. *Overcoming Depression,* 3rd ed. New York: HarperCollins, 1997.

Roth, Loren H. "A Commitment Law for Patients, Doctors, and Lawyers." *American Journal of Psychiatry* 136 (September 1979): 1121–1126.

Schneider Children's Hospital Child Psychiatry Inpatient Unit Parents' Guide. New Hyde Park, N.Y.

Torrey, E. Fuller. *Surviving Schizophrenia,* 3rd ed. New York: HarperCollins, 1983.

## CHAPTER 13

Academy of Child and Adolescent Psychiatry. "New Children's Health Program Becomes Effective October 1, 1997." Legislative Alert Issued by the Department of Government Affairs of the Academy, September 8, 1997.

Ammer, Christine, with Nathan T. Sidley. *The Common Sense Guide to Mental Health Care.* Brattleboro, Vt.: The Lewis Publishing Company, 1982.

Bazelon Center for Mental Health Law. *SSI: Help for Children with Disabilities.* Washington, D.C.: Bazelon Center Publications, 1997.

Bazelon Center for Mental Health Law. *Your Family and Managed Care.* Washington, D.C.: Bazelon Center Publications, 1996.

Beckett, Julie. Telephone conversation with Janice Papolos, February 12, 1999.

Center for Health Policy Studies. *Mandated Mental Health Benefits under Private Insurance: A Review of State Laws.* Prepared for the National Institute of Mental Health, December 1983.

Freudenheim, Milt. "H.M.O.'s Cope with a Backlash on Cost Cutting." *New York Times,* May 19, 1996.

Freudenheim, Milt. "Insurers Tighten Rules and Reduce Fees for Doctors." *New York Times,* June 28, 1998.

Freudenheim, Milt. "(Loosely) Managed Care Is in Demand." *New York Times,* September 29, 1998.

Gorman, Christine. "Playing the HMO Game." *Time,* July 13, 1998.

Greenley, Dianne. "Insurance and Other Third-Party Coverage for Persons Who Are Mentally Ill: Issues and Possibilities." Report written for the National Alliance for the Mentally Ill, February 1986.

Hall, Laura Lee, Elizabeth Edgar, and Laurie Flynn. *Stand and Deliver: Action Call to a Failing Industry.* Arlington, Va.: National Alliance for the Mentally Ill, September 1997.

Malloy, Michael. *Mental Illness and Managed Care: A Primer for Families and Consumers.* Arlington, Va.: National Alliance for the Mentally Ill, 1995.

National Committee for Quality Assurance. "Draft Accreditation Standards for Managed Care Behavioral Healthcare Organizations," April 1996.

Nerney, John. "Fire." *AMI-NYS News,* November 1995.

Papolos, Demitri F., and Janice Papolos. *Overcoming Depression,* 3rd ed. New York: HarperCollins, 1997.

Torrey, Fuller E. *Surviving Schizophrenia,* 3rd ed. New York: HarperCollins, 1995.

U.S. Department of Health and Human Services. *Disability Evaluation Under Social Security.* SSA Publication No. 64–039, January 1998.

U.S. Department of Health and Human Services. *Social Security Handbook.* SSA Publication No. 05–10135, July 1984.

## CHAPTER 14

Butterfield, Fox. "Prisons Replace Hospitals for the Nation's Mentally Ill." *New York Times,* March 5, 1998.

Pear, Robert. "Insurance Plans Skirt Requirement on Mental Health." *New York Times,* December 26, 1998.

# Index

© Nick Granito

# About the Authors

**Demitri Papolos, M.D.** is an associate professor of psychiatry at the Albert Einstein College of Medicine in New York City and the codirector of the Program in Behavioral Genetics. He is the director of research of the Juvenile Bipolar Research Foundation.

**Janice Papolos** is the author of three other books, all recognized as definitive in their fields, and is the editor of *The Bipolar Child Newsletter*.

The Papoloses are the authors of the classic text *Overcoming Depression,* now in its third edition. They live in Westport, Connecticut.